Please turn the page for more reviews. . . .

"This excellent anthology. . . . shimmers with interesting reading . . . Santiago has gracefully managed to pull together a collection that presents a united front while preserving the diversity of the individual voices."
—*Publishers Weekly*

"Bursts with the energy of Puerto Rican life. . . . This book is a must for every library worth its salt and for every serious student of literature."
—*Hispanic*

"Groundbreaking."
—*Essence*

"Deftly organized and sincerely moving, *Boricuas* is a fresh look at Puerto Rican life and culture. . . . A convincing and heart-warming testimony of not only Puerto Rican pride but also the unwavering faith in the triumphant humanity of all people subjected to adversity."
—*Quarterly Black Review*

"A rare collection."
—*Newsday*

"A lively sampling of Puerto Rican (and "Nuyorican") fiction, nonfiction, poetry, and drama."
—*The Cleveland Plain Dealer*

"Powerful . . . Brilliant."
—*The Herald* (Lake Worth, FL)

"Santiago has given voice to the history, struggles, hopes, joys, and pains of his Puerto Rican people. . . . *Boricuas* is a long-awaited voice that needs to be heard."
—*Class*

"By far the most brilliant aspect of Boricuas is the sheer variety of work it gathers together. . . . It salvages Puerto Rican identity from the multicultural blur of the 'Hispanic' and 'Latino' masses. . . . Each voice rings true and clear . . . snar[ing] the spirit of *boricua*."
—*Weekly Alibi*

BORICUAS

INFLUENTIAL PUERTO RICAN WRITINGS— AN ANTHOLOGY

EDITED BY
ROBERTO SANTIAGO

ONE WORLD
THE RANDOM HOUSE PUBLISHING GROUP · NEW YORK

A One World Book
Published by The Random House Publishing Group

Copyright © 1995 by Roberto Santiago
Illustrations copyright © 1995 by Clemente Flores

Published in the United States by One World Books, an imprint
of The Random House Publishing Group, a division of Random
House, Inc., New York, and simultaneously in Canada by
Random House of Canada Limited, Toronto.

One World is a registered trademark and the One World
colophon is a trademark of Random House, Inc.

www.oneworldbooks.net

Permission acknowledgments can be found on pages 358–61,
which constitute an extension of this copyright page.

Library of Congress Catalog Card Number: 95-94411

ISBN: 978-0-345-39502-3

Cover illustration by Frank Diaz Escalet
Cover design by Kristine Mills
Text design by Holly Johnson

First Edition: September 1995

147429898

This book is dedicated to Darcy Marousek, the beautiful and strong woman I adore, who has given me nothing but love and support.

To my parents, Fundador and Francisca Santiago, for giving me the self-esteem that—armed with an education, moral virtues, and discipline—helped me see that I could do anything in life.

To my autistic brothers, Gilberto and Nelson, for teaching me patience, kindness, and forgiveness.

And to my sister, Nilsa, who inspired me to become a writer and editor by having me read Edgar Allan Poe and John Steinbeck when I was eight years old.

CONTENTS

PART 2: HISTORY AND POLITICS

"I pray to the rain . . ./Return the remnants of my identity/Bathe me in self-discovered knowledge. . . ."
—FROM *IT IS RAINING TODAY* BY SANDRA MARIA ESTEVES

PART 3: IDENTITY AND SELF-ESTEEM

*"I am new. History made me . . ./I was born at the crossroads/and
I am whole."*
—FROM *CHILD OF THE AMERICAS* BY AURORA LEVINS MORALES

PART 4: ANXIETY AND ASSIMILATION

*"Always broke/Always owing/Never knowing/that they are
beautiful people/Never knowing/the geography of their
complexion . . ."*
—FROM *PUERTO RICAN OBITUARY* BY PEDRO PIETRI

PART 5: URBAN REALITY

"We accepted everybody . . . Nobody accepted us."
—FROM *CARLITO'S WAY* BY EDWIN TORRES

PART 6: LOVE, FAITH, AND TRANSCENDENCE

*"Who will be able to detain me with useless dreams/when my soul
begins to fulfill its task . . . ?"*
—FROM *POEM FOR MY DEATH* BY JULIA DE BURGOS

EPILOGUE: REDEMPTION

"And I will rise, holding a flag once a shroud"
—FROM *THE FINAL ACT* BY JOSÉ DE DIEGO

INTRODUCTION

"I am two parts/a person/boricua/spic/past and present/alive and oppressed . . ."

—SANDRA MARÍA ESTEVES
FROM *HERE*

For years, I was called a *Boricua*, never knowing what it meant. *Boricua* was what old men playing dominoes by the candy store called one another between smiles and sips of cold *malta*. *Boricua* was what local politicians told everyone in the neighborhood that they were when election time rolled around. *Boricua* was what nationalist activists chanted when they marched down Fifth Avenue during the Puerto Rican Day Parade. But above all, *Boricua* was the word that turned strangers into friends when used as a greeting. Whether it was addressed to a wealthy Puerto Rican man in Ponce or a Puerto Rican from the South Bronx, *Boricua* had the same indisputable impact.

I imagined that *Boricua* was just affectionate slang for *Puerto Rican*. I guessed that *Boricua* was just a word that proclaimed that you were down with your people and your culture—no different from *brother* and *sister*, the terms of endearment used by African Americans.

In New York City's Spanish Harlem in the 1960s and 1970s, guessing was the only way Puerto Ricans like me figured out our culture and history. School was a place where we learned about everyone else except ourselves. We learned about the Fourth of July and how the United States was founded by English people who proclaimed that, in this nation, all men were created equal. We learned about how the Europeans shared dinner with the Indians on Thanksgiving.

We learned about Christianity and how people who hold Christian values treat one another with love and respect. We learned about the environment and how important it is to keep the air and water clean.

But who we were as a people was never a consideration; it was a question that seldom entered our minds. Every other group except the Puerto Ricans—the Italians, the Irish, the Jews, the African Americans—seemed to have an idea who they were.

I'll never forget talking to a Jewish boy on the subway, who, like me, was nine years old. Proudly, he told me that he went to something called a "Yeshiva" school where he learned about the history of his people, about something called "oppression," and about how it was the responsibility of every Jewish person to rise and triumph no matter what the world dished out.

I'll never forget my confusion when he asked me what Puerto Rican culture and history was all about and what made Puerto Ricans special on this planet. All I could think of was salsa music, rice and beans, and the palm trees of Puerto Rico. How that boy stared at me. I remember wishing that there was a Yeshiva for Puerto Ricans so I could learn the answers to the boy's questions.

I wanted to find out what made Puerto Ricans special, but asking such questions in school only seemed to make teachers angry, especially the nuns and priests. At Commander Shea Grammar School in Spanish Harlem, a nun told me that Puerto Ricans had no culture. She made me feel stupid for even asking the question. "Oppressed," a priest told me, was what lazy people said they were so they could blame other people for their problems.

Twenty years later, as a reporter and thus entitled to ask as many questions as I wished, I stood in Havana, Cuba, talking with political exile Guillermo Morales, one of the leaders of the Puerto Rican revolutionary group, the FALN (Armed Forces for National Liberation). Morales was remembering his own experience in grade school. When he told his teacher that he wanted to do a report on Puerto Rican history instead of British or American history, the teacher laughed and told him that Puerto Rican people had no history.

Then I remembered an interview I'd read about Puerto Rican writer Abraham Rodriguez, Jr. He'd been told by a teacher that there was no such thing as a Puerto Rican writer.

It seemed that we were a worthless people. We had no history. No culture. No identity. And there were so many of us around, too, in cars, on the streets, crowded into small apartments. We would say that we were proud to be Puerto Rican, but we couldn't say why. And yet, I realized how powerfully we were all tied together by a common bond: the struggle to claim our identity against all odds.

I looked all around and I saw this mixture of colors, of languages, of ages; I saw integrity and docility, poverty and wealth, faith and frustration, humor and pain. But most of all, I saw fear. Fear rising from ourselves and others when we Puerto Ricans did something out of the ordinary. I saw that same fear when Puerto Ricans stood up and gave a speech that moved crowds. And I saw that fear again when Puerto Ricans waved poems they wrote and read them aloud.

One question began to haunt me: "What makes Puerto Ricans special on this planet?" I knew there had to be answers; I just hadn't found them yet.

In New York City I attended Xavier High School, an all boys, semi-military school run by the Jesuits. There, the priests taught me about patriotism, Christian values, and the military. I was shown a flag, told that I was an American, and that I should love my country and die for it. Then I was shown a crucifix and told I should turn the other cheek when faced with injustice. Finally, they told me that I was a Son of Xavier, that I belonged. But out in the halls I was called "nigger" and "spic" by the white boys who attended the school. And the Jesuits just looked the other way.

My classmates told me that I should go back where I came from.

That my people were all lazy welfare and food stamp cheats.

That my people were too stupid to learn English.

Over and over again, it was reinforced that being white meant being superior. Only years later did I realize that—if it hadn't been for their white skin—some of my classmates would have had nothing going for them.

Racism either makes you withdraw from yourself, hate yourself, or discover yourself. It was in the solitude of the Aguilar Library on 110th Street between Lexington and Third Avenue that I discovered myself through an odyssey of pain. Driven to books by the hatred and ignorance all around me, I read to survive. It was in that library that I first read Fidel Castro and Che Guevara and embraced progressive politics. It was in that library that, by accident, I discovered that there really were Puerto Rican writers.

Puerto Rican writers! Even now, years later, they still seem so subversive. All around me was this body of work: Puerto Rican poets and novelists, Puerto Rican orators, journalists, and academics. Puerto Rican playwrights, humorists, and essayists. Puerto Ricans wrote all these amazing things in all these great books, just like white people.

I felt a surge of excitement when I pulled from the shelves works from Piri Thomas, Pedro Pietri, Julia de Burgos, Jesus Colon, Miguel Piñero, Lola Rodriguez de Tio, Eugenio María de Hostos, Pedro Albizu Campos, Luis Muñoz Marín, José Luis Gonzalez. I held the stack of books in my arms for a long time, enjoying its weight. I let them tumble onto the desk. I watched these books by Puerto Rican writers spill over books by William Faulkner and Virginia Woolf, knowing that I was participating in a very solemn ceremony that would change my life forever. Oblivious to everyone around me, I saw only the books by Puerto Rican writers.

As fate would have it, the first book I read by a Puerto Rican author was the one the Jesuits at Xavier had denounced as pornographic and prejudiced against whites. I knew it had to be good. It was. The book was *Down These Mean Streets*, the autobiography of Puerto Rican writer Piri Thomas. He'd written about growing up in Spanish Harlem in the 1940s, but his experience was no different than mine thirty years later in the 1970s. And then there was that chapter, "Babylon for the Babylonians," where Thomas, a black-skinned Puerto Rican, faces his first painful encounter with a racism he doesn't understand, through the vicious words of a young white girl who masks her hatred with a smile.

Thomas's story brought back my own painful memories of racism, which I later wrote about in my essay, "Black *and* Latino":

My first encounter with this attitude about the race thing rode on horseback. I had just turned six years old and ran toward the bridle path in Central Park as I saw two horses about to trot past. "Yea! Horsie! Yea!" I yelled. Then I noticed one figure on horseback. She was white, and she shouted, "Shut up, you f_____g nigger! Shut up!" She pulled back on the reins and twisted the horse in my direction. I can still feel the spray of gravel that the horse kicked at my chest. And suddenly she was gone. I looked back, and, in the distance, saw my parents playing Whiffle Ball with my sister. They seemed miles away.

As I read *Down These Mean Streets*, I no longer felt alone. Through Piri Thomas's pain I was able to relive what I had so long suppressed, and this gave me new strength.

I read Pedro Pietri's "Puerto Rican Obituary" and understood for the first time what it meant to have to live in poverty. There I was, living in the Taft Projects on 114th Street and Madison Avenue, but it wasn't until I read this poem that I truly understood the reality of my surroundings.

———

To deserve a people's love, you must know them. You must learn to appreciate their history, their culture, their values, their aspirations for human advancement and freedom.

—JESUS COLON

FROM "HOW TO KNOW THE PUERTO RICANS"

Each piece of writing I found—the fiction, drama, essays, journalism, poetry, and speeches—filled in my gaps of knowledge about the range of racial, political, and cultural dynamics of the Puerto Rican people. In these writings I found everything we'd been told in school didn't exist.

And as I passionately devoured these books by Puerto Rican writers, I rediscovered a long-lost friend, the word *"Boricua."*

Sprinkled like pepper throughout many of these writings, that word, *"Boricua,"* radiated an extraordinary sense of power and confidence. The writings themselves may have talked about defeat, tragedy, and despair, but the underlying message was always that it was the responsibility of every *Boricua* to rise and triumph, no matter what the world dished out. At last I had an answer to that Yeshiva boy I'd met on the subway. And it was the same answer for my people as his.

Then, accidentally, in a tiny book tucked away on a dusty shelf in the Aguilar Library, I discovered what *"Boricua"* actually stood for. It meant "Brave Lord." *Boricua* was derived from the word *Borinquen*, or "Land of the Brave Lord," which is what the Puerto Rican natives—the Arawak Indians—called their island before Christopher Columbus confiscated it for the Spanish crown in 1493.

Once Columbus arrived, everything changed. He began by changing the island's name from Borinquen to San Juan Bautista. But in 1508 Spanish explorer Ponce de Leon renamed it Puerto Rico. He felt that "Rich Port" better expressed how he felt about the island.

Columbus had also renamed the Arawak Indians. He called them *"Taíno,"* meaning "Peace"—the first word with which they had greeted Columbus and his men as they stepped ashore on their island.

Columbus's next move was to enslave, christen, and convert the Taíno to Catholicism. Bravely, the Arawak fought back against superior armaments, and each time they were soundly defeated. In 1511 the only way Ponce de Leon managed to put down a major Arawak rebellion was to massacre 6,000 people. After that, the genocide continued unabated.

Faced with this enormous loss of manpower, Spain's Queen Isabella was forced to ship West African slaves to the Caribbean island Columbus had seized. Ponce de Leon needed them to harvest the rich crops of his "rich port"—sugar cane, coffee, ginger, and tobacco.

Over time, the remnants of the Arawak people intermarried with the Africans, who had themselves intermarried with the Spaniards. And thus a blending of Indian, black, and white bloodlines was forged to create a new race—the Puerto Ricans.

While political insurrections occurred throughout the years that followed, none was more significant than *El Grito de Lares*, an uprising that took place on September 23, 1868. A thousand Puerto Ricans had gathered in the town of Lares to demand their island's independence from Spain. They installed a provisional government and battled Spanish troops in the hills until—like the Arawaks before them, outmanned and outgunned—they were defeated. Down through the years, *El Grito de Lares* has become the symbol of the continuing struggle for Puerto Rican self-determination, identity, and nationalism.

I am not african. Africa is in me, but I cannot return.
I am not taína. Taíno is in me, but there is no way back.
I am not european. Europe lives in me, but I have no home there.

I am new. History made me. My first language was spanglish.
I was born at the crossroads
and I am whole.

—AURORA LEVINS MORALES
FROM *GETTING HOME ALIVE*

The racial dynamics of Puerto Ricans reflect our political dynamics. Being a little bit of three races and not enough of any one, we are often forced to deny our own racial identity to appease others who insist that we pledge allegiance to one race.

The problems date back to the Spanish-American War of 1898, when Puerto Rico became war booty for the United States, and ownership and control of the island changed hands. Still a colonial possession, Puerto Rico remains today a country and a people denied cultural and political self-determination.

Puerto Rico was declared a United States Protectorate in 1900 under the Foraker Act. And much against our will and desire for independence, the people of Puerto Rico were declared American citizens with a stroke of President Woodrow Wilson's pen in 1917, when he signed the Jones Act. This law gave the United States government the right to suppress armed rebellions on the island, and to dictate the political and economic policies that continue to affect the fate of the people of Puerto Rico. Ironically, despite their U.S. citizenship, Puerto Ricans have only limited political powers if they choose to remain on their native island.

Nevertheless, the tradition of armed rebellion remains active on the island as those who seek independence struggle against those who favor continued commonwealth status or statehood. From the 1930s and the impassioned oratory of Pedro Albizu Campos, Puerto Rico's greatest hero and most renowned nationalist, to the 1980s and the guerrilla campaigns by armed nationalists such as *Los Macheteros*, the message of *El Grito de Lares* lives on.

You're better off having a little bit of everything. That way you are what you have to be whenever you got to be. . . .

—EDWIN TORRES

FROM *CARLITO'S WAY*

What does it mean to be Puerto Rican? In the United States, children are raised to know everything about European history. But those of us who are of Puerto Rican descent often graduate from college ignorant of our own language, our own history, our own culture and its importance. A major reason for this is that information about us is so hard to find.

For me, this cultural quest has meant a lifetime's search for information. But as I struggled to learn about our people and our history, I began to understand why Puerto Ricans call themselves *Boricuas*, for they truly are Brave Lords, people who have fought, suffered, and survived. People who, in the end, have triumphed despite the odds. I learned that every Puerto Rican—from the old man playing dominoes with his *compadres*, to the young congresswoman introducing national legislation—is a Brave Lord.

I discovered that our history—our shared struggle—links all Puerto Ricans. It made no difference whether I was reading a poem by José de Diego written in the 1890s, a short story by Pedro Juan Soto from the 1950s, an essay by Jesus Colon from the 1960s, a scholarly essay by Clara E. Rodriguez from the 1970s, a play by Reinaldo Povod from the 1980s, or a 1990s screenplay by Joseph B. Vasquez.

Over the past hundred years our personal and societal struggles have not changed. We are still a people reclaiming our multiracial identity.

We are still a people struggling over our political destiny.

We are still a people trying to preserve and honor our culture.

We are still a people seeking freedom from foreign dominance.

———————

America should never have taught us how to read,
she should never have given us eyes to see.
                                    —FELIPE LUCIANO
                        FROM *PALANTE! YOUNG LORDS PARTY*

The prolific and exciting voices gathered in *BORICUAS: INFLUEN-TIAL PUERTO RICAN WRITINGS* tell us much about the Puerto Rican people. These *Boricuas*—a mix of revolutionaries, athletes, mothers, lawyers, journalists, ex-convicts, comedians, politicians, feminists, scholars, and actors—are the Brave Lords who maintain the spiritual continuum of our people. They have all recognized the importance of the printed word. And they have used their words to shape the societies in which they lived, building pride by championing such values as education and self-determination, and speaking out against racism and years of oppression.

These writers may, at first glance, seem to have little in common. But put their works together, and their words begin to jump off the page. Themes begin to reverberate as they are echoed, deflected, and reflected, revealing that these Puerto Rican writers have everything in common. They may represent different backgrounds, experiences, genders, and historical eras. They may use different words and different approaches. But they're all expressing the same message: We are a proud people sharing our cultural identity, our progress, and our unity of purpose.

These writers express the many aspects of the Puerto Rican experience. As we read them, we quickly begin to realize that it isn't possible to separate Puerto Rican art from its politics. Strip one aspect away and you're left with an incomplete portrait.

Take, for example, the work of nineteenth-century revolutionary poet José de Diego, who challenged the Puerto Rican people to raise their self-esteem, liberate themselves from foreign domination, and embrace their culture as a source of redemption. José de Diego was born and raised in Puerto Rico, but he was sent to Spain for his education. And while in Spain he fell under the spell of the *corrida*, the bullfights. He seriously considered shelving his education to become a bullfighter and went to a professional matador to seek advice.

> The young man told the bullfighter: "I want to face the challenge of life and death, sword in hand, as you do. It is a noble calling."
> "Pah!" the man replied. "There are greater callings. A bullfighter grasping a sword can only kill bulls in the ring. But a courageous person, with learning and with a pen in his hand, can topple kingdoms. Go back to your books!"

The writings by these forty *Boricuas* have all had tremendous influence in the Puerto Rican community. However, this anthology isn't simply intended to be an enlightening literary chronicle of the history of the Puerto Rican people. It's meant to be a stimulating read.

This anthology was born out of my life experiences, out of my career as a journalist and lecturer, and out of my concern that, for the most part, my people are unaware of the many Puerto Ricans who have written powerful and influential words that have shaped our society over the past hundred years. My aim is to present an overview of a select group of nineteenth- and twentieth-century authors whose writings bring new understanding to our recurring cultural themes.

As I assembled these works they seemed to fall naturally into six sections: Pride; History and Politics; Identity and Self-Esteem; Anxiety and Assimilation; Urban Realities; and Love, Faith, and Transcendence.

The book opens with a Prologue: Catharsis. The Puerto Rican experience requires catharsis—a purging of the emotions, a release of pent-up tensions. The struggle to birth our identity is painful, but it brings us to a greater understanding of ourselves and our people. I chose Sandra María Esteves's poem "Here" as a powerful expression of this catharsis. Although she mourns the theft of her "*isla* heritage," she knows that the act of writing down her feelings, of remembering her past, will teach her "to see, and will/bring me back to me."

PART 1: PRIDE

In this section writers from different centuries and three generations mirror one another in their messages of inspiration. José de Diego
did take the bullfighter's advice, and in 1880 he became a passionate
writer, championing the liberation of Puerto Rico from Spain, which
led to his arrest several times. Later, when the United States controlled
the island, his poetry kept the desire for independence alive by
making Puerto Ricans proud of their heritage. In his poem "To the
Persecuted," José de Diego exhorts us not to accept the role of victim,
despite racism and colonialism. He urges us to take charge of our own
lives—to "do as the bull in the face of adversity: Charge! . . ."

This is followed by Martita Morales's inspiring poem "The Sounds
of Sixth Street," in which she chronicles the education of a Puerto Rican girl confronted by injustice in her own family as well as in the
larger society. When she is "harassed by her teacher and two deans"
because she "does not stand up . . . to do the pledge of allegiance to
the amerikan flag," she takes charge of her own life and "rebels . . .
rebels . . ." against racism. "She keeps on fighting/yeah, she fights
and she fights/because she knows she is Right!"

Recognizing that the most revolutionary battles are often fought
within our own souls, José Torres, the former light heavyweight
champion of the world who went on to become a renowned sports-
writer, offers us his inspiring essay "A Letter to a Child Like Me." He
writes brilliantly about the challenges that Puerto Rican children
face, and how they can fight through their fears as he learned to do,
and emerge strong and successful. "Don't be ruled by other people's
low expectations of you!" he tells our young people. "The 21st century is yours. Go and get it!"

PART 2: HISTORY AND POLITICS

Here, an array of poetry, fiction, essays, and speeches brings the
history of the Puerto Rican people to life. These authors remind us of
the importance of history in shaping our identity, both as individuals
and as members of a community.

Poet Sandra María Esteves again reminds us that Puerto Rican culture has always been there. It's just a matter of discovering it for one-

self, of seeing and feeling what's already there. In her poem "It Is Raining Today," she prays "to the rain" to "bathe" her in "self-discovered
knowledge," to "return the remnants" of her lost history.

We then move into Jesus Colon's bittersweet essay, "How to Know
the Puerto Ricans," where he details with wry humor why our lives
are the way they are. He warns outsiders looking in that it isn't always easy to get to know us.

> "When you come to knock at the door of a Puerto Rican home,"
> he tells us, "you will be encountered by this feeling in the Puerto
> Rican—sometimes unconscious in himself—of having been
> taken for a ride for centuries. He senses that 99 persons out of
> 100 knock at his door because they want something from him
> and not because they desire to become his friend . . . that is why
> you must come many times to that door.

There's no better way to get *Boricuas* talking than to bring up the
age-old question: Should Puerto Rico be a state, a commonwealth, or
a free nation? Esmeralda Santiago doesn't take sides in her *New York
Times* Op Ed piece: "Island of Lost Causes." Her passionate advice to
her countrymen is to stop sitting on the fence. She warns that the on-
slaughts of the English language and American customs and morés
continue to undermine the already battered spirit of the Puerto Rican
people. Stop living in limbo, she tells us. Choose one path or the
other while we still have a culture to protect. We must choose our
own destiny if we are ever to solve our problems.

A century earlier, José de Diego's impassioned poem, "Hallelujahs,"
came up with a clear answer to the question of who owns Puerto
Rico: The Puerto Ricans—the same people who always owned
the island. He asks the "Gentlemen . . . from the north" to "go to the
Devil/and leave us with God."

This same powerful conviction was shared by 1930s' revolutionary
Pedro Albizu Campos. In his speech "Puerto Rican Nationalism," he
predicts that the future of the island will be bleak if Puerto Ricans let
dominion by the United States destroy their race and culture.

But not all *Boricuas* agree, as demonstrated by Luis Muñoz Marín's
1950 statement against nationalism, "On Recent Disturbances in
Puerto Rico." As the island's first elected governor, he denounced

armed rebellion and moved to tighten the bolts on Puerto Rico's remaining ties to the United States.

Nevertheless, Puerto Rican pride runs high in the soul of the boy who refuses to salute the American flag in "The Boy Without a Flag," a story by Abraham Rodriguez, Jr.

All these writers are protesting our island's fate in different ways.

In "Grand River of Loiza," Julia de Burgos, the greatest poet in the history of Puerto Rico, mourns for her enslaved people.

José Luis Gonzalez, in his fascinating essay "The *Lamento Borincaño*," examines the ways in which this popular song has become an acceptable expression of revolutionary fervor.

Revolutionary zeal explodes off the pages of Pablo Guzman's essay in *Palante! Young Lords Party*:

So we had no leadership, and we had no people—our people were dying from dope. But we knew that it was *there*, man, 'cause we knew that the fire was there.

In this same lineage, Ronald Fernandez writes with intelligence and vigor about the Puerto Rican freedom fighters of the 1980s. A scholar of Spanish ancestry, Fernandez is clearly *Boricua* in spirit. His highly influential book *Los Macheteros* is the finest work on the most powerful Puerto Rican armed nationalist group that ever existed. Leading us into the core of this organization—often dismissed as desperate terrorists—Fernandez reveals its members to be highly educated, disciplined men and women following in the spiritual footsteps of José de Diego and Pedro Albizu Campos.

Rosario Morales brings this journey through the history of our people full circle in her prose poem "Double Allegiance," by reminding us of the links between Puerto Ricans and other oppressed peoples, and of the inseparable nature of history and cultural identity.

PART 3: IDENTITY AND SELF-ESTEEM

This section shows how *Boricuas* view themselves in terms of color and culture. Are we Indio? Are we white? Are we black? Are we a rainbow people? What does this mean for us as a people and in the larger society?

It is horrifying that racism had so infected our souls that we could hate our own features, our own color, so much that we'd do anything to deny our African roots. This stigma still remains. I see it reflected out on the streets every day.

When I was growing up I'd hear ink-black Puerto Ricans say, "I'm not black! I'm Puerto Rican!" The anger and pain they associated with blackness hurt them more than any insult. After all, didn't the TV, the newspapers, our school teachers, and even our families and friends keep hammering into us that to be black was to be ugly, lazy, criminal?

I would hear Puerto Rican mothers sigh with relief when the dark-skinned men their daughters brought home turned out to be Puerto Rican. Their sons might be sitting there with ebony-colored skin and the nappiest afro you ever saw—but he wasn't black (whew!). He was Puerto Rican!

I always knew that I was both—a black and a Puerto Rican. Any time I forgot about it, the white boys I went to school with were sure to remind me. Tired of having to justify myself to Puerto Ricans and African Americans—who both said I was not black—I wrote an essay for *Essence* magazine in 1989 called "Black *and* Latino." There I proudly declared to the entire world that I was both of these things, because to deny any side of my race or my culture would be to deny my very being.

I received hundreds of letters from Puerto Ricans who had experienced the same thing. The letters thanked me, because before reading my essay they had felt all alone. Now they knew there were others—hundreds and thousands of others—who were also making peace with their dual identity.

All the writers in this section are expressing their struggles with their multicultural heritage.

Embracing her dual heritage on her own terms, Rosario Morales's daughter, Aurora Levins Morales, writes about being both Puerto Rican and Jewish in her 1986 book of poems and prose, *Getting Home Alive*. Speaking of her various heritages and identities, she feels they make her something new under the sun—a child of the Americas.

Julia de Burgos returns with her glorious and juicy paean to her racial identity: "Ay, Ay, Ay of the Kinky Negress," in which she radiates her immense pride in being African, in being a black woman, in being a Puerto Rican, and how this pride makes it possible for her to challenge injustice.

> Ay, ay, ay, that my black race escapes
> and with the white one runs to become dark;
> to become the one of the future
> brotherhood of America!

In her 1991 essay, "Puerto Ricans: Between Black and White," noted scholar Clara E. Rodriguez describes the conflicts inherent in being a member of a multicultural race.

Willie Perdomo returns to the same issues as Julia de Burgos, in "Nigger-Reecan Blues." As both Perdomo and then Piri Thomas remind us in "Babylon for the Babylonians," racists will always know that Puerto Ricans are both black and Latino even if they don't know it themselves, while Victor Hernández Cruz goes on to celebrate all things black in "African Things."

This section ends on a sober note. Judith Ortiz Cofer writes about the "Myth of the Latin Woman" in her 1993 essay that confronts the painful reality of living every day in a culture that devalues your worth, and the cruel stereotypes she and her sister *Boricuas* have to face—and resist.

Seriousness and humor blend in Nuyorican poet Miguel Algarín's seminal 1975 poem "A Mongo Affair," in which he examines the lives of Puerto Ricans who have allowed society to break them down.

Algarín, the founder of the Nuyorican Poets Cafe in New York City, is one of the most important *Boricuas* who has ever breathed city air. Over the past twenty years he has encouraged the work of hundreds of poets of all races in his Lower East Side coffee house. Many of these Nuyorican voices, who passionately express the American and native experience, have been collected in his anthology: *Aloud: Voices from the Nuyorican Poets Cafe*, which won the 1994 American Book Award.

PART 4: ANXIETY AND ASSIMILATION

This selection of writings shows how, faced with the endless pressures on their identity and self-esteem, some *Boricuas* try to assimilate and pass in white society, often successfully—but always at the cost of our identity as a people and a culture. When attempts to fit in are unsuccessful, or when one of us rebels, the anxiety can be overwhelming.

We must find our own dreams, or we will die trying to grab for the brass ring of the impossible American dream, as Pedro Pietri warns in the most famous poem ever written about the *Boricua* experience: "Puerto Rican Obituary." He speaks of five Puerto Rican men and women who died, beaten down by racism, never knowing themselves, never knowing the redemptive power of their culture.

Trying to fit how we look into the dominant culture can alienate us from our own people or from ourselves, as Piri Thomas shows us in his autobiographical story, "The Konk," about a boy whose racial self-hatred is so powerful that he wants to straighten his kinky black hair to look more like a white person's. Judith Ortiz Cofer continues this theme in "The Story of My Body," realizing in the end that she must gain her self-esteem from inside herself, since it isn't going to come from the world around her.

Sometimes our problems are so complex and so painful that writing is the only route to catharsis. Julia de Burgos writes about how difficult it is to be both a woman and an artist. She feels that she transcends her false self, which bows to the demands of husband, children, and society, only in her poetry.

In Joseph B. Vasquez's "Hangin' (Out) with the Homeboys," the central character has neither a strong sense of self nor a poetic alter ego. He's so ashamed of his Puerto Rican roots that he takes to calling himself "Vinnie," hoping others will think he's Italian.

Masking our identity may seem to be a smart move—if we can get away with it! Martin Espada's poem "Niggerlips" hauntingly describes the racism that follows us wherever we go because of the way white people perceive us.

Racism, and the anxiety it provokes, often makes us put a hold on our natural humanitarian instincts, as Jesus Colon describes in his essay "Little Things Are Big." He decides not to help a woman in difficulties because he's afraid of scaring her if he approaches. Ashamed of his nonaction, writing the essay becomes a catharsis for Colon. He vows never again to allow racial hatred to smother his benevolent instincts.

Are Puerto Ricans really the pushovers that scholar René Marqués makes them out to be in his seminal 1960 essay "The Docile Puerto Rican"? Do we inherently like being pushed around by other people—especially white Americans? Or are we actually a people who have been stripped of our history?

Esmeralda Santiago is anything but docile as she stages her own protest, refusing to eat the tasteless food the Americans try to serve her in "The American Invasion of Macun."

PART 5: URBAN REALITY

The poems, plays, and stories in this section form a living testament to how poverty and life on the streets eat away at the souls of *Boricuas*. Negative realities may be so ingrained in us that we come to dread "Monday Morning," as Pedro Pietri tells us in the poem of the same name.

Humor is one way we survive the realities of our everyday lives. And Freddie Prinze, still regarded as the best Puerto Rican comedian of all time, could always make us laugh. In his classic routine "Looking Good," he made light of all our serious problems and reminded us that no situation is hopeless, that every problem has a solution:

Most people buy German Shepherds because they're great with the
    door bell.
BUZZ!
'WOOF! WOOF! WOOF!'
Neighbors move.
I bought a Puerto Rican Shepherd. Very macho.
BUZZ!
'WHO IS IT!'
. . . The reason I knew he was a Puerto Rican Shepherd, if I took him
    out in the street, and he would see a French poodle, he'd go:
'BOW WOW! HONEY! OYE! LOOKING GOOD!'

Whether we're laughing or crying, the reality of the streets persists. And sometimes that reality ends in violence.

In *Carlito's Way*, N.Y. State Supreme Court Judge turned mystery writer, Edwin Torres, paints a powerful picture of the life of street hustler Carlos Brigante, a man who has somehow managed to keep his moral soul intact and who seeks redemption.

While doing time for armed robbery, real-life junkie and convict, Miguel Piñero, wrote "Short Eyes." It won the New York Drama Critics Circle Award for Best American Play in the 1973–74 season. In this riveting drama about prison life, the lives of several Puerto Rican and African American convicts are forever changed when a white child molester is brought into their cell block and they have to deal with the immorality of the man's actions.

The violence in our lives isn't always confined to the streets. It may be lurking in our own homes, destroying our families, as Reinaldo Povod shows us in his one-act play "Poppa Dio!" This drama about matricide in a dysfunctional family is part of Povod's gritty trilogy, *La Puta Vida—This Bitch of a Life*.

Or it may hit us out of the blue as we're going about our business trying to scratch out a living as best we can. In Pedro Juan Soto's heart-breaking story *"Bayaminiña,"* a street vendor is reduced to self-destructive rage when an arrogant white cop harasses him out of business.

Transformation and transcendence are possible, but not without their difficulties, as Felipe Luciano—who rose from poverty to become a prominent newscaster—reminds us in an essay that appeared in *Palante! Young Lords Party:*

> There's nothing extraordinary you know in my childhood— maybe just that I learned very early how to become accepted, how to rise above and beyond as they say.

PART 6: LOVE, FAITH, AND TRANSCENDENCE

Despite the harshness of our lives, we Boricuas persist, through stubbornness, ingeniousness, and the power of our loving and our faith. We go far beyond mere survival—we transcend our limitations and our surroundings.

In recognizing the gifts she has to offer the world, Julia de Burgos expresses love for herself and her future in her poem "I Became My Own Path." Migene González-Wippler's autobiographical account of her adolescent initiation into the practice of Santeria in *The Santeria Experience* explores the place where love and faith and magic meet.

Other writers in this section explore our relationships with those we love in a range that spans a fantasy connection to a remembered lover in Nicholasa Mohr's "Aunt Rosana's Rocker," to the quirky erotica of Ana Lydia Vega's "Aerobics for Love," where three, not two, make for tantalizing coupling and Ed Morales's bittersweet evocation of a dying love in his essay "My Old Flame."

In his moving ode to love and death entitled "HIV," Miguel Algarín's lovers wrestle with their pain and fear.

> Can it be that I am the bearer of plagues?
> Am I poison to desire?
> Do I have to deny yearning for firm full flesh
> so that I'll not kill what I love?

Love and death call to us again in Julia de Burgos's "Poem for My Death," where she longs for the joy that death—and its transcendence—will bring.

Other kinds of relationships are explored. A son expresses his love for his mother in Lucky CienFuegos's poem "Dedicated to María Rodriguez Martinez."

María Graniela de Pruetzel—Freddie Prinze's mother—shows her undying love for her brilliant and talented half Puerto Rican, half Hungarian son—"Hungarican" as he called himself. In her 1978 biography, *The Freddie Prinze Story*, she details how the pressures of success on the Hollywood fast track led to her son's tragic suicide at the age of twenty.

In 1976, investigative reporter, now talk-show host, Geraldo Rivera—himself a multicultural mix of Puerto Rican and Jewish—was horrified when he found himself face-to-face with the ugliness and abuse suffered by the mentally retarded incarcerated in a New Jersey institution called Willowbrook.

Bad as this was, Rivera was even less prepared for the injustice done a fellow *Boricua*, Bernard Carabello, who suffered from cerebral palsy. Incorrectly diagnosed as mentally retarded, Carabello had been confined in the living hell of Willowbrook for eighteen years.

In Rivera's groundbreaking book, *A Special Kind of Courage*, he tells the story of Carabello's harrowing ordeal and eventual release from Willowbrook. Rivera's investigations in the 1970s forever changed the way the United States would treat its mentally retarded citizens in government institutions.

Our concluding section ends with an ode to love and lust, "Loiza Aldea," by Victor Hernández Cruz.

EPILOGUE: REDEMPTION

And, finally, in the Epilogue, *BORICUAS: INFLUENTIAL PUERTO RICAN WRITINGS*, ends as it began—in catharsis. But this time our sigh of relief is much more hopeful and joyous, as our spiritual elder, José de Diego, tells us in "Final Act":

> ". . . there will arrive a great day when . . .
> My bony remains will lift that shield.
> And I will rise, holding a flag once a shroud
> Hoisted high, before the world, before Infinity."

"We accepted everybody. . . . Nobody accepted us."
—EDWIN TORRES
FROM *CARLITO'S WAY*

We often say that we're proud to be Puerto Ricans. But when we're challenged, we're at a loss to say why. It's been my deepest desire that the writings by the *Boricuas* in this anthology will provide us with answers to our innermost questions of identity, both as individuals and as a community—something we certainly don't pick up in school.

I look forward with hope and joy to the time that is dawning when we—as America's united multicultural race of whites, Indians, and blacks—fully understand and appreciate the beautiful seven letter word that chronicles our past, our present, and our future. When, armed with knowledge and power, each of us will stand proudly and say:

YO SOY BORICUA!

—Roberto Santiago
Cleveland, Ohio
1995

ACKNOWLEDGMENTS

Boricuas would not be in your hands if it were not for the work and dedication of three remarkably talented people who were there when the going got tough and believed in the importance of this anthology. My sincere thanks to the following:

My patient and brilliant editor Cheryl D. Woodruff, whose guidance and suggestions were always on target; assistant editor Leah Odze, whose editorial expertise, organizational skills, and work in securing author permissions was nothing short of miraculous; and my agent Marie Dutton Brown, whose common sense always set me at ease. Everyone at One World Books, especially Beverly Robinson designer Holly Johnson, Jennifer Richards, and Kristine Mills.

Artist Frank Diaz Escalet whose vibrant cover art reflects the unity and diversity of the Puerto Rican people. Artist Clemente Flores whose powerful original line drawings give special voice to the themes of the selections.

PROLOGUE

CATHARSIS

"... that reality .../teaches me to see, and will/bring me back to me."
—FROM *HERE* BY SANDRA MARIA ESTEVES

SANDRA MARIA ESTEVES

Here

I am two parts/a person
boricua/spic
past and present
alive and oppressed
given a cultural beauty
. . . and robbed of a cultural identity

I speak the alien tongue
in sweet boriqueño thoughts
know love mixed with pain
have tasted spit on ghetto stairways
. . . here, it must be changed
we must change it

I may never overcome
the theft of my isla heritage
dulce palmas de coco on Luquillo
sway in windy recesses I can only imagine
and remember how it was

But that reality now a dream
teaches me to see, and will
bring me back to me.

PART 1

PRIDE

"Do as the bull in the face of adversity:/charge...."
—FROM *TO THE PERSECUTED* BY JOSÉ DE DIEGO

JOSÉ DE DIEGO

To the Persecuted

Translation by Roberto Santiago

If suffering comes unabated,
if weariness weighs down your spirit,
do as the once barren tree:
flourish.
And like the planted seed:
rise.

Resurge, breathe, shout, walk, fight,
Vibrate, glide, thunder; shine forth . . .
Do as the river rich with new rainwater:
grow.
Or like the sea approaching a rocky shore:
strike.

Know how to face the angry thrust of storms,
not braying, like a frightened lamb,
but roaring, like a defiant beast.

Rise! Revolt! Resist!
Do as the bull in the face of adversity:
charge
with confident power.

MARTITA MORALES

The Sounds of Sixth Street

Kids with innocent minds
and their curiosity aroused

"¿Mami, porqué tú blanca y papi tan?"

your curiosity aroused you into asking the question
your curiosity was wandering
you wondered why all the spanish speaking people
are of many different colors

"Chocolate
hey nene
mira
Chocolate
hey mira
ven acá Chocolate"

but he kept on running
and
you had no knowledge
that
that wasn't his name
but the name of his color
which was Tan or Brown
you did not know
that
the Puerto Rican people

are a mixture of
many different races
you do not know
for you are
so young
and so innocent
and when your mother
would take you to the park
or in the summer
to the beach
where you play in the sand
with many different people
people—
men and women of your age
that range from about 3-5
you do not know
for they are all
beautiful people
because you can all play
get along
and be in a world of your own
but as the child gets older
she rebels
rebels against the fact
that
her parents will not let her have a boyfriend
with an afro
or con el pelo grifo
because he looks black
and black to them is dirty
but dead and silky blond hair
with blue eyes
and white skin
is supposed to be pure
and she rebels against the fact
that where she lives at
is a

95% Puerto Rican and
Black community
and the white
honky Ass-bourgeoisie
wants to take over
And she fights and she fights
for her
ARROZ CON GANDULES
for lunch
instead of that so-called lunch
peanut butter and jelly sandwiches
with peagreen soup
which looks like—CHURRAS
and she fights and
she fights
for what she thinks is right
she fights and
she rebels
and for this
she gets expelled
but she never gives up
no she never gives up
because in what they are doing
they are wrong and
she knows she is right
she fights
and she is in assembly in school
and because she does not stand up
like the rest of her fellow students
to do the pledge of allegiance to the amerikan flag
she is harassed by her teacher and two deans
she is almost expelled
at which she more fully rebels
and they ask her questions after questions
that she doesn't dig so she just gets up and she tips
cause she is tired of being harassed by that
    MOTHER FUCKING white ass
this is a Puerto Rican girl

trigueña and fifteen years old
this is a Puerto Rican girl
  to her, her flag is GOLD
and she rebels
and she rebels
and for this, they want her expelled
but she keeps on fighting
yeah, she fights and she fights
because she knows she is Right!

JOSÉ TORRES

A Letter to a Child Like Me

February 24, 1991

PARADE MAGAZINE

José Torres was born in an impoverished Barrio in Puerto Rico and rose to become the world light-heavyweight boxing champion in 1965, and, later, to distinguish himself as a writer. We asked Mr. Torres what he would say to a child, someone like the boy he was—we'll call him Pedrito—facing his future in today's world.

Dear Pedrito:

You're 13 now, and you must certainly be aware that there are some people in this country who refer to you as "Hispanic." That is, you're a member of a "minority group." You read newspapers and magazines, you watch television, so you know that the world is moving into the 21st century faced with big problems, enormous possibilities, huge mysteries. I worry that you might not be fully prepared for the journey.

The statistics are scary. They show us Hispanics facing a sea of trouble. The United States has 250 million people, a little more than 20 million of whom are of Hispanic descent. That's only 8 percent of this nation's total population. We're also the youngest ethnic group in the nation. We earn the lowest salaries, and, in cities where we have a large concentration of Hispanics, we have the highest school dropout rate. In New York City, for example, we comprise 25.7 percent of the high school dropouts, 42.7 percent of pregnant teenagers and 8.9 percent of the unemployed.

It should not be too hard for you to understand, my friend, that these statistics hurt us a lot. That means that many of our young people end up badly, as both victims and perpetrators. Some blame us for these conditions, despite our minuscule stock in this country and the fact the overwhelming majority of us are hardworking, decent, law-abiding citizens.

Still, you should realize that the world is not made up of statistics but of individuals. By the year 2030, you'll be my age, and what you do now is going to determine what you'll be doing then.

I've had my defeats; I've made my share of mistakes. But I've also learned something along the way. Let me tell you about a few of them. You didn't ask for this advice, but I'm going to give it to you anyway.

Let's start with a fundamental human problem, and I don't mean race or religion or origin. I mean fear. Fright, my young friend, may be the first serious enemy you have to face in our society. It's the most destructive emotional bogeyman there is. Cold feet, panic, depression, and violence are all symptoms of fear—when it's out of control. But this feeling, ironically, can also trigger courage, alertness, objectivity. You must learn not to try to rid yourself of this basic human emotion but to manipulate it for your own advantage. You cannot surrender to fear, but you *can* use it as a kind of fuel. Once you learn to control fear—to make it work for you—it will become one of your best friends.

I learned this the hard way. I was a boxer. I became a world champion, but on my way up the ladder I found Frankie Kid Anslem, a tough young Philadelphian made of steel. The match proceeded, to my increasing dismay, with me hitting and Anslem smiling. At one point, I remember, I let go a particularly left hook-right cross combination. The punches landed flush on his jaw, but he simply riposted with a smile—and some hard leather of his own.

Suddenly, I found myself struggling for my life. I was afraid. For two rounds—the eighth and ninth—Anslem and I seemed contestants in an evil struggle. My punches seemed to give him energy and pleasure! Unexpectedly, my chest began to burn, my legs weakened, my lungs gasped for air. I felt exhausted. I was dying! Thoughts of defeat and humiliation assailed me. I was grappling with these facts when I saw Anslem's jaw exposed and, reaching from somewhere beyond my terror, I threw a straight right with all my might. And Anslem lost his smile and dropped like an old shoe.

My fatigue disappeared. I felt good, happy, invigorated. Fear had overtaken me, been recognized, then resolved and manipulated for a positive result.

I was obliged to learn about handling fear through the brutal trade of boxing. I didn't have the option now open to you, my young friend. I was one of seven poor kids who lived under many layers of an underdeveloped subculture. I chose a tough profession because two black boxers—a heavyweight champion named Joe Louis, and a middleweight marvel called Sugar Ray Robinson—showed me the way. They lived far away from my hometown in Puerto Rico. But I knew them. I wanted to be like them.

Looking back, I wonder what my choice would have been if real alternatives had been available when I was your age. Don't get me wrong. I'm very proud of my first profession. To be recognized as the best in the world at what you do, even if only for a moment, is a wonderful experience. Still, I was very much aware that boxing was a temporary activity intended only for the young. And so I had a pretty good idea of what your choice should not be if you're given a chance to become an artist, a corporate executive, a doctor, a lawyer, an engineer, a writer, or a prizefighter—though it should be *my* choice.

Whatever your ambition, you must educate yourself. School is a great gift our society offers you. It provides the key for your future. You must accept this gift, not disdain it. School is where you'll learn about your country and your world and your life in both. You also discover the conflicts and contradictions of history. You'll unlock the treasure chest of the world's literature and begin to sense the beauty of music and art. You'll acquire the tools of abstract thinking, of science and mathematics—and the computer, perhaps the primary instrument of the world you'll inherit.

At home, you should learn about compassion and dignity and care. You should realize that the workings of an individual's heart and soul can be as important as the histories of the great battles, military generals, dictators and kings. Most of all, you should learn that it's *you* who are responsible for your future.

There is a basic principle you should never forget: Don't be ruled by other people's low expectation of you! It almost happened to me. I grew up in Playa de Ponce, a small *barrio* in the southern part of Puerto Rico, an island 100 miles long and 35 miles wide, with a dense population today of more than 3.3 million—1,000 human beings per square mile. I was only five when I first noticed the American military men— many of them tall, blond, and blue-eyed—wearing a variety of uniforms, roaming the streets of my neighborhood and picking up the prettiest girls. They seemed to own Playa de Ponce. Their attitude in the streets and their country's constant military victories, which we witnessed at the movie houses, became symbols of these young men's "obvious superiority." By comparison, we Puerto Ricans felt limited, inadequate.

To catch up, I volunteered to serve in the U.S. Army as soon as I became of age. And, for some mysterious reason, I joined its boxing team. My first four opponents were two compatriots and two black men from the Virgin Islands, all of whom I had no trouble disposing of. But just before my fifth fight—against one of those tall, blond, blue-eyed "superior" American soldiers, doubt started to creep into my mind. Yet, despite my worries, after three rounds of tough boxing, I overcame. I won! I had discovered the equality of the human race.

Your best defense against the ignorance of bigots and haters is pride in your own heritage. That's why you must learn your own history. Do it now. Don't wait until you are in college. You don't need teachers. Go to the library. Ask your parents and relatives and friends.

Be proud of your ethnicity and language. Don't be afraid to use it. Don't give up to the stupidity of those know-nothings who insist one language is better than two or three. You should know, and be proud, that in the Western Hemisphere more people speak Spanish than English; that *Español* was the language of the Hemisphere's first university—the Santo Tomás de Aquino University in the Dominican Republic, founded in 1538—and of the books in its first library. When you discover the long and honorable tradition to which you belong, your pride will soar.

So do not lose the language of your parents, which is also yours. Instead, refine your skill in it. If you're having trouble with grammar or writing, take courses in Spanish. Go to the library and read Cervantes' *Don Quixote*, the first full-fledged novel, or the works of the hundreds of great modern Hispanic authors, such as Gabriel García Márquez, Lola Rodriguez de Tió, Carlos Fuentes, Mario Vargas Llosa, Octavio Paz, Jorge Luis Borges, and Oscar Hijuelos, the 1990 Pulitzer Prize winner in fiction (who writes in English). Read them in both languages; know the strength of both. This is the treasure that no one can ever beat.

Puerto Rico is a nearly imperceptible dot on the map, my friend. Still, this small island recently had five boxing champions at the same time. And consider this: Baseball star Reggie Jackson; the great entertainer Sammy Davis, Jr.; Dr. Joaquín Balaguer, poet, writer and six-time president of the Dominican Republic; the renowned cellist Pablo Casals all had one thing in common—one of their parents was Puerto Rican. The film and stage star Rita Moreno, a Puerto Rican, is one of the few performers ever to win an Oscar, a Tony, a Grammy, and an Emmy award. José Ferrer, a proud Puerto Rican, was once selected as the American citizen with the finest English diction in the United States. Ferrer also won an Oscar for his brilliant performance in the classic film *Cyrano de Bergerac*. Dr. Raúl García Rinaldi, a physician of world prominence and a native Puerto Rican, helped invent six instruments now used in cardiovascular surgery. Arturo Alfonso Schomburg, a native Puerto Rican, made extensive investigation into Black history. In his honor, the New York Public Library system erected the Schomburg Center for Research in Black Culture.

The contribution of Hispanics to the development of the United States of America has been vast and unquestionable. But much more remains to be done, my friend. Every member of society must work together in order to survive together.

We live in a country where more than 27 million people can't read or write well enough to take a driving test, and many can't recognize "danger," or "poison." Every eight seconds of the school day a student drops out; every sixty seconds a teenager has a baby; every six minutes a child is arrested for drugs; every year, the schools graduate 700,000 who cannot read their diplomas.

Most of them are *not* Hispanics. Yet, many of these victims are the same people who, day after day, throw themselves in front of a TV set and become passive, docile ghosts, allowing their lives to be easily controlled by others. Television, with its emphasis on package images and quick bites, discourages thought and imagination. Studies indicate that chronic televiewers develop problems with their thinking processes and articulation. Excessive viewing dulls the most indispensable muscle—the brain.

Instead of watching TV, read and write. Words are the symbols of reality, and a well-read person, skilled at decoding those symbols, is better able to comprehend and think about the real world.

Many years ago, the great Japanese artist, Katsushika Hokusai lay on his deathbed at age 89. Experts say no one could paint better than Hokusai during his prime, and many are convinced that his work is as good as—or better than—today's top artists. But Hokusai was never satisfied with his triumphs and successes. "If I could live one more year," he said, "I could learn how to draw."

You, my young friend, would do well to become like Hokusai—a person who can lead a humble but useful and productive life, free of harm and, most important, free of the influences that generate hate, murder, suicide, and death. If you choose to spend your time not reading, thinking, and creating, but watching TV and learning how to deceive, cheat, and lie, then you become another person out there perpetuating the cycle of ignorance that leads to poverty, suffering, and despair. But if you commit yourself to a lifetime of honest work—if you assure yourself that a day in which you are unable to produce anything positive is a tragically misspent day—then, my friend, the 21st century is yours.

Go and get it!

PART 2

HISTORY AND POLITICS

"I pray to the rain . . ./Return the remnants of my identity/Bathe me in self-discovered knowledge. . . ."

—FROM *IT IS RAINING TODAY* BY SANDRA MARIA ESTEVES

SANDRA MARIA ESTEVES

It Is Raining Today

Each droplet contains a message
Soaks my clothing
The earth is crying
Or is it the sky washing down the clouds?
In the puddles lie reflections
Difficult to see thru oil film staining
Rainbow luminescence
Concentric circles expanding

La lluvia contains our history
In the space of each tear Cacique valleys and hills
Taíno, Arawak, Carib, Ife, Congo, Angola, Mesa
Mandinko, Dahome, Amer, African priests tribes
Of the past
Murdered ancestors
Today, voices in the mist

Where is our history?

What are the names washed down the sewer
In the septic flood?

I pray to the rain
Give me back my rituals
Give back truth
Return the remnants of my identity

Bathe me in self-discovered knowledge
Identify my ancestors who have existed suppressed
Invocate their spirits with power
Recreate the circle of the Ayreto
Reunite the family in a universal joining
A shower and penetrating waterfall
Rekindle the folklore
Candles of wisdom with never ending flames

Speak to me of rain.

JESUS COLON

How to Know the Puerto Ricans

One of the questions that we are most frequently asked is: "How can I get to the Puerto Ricans?" This is not a strange question to ask in a city like greater New York with more than 600,000 Puerto Ricans living, working, and struggling along with the rest of our city's inhabitants. This is a question that is crying for a correct answer, not only in our city, but in many other great cities throughout the nation where the Puerto Ricans have gone to live.

We have to admit from the start that we have no complete answer to open the door to the Puerto Ricans' houses, minds, and hearts. We have to confess that every day we are adding to that answer by our personal experience, by our going around with our American friends or by listening to what others have done—or have failed to do—in winning entrance to a Puerto Rican home and from there, to their confidence, friendship, and love. This, of course, is something that cannot be gotten in one day or in a number of weeks. Sometimes it takes months. Sometimes it takes years.

So, please excuse us if, in presenting what we have learned ourselves or added to our knowledge from the experience of others, we might sound at times a little critical, preachy or even sermonizing. The theme lends itself to committing such errors.

The first thing we must realize is that the Puerto Ricans have been exploited for hundreds of years. That strangers have been knocking at the door of the Puerto Rican nation for centuries, always in search of something, to get something or to take away something from Puerto Ricans. This has been done many times with the forceful and openly criminal way of the pirate.

Pirates with such tragically "illustrious" names as Cumberland and Drake. In one of those pirates' assaults around the middle of the seventeenth century, the bells of the cathedral in San Juan, Puerto Rico, were stolen and sold by one of their buccaneer ships in a little town known as New Amsterdam, just being built along the shores of the Hudson River.

So, in the words of one of my Puerto Rican friends, when one of those 200 percent Americans asks us why do Puerto Ricans have to come to New York? We can answer: "We come to take back our bells."

After the Spanish grandees, the French and English pirates and many others came to deprive us of whatever of value we have in our Puerto Rican land. Many came with the iron fist often hidden in the velvet glove. Many with the unctuous "love" and missionary ways of the do-gooders who come to "help" us. And we always had to listen to the chant that what was being done was "for our own good." Then came the imperialists: the pirates of the "American Century."

So when you come to knock at the door of a Puerto Rican home you will be encountered by this feeling in the Puerto Rican— sometimes unconscious in himself—of having been taken for a ride for centuries. He senses that 99 persons out of 100 knock at his door because they want something from him and not because they desire to be his friend—a friend solving mutual problems that affect them both.

That is why you must come many times to that door. You must prove yourself a friend, a worker who is also being oppressed by the same forces that keep the Puerto Rican down. Only then will the Puerto Rican open his heart to you. Only then will he ask you to have a cup of black coffee with him in his own kitchen.

Before you come to understand a person, to deserve a people's love, you must know them. You must learn to appreciate their history, their culture, their values, their aspirations for human advancement and freedom.

There is much you can learn by speaking to the Puerto Ricans every time you get a chance at work or in the casual contact of everyday life.

We must always be ready to learn from the colonial people. They have much to teach. We do not have to elaborate the point to readers of this column. Their grueling struggle against economic, political, and social oppression has steeled the colonial world and taught its people many a way to combat imperialism and war. We colonial people have also much to learn from the working class of the imperialist countries. But if you want to open that door, don't assume a know-it-all attitude and superior airs just because you were born in the United States. This "superiority" attitude of the imperialist exploiters is unfortunately reflected sometimes in the less developed members of our own working class.

You can acquire much information by reading what is published about the Puerto Ricans in our papers and in the progressive weekly and monthly publications. There are some books with much valuable factual information and many incorrect conclusions. We have to be careful about such books.

ESMERALDA SANTIAGO

Island of Lost Causes

On Oct. 30, 1950, 15 policemen and 25 National Guardsmen surrounded the Salón Boricua in Villa Palmeras, Puerto Rico, a barbershop owned by the nationalist leader Vidal Santiago Diaz. The windows of the shop were shuttered, but every once in a while gunfire erupted through the slats and was returned by the police and guards armed with pistols, machine guns, rifles and tear gas.

The siege lasted more than four hours. When the police were finally able to ax their way into the shop, they found a man slumped in a corner, his torso ripped by a grenade, his head bleeding. Two policemen dragged him out to the street and threw him on a stretcher.

Vidal Santiago Diaz was my uncle. As a child, I sat on his lap and stuck my index finger into the soft hole in the middle of his forehead, the scar left from a bullet.

In the 32 years since I left Puerto Rico for the United States, I haven't told many people about Tío Vidal. No one has ever asked me much about the island other than the location of the most charming hotels and whether we cook with hot chili peppers.

Lately, however, I've been grilled politely about the plebiscite taking place there today: Should Puerto Rico become the 51st state? Should it be an independent nation? Should it remain a commonwealth?

The vote is nonbinding—not much more than a recommendation to the U.S. Congress. But as the first referendum since 1967, it has excited intense interest, on the island as well as among Puerto Ricans now living in the U.S.

As a Puerto Rican born in San Juan but now living in New York, I'm not eligible to vote on these questions. If I could, however, I would be filled with ambivalence.

Puerto Rico has been a colony for 500 years, first of Spain, then, since 1898, the U.S. Today's plebiscite gives Puerto Ricans only the illusion of self-determination—an illusion that deflects attention from the basic problems on the island.

The reality of Puerto Rico is an unemployment rate of 17.3 percent; 862 murders in 1992—a number that is expected to rise in 1993; a language so quickly becoming Spanglish that we have an inferiority complex about the purity of our spoken tongue; rampant urbanization that has destroyed thousands of acres of farmland; American businesses that set up shop for as long as they can get tax breaks, then move on to another part of the world where there is no minimum wage and the workers don't expect as much.

Puerto Rico's unsettled political status is symptomatic of the internal conflicts its people struggle with every day, whether we live on the island or in the U.S. We are born American citizens but harbor an intense Latin American identity.

Yet we are looked down upon by some Latin American neighbors because our culture is a hodge-podge of American influences grafted onto 400 years of Spanish traditions. We are told that our island doesn't have the rich heritage of bloody struggles for independence that other countries do.

The truth is, we do have a history of struggle for independence, but the opposition has always won. The failure of our best hopes for independence through centuries of failed insurrections has caused many Puerto Ricans to simply give up.

To some, statehood seems a clear solution to the island's ambiguous commonwealth status and a way of making the U.S. accountable for our future. After all, many Americans already refer to Puerto Rico as "part of the United States," as if the island were attached to the North American continent, like Kansas or Nebraska.

We are taken for granted by the U.S., and that sharpens in us a stubborn nationalist streak—yet we don't demonstrate it at the ballot box. In our hearts, we want to believe independence is the right choice, but our history forces us to see it as a lost cause. Still, we are not willing to give up so completely as to vote for statehood. It would be the ultimate statement of surrender.

This is why so many Puerto Ricans will vote for the status quo. It fosters the illusion of choosing a destiny, neither capitulating nor fighting. But it continues to evade the question of who we are as a people.

An elusive cultural identity lies at the heart of our unwillingness to declare ourselves either a nation or a state. A vote for the commonwealth insures that we don't have to commit one way or the other.

Ironically, neither violent insurrection nor the democratic process seem able to solve that question. Tío Vidal had a belief in nationhood that drove him to risk his life. How many of us Puerto Ricans would go that far? We need to look at ourselves hard and to stop hiding behind the status quo. It is not a choice. It is a refusal to choose.

JOSÉ DE DIEGO

Hallelujahs

Translation by Roberto Santiago

Gentlemen from the powerful, bountiful North,
Our island is part of the world.

Our Caribbean island is part of the Americas.

In the Beginning, God raised our island from the sea,
when its waters were clear and undisturbed.

And, after centuries, coming from the East,
the Arawaks inhabited the island.

And, centuries after, quaking the seas, the Spanish
ships arrived.

Mighty ships, cursed with being Latin.

That day your Puritan ships did battle, our Spanish
fleet were no match; tiny.

That day, when the Spanish people sank, ships and all,
in the seas of the Americas.

That day when you came in your splendor,
You, the all powerful Gentlemen of the North.

Forgive, Gentlemen, the heavens and earth,
for having made this island, long before the war . . .

Forgive, that so many of us were born,
before the United States.

Born in the Americas, with nothing,
but the kindness of God.

We are not the strongest, nor are we the masters,
but we are sons of the *Conquistadors*.

We know the mysteries of philosophy
and of the Art of Holy Poetry

But we know nothing, in our land of the Sun,
of the government practiced in Tammany Hall.

Nor do we understand your creative doctrines,
that placed the Philippines within the boundaries of
California.

Forgive, Gentlemen, if we seem perplexed,
of your concept of the Right of the People.

We shun concepts that would reduce us to an Island of
Thieves.

We shun, despite your historical reversals, the language and the
spirit of the Anglo people.

We speak another language, with other thoughts,
with the power of the spirit
and the power of the wind.

And we have been telling you for a long time,

over and over,

to go to the Devil
and leave us with God.

PEDRO ALBIZU CAMPOS

Puerto Rican Nationalism

Translation by Roberto Santiago

SPEECH GIVEN BEFORE THE ASSOCIATED PRESS, 1936

Sixty-eight years ago, our republic was formed. On September 23, 1868, we declared our independence from Spain. Puerto Rico was rich in name and in soil. Our Christian foundation had created a family model that was to be a vanguard of modern civilization.

Influential, independent men have made a difference in our society. Men such as musician Morel Campos; intellectuals such as Eugenio Maria de Hostos; and poets like Gautier Benitez were among the great men who built and founded this nation.

The founders of our republic in 1868 held that our nation and its people would be sovereign—never belonging to another nation or people. This idea is not original, but is the basis of universal civilization, of international law. It is the basis of the family of free nations.

Our mother nation, Spain, founder of North and South American civilization, recognized this basic principle of sovereignty and, in 1868, paved the way for Puerto Rico to enter the family of free nations.

The United States (after the Spanish American War), on the other hand, saw Puerto Rico not as a nation, but as island property, and therefore took Puerto Rico through military intervention, and kept it.

Military intervention is the most brutal and abusive act that can be committed against a nation and a people. We demanded then, as we do today, the retreat of United States armed forces from Puerto Rico in order to embrace the liberty we held all too briefly in 1868.

We are not as fortunate as our forebears in 1868, who struggled to attain sovereignty. They never had a complaint against Spain, for Spain had every intention of granting Puerto Rico its liberty.

We stand today, docile and defenseless, because, since 1868, our political and economic power has been systematically stripped away by the United States for its own political and economic gain.

We stand as a nation forced not only to demand our liberty, but to demand reparations for having our political and economic liberty taken away.

We stand as a nation surrounded by industry, but with little of it belonging to our people. The business development in Puerto Rico since the United States intervention should have made the island one of the most prosperous islands in the world, but that is not the case.

The United States controls our economy, our commerce. Puerto Rico must determine a price for its products that is acceptable to the United States, while the United States issues their products to Puerto Rico at a rate that is comfortable to its own manufacturers and not the Puerto Rican consumer. The result is exploitation and abuses perpetrated at will, resulting in poverty for our people and wealth for the United States.

Seventy-six percent of the wealth is in the hands of United States corporations, and their stability is ensured by the United States military. This economic exploitation will have long-lasting impact. Our family structure will be weakened, and the intellectual, spiritual, and moral advancement of our race will be jeopardized as we are made to be more "North American."

Already United States government agencies, under the guise of Christian virtue and goodwill, are simply controlling our people, destroying its culture. By imposing its own culture and language, the United States destroys our own culture and language.

What will we have when we have nothing but dependency on those who destroyed us?

This is why I am dismayed by the effort among our own people to defeat the spirit of those who struggle for our liberation. Our own people see Puerto Rican nationalism as nothing but a path of terrorism and murder; but they defeat our spirit in denouncing themselves. They defeat our spirit by ignoring the historical terrorism and murder of the United States. In the end, they help only the United States, its industry, its imperialistic objectives.

It stands to reason—it stands to common sense—that we must be a free nation in order to survive as a people. The future of those not yet born depends on respecting the independence of Puerto Rico. That respect alone—the respecting of Puerto Rico's independence—is what Puerto Rican nationalism is all about.

LUIS MUÑOZ MARÍN

On Recent Disturbances in Puerto Rico

COAST-TO-COAST BROADCAST, NOVEMBER 1, 1950

The people of Puerto Rico are profoundly indignant at the attempt made at Blair House, in which two Puerto Rican nationalists were involved. We would feel ashamed of calling ourselves Puerto Ricans, if it were not for the fact that the nationalist gangsters are less than 500 in number, among the more than two million decent, democracy-loving American citizens that make up our community. We have a genuine admiration and affection for President Truman, not only because of his leadership in these troubled times of the world, but in a more intimate sense, because of his constant, fair-minded, generous attitude in helping Puerto Rico to help itself. We are deeply relieved that this criminal attempt was as futile as the violence that we have experienced from the same source and under the same guidance in Puerto Rico during the last two days. This crime confirms my conviction of the connection of these mad, grotesque, and futile nationalist violence-makers in Puerto Rico with communistic propaganda strategy all over the world.

The nationalists started violence and assassination last Monday in Puerto Rico. Twenty-seven people were killed and about ninety wounded. In numbers, they are an insignificant group favoring the independence of Puerto Rico. The issue in Puerto Rico is not between colonialism and independence. We are not a colony of the United States. We are citizens of the United States and our Island is associated on a basis of freedom with the United States. We are members of the independence of the United States.

The last time the Nationalist Party risked the hazard of democracy by going to the polls was in 1932. At that time they managed to get only 5,000 votes out of 400,000 votes cast. Since then, they have expressed the conviction that votes and democracy are not important. I am governor of Puerto Rico by a majority of 390,000 votes out of a total of 640,000, but my opponents, who polled the other 250,000, are one hundred percent with me in condemning this dastardly attempt on President Truman's life and all the criminal works of this communist-prompted lunacy. The nationalists have no political power. They have no votes and they hate votes. Votes to them are as repugnant as holy water to the devil. As decent Christians, as militant members of the democratic world, all Puerto Rico tonight is filled with wrath and indignation.

I have just talked to President Truman on the telephone and I expressed to him the joy of our people that the criminal attack was thwarted. I am happy to say that the President answered me that the facts are clearly understood by the people in the United States.

In the name of the people of Puerto Rico, I wish also to convey our grief to the family of the guard who lost his life at Blair House today.

ABRAHAM RODRIGUEZ, JR.

The Boy Without a Flag

—To Ms. Linda Falcón, wherever she is

Swirls of dust danced in the beams of sunlight that came through the tall windows, the buzz of voices resounding in the stuffy auditorium.

Mr. Rios stood by our Miss Colon, hovering as if waiting to catch her if she fell. His pale mouse features looked solemnly dutiful. He was a versatile man, doubling as English teacher and gym coach. He was only there because of Miss Colon's legs. She was wearing her neon pink nylons. Our favorite.

We tossed suspicious looks at the two of them. Miss Colon would smirk at Edwin and me, saying, "Hey, face front," but Mr. Rios would glare. I think he knew that we knew what he was after. We knew, because on Fridays, during our free period when we'd get to play records and eat stale pretzel sticks, we would see her way in the back by the tall windows, sitting up on a radiator like a schoolgirl. There would be a strange pinkness on her high cheekbones, and there was Mr. Rios, sitting beside her, playing with her hand. Her face, so thin and girlish, would blush. From then on, her eyes, very close together like a cartoon rendition of a beaver's, would avoid us.

Miss Colon was hardly discreet about her affairs. Edwin had first tipped me off about her love life after one of his lunchtime jaunts through the empty hallways. He would chase girls and toss wet bathroom napkins into classrooms where kids in the lower grades sat, trapped. He claimed to have seen Miss Colon slip into a steward's closet with Mr. Rios and to have heard all manner of sounds through the thick wooden door, which was locked (he tried it). He had told half the class before the day was out, the boys sniggering behind grimy hands, the girls shocked because Miss Colon was married, so married that she even brought the poor unfortunate in one morning as a kind of show-and-tell guest. He was an untidy dark-skinned Puerto Rican type in a colorful dashiki. He carried a paper bag that smelled like glue. His eyes seemed sleepy, his Afro an uncombed Brillo pad. He talked about protest marches, the sixties, the importance of an education. Then he embarrassed Miss Colon greatly by disappearing into the coat closet and falling asleep there. The girls, remembering him, softened their attitude toward her indiscretions, defending her violently. "Face it," one of them blurted out when Edwin began a new series of Miss Colon tales, "she married a bum and needs to find true love."

"She's a slut, and I'm gonna draw a comic book about her," Edwin said, hushing when she walked in through the door. That afternoon, he showed me the first sketches of what would later become a very popular comic book entitled "Slut at the Head of the Class." Edwin could draw really well, but his stories were terrible, so I volunteered to do the writing. In no time at all, we had three issues circulating under desks and hidden in notebooks all over the school. Edwin secretly ran off close to a hundred copies on a copy machine in the main office after school. It always amazed me how copies of our comic kept popping up in the unlikeliest places. I saw them on radiators in the auditorium, on benches in the gym, tacked up on bulletin boards. There were even some in the teachers' lounge, which I spotted one day while running an errand for Miss Colon. Seeing it, however, in the hands of Miss Marti, the pig-faced assistant principal, nearly made me puke up my lunch. Good thing our names weren't on it.

It was a miracle no one snitched on us during the ensuing investigation, since only a blind fool couldn't see our involvement in the thing. No bloody purge followed, but there was enough fear in both of us to kill the desire to continue our publishing venture. Miss Marti, a woman with a battlefield face and constant odor of Chiclets, made a forceful threat about finding the culprits while holding up the second issue, the one with the hand-colored cover. No one moved. The auditorium grew silent. We meditated on the sound of a small plane flying by, its engines rattling the windows. I think we wished we were on it.

It was in the auditorium that the trouble first began. We had all settled into our seats, fidgeting like tiny burrowing animals, when there was a general call for quiet. Miss Marti, up on stage, had a stare that could make any squirming fool sweat. She was a gruff, nasty woman who never smiled without seeming sadistic.

Mr. Rios was at his spot beside Miss Colon, his hands clasped behind his back as if he needed to restrain them. He seemed to whisper to her. Soft, mushy things. Edwin would watch them from his seat beside me, giving me the details, his shiny face looking worried. He always seemed sweaty, his fingers kind of damp.

"I toldju, I saw um holdin hands," he said. "An now lookit him, he's whispering sweet shits inta huh ear."

He quieted down when he noticed Miss Marti's evil eye sweeping over us like a prison-camp searchlight. There was silence. In her best military bark, Miss Marti ordered everyone to stand. Two lone, pathetic kids, dragooned by some unseen force, slowly came down the center aisle, each bearing a huge flag on a thick wooden pole. All I could make out was that great star-spangled unfurling, twitching thing that looked like it would fall as it approached over all those bored young heads. The Puerto Rican flag walked beside it, looking smaller and less confident. It clung to its pole.

"The Pledge," Miss Marti roared, putting her hand over the spot where her heart was rumored to be.

That's when I heard my father talking.

He was sitting on his bed, yelling about Chile, about what the CIA had done there. I was standing opposite him in my dingy Pro Keds. I knew about politics. I was eleven when I read William Shirer's book on Hitler. I was ready.

"All this country does is abuse Hispanic nations," my father said, turning a page of his *Post*, "tie them down, make them dependent. It says democracy with one hand while it protects and feeds fascist dictatorships with the other." His eyes blazed with a strange fire. I sat on the bed, on part of his *Post*, transfixed by his oratorical mastery. He had mentioned political things before, but not like this, not with such fiery conviction. I thought maybe it had to do with my reading Shirer. Maybe he had seen me reading that fat book and figured I was ready for real politics.

Using the knowledge I gained from the book, I defended the Americans. What fascism was he talking about, anyway? I knew we had stopped Hitler. That was a big deal, something to be proud of.

"Come out of fairy-tale land," he said scornfully. "Do you know what imperialism is?"

I didn't really, no.

"Well, why don't you read about that? Why don't you read about Juan Bosch and Allende, men who died fighting imperialism? They stood up against American big business. You should read about that instead of this crap about Hitler."

"But I like reading about Hitler," I said, feeling a little spurned. I didn't even mention that my fascination with Adolf led to my writing a biography of him, a book report one hundred and fifty pages long. It got an A-plus. Miss Colon stapled it to the bulletin board right outside the classroom, where it was promptly stolen.

"So, what makes you want to be a writer?" Miss Colon asked me quietly one day, when Edwin and I, always the helpful ones, volunteered to assist her in getting the classroom spiffed up for a Halloween party.

"I don't know. I guess my father," I replied, fiddling with plastic pumpkins self-consciously while images of my father began parading through my mind.

When I think back to my earliest image of my father, it is one of him sitting behind a huge rented typewriter, his fingers clacking away. He was a frustrated poet, radio announcer, and even stage actor. He had sent for diplomas from fly-by-night companies. He took acting lessons, went into broadcasting, even ended up on the ground floor of what is now Spanish radio, but his family talked him out of all of it. "You should find yourself real work, something substantial," they said, so he did. He dropped all those dreams that were never encouraged by anyone else and got a job at a Nedick's on Third Avenue. My pop the counterman.

Despite that, he kept writing. He recited his poetry into a huge reel-to-reel tape deck that he had, then he'd play it back and sit like a critic, brow furrowed, fingers stroking his lips. He would record strange sounds and play them back to me at outrageous speeds, until I believed that there were tiny people living inside the machine. I used to stand by him and watch him type, his black pompadour spilling over his forehead. There was energy pulsating all around him, and I wanted a part of it.

I was five years old when I first sat in his chair at the kitchen table and began pushing down keys, watching the letters magically appear on the page. I was entranced. My fascination with the typewriter began at that point. By the time I was ten, I was writing war stories, tales of pain and pathos culled from the piles of comic books I devoured. I wrote unreadable novels. With illustrations. My father wasn't impressed. I guess he was hard to impress. My terrific grades did not faze him, nor the fact that I was reading books as fat as milk crates. My unreadable novels piled up. I brought them to him at night to see if he would read them, but after a week of waiting I found them thrown in the bedroom closet, unread. I felt hurt and rejected, despite my mother's kind words. "He's just too busy to read them," she said to me one night when I mentioned it to her. He never brought them up, even when I quietly took them out of the closet one day or when he'd see me furiously hammering on one of his rented machines. I would tell him I wanted to be a writer, and he would smile sadly and pat my head, without a word.

"You have to find something serious to do with your life," he told me one night, after I had shown him my first play, eighty pages long. What was it I had read that got me into writing a play? Was it Arthur Miller? Oscar Wilde? I don't remember, but I recall my determination to write a truly marvelous play about combat because there didn't seem to be any around.

"This is fun as a hobby," my father said, "but you can't get serious about this." His demeanor spoke volumes, but I couldn't stop writing. Novels, I called them, starting a new one every three days. The world was a blank page waiting for my words to recreate it, while the real world remained cold and lonely. My schoolmates didn't understand any of it, and because of the fat books I carried around, I was held in some fear. After all, what kid in his right mind would read a book if it wasn't assigned? I was sick of kids coming up to me and saying, "Gaw, lookit tha fat book. Ya teacha make ya read tha?" (No, I'm just reading it.) The kids would look at me as if I had just crawled out of a sewer. "Ya crazy, man." My father seemed to share that opinion. Only my teachers understood and encouraged my reading, but my father seemed to want something else from me.

Now, he treated me like an idiot for not knowing what imperialism was. He berated my books and one night handed me a copy of a book about Albizu Campos, the Puerto Rican revolutionary. I read it through in two sittings.

"Some of it seems true," I said.

"Some of it?" my father asked incredulously. "After what they did to him, you can sit there and act like a Yankee flag-waver?"

I watched the Yankee flag making its way up to the stage over indifferent heads, my father's scowling face haunting me, his words resounding in my head.

"Let me tell you something," my father sneered. "In school, all they do is talk about George Washington, right? The first president? The father of democracy? Well, he had slaves. We had our own Washington, and ours had real teeth."

As Old Glory reached the stage, a general clatter ensued.

"We had our own revolution," my father said, "and the United States crushed it with the flick of a pinkie."

Miss Marti barked her royal command. Everyone rose up to salute the flag.

Except me. I didn't get up. I sat in my creaking seat, hands on my knees. A girl behind me tapped me on the back. "Come on, stupid, get up." There was a trace of concern in her voice. I didn't move.

Miss Colon appeared. She leaned over, shaking me gently. "Are you sick? Are you okay?" Her soft hair fell over my neck like a blanket.

"No," I replied.

"What's wrong?" she asked, her face growing stern. I was beginning to feel claustrophobic, what with everyone standing all around me, bodies like walls. My friend Edwin, hand on his heart, watched from the corner of his eye. He almost looked envious, as if he wished he had thought of it. Murmuring voices around me began reciting the Pledge while Mr. Rios appeared, commandingly grabbing me by the shoulder and pulling me out of my seat into the aisle. Miss Colon was beside him, looking a little apprehensive.

"What is wrong with you?" he asked angrily. "You know you're supposed to stand up for the Pledge! Are you religious?"

"No," I said.

"Then what?"

"I'm not saluting that flag," I said.

"What?"

"I said, I'm not saluting that flag."

"Why the . . . ?" He calmed himself; a look of concern flashed over Miss Colon's face. "Why not?"

"Because I'm Puerto Rican. I ain't no American. And I'm not no Yankee flag-waver."

"You're supposed to salute the flag," he said angrily, shoving one of his fat fingers in my face. "You're not supposed to make up your own mind about it. You're supposed to do as you are told."

"I thought I was free," I said, looking at him and at Miss Colon.

"You are," Miss Colon said feebly. "That's why you should salute the flag."

"But shouldn't I do what I feel is right?"

"You should do what you are told!" Mr. Rios yelled into my face. "I'm not playing no games with you, mister. You hear that music?

That's the anthem. Now you go stand over there and put your hand over your heart." He made as if to grab my hand, but I pulled away. .

"No!" I said sharply. "I'm not saluting that crummy flag! And you can't make me, either. There's nothing you can do about it."

"Oh yeah?" Mr. Rios roared. "We'll see about that!"

"Have you gone crazy?" Miss Colon asked as he led me away by the arm, down the hallway, where I could still hear the strains of the anthem. He walked me briskly into the principal's office and stuck me in a corner.

"You stand there for the rest of the day and see how you feel about it," he said viciously. "Don't you even think of moving from that spot!"

I stood there for close to two hours or so. The principal came and went, not even saying hi or hey or anything, as if finding kids in the corners of his office was a common occurrence. I could hear him talking on the phone, scribbling on pads, talking to his secretary. At one point I heard Mr. Rios outside in the main office.

"Some smart-ass. I stuck him in the corner. Thinks he can pull that shit. The kid's got no respect, man. I should get the chance to teach him some."

"Children today have no respect," I heard Miss Marti's reptile voice say as she approached, heels clacking like gunshots. "It has to be forced upon them."

She was in the room. She didn't say a word to the principal, who was on the phone. She walked right over to me. I could hear my heart beating in my ears as her shadow fell over me. Godzilla over Tokyo.

"Well, have you learned your lesson yet?" she asked, turning me from the wall with a finger on my shoulder. I stared at her without replying. My face burned, red hot. I hated it.

"You think you're pretty important, don't you? Well, let me tell you, you're nothing. You're not worth a damn. You're just a snotty-nosed little kid with a lot of stupid ideas." Her eyes bored holes through me, searing my flesh. I felt as if I were going to cry. I fought the urge. Tears rolled down my face anyway. They made her smile, her chapped lips twisting upwards like the mouth of a lizard.

"See? You're a little baby. You don't know anything, but you'd better learn your place." She pointed a finger in my face. "You do as you're told if you don't want big trouble. Now go back to class."

Her eyes continued to stab at me. I looked past her and saw Edwin waiting by the office door for me. I walked past her, wiping at my face. I could feel her eyes on me still, even as we walked up the stairs to the classroom. It was close to three already, and the skies outside the grated windows were cloudy.

"Man," Edwin said to me as we reached our floor, "I think you're crazy."

The classroom was abuzz with activity when I got there. Kids were chattering, getting their windbreakers from the closet, slamming their chairs up on their desks, filled with the euphoria of soon-home. I walked quietly over to my desk and took out my books. The other kids looked at me as if I were a ghost.

I went through the motions like a robot. When we got downstairs to the door, Miss Colon, dismissing the class, pulled me aside, her face compassionate and warm. She squeezed my hand.

"Are you okay?"

I nodded.

"That was a really crazy stunt there. Where did you get such an idea?"

I stared at her black flats. She was wearing tan panty hose and a black miniskirt. I saw Mr. Rios approaching with his class.

"I have to go," I said, and split, running into the frigid breezes and the silver sunshine.

At home, I lay on the floor of our living room, tapping my open notebook with the tip of my pen while the Beatles blared from my father's stereo. I felt humiliated and alone. Miss Marti's reptile face kept appearing in my notebook, her voice intoning, "Let me tell you, you're nothing." Yeah, right. Just what horrible hole did she crawl out of? Were those people really Puerto Ricans? Why should a Puerto Rican salute an American flag?

. I put the question to my father, strolling into his bedroom, a tiny M-1 rifle that belonged to my G.I. Joe strapped to my thumb.

"Why?" he asked, loosening the reading glasses that were perched on his nose, his newspaper sprawled open on the bed before him, his cigarette streaming blue smoke. "Because we are owned, like cattle. And because nobody has any pride in their culture to stand up for it."

I pondered those words, feeling as if I were being encouraged, but I didn't dare tell him. I wanted to believe what I had done was a brave and noble thing, but somehow I feared his reaction. I never could impress him with my grades, or my writing. This flag thing would probably upset him. Maybe he, too, would think I was crazy, disrespectful, a "smart-ass" who didn't know his place. I feared that, feared my father saying to me, in a reptile voice, "Let me tell you, you're nothing."

I suited up my G.I. Joe for combat, slipping on his helmet, strapping on his field pack. I fixed the bayonet to his rifle, sticking it in his clutching hands so he seemed ready to fire. "A man's gotta do what a man's gotta do." Was that John Wayne? I don't know who it was, but I did what I had to do, still not telling my father. The following week, in the auditorium, I did it again. This time, everyone noticed. The whole place fell into a weird hush as Mr. Rios screamed at me.

I ended up in my corner again, this time getting a prolonged, pensive stare from the principal before I was made to stare at the wall for two more hours. My mind zoomed past my surroundings. In one strange vision, I saw my crony Edwin climbing up Miss Colon's curvy legs, giving me every detail of what he saw.

"Why?" Miss Colon asked frantically. "This time you don't leave until you tell me why." She was holding me by the arm, masses of kids flying by, happy blurs that faded into the sunlight outside the door.

"Because I'm Puerto Rican, not American," I blurted out in a weary torrent. "That makes sense, don't it?"

"So am I," she said, "but we're in America!" She smiled. "Don't you think you could make some kind of compromise?" She tilted her head to one side and said, "Aw, c'mon," in a little-girl whisper.

"What about standing up for what you believe in? Doesn't that matter? You used to talk to us about Kent State and protesting. You said those kids died because they believed in freedom, right? Well, I feel like them now. I wanna make a stand."

She sighed with evident aggravation. She caressed my hair. For a moment, I thought she was going to kiss me. She was going to say something, but just as her pretty lips parted, I caught Mr. Rios approaching.

"I don't wanna see him," I said, pulling away.

"No, wait," she said gently.

"He's gonna deck me," I said to her.

"No, he's not," Miss Colon said, as if challenging him, her eyes taking him in as he stood beside her.

"No, I'm not," he said. "Listen here. Miss Colon was talking to me about you, and I agree with her." He looked like a nervous little boy in front of the class, making his report. "You have a lot of guts. Still, there are rules here. I'm willing to make a deal with you. You go home and think about this. Tomorrow I'll come see you." I looked at him skeptically, and he added, "to talk."

"I'm not changing my mind," I said. Miss Colon exhaled painfully.

"If you don't, it's out of my hands." He frowned and looked at her. She shook her head, as if she were upset with him.

I reread the book about Albizu. I didn't sleep a wink that night. I didn't tell my father a word, even though I almost burst from the effort. At night, alone in my bed, images attacked me. I saw Miss Marti and Mr. Rios debating Albizu Campos. I saw him in a wheelchair with a flag draped over his body like a holy robe. They would not do that to me. They were bound to break me the way Albizu was broken, not by young smiling American troops bearing chocolate bars, but by conniving, double-dealing, self-serving Puerto Rican landowners and their ilk, who dared say they were the future. They spoke of dignity and democracy while teaching Puerto Ricans how to cling to the great coat of that powerful northern neighbor. Puerto Rico, the shining star, the great lapdog of the Caribbean. I saw my father, the Nationalist hero, screaming from his podium, his great oration stirring everyone around him to acts of bravery. There was a shining arrogance in his eyes as he stared out over the sea of faces mouthing his name, a sparkling audacity that invited and incited. There didn't seem to be fear anywhere in him, only the urge to rush to the attack, with his armband and revolutionary tunic. I stared up at him, transfixed. I stood by the podium, his personal adjutant, while his voice rang through the stadium. "We are not, nor will we ever be, Yankee flag-wavers!" The roar that followed drowned out the whole world.

The following day, I sat in my seat, ignoring Miss Colon as she neatly drew triangles on the board with the help of plastic stencils. She was using colored chalk, her favorite. Edwin, sitting beside me, was beaning girls with spitballs that he fired through his hollowed-out Bic pen. They didn't cry out. They simply enlisted the help of a girl named Gloria who sat a few desks behind him. She very skillfully nailed him with a thick wad of gum. It stayed in his hair until Edwin finally went running to Miss Colon. She used her huge teacher's scissors. I couldn't stand it. They all seemed trapped in a world of trivial things, while I swam in a mire of oppression. I walked through lunch as if in a trance, a prisoner on death row waiting for the heavy steps of his executioners. I watched Edwin lick at his regulation cafeteria ice cream, sandwiched between two sheets of paper. I was once like him, laughing and joking, lining up for a stickball game in the yard without a care. Now it all seemed lost to me, as if my youth had been burned out of me by a book.

Shortly after lunch, Mr. Rios appeared. He talked to Miss Colon for a while by the door as the room filled with a bubbling murmur. Then, he motioned for me. I walked through the sudden silence as if in slow motion.

"Well," he said to me as I stood in the cool hallway, "have you thought about this?"

"Yeah," I said, once again seeing my father on the podium, his voice thundering.

"And?"

"I'm not saluting that flag."

Miss Colon fell against the doorjamb as if exhausted. Exasperation passed over Mr. Rios' rodent features.

"I thought you said you'd think about it," he thundered.

"I did. I decided I was right."

"*You* were right?" Mr. Rios was losing his patience. I stood calmly by the wall.

"I told you," Miss Colon whispered to him.

"Listen," he said, ignoring her, "have you heard of the story of the man who had no country?"

I stared at him.

"Well? Have you?"

"No," I answered sharply; his mouse eyes almost crossed with anger at my insolence. "Some stupid fairy tale ain't gonna change my mind anyway. You're treating me like I'm stupid, and I'm not."

"Stop acting like you're some mature adult! You're not. You're just a puny kid."

"Well, this puny kid still ain't gonna salute that flag."

"You were born here," Miss Colon interjected patiently, trying to calm us both down. "Don't you think you at least owe this country some respect? At least?"

"I had no choice about where I was born. And I was born poor."

"So what?" Mr. Rios screamed. "There are plenty of poor people who respect the flag. Look around you, dammit! You see any rich people here? I'm not rich either!" He tugged on my arm. "This country takes care of Puerto Rico, don't you see that? Don't you know anything about politics?"

"Do you know what imperialism is?"

The two of them stared at each other.

"I don't believe you," Mr. Rios murmured.

"Puerto Rico is a colony," I said, a direct quote of Albizu's. "Why I gotta respect that?"

Miss Colon stared at me with her black saucer eyes, a slight trace of a grin on her features. It encouraged me. In that one moment, I felt strong, suddenly aware of my territory and my knowledge of it. I no longer felt like a boy but some kind of soldier, my bayonet stained with the blood of my enemy. There was no doubt about it. Mr. Rios was the enemy, and I was beating him. The more he tried to treat me like a child, the more defiant I became, his arguments falling like twisted armor. He shut his eyes and pressed the bridge of his nose.

"You're out of my hands," he said.

Miss Colon gave me a sympathetic look before she vanished into the classroom again. Mr Rios led me downstairs without another word. His face was completely red. I expected to be put in my corner again, but this time Mr. Rios sat me down in the leather chair facing the principal's desk. He stepped outside, and I could hear the familiar clack-clack that could only belong to Miss Marti's reptile legs. They were talking in whispers. I expected her to come in at any moment, but the principal walked in instead. He came in quietly, holding a folder in his hand. His soft brown eyes and beard made him look compassionate, rounded cheeks making him seem friendly. His desk plate solemnly stated: Mr. Sepulveda, PRINCIPAL. He fell into his seat rather unceremoniously, opened the folder, and crossed his hands over it.

"Well, well, well," he said softly, with a tight-lipped grin. "You've created quite a stir, young man." It sounded to me like movie dialogue.

"First of all, let me say I know about you. I have your record right here, and everything in it is very impressive. Good grades, good attitude, your teachers all have adored you. But I wonder if maybe this hasn't gone to your head? Because everything is going for you here, and you're throwing it all away."

He leaned back in his chair. "We have rules, all of us. There are rules even I must live by. People who don't obey them get disciplined. This will all go on your record, and a pretty good one you've had so far. Why ruin it? This'll follow you for life. You don't want to end up losing a good job opportunity in government or in the armed forces because as a child you indulged your imagination and refused to salute the flag? I know you can't see how childish it all is now, but you must see it, and because you're smarter than most, I'll put it to you in terms you can understand.

"To me, this is a simple case of rules and regulations. Someday, when you're older," he paused here, obviously amused by the sound of his own voice, "you can go to rallies and protest marches and express your rebellious tendencies. But right now, you are a minor, under this school's jurisdiction. That means you follow the rules, no matter what you think of them. You can join the Young Lords later."

I stared at him, overwhelmed by his huge desk, his pompous mannerisms and status. I would agree with everything, I felt, and then, the following week, I would refuse once again. I would fight him then, even though he hadn't tried to humiliate me or insult my intelligence. I would continue to fight, until I . . .

"I spoke with your father," he said.

I started. "My father?" Vague images and hopes flared through my mind briefly.

"Yes. I talked to him at length. He agrees with me that you've gotten a little out of hand."

My blood reversed direction in my veins. I felt as if I were going to collapse. I gripped the armrests of my chair. There was no way this could be true, no way at all! My father was supposed to ride in like the cavalry, not abandon me to the enemy! I pressed my wet eyes with my fingers. It must be a lie.

"He blames himself for your behavior," the principal said. "He's already here," Mr. Rios said from the door, motioning my father inside. Seeing him wearing his black weather-beaten trench coat almost asphyxiated me. His eyes, red with concern, pulled at me painfully. He came over to me first while the principal rose slightly, as if greeting a head of state. There was a look of dread on my father's face as he looked at me. He seemed utterly lost.

"Mr. Sepulveda," he said, "I never thought a thing like this could happen. My wife and I try to bring him up right. We encourage him to read and write and everything. But you know, this is a shock."

"It's not that terrible, Mr. Rodriguez. You've done very well with him, he's an intelligent boy. He just needs to learn how important obedience is."

"Yes," my father said, turning to me, "yes, you have to obey the rules. You can't do this. It's wrong." He looked at me grimly, as if working on a math problem. One of his hands caressed my head.

There were more words, in Spanish now, but I didn't hear them. I felt like I was falling down a hole. My father, my creator, renouncing his creation, repentant. Not an ounce of him seemed prepared to stand up for me, to shield me from attack. My tears made all the faces around me melt.

"So you see," the principal said to me as I rose, my father clutching me to him, "if you ever do this again, you will be hurting your father as well as yourself."

I hated myself. I wiped at my face desperately, trying not to make a spectacle of myself. I was just a kid, a tiny kid. Who in the hell did I think I was? I'd have to wait until I was older, like my father, in order to have "convictions."

"I don't want to see you in here again, okay?" the principal said sternly. I nodded dumbly, my father's arm around me as he escorted me through the front office to the door that led to the hallway, where a multitude of children's voices echoed up and down its length like tolling bells.

"Are you crazy?" my father half whispered to me in Spanish as we stood there. "Do you know how embarrassing this all is? I didn't think you were this stupid. Don't you know anything about dignity, about respect? How could you make a spectacle of yourself? Now you make us all look stupid."

He quieted down as Mr. Rios came over to take me back to class. My father gave me a squeeze and told me he'd see me at home. Then, I walked with a somber Mr. Rios, who oddly wrapped an arm around me all the way back to the classroom.

"Here you go," he said softly as I entered the classroom, and everything fell quiet. I stepped in and walked to my seat without looking at anyone. My cheeks were still damp, my eyes red. I looked like I had been tortured. Edwin stared at me, then he pressed my hand under the table.

"I thought you were dead," he whispered.

Miss Colon threw me worried glances all through the remainder of the class. I wasn't paying attention. I took out my notebook, but my strength ebbed away. I just put my head on the desk and shut my eyes, reliving my father's betrayal. If what I did was so bad, why did I feel more ashamed of him than I did of myself? His words, once so rich and vibrant, now fell to the floor, leaves from a dead tree.

At the end of the class, Miss Colon ordered me to stay after school. She got Mr. Rios to take the class down along with his, and she stayed with me in the darkened room. She shut the door on all the exuberant hallway noise and sat down on Edwin's desk, beside me, her black pumps on his seat.

"Are you okay?" she asked softly, grasping my arm. I told her everything, especially about my father's betrayal. I thought he would be the cavalry, but he was just a coward.

"Tss. Don't be so hard on your father," she said. "He's only trying to do what's best for you."

"And how's this the best for me?" I asked, my voice growing hoarse with hurt.

"I know it's hard for you to understand, but he really was trying to take care of you."

I stared at the blackboard.

"He doesn't understand me," I said, wiping my eyes.

"You'll forget," she whispered.

"No, I won't. I'll remember every time I see that flag. I'll see it and think, 'My father doesn't understand me.' "

Miss Colon sighed deeply. Her fingers were warm on my head, stroking my hair. She gave me a kiss on the cheek. She walked me downstairs, pausing by the doorway. Scores of screaming, laughing kids brushed past us.

"If it's any consolation, I'm on your side," she said, squeezing my arm. I smiled at her, warmth spreading through me. "Go home and listen to the Beatles," she added with a grin.

I stepped out into the sunshine, came down the white stone steps, and stood on the sidewalk. I stared at the towering school building, white and perfect in the sun, indomitable. Across the street, the dingy row of tattered uneven tenements where I lived. I thought of my father. Her words made me feel sorry for him, but I felt sorrier for myself. I couldn't understand back then about a father's love and what a father might give to insure his son safe transit. He had already navigated treacherous waters and now couldn't have me rock the boat. I still had to learn that he had made peace with The Enemy, that The Enemy was already in us. Like the flag I must salute, we were inseparable, yet his compromise made me feel ashamed and defeated. Then I knew I had to find my own peace, away from the bondage of obedience. I had to accept that flag, and my father, someone I would love forever, even if at times to my young, feeble mind he seemed a little imperfect.

JULIA DE BURGOS

Mighty River of Loíza

Mighty River of Loíza! . . .Flow into my spirit
and let my soul dissolve within your little ripples
to seek the wellspring that stole you as a child
and then on impulse returned you to your course.

Eddy against my lips and let me drink you
to feel you as mine even for a brief moment,
I'll hide you from the world and inside you surge
to hear the awesome voices from the wind's mouth.

For little while, dismount your earthly summit,
behold the most intimate secret of my longing,
dizzy yourself in the whirl of my bird fantasy
and in my daydreams, leave me a rose of water.

Mighty River of Loíza! . . . My wellspring, my river,
ever since a maternal petal lifted me into this world,
my pale desires have been carried down river
from jagged crests, looking for fresh spun currents.
The whole of my youth was like a poem in a river
and a river appeared in the poem of my first dreams.

Adolescence arrived. Life surprised me
clinging to the widest span of your unceasing flow,
I was yours a thousand times and in a blissful romance,
when you kissed my body, you stirred my soul.

But where did you send those waters
that bathed me in sun rays sprouted at daybreak?

Who knows in what remote Mediterranean nation
some faun on the beach is now possessing me?

Who knows in what showers of some faraway land
I will be pouring myself out to flood fresh rapids;
or perhaps, weary from biting hearts,
be freezing into crystals of ice!

Mighty River of Loíza! . . . Blue. Brown. Red.
Blue mirror, shards fallen from the blue of the sky,
pale naked flesh that turns to black
each time night reclines in your bed,
or to a blood red streak when the hills
vomit their mud under torrential rains.

Man river, but a man with a river's purity,
you bestow your blue soul when you give your bluesy kiss.

My dear man, my river. Man river. The only man
who by kissing the length of my body, kisses my inner spirit.

Mighty River of Loíza! . . . Great river. A river of tears—
the most enduring of all our island laments, were mine
not a greater sorrow flowing through the eyes of my soul
weeping for my people still enslaved.

JOSÉ LUIS GONZALEZ

The "Lamento Borincano"

When I went to Mexico for the first time already more than thirty years ago, people there knew very little about Puerto Rico. However, there was one thing many Mexicans *did* know, which was that Puerto Rico was the home of Rafael Hernández. His "Lamento Borincano" then enjoyed and continues to enjoy today, in spite of the considerable time that has passed, a popularity equaled only by some of the songs of the best popular composers of the period such as Agustín Lara or Alberto Domínguez. But the fact remains that nowadays the "Lamento" continues to resurface on the radio programs of Mexico City and the provinces with an equal or greater frequency than it does in Puerto Rico itself, whereas even a "classic" of the genre like "Perfidia," which once took the world by storm in innumerable local versions, is a mere "nostalgia piece" in today's Mexico. (And if I may be permitted the autobiographical digression, how can I fail to remember that it was while dancing this bolero by Domínguez the summer of 1959 in a Prague nightclub that I began to court the young woman who a few months later agreed to join her life with mine?)

Personally, I believe that the durability—or perhaps even immortality, to use what is perhaps rather a startling word—of this song by our own Rafael Hernández has a sociological cause perhaps even more noteworthy than the artistic merits of the song itself. I stress *perhaps* because my extremely meager musical knowledge disqualifies me from giving an opinion on this subject with any show of authority. Still, I remember having once read that Hernández himself initially felt so dissatisfied with his "Lamento" that he was on the point of throwing it out, before he decided, no one knows why, to give it to the world. I cannot guarantee the truth of this story, but in any case, if the "Lamento Borincano" continues to exercise its spell over Latin American sensibilities in spite of changes in musical taste, one reason, though there are others, is that it expressed better than any other song a social reality that far from having become "past history" is still fully alive for most countries on that long-suffering continent. The tragedy of the Puerto Rican *jíbaro*, in the 1930s a helpless victim of poverty and spiritual malaise, is the tragedy of today's Salvadoran, Guatemalan, Bolivian, Paraguayan, or Ecuadoran peasant. (To set matters in their right perspective, we should add that in Puerto Rico this poverty has been dressed up in consumerist affluence, and this malaise in frivolity and unscrupulousness, but there is no Puerto Rican, however deluded and irresponsible, who does not feel them breathing down his neck.)

If I am not mistaken, the "Lamento" was Latin America's first "protest song" and I know of no other piece of music of the genre to which it belongs—a genre increasingly subject, I fear, to the claims of an industry run, like all industries, for profit—that can rival it in sustained popularity. Even today the Mexico where this native of Aguadilla spent his best years continues to remember him as "the little *jíbaro*," in homage to the song he wrote and to the country of his birth.

If the "Lamento" is in fact Latin America's first "protest song," then I should point out that there is an essential difference between it and most of the protest songs being written today. (I refer, of course, only to the lyrics, which is all I feel myself competent to give an opinion about without exposing myself to the charge of glaring ignorance.) The lyrics of the "Lamento," as we all know, narrate—*narrate* rather than *preach*, an important difference—a personal experience which only acquires a collective significance as it passes through the reader's—in this case, auditor's—consciousness, partly because this experience was a *typical* experience in a Puerto Rico then in the throes of an economic crisis, but above all, it seems to me, because the author refrains from making assertions about the causes or consequences of the situation his hero lives through and confines himself instead to a final question: "What will become of Borinquen, dear God, what will become of my children and my home?"

The question, of course, implied a commitment that, without forcing matters, we could term ideological, but the commitment was expressed at a human and individual level, which, merely by being human, grew to be social, so that Borinquen (the country, society in general) came to be identified with the more particular and intimate (the children and the home). There was no overt judgment in the song, but instead the reference to a reality that all Puerto Ricans could immediately recognize even if they hadn't all experienced it to the same degree. Nor did the lyrics voice an explicit demand for freedom. What they *did* voice was an accusation in the form of a "lament," which is the least aggressive, though by no means the least eloquent, of all forms of accusation. It is significant that a few years later the same Hernández composed the equally well-known and ever-popular "Preciosa," where the political protest is quite overt. In fact, it was so overt that the mean-spirited attempt to denature it (at whose instigation, I wonder?) by converting an easily identifiable "tyrant" into a vague "destiny" was promptly rejected by a public by then no longer willing to put up with such a shabby trick of substitution. "Preciosa" wasn't in fact composed in response to an economic crisis, as the "Lamento" had been, but instead, as now seems very obvious to me, in response to a crisis of political consciousness provoked by the nationalist movement and by the wave of repression unleashed against it by the colonial regime.

I find all of this interesting, because in today's Puerto Rico as elsewhere there is an ongoing debate on how to create a "political art" capable of reaching the masses at whom it is consciously aimed. I believe that the history of Puerto Rican literature at both the "cultivated" and "popular" levels can offer us some useful lessons here. Forty years before Rafael Hernández wrote the "Lamento Borincano," Lola Rodríguez and Pachín Marín cultivated an explicitly political, revolutionary poetry, intended, they declared, to awaken and inspire the independence movement then actively opposing Spanish colonial rule. Lola, as is well-known, tried to combine her poetic efforts with other forms of popular entertainment by writing new subversive lyrics (in the most honest and respectable sense of the word *subversive*) for "La Borinqueña." What now needs to be explained is why the poetry of Lola and Pachín never made an impression on the Puerto Rican masses as the "Lamento Borincano" and "Preciosa" were later to do.

One explanation may be that poetry is written to be read and cannot therefore reach a public that is illiterate, as were the great majority of Puerto Ricans in the last century. But this argument has never quite convinced me, since the popular masses in Argentina were also illiterate and yet made José Hernández's *Martín Fierro* very much their own by memorizing and transmitting it orally. Similarly, the Cuban masses took to their hearts much of the poetry of José Martí and in particular his *Versos sencillos*. The same Puerto Rican public, much more literate in the forties of this century than at the end of the nineteenth century (though still without a taste for reading), took to heart the "cultivated" verses of Lloréns Torres and of Palés Matos, when these two poets, each in his own manner, touched certain common chords. So, too, they lapped up the "popular" verses of Fortunato Vizcarrondo in which he reproached some Puerto Ricans (and how many of them there are!) for hiding grandmother in the kitchen *porque es prieta de verdá* ("because she's *so* black.")

Now, of course it's true that the popularity of Vizcarrondo's poetry owed much to the wide coverage it received on radio and in the theater as a result of the excellent recitations by Juan Boria, and that the poems of Lloréns and Palés enjoyed an ever-widening public once they had been included in the syllabus of Puerto Rico's public schools. For obvious reasons these advantages were denied to the seditious poems of Lola and Pachín during the Spanish colonial regime. But for all that, I think the basic reason why Lola and Pachín's revolutionary poetry never gained a following with the Puerto Rican masses lies in the difference between the ideological temperament of their poetry and that of the people. And I should make it clear that when I say *masses* I refer to the urban part of those masses. The rural parts, the countrymen who formed a demographic majority and lived in isolation from the country's cultural centers, certainly weren't alien to *"the"* culture, even though at the same time they were producing their own culture, which has so far only been studied as "folklore"—that is to say, from a point of view *external* to its own reality. But to return to the urban part, its ideological temperature last century reflected that of the creole ruling class in that it was reformist (i.e., autonomist) but not revolutionary (i.e., separatist), hence in no condition to assimilate the radical and subversive message expressed in the verses of Lola and Pachín. The political leaders of *these* masses were Muñoz Rivera and Barbosa rather than Betances and Hostos (both of whom had in any case been in political exile for a number of years).

Under the American colonial regime, when part of the creole ruling class found itself in conflict with the interests of the new metropolis, that same Muñoz Rivera together with José de Diego produced a patriotic poetry which achieved much greater popularity than anything written by Lola or Pachín, even though it never achieved unanimous or even near-unanimous acceptance. One reason for this last fact is that a considerable sector of the masses had already become republican or socialist, in other words as ideologically opposed to Muñoz Rivera as it was to José de Diego. Only in the 1930s, under the impact of an economic crisis that affected society as a whole, did an art of accusation and protest finally emerge that was "popular" in its forms and ideologically in tune with the masses, both urban and rural, in being reformist (though not exactly revolutionary). The "Lamento Borincano," in my opinion, was just such an art. In fact, it seems to me neither exaggerated nor untruthful to say that the true prophet (and remember that from *prophet* comes *prophecy*) of the political movement headed at the end of the 1930s by Luis Muñoz Marín was Rafael Hernández. Such a fact and its implications for the situation today doubtless deserve more attention than there is space for here. Let them therefore await another occasion—or better still, pens more authoritative than mine.

PABLO GUZMAN

The Party

FROM *PALANTE! YOUNG LORDS PARTY*

People always look for the beginnings of the party. We started the Young Lords because we just knew something had to be done. If we didn't find or create an organization that was gonna do something, then everybody was gonna get shot, see, because it would have gotten to the point that people got so frustrated, they would just jump on the first cop they saw, or just snap, do something crazy.

At first the only model we had to go on in this country was the Black Panther party. Besides that, we were all a bunch of readers, when we first came in we read Che, Fidel, Fanon, Marx, Lenin, Jefferson, the Bill of Rights, Declaration, Constitution—we read everything. Now there ain't too much time for reading.

We also felt that the potential for revolution had always been there for Puerto Rican people. If we had gone into the thing from a negative point of view, we wouldn't have made it, right. 'Cause a lot of times when things were really rough, it's been that blind faith in the people that keeps us going. The problem has been to tap that potential and to organize it into a disciplined force that's gonna really move on this government. Puerto Ricans had been psyched into believing this myth about being docile. A lot of Puerto Ricans were afraid to move, a lot of Puerto Ricans really thought that the man in blue was the baddest thing going.

Things were different in the gang days. Gang days, we owned the block, and nobody could tell us what to do with the street. Then dope came in and messed everything up, messed our minds up and just broke our backs—dope and antipoverty. Antipoverty wiped out a whole generation of what could have been Puerto Rican leaders in New York City.

For example, in '65, the time of the East Harlem riots, we held East Harlem for two days. We had the rooftops, the streets, and the community—no pigs could go through. It was like back in the old days. A lot of people really tripped off that, a lot of the junkies who had been in gangs remembered that shit. To end it they shipped in antipoverty. They brought it in full force, and they brought out a lot of the young cats who were leading the rebellions. A lot of dudes who were throwing bricks one day found themselves directors of antipoverty programs the next, or workers on Mayor Lindsay's Urban Action Core.

So we had no leadership, and we had no people—our people were dying from dope. But we knew that it was *there,* man, 'cause we knew that the fire was there. Those of us who got together to start the thing, we knew we weren't freaks—we didn't feel that we were all that much different from the people. There's a tendency to say *the people* and put the people at arm's length. When we say *people*, man, we're talking about ourselves. We're from these blocks, and we're from these schools, products of this whole thing. Some of us came back from college—it was like rediscovering where your parents had come from, rediscovering your childhood.

Our original viewpoint in founding the party was a New York point of view—that's where the world started and ended. As we later found out, New York is different from most other cities that Puerto Ricans live in. But even in New York, we found that on a grass-roots level a high degree of racism existed between Puerto Ricans and blacks, and between light-skinned and dark-skinned Puerto Ricans. We had to deal with this racism because it blocked any kind of growth for our people, any understanding of the things black people had gone through. So rather than watching Rap Brown on TV, rather than learning from that and saying, "Well, that should affect me, too," Puerto Ricans said, "Well, yeah, those blacks got a hard time, you know, but we ain't going through the same thing." This was especially true for the light-skinned Puerto Ricans. Puerto Ricans like myself, who are darker-skinned, who look like Afro-Americans, couldn't do that, 'cause to do that would be to escape into a kind of fantasy. Because before people called me a spic, they called me a nigger. So that was, like, one reason as to why we felt the Young Lords party should exist.

At first many of us felt why have a Young Lords party when there existed a Black Panther party, and wouldn't it be to our advantage to try to consolidate our efforts into getting Third World people into something that already existed? It became apparent to us that that would be impractical, because we wouldn't be recognizing the national question. We felt we each had to organize where we were at— so that Chicanos were gonna have to organize Chicanos, blacks were gonna have to organize blacks, Puerto Ricans Puerto Ricans, etc., until we came to that level where we could deal with one umbrella organization that could speak for everybody. But until we eliminate the racism that separates everybody, that will not be possible.

What happened was, in 1969 in the June 7 issue of the Black Panther newspaper, there was an article about the Young Lords Organization in Chicago with Cha Cha Jimenez as their chairman. Cha Cha was talking about revolution and socialism and the liberation of

Puerto Rico and the right to self-determination and all this stuff that I ain't *never* heard a spic say. I mean, I hadn't never heard no Puerto Rican talk like this—just Black people were talking this way, you know. And I said, "Damn! Check this out." That's what really got us started. That's all it was, man.

We started by trying to pick something that would introduce us to the community. It had to be an action. See—it was summer, it was hot, the people were just, like, sweltering in the heat, nobody was doing nothing. For four years there had been no action. Puerto Ricans hadn't had a good riot since 1965, not even a good fight, a good brawl. Something had to happen that would stun the community. It had to be something with a sense of drama, and flair, right—but it also had to be something that was real so the people would know that this wasn't just a bunch of young punks messin' around.

The best thing to hook into was garbage, 'cause garbage is visible and everybody sees it. It's there, you know. So we started out with this thing, "Well, we're gonna clean up the street." This brought the college people and the street people together, 'cause when street people saw college people pushing brooms and getting dirty, that blew their minds. It also got us out of our shyness. When we began, people said, "Well, what are you doing with those berets?" and "What are you doing with those buttons?" and "What does 'All Power to the People' mean?" and things like that. The bolder ones in our group would get out there and yell to people, and everybody else would jump with shock. It was frightening, man, to go on the street and to walk up to some strangers and just start rapping, and give 'em a leaflet—that's frightening shit. And we just forced ourselves to do it, and it got to a thing where nobody wanted to be the one who didn't talk that day, because everybody else would criticize you.

At first some people thought we were part of Lindsay's Urban Action Task Force, and some thought we were just a gang that was trying to be a social club. People couldn't figure us out, man. If we said, "All Power to the People," some of them who read the *Daily News* right away said, "Well, those are the Panthers, and they're communists." A lot of people thought we were the Panthers, and to that we got a bad reaction, 'cause they were afraid of us. But some people just came out and looked.

This is all we did for the first two Sundays—clean up the street, make it look nice, and put the stuff in garbage cans. We picked Sunday 'cause that was one of the few days when everybody could get together. Some of the members of the party got pissed. We'd have general meetings and they'd say, "I didn't do this for this *shit*, to clean up no garbage. I came here to off the pigs"; they were comin' from that, right. So, it was hard, man, 'cause we had a bunch of crazy people who just loved fighting, loved getting into shit. And cleaning garbage was not where it was at, so it was a kind of discipline for us, to go through that and learn patience. We didn't realize that what we were doing at that time was building the proper conditions for struggle. I mean, we could have gone underground and started blowing shit up—the thing is, nobody would have understood where it was coming from. Those people who didn't think it was the pig would think it was some lunatics, and they'd probably be right. So we were just getting ourselves known.

By the second time around, everybody said, "Hey, here they come again! Here come these nuts!" They were calling their friends out— "Look at these fools cleaning off the street!" It was a big thing. They were coming from blocks around. We cleaned 110th Street from Second to Third to Lexington.

By the third Sunday we did something we had learned from what we had read about the Chicago group, and that was to get the people involved through "observation and participation." This time we got the people to clean the shit up with us. We knew somehow we would take them through some kind of a struggle, we didn't know where the hell we were going, but we had to get them involved.

And then came the Sunday of July 27, when we had a lot of people and not enough brooms, and we went to the Sanitation Department. . . . Now understand this—for the Young Lords party, this July 27 is probably a historical date. It was a Sunday, right? When four of us went to pick up some brooms, they told us, "Well, you can't have any brooms." And we said, "Why?" and they said, "Because it's Sunday." Now the sanitation cats are just second cousins to the cats in blue, 'cept that they wear green. This fool at 106th Street, which was the nearest branch of the department, asks us, "What area are you cleaning up?" So we tell him 110th between Second and Third. He says, "That area is serviced by Seventy-third Street and York." So we had to go about a mile and a half outside where we were, when there was this place four blocks down. And the dude at Seventy-third and York says, "Well, you can't have any brooms." So, we were pissed, you know. We had gone through all the legal machinations, and now we were pissed. We were looking for a rationale for what was going to come next.

In the car on the way up, the four of us said, "Look, we're going to take the garbage and throw it in the street and that's all there is to it—we're just going to dump it." And that's what we did. We blocked Third Avenue to traffic, right. The people, they went and blocked 111th Street and Third Avenue, blocked 112th, and what was developing was a riot situation. When we saw that happening, we set up a line of garbage cans at the end of 112th Street and we set up a line of Lords and said, "We ain't lettin' nobody through." There was this one cat who said, "Let's go! Let's take it all the way up to the Bronx!" This cat was freaking out, and we were saying, "No, you ain't going noplace—we're stoppin' right here because if we keep going, this is what the pigs want, they just going to pick us off. You ain't got no guns, you know." And this guy kept saying, "No, no, let's go! We got all these people here!" 'Cause people had come out, they came from all over East Harlem for this, they moved a truck into the street, they turned cars over, they were ready to go crazy. The pigs showed up and didn't do nothing, 'cause the pigs believe that Puerto Ricans are docile, you know. We didn't know what kind of reaction we'd get. I mean, all we were doing was throwing some garbage in the street, but we saw that it turned the people loose, it was what they needed, it just set them going. So, we had a quick rally and signed up some recruits, and we said, "Well, we're gonna do this again next Sunday."

When we went back the next Sunday, more people came—but it was a different thing. This time it wasn't "Here come those nuts. . . ." but "Here come those people who started this shit last Sunday—let's get together." And people were just, like, waiting, waiting like this on the corner, waiting for us to throw the garbage so they could get involved in the shit.

The next day Lindsay's office called a meeting. Gottehrer and all those dudes came down to East Harlem to this poverty place. That's when we found out what poverty pimps were really about—they're like outposts in Indian territory, like Fort Apache and Fort Savage, they are the eyes and ears of the mayor of any city. And they're sup-

posed to keep the savages down, right. In this case, we weren't
working with the poverty pimps. This was coming from the people,
and the poverty pimps are far removed from the people. When they
couldn't explain to their masters what was going down in East
Harlem, they said, "Well, we have this under control . . . there are
these leaflets that are going around. . . ."

We found that a lot of people thought we were there just to throw
garbage in the street. They couldn't understand that we were really
there for a socialist revolution, we were really there to off the government of the United States. They just couldn't deal with that, you
know. So we tried setting up political education classes . . .

. . . When we talk about our role in terms of creating the American
Revolution, we are not saying we are going to take Puerto Rican people and ship them back to Puerto Rico. We are saying that we have
been here in this country for two generations—in some cases, maybe
three generations—we've been here for so long, right, that it would
be too convenient for us to move back now, and just create a revolution there. We're saying that we want payback for the years that we
have suffered, the years that we have put up with cockroaches and
rats. We had to put up with snow, we had to put up with English, we
had to put up with racism, with the general abuse of America. And
we are gonna hook up with everybody else in this country who's
fighting for their liberation—and that's a whole lot of people. We
know that the number-one group that's leading that struggle are
black people, 'cause black people—if we remember the rule that
says the most oppressed will take the vanguard role in the struggle—
black people, man, have gone through the most shit. Black people,
along with Chicanos and Native Americans, are the greatest ally we
can have. So we must build the Puerto Rican–black alliance. That is
the basis of the American Revolution for us. Actually, the first group
in America that we had a formal coalition with was the Black Panther
party. Also we must further the Latino ties, especially as we move
west, and here in New York City, we must work with Dominicans—
to further eliminate the racism that has deeply divided black people
and Spanish people.

We are also coming very close together with the struggle of Asians
in this country, Asians who have been disinherited from the land that
was theirs. Hawaii, for example, was made a state. One of our imme-

diate struggles is to prevent that from happening to Puerto Rico. The Asian struggle is, like, twice as hard, because now they have to free a state, which is different from freeing a colony, right. That's actually going in and busting up part of a union.

Now the time has come for the Young Lords party to begin organizing on the island. I mean, that's inevitable—we're not fighting just for Puerto Ricans in the States, we are fighting for all Puerto Ricans, you know, and in turn, we're fighting for all oppressed people. In the fourth point of our Thirteen Point Program and Platform, we say we are revolutionary nationalists, not racists. That also means that we recognize the struggle of white people.

One thing we always say in the Young Lords, "Don't ever let any particular hatred you have prevent you from working. Always take it into you and let it move you forward. And if it's strong, change it, because it stops your work." We tell all Puerto Rican youth to listen to this. High-school-age Puerto Ricans are into a *big* thing about whitey, and we tell them, "Man, it's not white *folk*. What we are trying to destroy is not white people, but a system created by white people, a capitalistic system that has run away from them to the point that it is now killing white people, too . . ."

. . . We try to encourage honesty in our relationships with white people. I think that we've gone a long way toward eliminating a lot of the shit in the Movement. And I think a lot of people get good vibes when they're around us. I think a lot of people in the Movement dig us because of that . . .

. . . You know, there was a way that the people used to walk in the street before 1969, before the Young Lords party began—people used to walk with their heads down like this, and the pigs would walk through the colonies, man, like they owned the block. They'd come in here with no kind of respect in their eyes. They'd *walk* through, they wouldn't ride through. See, when a pig *walks* through the street, that means they got less respect than if they gotta ride. But after the Garbage Offensive and the Peoples' Church it was a whole new game . . .

. . . Our people have been taught to believe that when they rounded up Albizu Campos and two thousand members of the Nationalist party, they broke the back of the Nationalist party. But now the people can think about Albizu and all of a sudden it seems like the Nationalist party has just been going through different kinds of changes for twenty years. "Well, man, we thought you all lost—it looks like we're gonna start winning." And, like, the concept of winning, right, that is the number-one contribution of the Young Lords party—that is what we are, man, the concept of winning . . .

. . . In this country, for example, racism is like a stick that the pigs are clubbing you on the head with. Now you got to grab the other end and hit them back with it—and the other end of the stick is nationalism. And if you do it righteously, if you do it with the interest of the people and with the backing of the people, then it becomes revolutionary. Now that's revolutionary nationalism—that is the kind of nationalism that says, "Yes, we are proud to be Puerto Rican, we are proud to be number one—but we want everybody else to be number one, too, and we're gonna help everyone else be number one." See, 'cause the other kind of nationalism is reactionary nationalism— where you say, "Well, I'm number one. Fuck everybody else . . ."

. . . We are not nihilists, you know, we're not just destroy, destroy, destroy. We're saying to our people, yes, we've got to destroy, but we have a new system that we're already starting to build, right. Taking the whole Puerto Rican nation into account, we're a small group, but inside that small group we're dealing socialistically with one another in a very human manner, and as we move, that influence is gonna spread out in many ways.

———

RONALD FERNANDEZ

Los Macheteros

Los Macheteros are a highly disciplined, well-organized, fully financed army of Puerto Rican revolutionaries. They expect no quick end to their struggle, and they fully anticipate defeats along the way, because no matter how careful, dedicated, and intelligent they are, Los Macheteros remain a small band of soldiers engaged in a war with the police and military forces of a superpower. Like Sisyphus with his rock, Los Macheteros knowingly face what appears to be an impossible task. But unlike Sisyphus, they have hope because their overall strategy is based on arousing the masses. Since the island does actually contain a large number of closet independentistas (an island adage I constantly heard repeated says, "After two or three drinks every Puerto Rican is pro-independence"), if Los Macheteros can stimulate a revolutionary consciousness, there is— so the reasoning goes—no sane way the United States could deny them. Eventually the costs would greatly outweigh whatever advantages the colony offers.

But how to arouse the masses? There's no simple answer to that one, says Victor Acosta, the head of Los Macheteros, because five hundred years of colonialism have so deeply instilled the twin myths of impotence and inferiority.

Los Macheteros agree that they are first and foremost revolutionaries of the mind. They are at war with the personal consequences of colonialism, and their actions cannot be understood until we recognize that they are reacting to images—of the inferior, impotent, docile Puerto Rican.

In an influential 1960 essay, "The Docile Puerto Rican," island playright Rene Marques defines docility "as the lack of strength or even the will to put up resistance to what others demand or command." Marques makes no attempt to explain why Puerto Ricans are docile. He only wants to prove it's a fact.

The Korean War had absolutely no bearing on any islander's life; Puerto Ricans had no right to vote in the federal elections that elected the representatives who decided where they were to risk their lives; and politicians like Albizu Campos told anyone willing to listen that Puerto Ricans were being shipped to Asia in numbers way out of proportion to their percentage of the total population. That islanders were used as cannon fodder in Korea is still a very touchy topic among independentistas. Yet Puerto Ricans not only showed up to fight, they consistently received awards for heroism in the service of American interests.

That sheepishness, turned upside down, is the self-destructive behavior manifested by the old-line nationalist movement. For Marques, the underside of docility is "repressing or inhibiting the normal aggressive impulse so as to direct it morbidly toward oneself." The docile lack strength, and instead of the effective political terrorism used by, say, the Algerians, Puerto Rican nationalists commit suicide. They engage in utterly futile actions (Marques cites the attempted assassination of President Truman as a conspicuous example) because at heart, their docile natures inhibit the discipline and methodology that lets other patriots succeed. Call it a "martyr complex," call it a "suicidal impulse." For Marques, the key is docility. If Puerto Ricans had the strength to truly resist American authority, they would stop tying their "bold and determined actions" to an obsession with certain death and create instead a methodical program capable of ushering in the revolution—and life after it, as well.

Is Marques correct? Do the data prove his point? Large numbers of dissident Puerto Ricans believe their brothers and sisters are the sheep described by Marques. As the head of Los Macheteros recently put it, their actions are specifically designed to create social consciousness by restoring pride in self and nation. When, as Marques suggested, poorly organized nationalists looked like bunglers, they acted "as an accomplice to the intelligence campaigns of the FBI." Failure after failure killed any budding faith in the possibility of radical change.

In sharp contrast to the almost ad hoc actions of a beloved nationalist like Albizu Campos, Los Macheteros are a crackerjack team of professional revolutionaries whose primary aim, at this stage of the revolution, is to successfully engage in one anticolonial strike after another. Eventually, like a Caribbean hurricane building up force, the inspirational effects of today's Taínos will move the masses to storm the manifestations of illegitimate American authority.

As examples of their efforts, Los Macheteros cite the "sledgehammer" blow delivered at Muñoz Airport . . . When the nine National Guard planes were destroyed, "our military action gave recognition to our organization on a national as well as an international level . . . And we were able to reactivate the fervor of our people . . . because this blow was the most severe given to the Yankees in North American territory since Pearl Harbor and outside the territory since the Tet offensive in Vietnam." On May 16, 1982, "four United States Navy enlisted men assigned to the U.S.S. *Pensacola* were attacked while returning to their ship which was docked in Old San Juan." They were shot—one man died, the other three were injured—by automatic rifle fire coming from a maroon Cadillac. Along with the Group for the Liberation of Vieques, Los Macheteros announced that the attack was in retaliation for the Navy exercise Ocean Venture 82.

On April 21, 1981, four individuals robbed a Wells Fargo armored car in Santurce, Puerto Rico, escaping with roughly $348,000 in cash. Los Macheteros soon announced they would use the expropriated funds to "promote the development and organization of the revolution in Puerto Rico."

On January 25, 1985, at roughly 10 A.M., an explosion occurred at the United States Courthouse in Old San Juan. By design, no one was injured, but Los Macheteros took credit for the action when they sent UPI a communiqué indicating that the attack was a memorial to the late poet and intimate of Albizu Campos, Juan Antonia Corretjer, "who had spent his entire life fighting against Yankee imperialism."

Since their first public announcement in 1978, Los Macheteros have averaged two or three incidents a year, and as with Victor and Wells Fargo, they welcome any opportunity to publicize their contempt for American authority. Soon after the attack on Muñoz Airport, for example, a San Juan television station played a videotape produced by Los Macheteros. It showed hooded figures in fatigue uniforms, and the voice-over indicated that eleven people had participated in the attack, with seven in charge of security and four in charge of demolition. Los Macheteros have flaunted every one of their "armed propaganda actions," because above all else, they seek to show that Puerto Ricans are not powerless, not submissive, not resigned to the poverty that is.

If Los Macheteros are first and foremost Puerto Rican nationalists, they are also socialists with a distinct Leninist tinge. Only a select, audacious, and agile few can serve as a revolutionary vanguard. Acting on the advice of Lenin—and the criticism of natives like Rene Marques—Los Macheteros are an exceedingly methodical and thoroughly trained group, with written guidelines for everything.

Consider a document entitled "Organization of the Puerto Rican People's Army." It details the group's structure with a precision that would make a mathematician smile with delight. At the bottom of the totem pole stands the combat unit, the basic building block of the

Macheteros army. Each unit contains five persons, but the leader is the only one that has to be a member of the Macheteros' political arm (more on that side of Los Macheteros later). This person controls the unit's arsenal—normally consisting of a short weapon, two automatic weapons, one semiautomatic rifle, and one shotgun—which allows the combat unit "to be in full capacity to fulfill a complete specific mission without needing additional elements."

The beauty of the combat unit is its size. It can easily operate under everyday circumstances (that is, actions in urban and semiurban areas); the five members can often meet to inconspicuously plan or train; and, using the car that is also part of any combat unit's standard equipment, the five (with, say, three in the car and two on foot) can blend so smoothly into human traffic that once a mission is over, a safe getaway is easily effected.

Combat units normally function as part of a group, the line cell, that sits in the middle of the Macheteros military hierarchy. At the center of the line cell is a squad of "five combatants": one political leader, one military leader, and three leaders of combat units. Thus a line cell has seventeen members, with a full complement of weapons that, ideally, "should be of the same caliber and, if possible, the same kind utilized by the enemy so as to facilitate the logistical supply."

Linked to the line cell is a group that rarely participates in combat action. The supporting cell is again composed of five members. Its role is to furnish "the logistic, organizational, and propaganda support" essential for the success of a Machetero mission. Only one member (the leader) belongs to the party. Support means "two or three medical or paramedic elements and a combatant whose principal responsibility includes providing typing, repairs, equipment, propaganda, printed matter, mimeographs, loudspeakers [say for the two Three Kings giveaways in Puerto Rico], radios, places to store equipment, explosives, etc."

The supporting cell, a mobile motorpool for Machetero needs, is controlled by a member of the party who is a part of a formation. Each formation contains five cells "of which four will be line and one support." This means 73 combatants (4 line cells × 17 equals 68, plus 5 in the supporting cell) led by an individual who is a member of the party. The advantage of the formation is that it allows members "to operate with major secretivity and dispersion in a geographical area of Puerto Rico composed of various towns." If, for example, members take an existing senatorial district, it is easy to see how "the formation could have its cells and its combat units dispersed in different towns."

If phrases like "major secretivity" bring to mind the managerial manuals of a modern bureaucracy, the resemblance between Los Macheteros and a well-run corporation is more than superficial. Each is an organization with precisely delimited and official jurisdictional areas, and each has a firmly ordered system of super- and subordination. But instead of lodging ultimate authority in the hands of one person, Los Macheteros have a military commission at the peak of their army's hierarchy.

Surprisingly, the organizational document I have does not specify the number of commission members on the military commission. Instead it focuses on their role, which is to prepare the units and cells for commencement of armed activity. The military commission has to create an "infra-logistical structure capable of surpassing all repressive intents of the enemy." There are subcommissions of military intelligence, military training, transportation, provisions, and general services. A subcommission of finances prepares budgets, establishes disbursement controls, and accounts for the funds in the group's treasury.

Quite often organizational documents bear no relationship to reality. Not so in the case of Los Macheteros. They operate in cells, they generally obey the designated chain of command, and they consistently carry a respect for precise rules and regulations into a wide variety of nonmilitary areas. Consider the payroll lists of monthly salaries for all full-time members. Bear in mind that wages are adjusted for inflation and that these are 1981 salaries:

1. Basic salary, single person: $400.
2. Basic salary, married and wife works: $400.
3. Basic salary, married and wife does not work: $500.
4. Basic salary, married with children and wife works: $35 additional for each child.
5. Basic salary, married with children and wife does not work: $60 additional for each child.

In a December 1981 amendment to the scale, Los Macheteros agreed to provide medical benefits—up to $500 per *approved* doctor—and they also paid for university training if the individual received commission approval. If a comrade was refused benefits, feelings of resentment sometimes surfaced. In an angry moment, Juan Segarra complained that "if you don't say something, it's forgotten and you get screwed. They [Macheteros policymakers] say, 'We can't be paying schools for the people,' but why did Juan get his paid, huh? No, no, it's not right."

The rigorous rules and regulations—which may seem surprising given the wild-eyed revolutionaries depicted by the media—exist because Los Macheteros are running an army. They are involved in a war, in which political considerations are always more important than any military mission.

Los Macheteros agree with Carl von Clausewitz (and with political figures as different as Henry Kissinger and Vladimir Lenin) that war is nothing but a continuation of politics by other means. Since their goal is to awaken the now docile Puerto Rican people, above the military commission, which carries out policy, sits a Central Committee, which makes policy. It is entirely possible that some Macheteros hold positions in both groups, but political decisions always dominate, because the Macheteros know there is no way they can win a purely military war with the United States. You defeat the Yankees only if you change people's minds. While the end (independence) justifies the means (killing American military personnel), the means are always guided by the supposed political results of any military action. For example, never use violence indiscriminately. Destroy objects of widespread resentment, because that generates "admiration" among the masses. And never forget that, in addition to three million Puerto Ricans, 240 million Americans read the papers and listen to Dan Rather. They too judge the independentistas, and their appraisal could be just as important as that made by the Puerto Rican people. As in Vietnam, the United States might leave because the human and material costs become too great. Or if Los Macheteros could do a better job with publicity, Americans might perceive the fundamental validity of the independence position.

If this sounds too rational, too methodical, too computerized (Los Macheteros keep large amounts of information stored on an Apple computer), remember how well scientific management served the cause of the machete wielders. It took nearly five years for the well-financed FBI to break through their cover; even then the authorities needed two lucky breaks (the ticket stub in the Blazer and the accidental safe-house haul); and, with only sixteen people under arrest, close to three hundred hardcore Macheteros are still at large.

This large organization has enjoyed a good deal of success because members of the group are consistently able to blend their revolutionary affiliation into a lifestyle that meshes with everyday Puerto Rican (and American) life. Some Macheteros do nothing but prepare for independence, but the vast majority of group members live normal lives that only when necessary are interrupted to make way for the revolution.

Although Pedro now lives in Chicago, he was born and grew up in a rural area of Puerto Rico that has long been a breeding ground for independentistas. He got his first military training from Uncle Sam. He left the island in 1979 because he wanted to avoid the government harassment nationalists often encounter. Pedro became a member of Los Macheteros in 1981, and since he joined, he has participated in no violent revolutionary activities. He works in a factory, lives quietly with his wife and three children, and waits for a call to action. Meanwhile, he openly supports groups who advocate a peaceful path to independence, and, like all Macheteros, spends a great deal of his free time looking over his shoulder. Since the arrest in 1983 of four Chicago members of the FALN shows that police and FBI spies are still trying to actively infiltrate the underground movement, Pedro shows his backstage self to very few people, and when a stranger appears in his life, Pedro checks him or her out. In one sense that's a waste of time, but it's a good deal better than being caught.

Pepe is sixty-eight years old. He has been an independentista since he first listened to Albizu Campos in the 1930s. He knows every prominent activist on the island and got involved with Los Macheteros when his daughter asked for his support. Day to day, Pepe runs a successful grocery store that provides a solid cover for his generally nonviolent assistance to Los Macheteros. He helps hide people who must remain underground, or finds the farms where new members are trained, or attends anticolonial gatherings—say at the local headquarters of the Puerto Rican Independence party—which are perfect occasions for recruiting new members. If Pepe spots someone who looks like a promising candidate, he makes an initial contact. Long before anything meaningful occurs, the individual is thoroughly checked out. Discreet questions may be asked of friends and relatives, Macheteros watch him in nonpolitical settings, and especially if the individual has spent time in the United States, efforts are made to investigate his foreign pursuits. One informant said that, given the level of suspicion and the need for airtight security, if an investigation turns up even a hint of questionable activity on the mainland, the potential recruit is immediately rejected.

Pepe is an old-time independentista. His daughter is a crackerjack revolutionary of the type Los Macheteros seek to nurture and sustain. At her father's urging, she attended the University of Puerto Rico in the late 1960s, and receptive to the Young Turks who resisted the draft and fought against the ROTC, Maria was quickly swept up in the militancy and passion of the island's pro-independence movement, the short-lived MPI *(El Movimiento Pro Independencia)*. From close up, Maria witnessed the transformation of the MPI into a Marxist-Leninist party—if the Cubans could succeed, why not the Puerto Ricans?—and, already in agreement with the overall ideology of Los Macheteros, she became a member in the late 1970s. Today, onstage, she holds an executive position in the island's government, while backstage, she provides cover for San Juan's Macheteros, oversees the disbursement of organizational funds, and helps develop strategy for the group's future activities.

Juan grew up and still lives in New York. His parents were apolitical, his teachers in Brooklyn told him nothing about colonialism in Puerto Rico, and on the streets, he learned more about drugs than independence. What changed Juan were too many experiences with prejudice, and a civil rights movement that produced not only Black Panthers but Puerto Rican Young Lords. Juan looked up to the Lords. They made his latent sense of pride manifest and got him interested in his culture. When Los Macheteros came calling in 1982, Juan quickly said yes. Today he has his own handyman business, but between jobs, Juan has trained in Cuba and helped recruit new Macheteros. If needed, he's ready to further the cause by robbing another branch of Wells Fargo or, as at Sebana Seca, participating in retaliatory attacks against the enemies of independence.

As these portraits suggest, many Macheteros spend most of their time "laying low." They hold down a job, live quiet, nondescript lives, keep in shape by constant exercise and infrequently attend meetings that are held only when necessary. When meetings do occur, all Macheteros behave in accordance with specific and exacting instructions about the character and use of any safe house.

Since the safe-house apartment, home, or office should never be located in a "hot" area, Macheteros learn to stay away from any location containing drug trafficking, prostitution, or other illegal activities. They also stay away from police stations, "repressive agency offices," armories, or facilities used by groups of nationalists or leftists.

The idea is to inconspicuously blend into the community. Macheteros try to avoid attracting attention by choosing meeting spots in private places in publicly respectable areas. If it's an apartment house, they make sure it's a big one, with lots of apartments, many entrances, and no crowds of people gathered outside. They try to stay away from places with meddlesome neighbors, and if they see people, they exchange the meaningless pleasantries that are a part of everyday etiquette. Rudeness stands out; polite nothings are, like the elevator ride to the apartment or office, taken for granted.

Once a safe house is found, members must be quite careful before they enter it. A thorough check for surveillance is mandatory, "dry cleaning" tactics should be routinely employed, "cars should be parked as far away from the safe house as possible," arrival times should be staggered, participants should use different entrances, some climbing stairs and others riding elevators, and, especially important, if a meeting includes comrades from other combat units, members must remember to put on the hoods that guarantee anonymity. Don't learn who the other soldiers are, and in the event of capture, you can truthfully say, even to a lie detector, that you don't know any Macheteros.

Or in the event that you turn out to be a squealer, the hoods, along with the use of code names, protect loyal Macheteros. When former member Carlos Rodriguez-Rodriguez was found guilty of bank fraud in 1984, his fifty-seven-year sentence turned him into a *chota* (a squealer). He apparently cooperated as much as possible with the FBI, but in many instances he could provide only useless information. Yes, he'd met a Rita, a Diana, and a Pancho, but what good did that do the authorities unless they could link the names to facial descriptions or true identities?

Los Macheteros wisely operate on a need-to-know basis. One combat unit often knows nothing about another's membership and projects, and if it does, the intelligence available is too general to allow an indictment. In Los Macheteros political and military information flows down only when necessary and, using the beepers strapped to the sides of many full-time members, knowledgeable comrades can sometimes alert one another to a likely search and seizure. If you possess incriminating evidence, the material is to be destroyed before the authorities arrive. Police might also miss important notes because a member used the invisible ink fountain pens that are a standard tool of clandestine groups.

To protect their identities when on a mission, Los Macheteros say it is best to avoid false IDs. The organization can provide, to a limited extent, some basic false documents, but the best identification is a legitimate one obtained through official channels. That is what Ojeda Rios allegedly did when he registered the Superior Motor Home in Texas. To get a legitimate license and registration, a Machetero would follow this kind of advice. Obtain a post office box or a cold (safe) address that guarantees risk-free receipt of the documents. Rent everything in an assumed name, and in dealing with the address problem—there's always one needed for a license or vehicle registration—use one in an area where mail is not distributed house by house or, as a neat alternative, report a broken mailbox at X address in a manner that would justify the request that your mail be kept at the post office.

With such IDs, members can travel anonymously, rapidly disappear when necessary, and purchase materials that they do not wish to be associated with them. And a false ID can allow time for the organization to contend with security measures in case of arrest. Assuming no bugs or double agents, other Macheteros can go to your real home—authorities would theoretically be at the false address—and comrades could tidy up before the authorities arrived.

While many skills can be learned from a manual, others require on-site training. For members not trained by Uncle Sam, Los Macheteros offer courses in the following areas: first aid, locksmithing, forgery, photography, scuba diving, makeup, the handling and use of explosives, the handling and use of firearms, and the manufacture of automobile license plates. Once individuals complete the military training, they are full members of the group. They're now ready for action, but only when called, which isn't often.

To store their supplies of *manteca* (literally, "butter" or "lard," the code name for weapons) and *libreta* (literally, "notebook," the code name for explosives), Los Macheteros purchased a farmhouse, brought in their construction crew, and when the work was done, *La Palangana* (the Washbowl) had a new bathroom, gratings in all the upstairs and downstairs windows, and a workshop for production and experimentation. The construction crew wrote a pleasing final report for the commanders. "While one of the projects of greatest difficulty" was a hiding place for the weapons, the task "was finished and it is a very good place, although there are still some problems to be resolved to eliminate the humidity which filters in."

Presumably Los Macheteros solved the humidity problem, but they failed to keep out the "petty thieves" who soon stole weapons, scanners, and communication equipment from the Washbowl. Crime is such a serious problem on the island that besides bars on all the windows, many city and rural residents use wrought iron to literally fence in their homes. Beautiful houses are covered with bars as inviting as those on a bank vault. It's a necessary evil, and perhaps the route Los Macheteros took because their final report states that they were "initiating a plan to eliminate security problems." In the meantime, those in command could rest assured that the custodial staff were cleaning up La Palangana, and they moved the comrade who acted as a front for the farm to a safer location.

To fund these operations, Los Macheteros provided one another with detailed budgets. In the farmhouse report mentioned above, the writer discusses a bathroom and other "final touches" (painting, plastering) that were not listed in the original request, but luckily "money was obtained from elsewhere." All available evidence indicates that Los Macheteros are as careful in their accounting procedures as the FBI. Joseph Rodriguez, the agent in charge on the island, indicated that "it kind of reminds you of the bureau, where you have to produce receipts for everything that you submit."

Recall the toy giveaway in Hartford. The FBI says that Norman Ramirez left for New York with $12,000. Out of that he had to furnish air fares for a number of people, rent the truck, buy the toys, and purchase meals. When he returned home, Norman had to account for literally every dollar he had spent, down to the sunglasses he bought to disguise his companions. His comrades seemed upset when, out of the $12,000, Norman had failed to account for $22.75. Aware of the microscopes that would soon be turned on their financial records, the Taínos combat unit found a pigeonhole (food) for the missing $22.75. Now they would have the approval of the auditing department.

One reason to act like Ebenezer Scrooge is scarce resources. Even with $7 million, Los Macheteros had to keep a tight rein on expenditures. Law rockets cost good money. So do mortars, the equipment in the farm workshop, the monthly payroll for full-time members, and the rental fees—$2,000 a month in one location—for safe houses. They watched every penny spent to assure the group's long-term survival. They could hardly take Victor's haul to a bank and fund expenditures with the interest earned on Wells Fargo's principal.

But the group's strict accounting procedures are more than anything a result of the profound commitment to the revolution displayed by virtually all Macheteros. FBI agents call them terrorists, but no one calls a Machetero a thief. They did take $7 million, but if you consider the fact that no Machetero accepts the legitimacy of federal authority, you enter a different world with its own moral standards. It is unthinkable for a Machetero to steal from the movement.

Dedication to the cause does not mean that Macheteros are fanatics or zealots. Those words connote an absence of perspective and a sense of rigidity. Juan Segarra, for example, rightly had a reputation as a ladies' man; besides a wife and two kids on the island, he supposedly had a lover in Boston, and when, after his arrest, Anne Gassin reportedly agreed to help the FBI, one of Segarra's friends said: "I always told him his cock would get him in trouble."

Los Macheteros are neither saints nor ascetics. They have faults, and they enjoy life. But a puritanical streak does run through the movement because this is, by its own definition, a serious and responsible organization. Macheteros condemn alcohol as passionately as AA, they totally reject the use of drugs, they abhor the crime that forces islanders to lock out the world with wrought-iron bars, they greatly value hard work, and they applaud sharp discipline in personal and social behavior.

Despite the open and violent rejection of American beliefs and values, many Macheteros are still determined by them. If you condemn indulging in alcohol because "they will think that's what all Puerto Ricans do" or applaud fidelity because "they will think all islanders come from unstable, unloving families," then your moral ideology is still guided by the presumed attitudes of the Americans Los Macheteros claim to reject.

The puritanical streak, the precise bookkeeping, the factions, the weapons used to kill: These are all sides of Los Macheteros, but the group's essence is best described by Norman Ramirez Talavera. He's an intelligent, articulate man who reportedly got caught putting these words into the FBI's tape machine: "I will not be arrested. I am not going to permit anyone to take me abroad. They will have to take me dead. I won't be caught alive. I couldn't stand being out there."

These words describe the passion any Machetero has for his or her homeland. These people are nourished by contact with their native soil, and like Norman Ramirez, they fear the debilitating spiritual consequences of living abroad, in an alien world.

That's easy to understand and even easier to applaud. What makes Los Macheteros Public Enemy Number One is the group's tactics and revolutionary goals, which by the FBI's definition, merit the label terrorist. As the bureau sees it, Los Macheteros are neither patriots nor freedom fighters. They are brutes in search of a target, and they deserve no mercy because their terrorist tactics make them international pariahs. As one person suggested, the only homeland a terrorist deserves is a small cell on a deserted island.

That may be true. In a world otherwise full of differences, violent tactics breed consensus. Virtually everyone agrees that terrorism is inhuman, but in a world overflowing with contemptible governments, there is also a widespread consensus among even "establishment" figures that revolutionary violence is sometimes legitimate. President Reagan not only funds the Contra effort in Nicaragua, he calls those "soldiers" freedom fighters. And Menachem Begin, the former prime minister of Israel, wrote that "substantial quantities of explosives were the main weapon in the struggle for liberation."

If violence is sometimes a legitimate revolutionary tool, a definition of terrorism is essential. Otherwise brutes and patriots get placed in the same inhuman category, and blinded by the terrorist label, interested observers miss the possibly legitimate reasons for revolutionary violence.

A good definition of terrorism is found in *Terrorism: How the West Can Win* (edited by Benjamin Netanyahu). Published in 1986, this volume arguably has a conservative bias (it includes, for example, essays by Secretary of State George Shultz, former United States American Ambassador to the United Nations Jeane Kirkpatrick, and FBI Director William Webster), but it does offer an accurate and widely accepted analysis of what terrorism is.

"Civilians are the key to the terrorists' strategy." Men, women, children, the handicapped, no one is excluded. "What distinguishes terrorism is the *willful* and *calculated* choice of innocents as targets." A guerilla is not a terrorist, because "guerrillas pit themselves against far superior combatants." But terrorists aim for "anybody except soldiers," and they do so with a specific goal in mind: fear. Terrorists try to scare their opponents into submission. To summarize: "Terrorism is the deliberate and systematic murder, maiming, and menacing of the innocent to inspire fear for political ends."

By that definition, Los Macheteros are definitely not terrorists. Rather than fear, they aim to create courage and pride; they're trying to arouse the Puerto Rican people, not scare them.

ROSARIO MORALES

Double Allegiance

I was torn, quite literally, the tear starting somewhere behind my left ear where my mother whispered duérmete nena to an afro beat when I was a little white-skinned spik with brown cousins cruising in my veins. And it was wrenched from my other ear, the one fed with yiddish-accented english sung in the streets of my adolescence. The raspy sound of cartilage parting from bone distracted me from the conference room where they stood up one after the other, jewish woman or woman of color, black or latina or any of the amazing mixtures of our various diasporas, ripping off sleeves to show the numbers tattooed on the bare skin, numbers passed on with hair color and the urge to hide, or pulling off blouses to bare ancient whip marks down black spines. A workshop, to heal our differences, I'd thought, but the noises were war cries, were competition for the one-down spot, each trying to prove to the other how much more oppressed *she* was, to prove she was the *only* one oppressed.

"Sure," I heard one cut in, "sure you're black and you get shit every day on your dark face, but they never tried to wipe you out, every one of you, every one," and sat down.

"Oh yes," the answer flicked out, "and so you say *history, history*. Something that you heard about, something that happened someplace else to someone else. And then you'll just sashay outa here in your bright white skin, step right over me where I'm getting my dark face ground into the dirt today, you hear, today." Oppression thrown at each other's faces like slaps.

Neither of them heard me ripping, heard my whimper, trying not to cry out loud from pain, heard the other women trying to hold my seams together with kindness.

But I heard two more voices pulling me apart. The first voice, jewish, stinging from this crack slung across her face: *You* can always get a nose job. She spoke:

Hear.

I am frightened. I know I can be boxcarted off, imprisoned shot gassed like my aunt Tessie, like Samuel of the round face. I've worked so hard to shape myself into anglosaxon the way my aunt Tessie shaped herself into aryan into middle class, conforming, accepting. But I know they'll search me out, they'll find me the way they do in my dreams and they will put a yellow star upon my brow.

The second voice, dark-skinned, darker than my kin, but close enough for comfort:

If you have a black skin or a brown skin or a yellow skin or a red, that's it, baby. No use worrying about when or where they'll find you. They find me every day. I get it every day. You've got a white skin and you pretend it isn't safety in the street, money in the bank, a leg up in any job, anytime.

Hear me.

I am dark in a racist society and I have no place to hide. Now. This minute. And all the minutes of my life.

Each spoke and then sat down with her hands on her ears while mine tore slowly and painfully. So that I had to go home to sew myself together with the thread we'd spun, my jewish girlfriends and I, made out of our games and fantasies, of tastes of each other's foods and each other's tears, of our parent's memories of cities hastily abandoned—Naranjito, Kiev, Munich—of yiddish-spanish accents in our speech, of browning photographs of grandparents we hardly knew, of the feel of our arms around each other. I ran small running stitches up my scalp, small chain stitches down my face, then stopped and wound what thread was left carefully onto the spool. It was about time, I thought, to give part of it away. No, all of it. I can make more.

PART 3

IDENTITY AND SELF-ESTEEM

"I am new. History made me . . . /I was born at the crossroads/and I am whole."

—FROM *CHILD OF THE AMERICAS* BY AURORA LEVINS MORALES

AURORA LEVINS MORALES

Child of the Americas

GETTING HOME ALIVE BY AURORA LEVINS MORALES
AND ROSARIO MORALES

I am a child of the Americas,
a light-skinned mestiza of the Caribbean,
a child of many diaspora, born into this continent at a crossroads.

I am a U.S. Puerto Rican Jew,
a product of the ghettos of New York I have never known.
An immigrant and the daughter and granddaughter of immigrants.
I speak English with passion: it's the tongue of my consciousness,
a flashing knife blade of crystal, my tool, my craft.

I am Caribeña, island grown. Spanish is in my flesh,
ripples from my tongue, lodges in my hips:
the language of garlic and mangoes,
the singing in my poetry, the flying gestures of my hands.
I am of Latinoamerica, rooted in the history of my continent:
I speak from that body.

I am not african. Africa is in me, but I cannot return.
I am not taína. Taíno is in me, but there is no way back.
I am not european. Europe lives in me, but I have no home there.

I am new. History made me. My first language was spanglish.
I was born at the crossroads
and I am whole.

JULIA DE BURGOS

Ay Ay Ay for the Kinky Black Woman

Ay ay ay, I'm kinky-haired and pure black;
proud my hair is kinky, proud of my fierce lips
and flat Mozambican nose.

Black woman of immaculate hue, I laugh and cry
at the notion of being a black monument;
a chunk of night in which my white
teeth sparkle;
being black cane
that entwines with blackness
weaving the black nest
where the black raven rests.
I sculpt myself out of a black chunk of blackness
Ay ay ay, so that my statue is totally black.

They say my grandfather was a slave
for whom his owner paid thirty coins.
Ay ay ay, that my grandfather was the slave
is my anguish, my immense sorrow.
If he'd been the slave owner,
it would be my shame.
For with people, the same as nations,
if being a slave means you have no rights,
being a slave owner means you have no conscience.

Ay ay ay, that the white king's sins
be washed away by the black queen's tears.

Ay ay ay, that my blood escapes me
and headed toward whiteness dives into clear water;
or perhaps whiteness will darken into black.

Ay ay ay, the black in me runs away
and with the white melds into wheaten
to be the kindred future of our Americas!

CLARA E. RODRIGUEZ
Puerto Ricans: Between Black and White

The experience of Puerto Ricans in New York City points up more clearly than any researched materials the chasm that exists between whites and blacks in the United States and the racism that afflicts both groups. For within the U.S. perspective, Puerto Ricans, racially speaking, belong to both groups; however, ethnically, they belong to neither. Thus placed, Puerto Ricans find themselves caught between two polarities and at a dialectical distance from both. Puerto Ricans are between white and black; Puerto Ricans are neither white nor black.

RACIAL HISTORY AND CONTRASTS

The degree to which racial heterogeneity is an integral factor of Puerto Rican life must be appreciated. It is not just a matter of black and white families within a community; it is more often a matter of a Negro-appearing brother and his Anglo-appearing sister attending the same school. The variety of racial types in the Puerto Rican community is the biological result of a still-not-clearly-analyzed history of racial mixing. Although a number of works have touched upon the issue of racial mixing in Puerto Rico, there is no real consensus in this area. Puerto Rican and American researchers have assumed or found Puerto Rico to be everything from a mulatto country to a predominantly white country with small subgroups of blacks and mulattos. Nevertheless, the process of racial mixing has continued and the existence of significant racial heterogeneity continues.

This same history has also yielded a unique set of social attitudes which have created a racial ambience quite different from that in the U.S. This ambience is vital to the understanding of the Puerto Rican experience in New York. A few of these points of contrast might bring about a better understanding of the racial ambience from which Puerto Ricans come and hence the racial attitudes that accompany racially heterogeneous Puerto Ricans to New York.

Perhaps the primary point of contrast is that, in Puerto Rico, racial identification is subordinate to cultural identification, while in the U.S., racial identification, to a large extent, determines cultural identification. Thus when asked that divisive question "What are you?" Puerto Ricans of all colors and ancestry answer, "Puerto Rican," while most New Yorkers answer, black, Jewish, or perhaps, "of Italian descent." This is not to say that Puerto Ricans feel no racial identification, but rather that cultural identification supersedes it.

Analyzing the system of racial classification in Puerto Rico, we see that it is based more on phenotypic and social definitions of what a person is than on genotypic knowledge about a person. In other words, physical and social appearance are the measures used to classify instead of the biological-descent classification (i.e., "one drop of Negro blood makes you Negro") used in the U.S. Thus in the U.S. the white-appearing offspring of an interracial couple is classified "Negro."[1] In Puerto Rico, he would probably be white. Alternatively, an obviously dark or "colored" person in the U.S. may not be seen as dark in Puerto Rico, especially if there are other mitigating circumstances, class for example. Many other examples of the contrasting racial classification criteria could be cited, but these two serve to point up the main differences.[2]

Another aspect of racial classification in Puerto Rico is that racial categories are based on color, class, facial features, and texture of hair. This is quite in contrast to the mainly color-based, white-nonwhite, or white, black, yellow, red, and brown classifications of the U.S. This makes for a spectrum of racial types in Puerto Rico. There are *blancos,* the equivalent of whites in this country;[3] *indios* are similar to the U.S. conception of East Indians, i.e., dark-skinned and straight-haired; *morenos* are dark-skinned, with a variety of features, Negroid and Caucasian; *negros* are the black, black men in the U.S. (As an aside, it is interesting that this latter term is also used as a term of endearment, at which time it bears no connotation of color whatsoever and can be used to refer to any of the racial types.) It can also, however, be used, depending on the tone, as a derogative term, like "nigger." Lastly, is the term *trigueño,* which can be applied to what would be considered brunettes in this country or to Negroes or *negros* who have high social status. Despite this term's lack of congruity with physical characteristics, it is still considered a term of racial classification; it just goes both ways.

The fact that this term goes both ways is indicative of the relationship between class and race. A "black" or "Negro" person becomes "white" by achieving economic status or one's friendship. It is an obvious form of "passing" without, however, the connotations given to that term in the U.S. In this country, a person who passes has become outwardly white. His physical appearance and cultural ways are white. In Puerto Rico a *trigueño,* who is Negro and moves up the status ladder, has not changed and is not furtively seeking escape from identification as a Negro.

Next, there is the contrast of a biracial, multiethnic society versus a homogeneous society. While in the U.S. racial/ethnic minorities have traditionally been segregated, there has never been any such tradition in Puerto Rico. Thus blacks in Puerto Rico are not a distinguishable ethnic group. This is not to say blacks are evenly distributed throughout the social structure, for there is, at present, some debate on this issue. But in terms of housing, institutional treatment, political rights, government policy, and cultural identification, black, white, and tan Puerto Ricans are not different. And race is not perceived as an issue on the island by Puerto Ricans of any pigmentation. Perhaps the clearest testament to this situation is the lack of response of dark Puerto Ricans on the island to the black-power movement. This is in contrast to the high degree of involvement in the black movement evidenced by Puerto Ricans of all colors in New York. Thus, while dark Puerto Ricans on the island are not a distinct ethnic group, Puerto Ricans of all colors in New York are.

One reflection of this unified society is that there is not the same taboo on intermarriage between white and black that exists in the U.S. Thus Puerto Ricans have intermarried and continue to inter-marry at what is probably a higher frequency than the U.S. And the strong emphasis on close family ties tends to make the world of most Puerto Rican children one that is inhabited by people of many colors, and these colors are not associated with different ranks.[4] This inter-mingled white, black, and tan world is foreign to most children in the U.S.

ONE-WAY STREET

This leads us into another area of contrast: two-way integration as opposed to one-way integration. In the U.S., one-way integration has been and is the norm. That is, blacks are usually sent to white schools, not vice versa; blacks integrate into white America, not whites into black America. For example, in this country a black couple almost never adopts a white child. The number of white babies available for adoption and the limited income of many blacks tend to discourage this action. In most adoption agencies the action is not permitted and the reverse is encouraged. In Puerto Rico, it is a fairly common occurrence to rear other people's children as one's own. These *hijos de crianza* come in all colors. Thus, a "dark" couple may rear the lighter, orphaned children of a relative or neighbor and a "white" couple may be rearing their own or another's "dark" child.

Furthermore, blacks or their contributions to U.S. culture are often whitewashed. Blacks in the U.S. have become more and more aware of how their cultural contributions to U.S. music, for example, have been "stolen," commercialized, denigrified. In Puerto Rico, the island music is a synthesis of Indian, African, and Spanish elements and is perceived as Puerto Rican. A similar type of synthesis is evolving in the New York Puerto Rican community; the new Latin sound incorporates Afro-Cuban, white rock, black soul, and the Latin rhythms. All Puerto Ricans in New York—white, black, and tan—continue to dance to this new music in the same way. This is quite different from the situation that has traditionally existed in the U.S., where blacks and whites not only tend to dance differently, but to different music. Thus while jazz split into white and black, Puerto Rican music development in New York and Puerto Rico was unitive. The rip-off process of whites and the indignation of blacks are possible only in a biracial, one-way society.

These descriptions of the racial climate in Puerto Rico should not be taken to imply the complete lack of discrimination in Puerto Rico. There is, at present, substantial debate over the "prejudice of no prejudice in Puerto Rico."[5] Some of the important questions currently being raised are: Have Indian and African elements been destroyed or integrated into society? Is the race issue in Puerto Rico dealt with by ignoring it, or is it really not an issue? Do all Puerto Ricans have some African ancestry? Is this condition necessary for harmonious "race" relations? Is there prejudice against Africanisms in Puerto Rico? Is this prejudice an American import? Is there an unrecognized color gradient as one moves up the income scale? If so, is this due to Puerto Rican preferential policies for light Puerto Ricans, discriminatory policies against blacks, inequalities inherited from slavery days, or the result of American imperialism? Is the whole debate over whether there is prejudice in Puerto Rico the result of a colonialized mentality?

PERCEPTUAL DISSONANCE

Despite the debate, the contrasts in racial climates in the U.S. and Puerto Rico exist and persist. Consequently these two climates have led to the development of widely different racial attitudes on the part of Puerto Ricans and other New Yorkers. These attitudinal differences coupled with the racial heterogeneity of Puerto Ricans have created a perceptual incongruence, with the inevitable strains accruing mainly to Puerto Ricans in New York. Given the racist perceptions in New York (and the U.S.), Puerto Ricans are not accepted by blacks or whites as a culturally distinct, racially integrated group, but are rather perceived and consequently treated as either black or white Puerto Ricans. Racial distinctions are heightened to a degree unnatural to Puerto Ricans (although blacks may be more aware of the cultural distinctness of Puerto Ricans, they still *perceive* in American racial terms). Given their racial heterogeneity, different racial perceptions, and awareness of the negative effects of racial reclassification in the U.S., Puerto Ricans generally exhibit considerable resistance to these divisive racial perceptions.

Thus there are only two options open in biracial New York—to be white or black. These options negate the cultural existence of Puerto Ricans and ignore their insistence on being treated, irrespective of race, as a culturally intact group. Thus, U.S. racial attitudes necessarily make Puerto Ricans either white or black, attitudes and culture make them neither white nor black, and our own resistance and struggle for survival places us between whites and blacks.[6]

This struggle for survival has not left Puerto Ricans unaffected. On the contrary, this in-between position has affected individual perceptions as well as group identity. Historically, Puerto Ricans arriving in New York have found themselves in a situation of perceptual incongruence—that is, they saw themselves differently than they were seen.

Some recently gathered data attest to the persistence of this situation. Fifty-two first- and second-generation Puerto Ricans in New York were asked to classify themselves in terms of color; meanwhile, the interviewer also classified respondents in terms of color using, however, U.S. racial classifications. The U.S. racial categorizations were based on whether or not the person would be considered white by white Americans in a white setting. Thus, those in the first category would pass without any question. Those in the second category might pass for white but would stand out a little. Those in the third category are noticeably not white, but also are not black, e.g., Filipino and South Pacific types. And in the fourth category are those with strong traces of African ancestry.

To the extent that the respondents were correctly classified in terms of U.S. standards, the results are intriguing. The only category in which there was no difference of opinion with respect to racial identification was the fourth. That is to say, a substantial proportion of respondents had self-perceptions of their color that differed from the U.S. perspective; however, all those with visible African ancestry perceived themselves as black. Many who were not seen as black, according to U.S. standards, saw themselves as black; hence while 13 percent of the respondents saw themselves as black the interviewer saw only 5 percent of the respondents as black.

On the other side of the color spectrum, more people saw themselves as "unquestionably white" than were thus classified—37 percent compared with 29 percent. However, some who were classified "unquestionably white" saw themselves as brown or tan. This indicates a "browning" tendency on the part of these "unquestionably white" Puerto Ricans; the so-called U.S. melting pot seems to "brown" Puerto Ricans. There were none classified "unquestionably white" who saw themselves as black.

There was, on the whole, however, a very strong tendency for respondents of both generations to classify themselves as darker than perceived by the interviewer. This was most evident in the "white, possibly" category. This (as defined by U.S. standards) was the most fluctuating and largest category of respondents. It was here that a significant number perceived themselves as brown, black, and Indian. However, it was also here that some perceived themselves as "unquestionably white."[7] Thus while this was the only category in which a few respondents saw themselves as lighter than they were seen, many people in this category also saw themselves as darker than they were seen.

It is possible that for these "white, possibly" Puerto Ricans, color has never been as issue. Perhaps they have not been periodically excluded from white groups or automatically included in black groups. (Nor have they been automatically included in white groups and excluded from black groups.) It is also possible that these "light" Puerto Ricans are members of a group which they think is considered nonwhite and so might, therefore, categorize themselves as darker. Furthermore, it is possible that they are perceived as darker than they are, when it becomes known they are Puerto Rican. Both situations would result in a darker racial self-image.

These still-tentative results do indicate that there exists important perceptual dissonance between Puerto Ricans and Americans. For although not all respondents had perceptions of their color that differed from those of the U.S., most did. There was, in addition, one respondent who said he did not know what his color was—a rather unusual reply in the U.S. This was perhaps indicative of a refusal to be slotted into black-white categories.

Given the racial heterogeneity of many Puerto Rican families, it would seem that family makeup also has much to do with their racial self-perception. Often the darkest or darker *in the family* usually do see themselves as nonwhite and/or darker than their actual color. This tended to be true for both first- and second-generation groups.

Although this small study raises more questions than it answers, its principal conclusion is clear: Puerto Ricans see themselves very differently than they are seen by American standards.

PUERTO RICANS, NEW YORICANS, AND RICANS

This perceptual incongruence points up the different mental-racial environment within which Puerto Ricans have functioned since they came to New York. Puerto Ricans living in the U.S. in the seventies have a considerably different mind-set than those who were among the early migrants.

The early-migrating Puerto Ricans entered a biracial society that strictly associated white with positive and black with negative. The migrating Puerto Rican saw that this association permeated every aspect of American life. There were the "nice" neighborhoods and the Negro neighborhoods. There were the Americans and the Negroes. There were also innumerable times he learned he was being given preference over a black—while, on the other hand, finding himself accepted and treated as a black, racially or socially.

The result of this situation was that the migrant Puerto Rican held on to his cultural identity very strongly and rejected racial identification on American terms. This prompted a bitter reaction from the black community capsuled in the words, "Trouble is they (Puerto Ricans) won't call themselves colored and we won't call them white." For the migrant Puerto Rican this racial identification, and all it implied, was not only foreign to his cultural and perceptual frame of reference, it was also damning.

However, with the black renaissance and black-power movement of the sixties, there have been significant changes. These changes are more apparent in the New York–bred second generation, but they are also visible in the first generation. A new response to perceptual incongruence appears to be developing. This is exemplified in the growing acceptance of the term *nonwhite* to describe New York Puerto Ricans.[8] The "browning process" found in the data cited previously appears to be consistent with this development.

Seen within a dialectical framework, darker racial self-perceptions and the acceptance of a nonwhite categorization appear to be indicative of a nascent synthesis of two diametrically opposed perceptions of Puerto Ricans. Puerto Ricans, a culturally homogeneous, racially integrated group, find themselves opposed to the demand that they become racially divided and culturally "cleansed" of being Puerto Rican.

What does the term *nonwhite* mean? Is this a racial term? Nonwhite is to New York Puerto Ricans what Puerto Ricans and blacks are; "white" is what Puerto Ricans and blacks are not. However, "black" is what blacks are and Puerto Ricans are not. This increasingly common definition of Puerto Ricans as "nonwhite" can also be seen as an evolution of racial perceptions and classifications engendered in Puerto Rico. For the predominance of cultural over racial considerations is evident in the development of this new "racial" term, which embraces all colors and types of Puerto Ricans.

The extent to which this growing acceptance of nonwhite categorization and the extent to which the "browning process" has been affected by political as well as historical and cultural forces can also be seen. For many New York Puerto Ricans have come of age at a time when black consciousness was in its renaissance—when the strength of black power was evident from the frightened faces of whites. The clear messages of these movements placed the option of assimilation in a different light and, more importantly, provided the possibility and example of an alternative to white-defined identities.[9]

An increasing number of (white, black, and tan) New York Puerto Ricans began identifying themselves as New Yoricans or Ricans—people who claim pride in being Puerto Rican but who acknowledge their New York soul. Implied in these terms is an acceptance of a nonwhite and ghetto status, with all its positive and negative consequences (this step would have been an impossible one for many Puerto Ricans reared on the island). For Puerto Ricans, this is the start of a new, self-defined position—an attempt to remain a unified whole and evolve from our own roots, between blacks and whites.

It is not clear where this change will lead, or what political implications it will have for Puerto Ricans. However, the commonly predicted routes for Puerto Rican identity resolution have changed. For it is no longer clear that "black" Puerto Ricans will assimilate into black American culture and that "white" Puerto Ricans will disappear in the white suburbs, while the various beiges, tans, and browns in between will hold on as the standard bearers of the New York Puerto Rican culture. Although these channels of assimilation still exist and exert pressures upon Puerto Ricans choosing and creating mind worlds and life spaces, it is no longer probable that people will follow these paths without question.

NOTES

1. And assuming in both instances that culture is held constant, i.e., an American white or black may not be judged within the Puerto Rican cultural framework. However, in Puerto Rico, the white-appearing offspring of an interracial American couple may still be seen as Negro because that is the culture he bears; that is how he has been socialized.

2. Most authors take the position that racial classification in Puerto Rico is class-influenced. But Harris (1970) concludes that color categories in Brazil (which are similar to those in Puerto Rico) cannot be seen in American terms.

3. There would probably be disagreement between Puerto Ricans and Americans on whether some *blancos* were the equivalent of whites in the U.S.

4. Felipe Luciano, former member of the Young Lords, describes Puerto Ricans as the "Rainbow People."

5. This term implies that claiming that no prejudice exists may in itself be a prejudicial act.

6. These same issues were underscored in the recent contesting of the U.S. Census count of Puerto Ricans. Puerto Rican groups demanded that third-generation Puerto Ricans should be included in

the count, pointing out that blacks are counted as blacks regardless of generation. The census considered Puerto Ricans as it has previous immigrant groups. However, as one community leader stated: "We are still considered Puerto Ricans no matter how long we are here." *New York Times*, July 3, 1972.

7. Those in this category going to a lighter categorization tended to be more favorably inclined to assimilation.

8. Though we know Puerto Ricans with obvious African ancestry are categorized as blacks, we don't really have data on how other Puerto Ricans are viewed when it is known they are Puerto Rican. Personal experiences of Puerto Ricans in New York indicate, however, that New Yorkers perceive Puerto Ricans as darker once they know the person is Puerto Rican.

9. I believe this was true not just for Puerto Ricans but for other "unmeltable ethnics" as well.

REFERENCE

Harris, Marvin. "Referential ambiguity in the calculus of Brazilian racial identity," in Norman E. Whitten, Jr. and John F. Szwed, eds., *Afro-American Anthropology*, New York: The Free Press. 1970.

WILLIE PERDOMO

Nigger-Reecan Blues

for Piri Thomas

Hey, Willie. What are you, man? Boricua? Moreno? Que?

I am.

No, silly. You know what I mean: What are you?

I am you. You are me. We the same. Can't you feel our veins drinking the same blood?

—But who said you was a Porta Reecan?
—Tú no eres Puerto Riqueño, brother.
—Maybe Indian like Gandhi Indian.
—I thought you was a Black man.
—Is one of your parents white?
—You sure you ain't a mix of something like
—Portuguese and Chinese?
—Naaaahhhh . . . You ain't no Porta Reecan.
—I keep telling you: The boy is a Black man with an accent.

If you look closely you will see that your spirits are standing right next to our songs. Yo soy Boricua! Yo soy Africano! I ain't lyin'. Pero mi pelo es kinky y kurly y mi skin no es negra pero it can pass . . .

—Hey, yo. I don't care *what* you say—you Black.

I ain't Black! Everytime I go downtown la madam blankeeta de madeeson avenue sees that I'm standing right next to her and she holds her purse just a bit tighter. I can't even catch a taxi late at night and the newspapers say that if I'm not in front of a gun, chances are that I'll be behind one. I wonder why . . .

—Cuz you Black, nigger.

I ain't Black, man. I had a conversation with my professor. Went like this:

—Where are you from, Willie?
—I'm from Harlem.
—Ohh! Are you Black?
—No, but—
—Do you play much basketball?

Te lo estoy diciendo, brother. Ese hombre es un moreno! Míralo!

Mira yo no soy moreno! I just come out of Jerry's Den and the coconut
spray off my new shape-up sails around the corner, up to the Harlem
River and off to New Jersey. I'm lookin' slim and I'm lookin' trim
and when my homeboy Davi saw me, he said: "Coño, Papo. Te parece como
un moreno, brother. Word up, bro. You look like a stone black kid."

—I told you—you was Black.

Damn! I ain't even Black and here I am sufferin' from the young
Black man's plight/the old white man's burden/and I ain't even Black,
man/a Black man/I am not/Boricua I am/ain't never really was/
Black/like me . . .

—Leave that boy alone. He got the Nigger-Reecan Blues

I'm a Spic!
I'm a Nigger!
Spic! Spic! No different than a Nigger!
Neglected, rejected, oppressed and depressed
From banana boats to tenements
Street gangs to regiments . . .
Spic! Spic! I ain't nooooo different than a Nigger.

ROBERTO SANTIAGO

Black *and* Latino

"There is no way that you can be black and Puerto Rican at the same
time." What? Despite the many times I've heard this over the years,
that statement still perplexes me. I *am* both and always have been.
My color is a blend of my mother's rich, dark skin tone and my fa-

ther's white complexion. As they were both Puerto Rican, I spoke Spanish before English, but I am totally bilingual. My life has been shaped by my black and Latino heritages, and despite other people's confusion, I don't feel I have to choose one or the other. To do so would be to deny a part of myself.

There has not been a moment in my life when I did not know that I looked black—and I never thought that others did not see it, too. But growing up in East Harlem, I was also aware that I did not "act black," according to the African-American boys on the block.

My lighter-skinned Puerto Rican friends were less of a help in this department. "You're not black," they would whine, shaking their heads. "You're a *boricua*, you ain't no *moreno* [black]." If that was true, why did my mirror defy the rules of logic? And most of all, why did I feel that there was some serious unknown force trying to make me choose sides?

Acting black. Looking black. Being a real black. This debate among us is almost a parody. The fact is that I am black, so why do I need to prove it?

The island of Puerto Rico is only a stone's throw away from Haiti, and, no fooling, if you climb a palm tree, you can see Jamaica bobbing on the Atlantic. The slave trade ran through the Caribbean basin, and virtually all Puerto Rican citizens have some African blood in their veins. My grandparents on my mother's side were the classic *negro como carbón* (black as carbon) people, but despite the fact that they were as dark as can be, they are officially not considered black.

There is an explanation for this, but not one that makes much sense, or difference, to a working-class kid from Harlem. Puerto Ricans identify themselves as Hispanics—part of a worldwide race that originated from eons of white Spanish conquests—a mixture of white, African, and *Indio* blood, which, categorically, is apart from black. In other words, the culture is the predominant and determinant factor. But there are frustrations in being caught in a duo-culture, where your skin color does not necessarily dictate what you are. When I read Piri Thomas's searing autobiography, *Down These Mean Streets*, in my early teens, I saw that he couldn't figure out other people's attitudes toward his blackness, either.

My first encounter with this attitude about the race thing rode on horseback. I had just turned six years old and ran toward the bridle path in Central Park as I saw two horses about to trot past. "Yea! Horsie! Yea!" I yelled. Then I noticed one figure on horseback. She was white, and she shouted, "Shut up, you f—g nigger! Shut up!" She pulled back on the reins and twisted the horse in my direction. I can still feel the spray of gravel that the horse kicked at my chest. And suddenly she was gone. I looked back, and, in the distance, saw my parents playing Whiffle Ball with my sister. They seemed miles away.

They still don't know about this incident. But I told my Aunt Aurelia almost immediately. She explained what the words meant and why they were said. Ever since then I have been able to express my anger appropriately through words or action in similar situations. Self-preservation, ego, and pride forbid me from ever ignoring, much less forgetting, a slur.

Aunt Aurelia became, unintentionally, my source for answers I needed about color and race. I never sought her out. She just seemed to appear at my home during the points in my childhood when I most needed her for solace. "Puerto Ricans are different from American blacks," she told me once. "There is no racism between what you call white and black. Nobody even considers the marriages interracial." She then pointed out the difference in color between my father and mother. "You never noticed that," she said, "because you were not raised with that hang-up."

Aunt Aurelia passed away before I could follow up on her observation. But she had made an important point. It's why I never liked the attitude that says I should be exclusive to one race.

My behavior toward this race thing pegged me as an iconoclast of sorts. Children from mixed marriages, from my experience, also share this attitude. If I have to bear the label of iconoclast because the world wants people to be in set categories and I don't want to, then I will.

A month before Aunt Aurelia died, she saw I was a little down about the whole race thing, and she said, "Roberto, don't worry. Even if—no matter what you do—black people in this country don't, you can always depend on white people to treat you like a black."

PIRI THOMAS

Babylon for the Babylonians

(FROM *DOWN THESE MEAN STREETS*)

In 1944 we moved to Long Island. Poppa was making good money at the airplane factory, and he had saved enough bread for a down payment on a small house.

As we got our belongings ready for the moving van, I stood by watching all the hustling with a mean feeling. My hands weren't with it; my fingers played with the top of a cardboard box full of dishes. My face tried hard not to show resentment at Poppa's decision to leave my streets forever. I felt that I belonged in Harlem; it was my kind of kick. I didn't want to move out to Long Island. My friend Crutch had told me there were a lot of paddies out there, and they didn't dig Negroes or Puerto Ricans.

"Piri," Momma said.

"Yeah, Moms." I looked up at Momma. She seemed tired and beat. Still thinking about Paulie all the time and how she took him to the hospital just to get some simple-assed tonsils out. And Paulie died. I remember she used to keep repeating how Paulie kept crying, "Don't leave me, Mommie," and her saying, "Don't worry, *nene*, it's just for a day." Paulie—I pushed his name out of my mind.

"*Dios mío*, help a little, *hijo*," Momma said.

"Moms, why do we gotta move outta Harlem? We don't know any other place better'n this."

"*Caramba!* What ideas," Momma said. "What for you talk like that? Your Poppa and I saved enough money. We want you kids to have good opportunities. It is a better life in the country. No like Puerto Rico, but it have trees and grass and nice schools."

"Yeah, Moms. Have they got Puerto Ricans out there?"

"*Sí*, I'm sure. Señora Rodriguez an' her family, an' Otelia—remember her? She lived upstairs."

"I mean a lotta *Latinos*, Moms. Like here in the *Barrio*. And how about *morenos*?"

"*Muchacho*, they got all kind." Momma laughed. "Fat and skinny, big and little. And—"

"Okay, Momma," I said. "You win. Give me a kiss."

So we moved to Babylon, a suburb on the south shore of Long Island. Momma was right about the grass and trees. And the school, too, was nice-looking. The desks were new, not all copped up like the ones in Harlem, and the teachers were kind of friendly and not so tough-looking as those in Patrick Henry.

I made some kind of friends with some paddy boys. I even tried out for the school baseball team. There were a lot of paddy boys and girls watching the tryouts and I felt like I was the only one trying out. I dropped a fly ball in the outfield to cries of "Get a basket," but at bat I shut everybody out of my mind and took a swing at the ball with all I had behind it and hit a home run. I heard the cheers and made believe I hadn't.

I played my role to the most, and the weeks turned into months. I still missed Harlem, but I didn't see it for six months. *Maybe,* I thought, *this squeeze livin' ain't as bad as Crutch said.* I decided to try the lunchtime swing session in the school gym. The Italian paddy, Angelo, had said they had hot music there. I dug the two-cents admission fee out of my pocket and made it up the walk that led to the gym.

"Two cents, please," said a little *muchacha blanca*.

"Here you are."

"Thank you," she smiled.

I returned her smile. Shit, man, Crutch was wrong.

The gym was whaling. The music was on wax, and it was a mambo. I let myself react. It felt good to give in to the natural rhythm. Maybe there were other worlds besides the mean streets, I thought. I looked around the big gym and saw some of the kids I knew a little. Some of them waved; I waved back. I noticed most of the paddy kids were dancing the mambo like stiff. Then I saw a girl I had heard called Marcia or something by the other kids. She was a pretty, well-stacked girl, with black hair and a white softness which set her hair off pretty cool. I walked over to her. "Hi," I said.

"Huh? Oh, hi."

"My first time here."

"But I've seen you before. You got Mrs. Sutton for English."

"Yeah, that's right. I meant this is my first time to the gym dance."

"I also was at the field when you smashed that ball a mile."

"That was *suerte*," I said.

"What's that?" she asked.

"What?"

"What you said—'swear-tay.' "

I laughed. "Man, that's Spanish."

"Are you Spanish? I didn't know. I mean, you don't look like what I thought a Spaniard looks like."

"I ain't a Spaniard from Spain," I explained. "I'm a Puerto Rican from Harlem."

"Oh—you talk English very well," she said.

"I told you I was born in Harlem. That's why I ain't got no Spanish accent."

"No-o, your accent is more like Jerry's."

What's she tryin' to put down? I wondered. Jerry was the colored kid who recently had moved to Bayshore.

"Did you know Jerry?" she asked. "Probably you didn't get to meet him. I heard he moved away somewhere."

"Yeah, I know Jerry," I said softly. "He moved away because he got some girl in trouble. I know Jerry is colored and I know I got his accent. Most of us in Harlem steal from each other's language or style or stick of living. And it's *suerte*, s-u-e-r-t-e. It means 'luck.' " *Jesus, Crutch, you got my mind messed up a little. I keep thinking this broad's tryin' to tell me something shitty in a nice dirty way. I'm gonna find out.* "Your name is Marcia or something like that, eh?" I added.

"Ahuh."

"Mine's Piri. Wanna dance?"

"Well, this one is almost over."

"Next one?"

"Well, er—I, er—well, the truth is that my boyfriend is sort of jealous and—well, you know how—"

I looked at her and she was smiling. I said, "Jesus, I'm sorry. Sure, I know how it is. Man, I'd feel the same way."

She smiled and shrugged her shoulders pretty-like. I wanted to believe her. I did believe her. I had to believe her. "Some other time, eh?"

She smiled again, cocked her head to one side and crinkled her nose in answer.

"Well, take it easy," I said. "See you around."

She smiled again, and I walked away not liking what I was feeling, and thinking that Crutch was right. I fought against it. I told myself I was still feeling out of place here in the middle of all these strangers, that paddies weren't as bad as we made them out to be. I looked over my shoulder and saw Marcia looking at me funny-like. When she saw me looking, her face changed real fast. She smiled again. I smiled back. I felt like I was plucking a mental daisy:

> You're right, Crutch
> You're wrong, Crutch
> You're right, Crutch
> You're wrong, Crutch.

I wanted to get outside and cop some sun and I walked toward the door.

"Hi, Piri," Angelo called. "Where you going? It's just starting."

"Aw, it's a little stuffy," I lied. "Figured on making it over to El Viejo's—I mean, over to the soda fountain on Main Street."

"You mean the Greek's?"

"Yeah, that's the place."

"Wait a sec till I take a leak and I'll go over with you."

I nodded okay and followed Angelo to the john. I waited outside for him and watched the kids dancing. My feet tapped out time and I moved closer to the gym and I was almost inside again. Suddenly, over the steady beat of the music, I heard Marcia say, "Imagine the nerve of that black thing."

"Who?" someone asked.

"That new colored boy," said another voice.

They must have been standing just inside the gym. I couldn't see them, but I had that for-sure feeling that it was me they had in their mouths.

"Let's go, Piri," Angelo said. I barely heard him. "Hey fella," he said, "what's the matter?"

"Listen, Angelo. Jus' listen," I said stonily.

". . . do you mean just like that?" one of the kids asked.

"Ahuh," Marcia said. "Just as if I was a black girl. *Well!* He started to talk to me and what could I do except be polite and at the same time not encourage him?"

"Christ, first that Jerry bastard and now him. We're getting invaded by niggers," said a thin voice.

"You said it," said another guy. "They got some nerve. My dad says that you give them an inch them apes want to take a yard."

"He's not so bad," said a shy, timid voice. "He's a polite guy and seems to be a good athlete. And besides, I hear he's a Puerto Rican."

"Ha—he's probably passing for Puerto Rican because he can't make it for white," said the thin voice. "Ha, ha, ha."

I stood there thinking who I should hit first. *Marcia. I think I'll bust her jaw first.*

"Let's go, Piri," Angelo said. "Those creeps are so fuckin' snooty that nobody is good enough for them. Especially that bitch Marcia. Her and her clique think they got gold-plated assholes."

". . . no, *really!*" a girl was saying. "I heard he's a Puerto Rican, and they're not like Neg—"

"There's no difference," said the thin voice. "He's still black."

"Come on, Piri, let's go," Angelo said. "Don't pay no mind to them."

"I guess he thought he was another Jerry," someone said.

"He really asked me to dance with him," Marcia said indignantly. "I told him that my boyfriend . . ."

The rest of the mean sounds faded as I made it out into the sun. I walked faster and faster. I cut across the baseball field, then ran as fast as I could. I wanted to get away from the things running to mind. My lungs were hurting—not from running but from not being able to scream. After a while I sat down and looked up at the sky. How near it seemed. I heard a voice: "Piri! Holy hell, you tore up the ground running." I looked up and saw Angelo. He was huffing and out of wind. "Listen, you shouldn't let them get you down," he said, kneeling next to me. "I know how you feel."

I said to him very nicely and politely, "Do me a favor, you

motherfuckin' paddy, get back with your people. I don't know why the fuck you're here, unless it's to ease your—oh, man, just get the fuck outta here. I hate them. I hate you. I hate all you white motherjumps."

"I'm sorry, Piri."

"Yeah, *blanco* boy, I know. You know how I feel, ain't that right? Go on, paddy, make it."

Angelo shook his head and slowly got up. He looked at me for a second, then walked away. I dug the sky again and said to it, "I ain't ever goin' back to that fuckin' school. They can shove it up their asses." I plucked the last mental daisy: *You was right, Crutch.*

VICTOR HERNÁNDEZ CRUZ

African Things

o the wonder man   rides his space ship/

                  brings his power through

many moons

           carries in soft blood   african spirits

dance & sing in my mother's house. in my cousin's house.

black as night can be/   what was Puerto Rican all about.

                  all about the

indios & you better believe it the african things

                black & shiny

grandmother speak to me & tell me of african things

              how do latin

boo-ga-loo sound   like you

            conga drums in the islands   you know

the traveling through many moons

            dance & tell me black african things

i know you know.

JUDITH ORTIZ COFER

The Myth of the Latin Woman:
I Just Met a Girl Named María

On a bus trip to London from Oxford University, where I was earning some graduate credits one summer, a young man, obviously fresh from a pub, spotted me and as if struck by inspiration went down on his knees in the aisle. With both hands over his heart he broke into an Irish tenor's rendition of "María" from *West Side Story.* My politely amused fellow passengers gave his lovely voice the round of gentle applause it deserved. Though I was not quite as amused, I managed my version of an English smile: no show of teeth, no extreme contortions of the facial muscles—I was at this time of my life practicing reserve and cool. Oh, that British control, how I coveted it. But María had followed me to London, reminding me of a prime fact of my life: you can leave the Island, master the English language, and travel as far as you can, but if you are a Latina, especially one like me who so obviously belongs to Rita Moreno's gene pool, the Island travels with you.

This is sometimes a very good thing—it may win you that extra minute of someone's attention. But with some people, the same things can make *you* an island—not so much a tropical paradise as an Alcatraz, a place nobody wants to visit. As a Puerto Rican girl growing up in the United States and wanting like most children to "belong," I resented the stereotype that my Hispanic appearance called forth from many people I met.

Our family lived in a large urban center in New Jersey during the sixties, where life was designed as a microcosm of my parents' casas on the island. We spoke in Spanish, we ate Puerto Rican food bought at the bodega, and we practiced strict Catholicism complete with Saturday confession and Sunday mass at a church where our parents were accommodated into a one-hour Spanish mass slot, performed by a Chinese priest trained as a missionary for Latin America.

As a girl, I was kept under strict surveillance, since virtue and modesty were, by cultural equation, the same as family honor. As a teenager I was instructed on how to behave as a proper señorita. But it was a conflicting message girls got, since the Puerto Rican mothers also encouraged their daughters to look and act like women and to dress in clothes our Anglo friends and their mothers found too "mature" for our age. It was, and is, cultural, yet I often felt humiliated when I appeared at an American friend's party wearing a dress more suitable to a semiformal than to a playroom birthday celebration. At Puerto Rican festivities, neither the music nor the colors we wore could be too loud. I still experience a vague sense of letdown when I'm invited to a "party" and it turns out to be a marathon conversation in hushed tones rather than a fiesta with salsa, laughter, and dancing—the kind of celebration I remember from my childhood.

I remember Career Day in our high school, when teachers told us to come dressed as if for a job interview. It quickly became obvious that to the barrio girls, "dressing up" sometimes meant wearing ornate jewelry and clothing that would be more appropriate (by mainstream standards) for the company Christmas party than as daily office attire. That morning, I had agonized in front of my closet, trying to figure out what a "career girl" would wear because, essentially, except for Marlo Thomas on TV, I had no models on which to base my decision. I knew how to dress for school: at the Catholic school I attended we all wore uniforms; I knew how to dress for Sunday mass, and I knew what dresses to wear for parties at my relatives' homes. Though I do not recall the precise details of my Career Day outfit, it must have been a composite of the above choices. But I remember a comment my friend (an Italian-American) made in later years that coalesced my impressions of that day. She said that at the business school she was attending, the Puerto Rican girls always stood out for wearing "everything at once." She meant, of course, too much jewelry, too many accessories. On that day at school, we were simply made the negative models by the nuns who were themselves not credible fashion experts to any of us. But it was painfully obvious to me that to the others, in their tailored skirts and silk blouses, we must have seemed "hopeless" and "vulgar." Though I now know that most adolescents feel out of step much of the time, I also know that for the Puerto Rican girls of my generation that sense was intensified. The way our teachers and classmates looked at us that day in school was just a taste of the culture clash that awaited us in the real world, where prospective employers and men on the street would often misinterpret our tight skirts and jingling bracelets as a come-on.

Mixed cultural signals have perpetuated certain stereotypes—for example, that of the Hispanic woman as the "Hot Tamale" or sexual firebrand. It is a one-dimensional view that the media have found easy to promote. In their special vocabulary, advertisers have designated "sizzling" and "smoldering" as the adjectives of choice for describing not only the foods but also the women of Latin America. From conversations in my house, I recall hearing about the harassment that Puerto Rican women endured in factories where the "boss men" talked to them as if sexual innuendo was all they understood, and worse, often gave them the choice of submitting to advances or being fired.

It is custom, however, not chromosomes, that leads us to choose scarlet over pale pink. As young girls, we were influenced in our decisions about clothes and colors by the women—older sisters and mothers who had grown up on a tropical island where the natural environment was a riot of primary colors, where showing your skin was one way to keep cool as well as to look sexy. Most important of all, on the island, women perhaps felt freer to dress and move more provocatively, since, in most cases, they were protected by the traditions, mores, and laws of a Spanish/Catholic system of morality and machismo whose main rule was: *You may look at my sister, but if you touch her I will kill you.* The extended family and church structure could provide a young woman with a circle of safety in her small pueblo on the island; if a man "wronged" a girl, everyone would close in to save her family honor.

This is what I have gleaned from my discussions as an adult with older Puerto Rican women. They have told me about dressing in their best party clothes on Saturday nights and going to the town's plaza to promenade with their girlfriends in front of the boys they liked. The males were thus given an opportunity to admire the women and to express their admiration in the form of *piropos*: erotically charged street poems they composed on the spot. I have been subjected to a few piropos while visiting the Island, and they can be outrageous, although custom dictates that they must never cross into obscenity. This ritual, as I understand it, also entails a show of studied indifference on the woman's part; if she is "decent," she must not acknowledge the man's impassioned words. So I do understand how things can be lost in translation. When a Puerto Rican girl dressed in her idea of what is attractive meets a man from the mainstream culture who has been trained to react to certain types of clothing as a sexual signal, a clash is likely to take place. The line I first heard based on this aspect of the myth happened when the boy who took me to my first formal dance leaned over to plant a sloppy overeager kiss painfully on my mouth, and when I didn't respond with sufficient passion, said in a resentful tone: "I thought you Latin girls were supposed to mature early"—my first instance of being thought of as a fruit or vegetable—I was supposed to *ripen*, not just grow into womanhood like other girls.

It is surprising to some of my professional friends that some people, including those who should know better, still put others "in their place." Though rarer, these incidents are still commonplace in my life. It happened to me most recently during a stay at a very classy metropolitan hotel favored by young professional couples for their weddings. Late one evening after the theater, as I walked toward my room with my new colleague (a woman with whom I was coordinating an arts program), a middle-aged man in a tuxedo, a young girl in satin and lace on his arm, stepped directly into our path. With his champagne glass extended toward me, he exclaimed, "Evita!"

Our way blocked, my companion and I listened as the man half-recited, half-bellowed, "Don't Cry for Me, Argentina." When he finished, the young girl said: "How about a round of applause for my daddy?" We complied, hoping this would bring the silly spectacle to a close. I was becoming aware that our little group was attracting the attention of the other guests. "Daddy" must have perceived this too, and he once more barred the way as we tried to walk past him. He began to shout-sing a ditty to the tune of "La Bamba"—except the lyrics were about a girl named María whose exploits all rhymed with her name and gonorrhea. The girl kept saying "Oh, Daddy" and looking at me with pleading eyes. She wanted me to laugh along with the others. My companion and I stood silently waiting for the man to end his offensive song. When he finished, I looked not at him but at his daughter. I advised her calmly never to ask her father what he had done in the army. Then I walked between them and to my room. My friend complimented me on my cool handling of the situation. I confessed to her that I really had wanted to push the jerk into the swimming pool. I knew that this same man—probably a corporate executive, well-educated, even worldly by most standards—would not have been likely to regale a white woman with a dirty song in public. He would perhaps have checked his impulse by assuming that she could be somebody's wife or mother, or at least *somebody* who might take offense. But to him, I was just an Evita or a María: merely a character in his cartoon-populated universe.

Because of my education and my proficiency with the English language, I have acquired many mechanisms for dealing with the anger I experience. This was not true for my parents, nor is it true for the many Latin women working at menial jobs who must put up with stereotypes about our ethnic group such as: "They make good domestics." This is another facet of the myth of the Latin woman in the United States. Its origin is simple to deduce. Work as domestics, waitressing, and factory jobs are all that's available to women with little English and few skills. The myth of the Hispanic menial has been sustained by the same media phenomenon that made "Mammy" from *Gone with the Wind* America's idea of the black woman for generations; María, the housemaid or counter girl, is now indelibly etched into the national psyche. The big and the little screens have presented us with the picture of the funny Hispanic maid, mispronouncing words and cooking up a spicy storm in a shiny California kitchen.

This media-engendered image of the Latina in the United States has been documented by feminist Hispanic scholars, who claim that such portrayals are partially responsible for the denial of opportunities for upward mobility among Latinas in the professions. I have a Chicana friend working on a Ph.D. in philosophy at a major university. She says her doctor still shakes his head in puzzled amazement at all the "big words" she uses. Since I do not wear my diplomas around my neck for all to see, I too have on occasion been sent to that "kitchen," where some think I obviously belong.

One such incident that has stayed with me, though I recognize it as a minor offense, happened on the day of my first public poetry reading. It took place in Miami in a boat-restaurant where we were having lunch before the event. I was nervous and excited as I walked in with my notebook in my hand. An older woman motioned me to her table. Thinking (foolish me) that she wanted me to autograph a copy of my brand new slender volume of verse, I went over. She ordered a cup of coffee from me, assuming that I was the waitress. Easy enough to mistake my poems for menus, I suppose. I know that it wasn't an intentional act of cruelty, yet of all the good things that happened that day, I remember that scene most clearly, because it reminded me of what I had to overcome before anyone would take me seriously. In retrospect I understand that my anger gave my reading fire, that I have almost always taken doubts in my abilities as a challenge—and that the result is, most times, a feeling of satisfaction at having won a convert when I see the cold, appraising eyes warm to my words, the body language change, the smile that indicates that I have opened some avenue for communication. That day, I read to that woman and her lowered eyes told me that she was embarrassed at her little faux pas, and when I willed her to look up at me, it was my victory, and she graciously allowed me to punish her with my full attention. We shook hands at the end of the reading, and I never saw her again. She has probably forgotten the whole thing, but maybe not.

Yet I am one of the lucky ones. My parents made it possible for me to acquire a stronger footing in the mainstream culture by giving me the chance at an education. And books and art have saved me from the harsher forms of ethnic and racial prejudice that many of my Hispanic *compañeras* have had to endure. I travel a lot around the United States, reading from my books of poetry and my novel, and the reception I most often receive is one of positive interest by people who want to know more about my culture. There are, however, thousands of Latinas without the privilege of an education or the entrée into society that I have. For them life is a struggle against the misconceptions perpetuated by the myth of the Latina as whore, domestic or criminal. We cannot change this by legislating the way people look at us. The transformation, as I see it, has to occur at a much more individual level. My personal goal in my public life is to try to replace the old pervasive stereotypes and myths about Latinas with a much more interesting set of realities. Every time I give a reading, I hope the stories I tell, the dreams and fears I examine in my work, can achieve some universal truth which will get my audience past the particulars of my skin color, my accent, or my clothes.

I once wrote a poem in which I called us Latinas "God's brown daughters." This poem is really a prayer of sorts, offered upward, but also, through the human-to-human channel of art, outward. It is a prayer for communication, and for respect. In it, Latin women pray "in Spanish to an Anglo God / with a Jewish heritage," and they are "fervently hoping / that if not omnipotent, / at least He be bilingual."

MIGUEL ALGARÍN

A Mongo Affair

On the corner by the plaza
in front of
the entrance to Gonzalez-Padín
in old San Juan
a black Puerto Rican talks
about "the race"
he talks of Boricuas
who are in New York on welfare
and on lines waiting for food stamps,
"yes, it's true, they've been taken out
and sent abroad and those that
went over tell me that they're
doing better over there than here
they tell me they get money
and medical aid
that their rent is paid
that their clothes get bought
that their teeth get fixed

is that true?"
on the corner by
the entrance to Gonzalez-Padín
I have to admit that he has been
lied to, misled,
that I know that all the goodies
he named humiliate the receiver,
that a man is demoralized
when his woman and children
beg for weekly checks
that even the fucking a man does
on a government bought mattress
draws the blood from his cock
cockless, sin espina dorsal,
mongo—that's it!
a welfare fuck is a mongo affair!
mongo means flojo
mongo means bloodless
mongo means soft
mongo can not penetrate
mongo can only tease
but it can't tickle
the juice of the earth-vagina
mongo es el bicho Taíno
porque murió
mongo es el borinqueño
who's been moved
to the inner-city jungles
of north american cities
mongo is the rican who survives
in the tar jungle of Chicago
who cleans, weeps, crawls,
gets ripped off,
sucks the eighty dollars a week
from the syphilitic
down deep frustrated
northern man—
viejo negro africano,

Africa Puerto Rico
sitting on department store entrances
don't believe the deadly game
of Northern cities paved with gold and plenty
don't believe the fetching dream
of life improvement in New York
the only thing you'll find in Boston
is a soft leather shoe up your ass,
viejo, anciano africano, Washington
will send you in your old age
to clean the battlefields
in Korea and Vietnam
you'll be carrying a sack
and into that canvas
you'll pitch las uñas
los intestinos
las piernas
los bichos mongos
of Puerto Rican soldiers
put at the front to face
sí!
to face the bullets, bombs, missiles,
sí! the artillery
sí!
to face the violent hatred of Nazi Germany
to confront the hungry anger of the world
viejo negro
viejo puertorriqueño
the north offers us pain
and everlasting humiliation
IT DOES NOT COUGH UP
THE EASY LIFE: THAT IS A LIE
viejo que has visto la isla '
perder sus hijos
are there guns to deal with
genocide, expatriation?
are there arms to hold
the exodus of borinqueños

from Borinquen?
we have been moved
we have been shipped
we have been parcel posted
first by water then by air
el correo has special prices
for the "low island element" to be
removed, then dumped
into the inner-city ghettos
Viejo, Viejo, Viejo
we are the minority
here in Borinquen
we, the Puerto Rican,
the original man of this island
is in the minority
I writhe with pain
I jump with anger
I know
I see
I am "la minoría de la isla"
viejo, viejo anciano
do you hear me?
there are no more Puerto Ricans
in Borinquen
I am the minority everywhere
I am among the few in all societies
I belong to a tribe of nomads
that roam the world without
a place to call a home,
there is no place that is ALL MINE
there is no place that I can
call mi casa,
I, yo, Miguel ¡ Me oyes viejo!
I, yo, Miguel
el hijo de Maria Socorro y Miguel
is homeless, has been homeless
will be homeless
in the to be

and the to come
Miguelito, Lucky, Bimbo
you like me have lost
your home
and to the first idealist
I meet
I'll say
don't lie to me
don't fill me full of vain
disturbing love for an island
filled with Burger Kings
for I know
there are no cuchifritos
in Borinquen
I remember last night
viejito lindo
when your eyes fired me
with trust
do you hear that?
with trust
and when you said
that you would stand by me
should any danger threaten
I halfway threw myself
into your arms to weep
mis gracias
I loved you
viejo negro
I would have slept
in your arms
I would have caressed
your curly gray hair
I wanted to touch
your wrinkled face
when your eyes fired me
with trust
viejo corazón puertorriqueño
your feelings cocinan

en mi sangre
el poder de realizarme
and when you whispered
your anger into my ears
when you spoke of
"nosotros los que estamos
preparados con las armas"
it was talk of future
happiness
my ears had not till
that moment heard such
words of promise and of guts
in all of Puerto Rico
old man with the golden chain
and the medallion with an indian
on your chest
I love you
I see in you
what has been
what is coming
and will be
and over your grave
I will write
HERE SLEEPS
A MAN
WHO SEES ALL OF
WHAT EXISTS
AND THAT WHICH WILL EXIST.

PART 4

ANXIETY AND ASSIMILATION

"Always broke/Always owing/Never knowing/that they are beautiful people/Never knowing/the geography of their complexion . . ."

—FROM *PUERTO RICAN OBITUARY* BY PEDRO PIETRI

PEDRO PIETRI

Puerto Rican Obituary

They worked
They were always on time
They were never late
They never spoke back
when they were insulted
They worked
They never took days off
that were not on the calendar
They never went on strike
without permission
They worked
ten days a week
and were only paid for five
They worked
They worked
They worked
and they died
They died broke
They died owing
They died never knowing
what the front entrance
of the first national city bank looks like

Juan
Miguel

Milagros
Olga
Manuel
All died yesterday today
and will die again tomorrow
passing their bill collectors
on to the next of kin
All died
waiting for the garden of eden
to open up again
under a new management
All died
dreaming about america
waking them up in the middle of the night
screaming: Mira Mira
your name is on the winning lottery ticket
for one hundred thousand dollars
All died
hating the grocery stores
that sold them make-believe steak
and bullet-proof rice and beans
All died waiting dreaming and hating

Dead Puerto Ricans
Who never knew they were Puerto Ricans
Who never took a coffee break
from the ten commandments
to KILL KILL KILL
the landlords of their cracked skulls
and communicate with their latino souls

Juan
Miguel
Milagros
Olga
Manuel
From the nervous breakdown streets
where the mice live like millionaires

and the people do not live at all
are dead and were never alive

Juan
died waiting for his number to hit
Miguel
died waiting for the welfare check
to come and go and come again
Milagros
died waiting for her ten children
to grow up and work
so she could quit working
Olga
died waiting for a five dollar raise
Manuel
died waiting for his supervisor to drop dead
so he could get a promotion

Is a long ride
from Spanish Harlem
to long island cemetery
where they were buried
First the train
and then the bus
and the cold cuts for lunch
and the flowers
that will be stolen
when visiting hours are over
Is very expensive
Is very expensive
But they understand
Their parents understood
Is a long non-profit ride
from Spanish Harlem
to long island cemetery

Juan
Miguel

Milagros
Olga
Manuel
All died yesterday today
and will die again tomorrow
Dreaming
Dreaming about queens
Clean-cut lily-white neighborhood
Puerto Ricanless scene
Thirty-thousand-dollar home
The first spics on the block
Proud to belong to a community
of gringos who want them lynched
Proud to be a long distance away
from the sacred phrase: Que Pasa

These dreams
These empty dreams
from the make-believe bedrooms
their parents left them
are the after-effects
of television programs
about the ideal
white american family
with black maids
and latino janitors
who are well train
to make everyone
and their bill collectors
laugh at them
and the people they represent

Juan
died dreaming about a new car
Miguel
died dreaming about new anti-poverty programs
Milagros
died dreaming about a trip to Puerto Rico

Olga
died dreaming about real jewelry
Manuel
died dreaming about the irish sweepstakes

They all died
like a hero sandwich dies
in the garment district
at twelve o'clock in the afternoon
social security number to ashes
union dues to dust

They knew
they were born to weep
and keep the morticians employed
as long as they pledge allegiance
to the flag that wants them destroyed
They saw their names listed
in the telephone directory of destruction
They were train to turn
the other cheek by newspapers
that mispelled mispronounced
and misunderstood their names
and celebrated when death came
and stole their final laundry ticket

They were born dead
and they died dead

Is time
to visit sister lopez again
the number one healer
and fortune card dealer
in Spanish Harlem
She can communicate
with your late relatives
for a reasonable fee
Good news is guaranteed

Rise Table Rise Table
death is not dumb and disable
Those who love you want to know
the correct number to play
Let them know this right away
Rise Table Rise Table
death is not dumb and disable
Now that your problems are over
and the world is off your shoulders
help those who you left behind
find financial peace of mind
Rise Table Rise Table
death is not dumb and disable
If the right number we hit
all our problems will split
and we will visit your grave
on every legal holiday
Those who love you want to know
the correct number to play
Let them know this right away
We know your spirit is able
Death is not dumb and disable
RISE TABLE RISE TABLE

Juan
Miguel
Milagros
Olga
Manuel
All died yesterday today
and will die again tomorrow
Hating fighting and stealing
broken windows from each other
Practicing a religion without a roof
The old testament
The new testament
according to the gospel
of the internal revenue

the judge and jury and executioner
protector and eternal bill collector

Secondhand shit for sale
Learn how to say Como Esta Usted
and you will make a fortune
They are dead
They are dead
and will not return from the dead
until they stop neglecting
the art of their dialogue
for broken english lessons
to impress the mister goldsteins
who keep them employed
as lavaplatos porters messenger boys
factory workers maids stock clerks
shipping clerks assistant mailroom
assistant, assistant assistant
to the assistant's assistant
assistant lavaplatos and automatic
artificial smiling doormen
for the lowest wages of the ages
and rages when you demand a raise
because is against the company policy
to promote SPICS SPICS SPICS

Juan
died hating Miguel because Miguel's
used car was in better running condition
than his used car
Miguel
died hating Milagros because Milagros
had a color television set
and he could not afford one yet
Milagros
died hating Olga because Olga
made five dollars more on the same job
Olga

died hating Manuel because Manuel
had hit the numbers more times
than she had hit the numbers
Manuel
died hating all of them
Juan
Miguel
Milagros
and Olga
because they all spoke broken english
more fluently than he did

And now they are together
in the main lobby of the void
Addicted to silence
Off limits to the wind
Confine to worm supremacy
in long island cemetery
This is the groovy hereafter
the protestant collection box
was talking so loud and proud about

Here lies Juan
Here lies Miguel
Here lies Milagros
Here lies Olga
Here lies Manuel
who died yesterday today
and will die again tomorrow
Always broke
Always owing
Never knowing
that they are beautiful people
Never knowing
the geography of their complexion

PUERTO RICO IS A BEAUTIFUL PLACE
PUERTORRIQUENOS ARE A BEAUTIFUL RACE

If only they
had turned off the television
and tune into their own imaginations
If only they
had used the white supremacy bibles
for toilet paper purpose
and make their latino souls
the only religion of their race
If only they
had return to the definition of the sun
after the first mental snowstorm
on the summer of their senses
If only they
had kept their eyes open
at the funeral of their fellow employees
who came to this country to make a fortune
and were buried without underwears

Juan
Miguel
Milagros
Olga
Manuel
will right now be doing their own thing
where beautiful people sing
and dance and work together
where the wind is a stranger
to miserable weather conditions
where you do not need a dictionary
to communicate with your people
Aqui Se Habla Espanol all the time
Aqui you salute your flag first
Aqui there are no dial soap commercials
Aqui everybody smells good
Aqui tv dinners do not have a future
Aqui the men and women admire desire
and never get tired of each other
Aqui Que Pasa Power is what's happening

Aqui to be called negrito
means to be called LOVE

PIRI THOMAS

The Konk

When I was a kid, many folks spent a lot of time, effort, and money trying to pass for white. Very few homes did not have some kind of skin-bleaching cream. If poverty prevented its purchase, raw lemon juice would suffice. Cream or juice was liberally applied to the skin with the hope of turning it yellow, which was light, if not white.

Parents were constantly pinching the noses of their children so that flat, wide nostrils could be unnaturally forced into sculptured images of white folks' noses.

Running neck and neck were hair-straightening and coloring effects. The very poor made up batches of Vaseline, lye, and harsh brown octagon soap for their hair-straightening. For those who could afford it, there were jars of heavy white cream with "You too can have beautiful hair" advertised on the label.

Even more money could buy a marcel, which straightened curly hair by pressing it out with iron-hot combs after dipping one's head in oil. The smell of burnt hair often overpowered the odors of garbage-littered alleyways. Even comic books carried ads for beauty care. One could earn a Red Ryder B.B. rifle or a bicycle if one sold enough of a particular brand of lightening cream.

By the time I was fourteen, I had grown tired of my curly hair being called "nappy," *pasas* (raisins), or *pelo malo* (bad hair). One day I decided to take the plunge. I went to a barbershop way up in the wilds of the South Bronx, recommended by some walking exponents of one hair-straightening process known as the "konk."

At Prospect Avenue station, I made my exit and headed for the barbershop, located on Westchester Avenue. A huge sign in the window advertised its specialty.

ROY'S BARBERSHOP—HAIR STRAIGHTENED
KONKS—FIVE DOLLARS—SATISFACTION
GUARANTEED

Overcoming my hesitancy, I marched into that barbershop like I copped konks every day. On the walls were photographs of all kinds of celebrities, including fighters like Kid Gavilan and Ray Robinson. They flashed big smiles signifying their joy at sporting straight hair via konks or marcels.

Some sad blues were being wailed by Billie Holiday from an antique radio. I figured Billie was saying konking was all right too. Two young black men wearing white barbershop jackets were playing checkers. One of them looked at me with a smile and in singsong asked, "What will it be, li'l brother? A trim trip or the works?"

"Gimme a konk," I said, as if I'd invented the word.

"Sit right there, li'l brother." He pointed to a mid-Victorian barbershop chair. "We'll get you straightened out in no time at all."

With cool-breeze apprehension, I lightly eased myself into the chair, which in my vivid imagination resembled the hot seat at Sing Sing.

"I'm Roy, bro. What's yours?"

"Mine's Piri," I answered, my eyes glued to his own natural unprocessed hair.

Roy put on some rubber gloves like doctors use when they have to touch something they don't really want to.

"Umhh." He frowned. "This won't do . . . won't do at all."

I wondered if my Puerto Rican hair was going to be left out of konk too. "What's the matter?"

"Too much grease, son. You got grease on your head that's been there from the year one. Gotta give you an A-1 Shampoo first, okay? It's $2.50 extra."

Too deeply involved by now to say no, I agreed and Roy proceeded to do his art. After the final rinsing, he squeaked my hair between his thumb and forefinger. "It's clean now."

I had to admit my curly hair had not looked that clean in a long time. Seeing my reflection in the mirror, I grunted approval.

Roy examined my scalp carefully, arousing my anxiety.

"You got lots of good hair to work with."

I bubbled with pleasure. At last my hair pleased somebody, even if it were just for a konk. Roy took out a huge jar of Dixie Peach Hair Pomade. He plunged his right hand in and came out with a gigantic blob of its thick yellow substance. I staggered under its weight as he worked close to a pound into my hair.

"Man, you sure are heavy on that grease," I protested.

"Got to, li'l man, 'cause without the Dixie Peach, the konk can burn your scalp right off your head. In fact, bro, it can cause your hair to fall right off your head or turn it red along with your scalp."

"Jesus Christ," I said, forcing my voice to stay without panic. Like I never thought it was going to be dangerous.

"A lot of bad can happen if it's not done right." My artist brother droned on, confident in his art. "If you want white man's hair, there's a price you gotta pay. Whatcha say? Now's the time to stop or go."

I smiled bravely and said, "Go, bro. But say, man. How come you don't konk your hair, seeing as you're in the business?"

Roy just mumbled. "No way, man. Konks or marcels ain't my stick. I just do it for others 'cause it's part of my living wages."

Satisfied that my head was greased to his satisfaction, Roy unscrewed the top of a large blue jar. I observed a soft whitish cream that smelled like sulfuric acid. With a comb, he began working it into my curly, terror-stricken, cringing hairs.

"Now, li'l brother, relax and listen. Soon as you start feeling your scalp begin burning, just gimme a holler. I sure don't want to be responsible for your hair turning red, let alone dropping out. Don't get scared if you just feel your scalp warming up. That's just the konk doing its thing. Only holler when it really starts to burn. Some scalps are tender, others can—"

Just then a voice interrupted from the doorway. "Good morning, gentlemen. Anybody feeling lucky today?"

In the mirror, I saw a boy. He was a numbers runner just a few years older than my fourteen, high yellow of color with soft reddish natural brown hair. He thoughtfully checked out my reflection, his eyes glued compassionately to the top of my head, by now a smoldering mass of plaster of paris.

The smell of burning, agonizing hair permeated the barbershop. I strained my neck out with a grin after what seemed like hours instead of minutes. "Hey, man. My hair is starting to burn."

Damnit. I wasn't being heard. Roy the artful barber was too busy checking out the numbers game.

"Yeah, I sure feel lucky today. Gimme 50¢ on 347, 50¢ on 656, and a buck combination on 437."

"Hey, man. My head's burning."

If he refused to hear me, he should at least be able to smell the smoke. I waited coolly as I could for a couple of more suffering seconds and then without any kind of embarrassment began to let out all kinds of yells.

"Hey, man. I ain't shitting. My head's on fire."

"Listen, George," Roy went on rapping to the young numbers runner, "I guess that's all for now. No, wait, George, hold on. Gimme 50¢ on 333. I really feel lucky today."

I wished I felt that lucky. I was already heading for the faucet with my head on fire. Roy finally got hip to the seriousness of the situation and got to the sink with me.

Attempting to comfort me, he said, "It's supposed to burn a little. You want it to come out cool, don't ya?"

He brought the three-alarm fire that was my scalp under control by life-saving, cold-water rinsing. He toweled my hair dry. I stared into the mirror, amazed. My short coils of curls no longer than a couple of inches around my ears were now a waterfall of hair, dead straight and hanging limply down to my shoulders.

Roy combed while I inwardly swore I looked like Cochise, if not Prince Valiant.

"Now for a haircut, bro. Do you want it long or short?"

"Long, man," I said. "Long enough for a pompadour in front and a duck's ass in the back."

"Gotcha."

Snip, snip, snip. Comb, comb, comb. Clip, clip, clip.

Straight razor, sweet-smelling hair lotion, some more combing, a pat here, a pat there.

"Okay, man. That's it. You got a Roy Special. Hey, man, open your eyes. Check yourself out."

Roy's voice sounded so pleased that I opened them in good faith. I ran my fingers through my hair. It was like fine silk. Roy expertly brushed away loose hairs and with a final flourish liberally splashed me with fragrant aftershave lotion. He held up a large mirror in back of me, which allowed me to see in my reflection the glory of his work.

Good God Almighty! I was sure looking good. I now had the biggest, softest, silkiest pompadour in the whole world, and a duck-ass style that would force vain ducks to drown themselves in sheer envy.

"Compliments of the house, li'l brother," Roy said, handing me a long slim-jim barber's comb that a short while back could only have been used to comb my eyebrows.

"Gee, thanks, man." I combed my hair in the mirror just like the cat going to the electric chair in the film *Knock on Any Door*.

"What's the tab, bro?"

"Five dollars, li'l brother, plus $2.50 for A-1 Shampoo."

I gave him $9.50; the extra two was to cover some inner shame I was somehow feeling.

"Thank you, bro." Roy saluted me.

George smiled friendly at me as I walked toward the door.

"Feeling lucky today? I always pay off, so no worries."

"Yeah," I said. "Gimme a dime on 692."

I didn't check his face out. A dime is pretty cheap. But how was he to know my hair konk had damn near broken me financially?

Roy called out some last minute professional advice.

"Hey, li'l brother. Don't forget you gotta keep the treatment up or your hair will definitely return to its nappy self."

"Yeah, sure," I called back, moving fast away from Roy's Barbershop. I began checking myself out in store windows, combing and recombing my newly reconstructed hair. I dropped my comb more than once—bending over mussed up hair, providing another excuse to recomb it.

Going home, I purposely rode between the rumbling cars of the subway train so that the blast of air caused my new hair to rise and fly. It was no longer bound to the greasy gravity of Dixie Peach.

Leaving the train at 103rd Street, I walked into my block of 104th Street where most everybody knew me. Heads began snapping my way, and smiles grew into jeering shouts of "Hey, monkey, what's that shit on your haid?" One renamed me "Konko Pete" on the spot followed by "Just wait until your hair turns red and your scalp drops dead."

I really felt like punching the insulters out but cooled the idea as being suicidal. I couldn't fight a whole block. As I climbed the stairs to my apartment, I braced myself for whatever else was ahead. I paused a long second outside my door and then strolled in, hoping no one would notice me. My two brothers were busy playing a card game of knuckles. My sister was into her Wonder Woman comics. They looked up at me vaguely, but it was enough for them to spot my new hairstyle. I dared them with my eyes to say anything that would put me down.

My brothers kept quiet although bursting to laugh. My sister, however, could not contain herself, blurting out, "*Mira, mira*, Piri's got a wig."

"Wig, shit," I snarled. "This ain't no wig. This here is my new hair."

There was no way my brothers could contain themselves any longer. Their laughter came out roaring like wheels on a subway train. Tears of rage mixed with embarrassment jumped out of my eyes. I wished the living room floor would swallow me up.

I hit out at Ray, causing my hair to come trembling down over my face. Their laughter increased. All I could do was stand there with my new straight hair stuck like wires of black spaghetti to my angry, sweaty face.

The noise brought in Momma, followed by Poppa still chewing on his supper. Suddenly everybody was silent. I walked slowly over to the sofa and plunked down heavily on it, feeling old and tired at fourteen and wondering why my strong young legs refused to hold me up.

Poppa shook his head. He knew what my hurting was all about. Momma sat down by my side and caressed my wilted, abused hair. Then hugging me close, she allowed my tears of hurt and shame to be absorbed by her big momma breasts. She whispered to me, "*Hijo*, what have you done to your beautiful hair?"

"Oh, Moms," I whispered back. "I just didn't want to be different anymore. I'm so tired of being called names. I ain't no raisinhead or nothing like that."

Momma hugged me very closely and said out loud, "Don't you ever be ashamed of being you. You want to know something, *negrito*? I wouldn't trade you for any *blanquitos*."

The next day found me playing stickball with a red bandanna around my forehead, sporting the baldest head in town.

JUDITH ORTIZ COFER

The Story of My Body

Migration is the story of my body.

—VÍCTOR HERNÁNDEZ CRUZ

SKIN

I was born a white girl in Puerto Rico but became a brown girl when I came to live in the United States. My Puerto Rican relatives called me tall; at the American school, some of my rougher classmates called me Skinny Bones, and the Shrimp because I was the smallest member of my classes all through grammar school until high school, when the midget Gladys was given the honorary post of front row center for class pictures and scorekeeper, bench warmer, in P.E. I reached my full stature of five feet in sixth grade.

I started out life as a pretty baby and learned to be a pretty girl from a pretty mother. Then at ten years of age I suffered one of the worst cases of chicken pox I have ever heard of. My entire body, including the inside of my ears and in between my toes, was covered with pustules which in a fit of panic at my appearance I scratched off my face, leaving permanent scars. A cruel school nurse told me I would always have them—tiny cuts that looked as if a mad cat had plunged its claws deep into my skin. I grew my hair long and hid behind it for the first years of my adolescence. This was when I learned to be invisible.

COLOR

In the animal world it indicates danger: the most colorful creatures are often the most poisonous. Color is also a way to attract and seduce a mate. In the human world color triggers many more complex and often deadly reactions. As a Puerto Rican girl born of "white" parents, I spent the first years of my life hearing people refer to me as *blanca*, white. My mother insisted that I protect myself from the intense island sun because I was more prone to sunburn than some of my darker, *trigueño* playmates. People were always commenting within my hearing about how my black hair contrasted so nicely with my "pale" skin. I did not think of the color of my skin consciously except when I heard the adults talking about complexion. It seems to me that the subject is much more common in the conversation of mixed-race peoples than in mainstream United States society, where it is a touchy and sometimes even embarrassing topic to discuss, except in a political context. In Puerto Rico I heard many conversations about skin color: A pregnant woman could say, "I hope my baby doesn't turn out *prieto*" (slang for "dark" or "black") "like my husband's grandmother, although she was a good-looking *negra* in her time." I am a combination of both, being olive-skinned—lighter than my mother yet darker than my fair-skinned father. In America, I am a person of color, obviously a Latina. On the Island I have been called everything from a *paloma blanca,* after the song (by a black suitor), to *la gringa.*

My first experience of color prejudice occurred in a supermarket in Paterson, New Jersey. It was Christmastime, and I was eight or nine years old. There was a display of toys in the store where I went two or three times a day to buy things for my mother, who never made lists but sent for milk, cigarettes, a can of this or that, as she remembered from hour to hour. I enjoyed being trusted with money and walking half a city block to the new, modern grocery store. It was owned by three good-looking Italian brothers. I liked the younger one with the crew-cut blond hair. The two older ones watched me and the other Puerto Rican kids as if they thought we were going to steal something. The oldest one would sometimes even try to hurry me with my purchases, although part of my pleasure in these expeditions came from looking at everything in the well-stocked aisles. I was also teaching myself to read English by sounding out the labels in packages: L&M cigarettes, Borden's homogenized milk, Red Devil potted ham, Nestle's chocolate mix, Quaker oats, Bustelo coffee, Wonder bread, Colgate toothpaste, Ivory soap, and Goya (makers of products used in Puerto Rican dishes) everything—these are some of the brand names that taught me nouns. Several times this man had come up to me, wearing his blood-stained butcher's apron, and towering over me had asked in a harsh voice whether there was something he could help me find. On the way out I would glance at the younger brother who ran one of the registers and he would often smile and wink at me.

It was the mean brother who first referred to me as "colored." It was a few days before Christmas, and my parents had already told my brother and me that since we were in Los Estados now, we would get our presents on December 25 instead of Los Reyes, Three Kings Day, when gifts are exchanged in Puerto Rico. We were to give them a wish list that they would take to Santa Claus, who apparently lived in the Macy's store downtown—at least that's where we had caught a glimpse of him when we went shopping. Since my parents were timid about entering the fancy store, we did not approach the huge man in the red suit. I was not interested in sitting on a stranger's lap anyway. But I did covet Susie, the talking schoolteacher doll that was displayed in the center aisle of the Italian brothers' supermarket. She talked when you pulled a string on her back. Susie had a limited repertoire of three sentences: I think she could say: "Hello, I'm Susie Schoolteacher," "Two plus two is four," and one other thing I cannot remember. The day the older brother chased me away, I was reaching to touch Susie's blonde curls. I had been told many times, as most children have, not to touch anything in a store that I was not buying. But I had been looking at Susie for weeks. In my mind, she was my doll. After all, I had put her on my Christmas wish list. The moment is frozen in my mind as if there were a photograph of it on file. It was not a turning point, a disaster, or an earthshaking revelation. It was simply the first time I considered—if naively—the meaning of skin color in human relations.

I reached to touch Susie's hair. It seems to me that I had to get on tiptoe, since the toys were stacked on a table and she sat like a princess on top of the fancy box she came in. Then I heard the booming "Hey, kid, what do you think you're doing!" spoken very loudly from the meat counter. I felt caught, although I knew I was not doing anything criminal. I remember not looking at the man, but standing there, feeling humiliated because I knew everyone in the store must have heard him yell at me. I felt him approach, and when I knew he was behind me, I turned around to face the bloody butcher's apron. His large chest was at my eye level. He blocked my way. I started to run out of the place, but even as I reached the door I heard him shout after me: "Don't come in here unless you gonna buy something. You PR kids put your dirty hands on stuff. You always look dirty. But maybe dirty brown is your natural color." I heard him laugh and someone else too in the back. Outside in the sunlight I looked at my hands. My nails needed a little cleaning as they always did, since I liked to paint with watercolors, but I took a bath every night. I thought the man was dirtier than I was in his stained apron. He was also always sweaty—it showed in big yellow circles under his shirtsleeves. I sat on the front steps of the apartment building where we lived and looked closely at my hands, which showed the only skin I could see, since it was bitter cold and I was wearing my quilted play coat, dungarees, and a knitted navy cap of my father's. I was not pink like my friend Charlene and her sister Kathy, who had blue eyes and light brown hair. My skin is the color of the coffee my grandmother made, which was half milk, *leche con café* rather than *café con leche*. My mother is the opposite mix. She has a lot of café in her color. I could not understand how my skin looked like dirt to the supermarket man.

I went in and washed my hands thoroughly with soap and hot water, and borrowing my mother's nail file, I cleaned the crusted watercolors from underneath my nails. I was pleased with the results. My skin was the same color as before, but I knew I was clean. Clean enough to run my fingers through Susie's fine gold hair when she came home to me.

SIZE

My mother is barely four feet eleven inches in height, which is average for women in her family. When I grew to five feet by age twelve, she was amazed and began to use the word tall to describe me, as in "Since you are tall, this dress will look good on you." As with the color of my skin, I didn't consciously think about my height or size until other people made an issue of it. It is around the preadolescent years that in America the games children play for fun become fierce competitions where everyone is out to "prove" they are better than others. It was in the playground and sports fields that my size-related problems began. No matter how familiar the story is, every child who is the last chosen for a team knows the torment of waiting to be called up. At the Paterson, New Jersey, public schools that I attended, the volleyball or softball game was the metaphor for the battlefield of life to the inner city kids—the black kids versus the Puerto Rican kids, the whites versus the blacks versus the Puerto Rican kids; and I was 4F, skinny, short, bespectacled, and apparently impervious to the blood thirst that drove many of my classmates to play ball as if their lives depended on it. Perhaps they did. I would rather be reading a book than sweating, grunting, and running the risk of pain and injury. I simply did not see the point in competitive sports. My main form of exercise then was walking to the library, many city blocks away from my barrio.

Still, I wanted to be wanted. I wanted to be chosen for the teams. Physical education was compulsory, a class where you were actually given a grade. On my mainly all A report card, the C for compassion I always received from the P.E. teachers shamed me the same as a bad grade in a real class. Invariably, my father would say: "How can you make a low grade for *playing games*?" He did not understand. Even if I had managed to make a hit (it never happened) or get the ball over that ridiculously high net, I already had a reputation as a "shrimp," a hopeless nonathlete. It was an area where the girls who didn't like me for one reason or another—mainly because I did better than they on academic subjects—could lord it over me; the playing field was the place where even the smallest girl could make me feel powerless and inferior. I instinctively understood the politics even then; how the *not* choosing me until the teacher forced one of the team captains to call my name was a coup of sorts—there, you little show-off, tomorrow you can beat us in spelling and geography, but this afternoon you are the loser. Or perhaps those were only my own bitter thoughts as I sat or stood in the sidelines while the big girls were grabbed like fish and I, the little brown tadpole, was ignored until Teacher looked over in my general direction and shouted, "Call Ortiz," or, worse, "Somebody's *got* to take her."

No wonder I read Wonder Woman comics and had Legion of Super Heroes daydreams. Although I wanted to think of myself as "intellectual," my body was demanding that I notice it. I saw the little swelling around my once-flat nipples, the fine hairs growing in secret places; but my knees were still bigger than my thighs, and I always wore long- or half-sleeve blouses to hide my bony upper arms. I wanted flesh on my bones—a thick layer of it. I saw a new product advertised on TV. Wate-On. They showed skinny men and women before and after taking the stuff, and it was a transformation like the ninety-seven-pound-weakling-turned-into-Charles-Atlas ads that I saw on the back covers of my comic books. The Wate-On was very expensive. I tried to explain my need for it in Spanish to my mother, but it didn't translate very well, even to my ears—and she said with a tone of finality, eat more of my good food and you'll get fat—anybody can get fat. Right. Except me. I was going to have to join a circus someday as Skinny Bones, the woman without flesh.

Wonder Woman was stacked. She had a cleavage framed by the spread wings of a golden eagle and a muscular body that has become fashionable with women only recently. But since I wanted a body that would serve me in P.E., hers was my ideal. The breasts were an indulgence I allowed myself. Perhaps the daydreams of bigger girls were more glamorous, since our ambitions are filtered through our needs, but I wanted first a powerful body. I daydreamed of leaping up above the gray landscape of the city to where the sky was clear and blue, and in anger and self-pity, I fantasized about scooping my enemies up by their hair from the playing fields and dumping them on a barren asteroid. I would put the P.E. teachers each on their own rock in space too, where they would be the loneliest people in the universe, since I knew they had no "inner resources," no imagination, and in outer space, there would be no air for them to fill their deflated volleyballs with. In my mind all P.E. teachers have blended into one large spiky-haired woman with a whistle on a string around her neck and a volleyball under one arm. My Wonder Woman fantasies of revenge were a source of comfort to me in my early career as a shrimp.

I was saved from more years of P.E. torment by the fact that in my sophomore year of high school I transferred to a school where the midget, Gladys, was the focal point of interest for the people who must rank according to size. Because her height was considered a handicap, there was an unspoken rule about mentioning size around

Gladys, but of course, there was no need to say anything. Gladys knew her place: front row center in class photographs. I gladly moved to the left or to the right of her, as far as I could without leaving the picture completely.

LOOKS

Many photographs were taken of me as a baby by my mother to send to my father, who was stationed overseas during the first two years of my life. With the army in Panama when I was born, he later traveled often on tours of duty with the navy. I was a healthy, pretty baby. Recently, I read that people are drawn to big-eyed round-faced creatures, like puppies, kittens, and certain other mammals and marsupials, koalas, for example, and, of course, infants. I was all eyes, since my head and body, even as I grew older, remained thin and small-boned. As a young child I got a lot of attention from my relatives and many other people we met in our barrio. My mother's beauty may have had something to do with how much attention we got from strangers in stores and on the street. I can imagine it. In the pictures I have seen of us together, she is a stunning young woman by Latino standards: long, curly black hair, and round curves in a compact frame. From her I learned how to move, smile, and talk like an attractive woman. I remember going into a bodega for our groceries and being given candy by the proprietor as a reward for being *bonita,* pretty.

I can see in the photographs, and I also remember, that I was dressed in the pretty clothes, the stiff, frilly dresses, with layers of crinolines underneath, the glossy patent leather shoes, and, on special occasions, the skull-hugging little hats and the white gloves that were popular in the late fifties and early sixties. My mother was proud of my looks, although I was a bit too thin. She could dress me up like a doll and take me by the hand to visit relatives, or go to the Spanish mass at the Catholic church, and show me off. How was I to know that she and the others who called me "pretty" were representatives of an aesthetic that would not apply when I went out into the mainstream world of school?

In my Paterson, New Jersey, public schools there were still quite a few white children, although the demographics of the city were changing rapidly. The original waves of Italian and Irish immigrants, silk-mill workers, and laborers in the cloth industries had been "assimilated." Their children were now the middle-class parents of my peers. Many of them moved their children to the Catholic schools that proliferated enough to have leagues of basketball teams. The names I recall hearing still ring in my ears: Don Bosco High versus St. Mary's High, St. Joseph's versus St. John's. Later I too would be transferred to the safer environment of a Catholic school. But I started school at Public School Number 11. I came there from Puerto Rico, thinking myself a pretty girl, and found that the hierarchy for popularity was as follows: pretty white girl, pretty Jewish girl, pretty Puerto Rican girl, pretty black girl. Drop the last two categories; teachers were too busy to have more than one favorite per class, and it was simply understood that if there was a big part in the school play, or any competition where the main qualification was "presentability" (such as escorting a school visitor to or from the principal's office), the classroom's public address speaker would be requesting the pretty and/or nice-looking white boy or girl. By the time I was in the sixth grade, I was sometimes called by the principal to represent my class because I dressed neatly (I knew this from a progress report sent to my mother, which I translated for her) and because all the "presentable" white girls had moved to the Catholic schools (I later surmised this part). But I was still not one of the popular girls with the boys. I remember one incident where I stepped out into the playground in my baggy gym shorts and one Puerto Rican boy said to the other: "What do you think?" The other one answered: "Her face is OK, but look at the toothpick legs." The next best thing to a compliment I got was when my favorite male teacher, while handing out the class pictures, commented that with my long neck and delicate features I resembled the movie star Audrey Hepburn. But the Puerto Rican boys had learned to respond to a fuller figure: long necks and a perfect little nose were not what they looked for in a girl. That is when I decided I was a "brain." I did not settle into the role easily. I was nearly devastated by what the chicken pox episode had done to my self-image. But I looked into the mirror less often after I was told that I would always have scars on my face, and I hid behind my long black hair and my books.

After the problems at the public school got to the point where even nonconfrontational little me got beaten up several times, my parents enrolled me at St. Joseph's High School. I was then a minority of one among the Italian and Irish kids. But I found several good friends there—other girls who took their studies seriously. We did our homework together and talked about the Jackies. The Jackies were two popular girls, one blonde and the other red-haired, who had women's bodies. Their curves showed even in the blue jumper uniforms with straps that we all wore. The blonde Jackie would often let one of the straps fall off her shoulder, and although she, like all of us, wore a white blouse underneath, all the boys stared at her arm. My friends and I talked about this and practiced letting our straps fall off our shoulders. But it wasn't the same without breasts or hips.

My final two and a half years of high school were spent in Augusta, Georgia, where my parents moved our family in search of a more peaceful environment. There we became part of a little community of our army-connected relatives and friends. School was yet another matter. I was enrolled in a huge school of nearly two thousand students that had just that year been forced to integrate. There were two black girls and there was me. I did extremely well academically. As to my social life, it was, for the most part, uneventful—yet it is in my memory blighted by one incident. In my junior year, I became wildly infatuated with a pretty white boy. I'll call him Ted. Oh, he was pretty: yellow hair that fell over his forehead, a smile to die for— and he was a great dancer. I watched him at Teen Town, the youth center at the base where all the military brats gathered on Saturday nights. My father had retired from the navy, and we had all our base privileges—one other reason we had moved to Augusta. Ted looked like an angel to me. I worked on him for a year before he asked me out. This meant maneuvering to be within the periphery of his vision at every possible occasion. I took the long way to my classes in school just to pass by his locker, I went to football games, which I detested, and I danced (I too was a good dancer) in front of him at Teen Town—this took some fancy footwork, since it involved subtly moving my partner toward the right spot on the dance floor. When Ted finally approached me, "A Million to One" was playing on the jukebox, and when he took me into his arms, the odds suddenly turned in my favor. He asked me to go to a school dance the following Saturday. I said yes, breathlessly. I said yes, but there were obstacles to surmount at home. My father did not allow me to date casually. I was allowed to go to major events like a prom or a concert with a boy who had been properly screened. There was such a boy in my life, a neighbor who wanted to be a Baptist missionary and was practicing his anthropological skills on my family. If I was desperate to go somewhere and needed a date, I'd resort to Gary. This is the type of religious nut that Gary was: when the school bus did not show up one day, he put his hands over his face and prayed to Christ to get us a way to get to school. Within ten minutes a mother in a station wagon, on her way to town, stopped to ask why we weren't in school. Gary informed her that the Lord had sent her just in time to find us a way to get there in time for roll call. He assumed that I was impressed. Gary was even good-looking in a bland sort of way, but he kissed me with his lips tightly pressed together. I think Gary probably ended up marrying a native woman from wherever he may have gone to preach the Gospel according to Paul. She probably believes that all white men pray to God for transportation and kiss with their mouths closed. But it was Ted's mouth, his whole beautiful self, that concerned me in those days. I knew my father would say no to our date, but I planned to run away from home if necessary. I told my mother how important this date was. I cajoled and pleaded with her from Sunday to Wednesday. She listened to my arguments and must have heard the note of desperation in my voice. She said very gently to me: "You better be ready for disappointment." I did not ask what she meant. I did not want her fears for me to taint my happiness. I asked her to tell my father about my date. Thursday at breakfast my father looked at me across the table with his eyebrows together. My mother looked at him with her mouth set in a straight line. I looked down at my bowl of cereal. Nobody said anything. Friday I tried on every dress in my closet. Ted would be picking me up at six on Saturday: dinner and then the sock hop at school. Friday night I was in my room doing my nails or something else in preparation for Saturday (I know I groomed myself nonstop all week) when the telephone rang. I ran to get it. It was Ted. His voice sounded funny when he said my name, so funny that I felt compelled to ask: "Is something wrong?" Ted blurted it all out without a preamble. His father had asked who he was going out with. Ted had told him my name. "Ortiz? That's Spanish, isn't it?" the father had asked. Ted had told him yes, then shown him my picture in the yearbook. Ted's father had shaken his head. No. Ted would not be taking me out. Ted's father had known Puerto Ricans in the army. He had lived in New York City while studying architecture and had seen how the spics lived. Like rats. Ted repeated his father's words to me as if I should understand *his* predicament when I heard why he was breaking our date. I don't remember what I said before hanging up. I do recall the darkness of my room that sleepless night and the heaviness of my blanket in which I wrapped myself like a shroud. And I remember my parents' respect for my pain and their gentleness toward me that weekend. My mother did not say "I warned you," and I was grateful for her understanding silence.

In college, I suddenly became an "exotic" woman to the men who had survived the popularity wars in high school, who were now practicing to be worldly: they had to act liberal in their politics, in their lifestyles, and in the women they went out with. I dated heavily for a while, then married young. I had discovered that I needed stability more than social life. I had brains for sure and some talent in writing. These facts were a constant in my life. My skin color, my size, and my appearance were variables—things that were judged according to my current self-image, the aesthetic values of the times, the places I was in, and the people I met. My studies, later my writing, the respect of people who saw me as an individual person they cared about, these were the criteria for my sense of self-worth that I would concentrate on in my adult life.

JULIA DE BURGOS

To Julia de Burgos

Already people whisper that I am your enemy
because they say in poetry I give you to the world.

They lie, Julia De Burgos. They lie, Julia De Burgos.
The voice that rises up in my poems is not yours. It's my voice
because you are the garment and I am the essence
and between us stretches the deepest chasm.

You are the cold doll of social deceit
and I, the vivacious spark of human truth.

You,the syrup of courtly hypocrisies, not I.
In all my poems I simply bare my heart.

You are all greed and ego like your world, not I.
I gamble everything to be what I am.

You are just a proper grande dame.
Not I. I am life. I am strength. I am woman.

You belong to your husband, to the master of the house.
Not I. I belong to no one, or to everyone and everything.
In clean feelings and unsullied thoughts, I give myself.

You curl your hair and dabble on makeup. Not I.
The wind curls my hair and the sun colors my skin.

You are housewife, resigned, submissive,
bound by men's sexism, Not I.
Unbridled, I am a Rocinante running wild
nuzzling the horizons of God's justice.

You do have any say over yourself, everyone rules you—
your husband, your parents, your family,
the priest, the dressmaker, the theater, the casino,
the car, fine furnishings, baubles, banquets, champagne,
heaven and hell, but also society's "What will they say?"

Not I. I am simply governed by my heart,
by the overriding thought—who rules me is me.

You, the uppercrust creme de la creme,
and I, a flower of the people.
You have all you could wish for and owe this to everyone,
while my bit of nothing I owe to no one.

You, fixed with the inheritance of stable dividends
and I, a single cipher from across the social divide,
join in a duel to the death that approaches fatally.

But when the multitudes run frenzied
leaving behind their anguish burnt to ashes,
and with a torch of seven virtues,
the multitudes pursue the seven sins against you,
against everyone who's unjust of inhumane.
I will be among them with a torch in hand.
or maybe my lips will need to nourish lilies.

What shall I be called when all that remains
is remembering myself on the rock of a deserted island?
A carnation placed between my shadow and the wind—
death's child and mine will call me poet.

JOSEPH B. VASQUEZ

Hangin' (Out) with the Homeboys

FIRST DRAFT SCREENPLAY

CUT TO: INT. TENEMENT BUILDING – BEDROOM – DUSK

Our CAMERA pans over to a dresser and focuses on its mirror, which holds small pictures of different young women. There must be at least thirty pictures surrounding the framework of the mirror. The CAMERA pans to a bed, where a man's body lies, back to CAMERA, covered by a sheet. Title appears: "FERNANDO." The title is immediately crossed out in red marker, and under it, a new name is written: "VINNY." Title soon fades away, and a new title appears: "7:59 P.M." CAMERA moves to a clock radio beside the bed, which changes from 7:59 to 8:00, and bursts forth loud, throbbing disco music. VINNY quickly jumps up and turns off the radio, revealing that he is wearing dark, black sunglasses in bed. He sluggishly sits up in bed, and pulls off his shades, revealing his twenty-five-year-old, Hispanic face. He reaches over to his telephone, which sits on a night table near him. The phone receiver is off the hook. He places it back on, and it immediately rings. He answers it.

VINNY *(drowsily)* Hello . . . Oh, Candy, how you doin', baby? Yeah . . . Ha? Tonight? Oh, baby, I can't tonight I'm hangin' out with the fellas. . . . What? When did I promise tonight! . . . Oh! Well, baby, you can't count anything I say when we're doin' that . . . Hello?

VINNY shrugs, hangs up the phone, and begins to rise from the bed when the phone rings again. VINNY sits back down tiredly and answers it.

VINNY Hello . . . Oh, Wendy. Hey, baby, how you doin'? Ha? . . . Tonight? . . . Oh, baby, I can't tonight. What? C'mon, baby, when did I say that? When did I promise tonight? . . . Oh, figures! Well, look, I'm sorry, I can't . . . I can't . . . Yeah, I know what I said, I lied, whatta ya want! . . . Hello?

VINNY sighs, then again starts to rise from the bed, and again, the phone rings. VINNY groans angrily, grabs the phone, and savagely throws it against the wall. He lets out a sigh of relief for the joys of silence, then rises out of bed and exits his bedroom . . .

. . . VINNY looks out the car window. His eyes bulge at the sight of two pretty young Hispanic GIRLS walking up the sidewalk. Both girls must be about sixteen, but their bodies are extremely well developed.

VINNY Oh, my God! Look at that shit! You gonna tell me that shit looks innocent to you! Slow down the car.

TOM slows down as VINNY shoves his upper body out the window.

EXT. CAR – STREET

TOM slows down the car, driving alongside the GIRLS, as VINNY calls out to them.

VINNY Yo, baby! Talk to me, baby! Talk to me!

The GIRLS giggle to themselves.

VINNY   Hey, what's your names? I'm Vinny. I'm from Italy.

GIRL #1   Yeah? What part of Italy?

VINNY's face goes blank. He searches for an answer.

VINNY   Italy, Italy. You know? Where all the Italians come from.

The GIRLS giggle again. In the car, JOHNNY's eyes roll in disgust.

VINNY   Hey, why don't you come in for a ride?

GIRL #2   No, thank you.

VINNY   Come on, babies. You could sit on my lap. Come on, c'mon!

The GIRLS soon reach the front of a broken-down tenement building, where a fat, hairy, middle-aged Hispanic MAN meets them, and leads them into the building. He looks at VINNY with complete hatred.

MAN   *(Furiously; with Spanish accent)* What you doin'! You tryin' to pick up my daughters, ha!

VINNY stares at the hairy ape in shock.

MAN   Ha? Hey! You tryin' to pick up my daughters, ha! Ya son-of-a-bitch, ha!

VINNY swings back in the car as the MAN starts to quickly walk toward the car.

INT. CAR

Everyone is laughing hysterically.

VINNY   *(To TOM)* Yo, man, get the fuck outta here!

TOM   *(Laughing)* No, man. I like this neighborhood. Let's stay.

VINNY   Man, move the fuckin' car, man!

TOM laughs loudly, until he sees, in his rearview mirror, the MAN grab two large bottles out of a nearby garbage can.

TOM   Oh, shit!

TOM hits the gas hard.

EXT. CAR – STREET

The car flies down the street as the MAN fires the two bottles into the air. They miss the car by inches, as it turns onto another street.

INT. CAR

TOM Yo, Vinny, man, if those bottles would've hit my car, I woulda kicked your ass!

VINNY Yo, bro, it wasn't my fault.

WILLIE It was your fault, 'cause you the one that made that crazy Puerto Rican come over.

JOHNNY Ayyyy, ayyy, ayyyy! Watch it with that stuff, all right.

WILLIE What stuff? All I said is crazy Puerto Rican.

JOHNNY Ayyy, man, watch the way you talk about my people, all right! *(To VINNY)* Damn, man, you hear the way he's talkin' about us?

VINNY shrugs his shoulders.

JOHNNY You don't care, do you?

VINNY What, man. What am I suppose to say to that?

JOHNNY You don't care because you don't think you're Puerto Rican, do you?

There is a moment of silence.

VINNY Why you wanna fuck wit' me, man? What the hell I'd do to you, bro! Leave me alone, please!

There is another moment of silence.

TOM He thinks he's Italian.

VINNY No, I don't think I'm Italian, all right! I don't think I'm Italian! I know what I am. Ask anybody, okay. Ask Willie. Hey, Willie, tell them I know what the hell I am!

WILLIE Well, man—

VINNY *(Interrupts)* What I'd tell you before, Willie? Ha? Remember? What I'd tell you before? In the street.

WILLIE thinks for a brief moment, then turns to look at JOHNNY. He nods his head vigorously.

VINNY Thank you, thank you. There you have it! Now just leave me the fuck alone!

WILLIE How come you don't like it when people call you Fernando?

VINNY How come you don't like it when people call you an ugly motherfucker!

JOHNNY   You will just deny that you're a Puerto Rican. Go 'head. Say it. Say "I'm a Puerto Rican." Go 'head.

VINNY   *(Quietly)* Look, I don't have to say shit to you, now leave me alone.

JOHNNY   Say it. Say "I'm a Puerto Rican."

VINNY   *(To WILLIE)* Willie! You see this shit, Willie! You see this! You know who's responsible for this shit right here, right, Willie? Ha!

JOHNNY   Why did you tell those girls you were Italian?

VINNY   You wanna know why, ha! You wanna know why?

JOHNNY   Yeah, I wanna know.

VINNY   Fine, I'll tell you! It just so happens at this moment in time, all women are goin' crazy for Italian men, okay!

JOHNNY   What?

TOM   Get the fuck outta here!

VINNY   It's true, man. Women think they're great lovers. They're crazy about 'em. So that's what I'm gonna be! Now, when the day comes that somebody else takes over that role of drivin' women crazy, let's say the black man, then that's the day that I'll become Ossie "motherfuckin' " Davis, but until that day, I'm Vinny, all right!

WILLIE   Man, you are crazy!

TOM   Yo, any of you guys got any more brews back there?

JOHNNY   Nahhhh, we're out.

TOM   I'm gonna stop. We'll get some more, all right . . .

. . . CUT TO: INT. SUBWAY STATION

The fellas walk down a staircase and head toward the turnstiles. They take a brief look around, then all jump the turnstiles.

SUBWAY BOOTH CLERK   Hey! Pay your fare!

WILLIE   The fare ain't fair, man!

Suddenly, from out of a corner room, bust forth two POLICE OFFICERS. The fellas try to run, but the officers quickly round them up and shove them into the room.

TIME CUT: INT. ROOM

The fellas are seated, with the POLICE OFFICERS standing above them.

POLICEMAN #1   Okay, fellas, let me see some ID.

They all pull out their wallets, find a piece of identification, and hand it to the OFFICERS. The OFFICERS immediately start writing tickets.

WILLIE   Oh, man. What a night.

VINNY starts to chuckle. Soon JOHNNY joins in.

POLICEMAN #1   Is there somethin' funny, here?
TOM   *(To his friends; scared)* Yo, man, why don't y'all cut it out!

They laugh even harder now.

POLICEMAN #1   You think this is amusing?
TOM   *(Whining)* Y'all gonna get us in trouble, man. Why don't y'all cut it out!

The chuckling soon ends.

POLICEMAN #2   Thomas McNeil.
TOM   Yeah?
POLICEMAN #2   What's your profession?
TOM   I'm an actor.
VINNY   Can't you tell. He's acting terrified.

They all chuckle again, except for TOM.

TOM   Yo, Vinny, man! Why don't you stop that shit, man! Damn, Vinny!

Soon, they become quiet again. The POLICE OFFICERS whisper to each other for a moment, then soon they hand out tickets to everyone but VINNY. They both walk over to VINNY and stand directly over him.

POLICEMAN #1   Do you know why I haven't given you a ticket?
VINNY   Because you think I'm pretty?

The OFFICERS exchange looks.

POLICEMAN #1   I have an ID in my hands that has your picture on it, but says Fernando Cuervas.
VINNY   Yeah, so?
POLICEMAN #1   We just heard your friend over there call you VINNY.

The guys all look at one another.

VINNY   Yeah, well, that's like a nickname.

POLICEMAN #1   I don't believe you. This is a fake ID, isn't it?

VINNY   No, it's not a fake ID. My name is . . . *(He reluctantly says it)* Fernando Cuervas.

POLICEMAN #1   I don't believe you.

VINNY   Look, man, you can ask anybody, all right. Willie, will you tell him my name is . . . *(He struggles to say it)* Fernando.

WILLIE starts to speak, but then thinks for a moment. He then nods his head vigorously, without saying a word.

VINNY   *(To himself)* Asshole!

POLICEMAN #1 studies VINNY's ID carefully.

POLICEMAN #1   *(Looking at ID)* What's your nationality?

There is a brief silence. VINNY looks over at his friends, who are leaning forward in their seats, paying strict attention.

VINNY   I'm Puerto Rican.

WILLIE   Oh, my God!

JOHNNY   I thought I'd never live to hear him say it.

POLICEMAN #1   *(Looking at ID)* What's your address, Fernando?

VINNY winces from hearing the name.

VINNY   It's two, three, four Willis Avenue.

The POLICEMAN nods.

POLICEMAN #1   Why did your friend call you Vinny?

VINNY   It's just a nickname, that's all.

POLICEMAN #1   From Fernando to Vinny. Wouldn't it be somethin' more like, ahhh, Fermin, or Furball, or somethin'?

WILLIE and JOHNNY struggle to hold in their laughter.

VINNY   *(To POLICEMAN #1)* No. It's Vinny. It's just a nickname.

POLICEMAN #1 walks over to TOM.

POLICEMAN #1   Is he tellin' the truth?

TOM   *(Scared)* What, man? I ain't do nothin', man!

POLICEMAN #1 I didn't say you did anything. I asked you a question. Why do you call this guy Vinny, if his name is Fernando?

TOM Oh. Well, ahhh, ya see, he, ahhh, he thinks he's Italian.

POLICEMAN #1 *(Laughing)* He thinks he's Italian.

TOM . . . Yeah.

The OFFICER *walks back over to* VINNY.

POLICEMAN #1 So, you think you're Italian, ha?

VINNY *smirks.*

POLICEMAN #1 Well, let me tell you somethin'. I'm Italian, okay. See that name. (Points to nameplate on uniform) Sannanelli. I'm Italian, and I'm gonna tell ya that no matter what you do, or what you say, you could never be an Italian. Scum like you could never be in with the same kinda company as me, you understand that?

VINNY *is angry, but stays silent.*

POLICEMAN #1 Kid's got a lot of nerve. Look at ya. For one thing, you don't look like an Italian. And then, you don't act like an Italian.

WILLIE *(Under his breath)* He don't smell like an Italian.

POLICEMAN #1 *(To* WILLIE*)* What was that?

WILLIE Nothin'. Nothin'.

POLICEMAN #1 You could never be an Italian. Remember that, okay. Never. I'm gonna write you out a ticket now, all right?

VINNY Thank you. I'm thrilled.

MARTIN ESPADA

Niggerlips

Niggerlips was the high school name
for me.
So called by Douglas

the car mechanic, with green tattoos
on each forearm,
and the choir of round pink faces
that grinned deliciously
from the back row of classrooms,
droned over by teachers
checking attendance too slowly.

Douglas would brag
about cruising his car
near sidewalks of black children
to point an unloaded gun,
to scare niggers
like crows off a tree,
he'd say.

My great-grandfather Luis
was un negrito too,
a shoemaker in the coffee hills
of Puerto Rico, 1900.
The family called him a secret
and kept no photograph.
My father remembers
the childhood white powder
that failed to bleach
his stubborn copper skin,
and the family says
he is still a fly in milk.

So Niggerlips has the mouth
of his great-grandfather,
the song he must have sung
as he pounded the leather and nails,
the heat that courses through copper,
the stubbornness of a fly in milk,
and all you have, Douglas,
is that unloaded gun.

JESUS COLON

Little Things Are Big

It was very late at night on the eve of Memorial Day. She came into the subway at the Thirty-fourth Street Pennsylvania Station. I am still trying to remember how she managed to push herself in with a baby on her right arm, a valise in her left hand, and two children, a boy and a girl about three and five years old, trailing after her. She was a nice-looking white lady in her early twenties.

At Nevins Street, Brooklyn, we saw her preparing to get off at the next station—Atlantic Avenue—which happened to be the place where I, too, had to get off. Just as it was a problem for her to get on, it was going to be a problem for her to get off the subway with two small children to be taken care of, a baby on her right arm and a medium-sized valise in her left hand.

And there I was, also preparing to get off at Atlantic Avenue, with no bundles to take care of—not even the customary book under my arm without which I feel that I am not completely dressed.

As the train was entering the Atlantic Avenue station, some white man stood up from his seat and helped her out, placing the children on the long, deserted platform. There were only two adult persons on the long platform sometime after midnight on the eve of last Memorial Day.

I could perceive the steep, long concrete stairs going down to the Long Island Railroad or into the street. Should I offer my help as the American white man did at the subway door, placing the two children outside the subway car? Should I take care of the girl and the boy, take them by their hands until they reached the end of the steep long concrete stairs of the Atlantic Avenue station?

Courtesy is a characteristic of the Puerto Rican. And here I was—a

Puerto Rican—hours past midnight, a valise, two white children and a white lady with a baby on her arm palpably needing somebody to help her at least until she descended the long concrete stairs.

But how could I, a Negro and a Puerto Rican, approach this white lady who very likely might have preconceived prejudices against Negroes and everybody with foreign accents, in a deserted subway station very late at night?

What would she say? What would be the first reaction of this white American woman, perhaps coming from a small town with a valise, two children, and a baby on her right arm? Would she say: Yes, of course, you may help me. Or would she think that I was just trying to get too familiar? Or would she think worse than that perhaps? What would I do if she let out a scream as I went toward her to offer my help?

Was I misjudging her? So many slanders are written every day in the daily press against the Negroes and Puerto Ricans. I hesitated for a long, long minute. The ancestral manners that the most illiterate Puerto Rican passes on from father to son were struggling inside me. Here was I, way past midnight, face-to-face with a situation that could very well explode into an outburst of prejudices and chauvinistic conditioning of the "divide and rule" policy of present-day society.

It was a long minute. I passed on by her as if I saw nothing. As if I was insensitive to her need. Like a rude animal walking on two legs, I just moved on, half running by the long subway platform, leaving the children and the valise and her with the baby on her arm. I took the steps of the long concrete stairs in twos until I reached the street above and the cold air slapped my warm face.

This is what racism and prejudice and chauvinism and official artificial divisions can do to people and to a nation!

Perhaps the lady was not prejudiced after all. Or not prejudiced enough to scream at the coming of a Negro toward her in a solitary subway station a few hours past midnight.

If you were not that prejudiced, I failed you, dear lady. I know that there is a chance in a million that you will read these lines. I am willing to take that millionth chance. If you were not that prejudiced, I failed you, lady, I failed you, children. I failed myself to myself.

I buried my courtesy early on Memorial Day morning. But here is a promise that I make to myself here and now: If I am ever faced with an occasion like that again, I am going to offer my help regardless of how the offer is going to be received.

Then I will have my courtesy with me again.

RENÉ MARQUÉS

The Docile Puerto Rican—
Literature and Psychological Reality

Docile, from the latin *docilis*, means "obedient" or "fulfilling the wishes of the one who commands." Sainz de Robles cites, among other synonyms of the word, "meek" and "submissive," which seem to be characteristic of the most generally held meaning. For *docility* (the quality of being docile), the same scholar gives us "subordination," "meekness," "submission."

In Roque Barcia's work we find that the word *docility* is given a broader range of meaning: "Docility is to lack the strength or even the will to put up resistance to what others demand, insinuate, or command; a propensity to obey, to follow the example, the opinion, the advice of others, which arises either from one's own weakness or failings, or from ignorance, or from lack of confidence in one's own intelligence, knowledge, or strength."

From this definition, we can deduce that the submissive, meek, or docile man is necessarily a weak person ("he lacks the strength or even the will") or an ignorant one ("which arises . . . from ignorance") or the victim of a pathetic inferiority complex ("lack of confidence in one's own intelligence, knowledge, or strength") . . .

. . . It is always interesting in Puerto Rico to observe a Puerto Rican and a North American communicating with each other when a business transaction is not involved. When it is, the North American's business sense may force him to use the typical salesman's approach of psychological concessions and flattery toward his client, which necessarily conceal the latter's inferior position from the eyes of the casual observer. In other circumstances, however, when the conversation is not directly related to the economic advantages which the North American hopes to gain, the respective national guilt complexes come to the surface in one way or another.

The North American in Puerto Rico feels himself guilty, although never consciously, of imperialism. This guilt is translated into one of two extreme attitudes. He may exhibit the aggressive arrogance of the "superior" man who must prove to himself the validity and morality of his position, saying, in effect: "I am an imperialist because, after all, I *am* superior." On the other hand, he may become benevolently condescending in his desire to prove *to others* the legitimacy and advantages of the imperialist policy. This consists of a humanitarian concern to help the weak or "inferior" person. (He cannot, of course, be helped a lot, because this would endanger the imperialist's insecure position of "superiority.") The North American himself has called this spiritual posturing a "patronizing attitude" (while in Spanish we would call it, with greater accuracy than the term might reveal at first glance, an "attitude of patronal benevolence").

It seems opportune to point out in this respect that so-called North American humanitarianism operates almost always on the material or economic plane, very rarely on the ethical or spiritual one. A study of the process of contemporary North American Caesarism brings one to the conclusion that the North American has restricted the term *freedom* to a narrow economic definition: freedom from hunger. In practice, this freedom can be condensed in an axiom: the nation which buys what it consumes in the United States market is "free" and "democratic." If it occurs to one of the nations under North American tutelage—and it does not have to be literally a colony like Puerto Rico—to carry the term *freedom* to the spiritual and ethical plane, alleging either that man does not live by bread alone or that the most tasty or most worthy bread is one's own, although it may be less soft and less white, North American "humanitarianism" feels wounded to the core. The power of the empire moves diligently to crush that nation which dared to violate the North American dogma of "freedom." (In this respect, Cuba and Puerto Rico may not be "of one bird, two wings," but they have certainly been two very similar feathers in the ostentatious plumage of the same imperial bird.) We have, then, to realize that United States "humanitarianism" is to a great extent nothing but a rationalization of the peremptory necessities of its economic empire. Each country "freed" from hunger by the United States becomes a captive market within the complex North American economic network. Any attempt by that country to overstep the bounds in its attainment of freedom (most especially national economic freedom) constitutes a grave offense against "democracy," that is, against the United States' imperial economy. It will have to pay for this offense, if it is in the United States' power to make it do so. The punishment will be economic aggression, or a hunger siege, from which it will again be "freed" once it accepts the conditions of North American "humanitarianism" which it before had the audacity to refuse.

All of this, which is very tragic, and very real for the parties involved, forms an unexamined and unreasoned psychological sediment in the mind of the North American in Puerto Rico. Such conflicts and ambivalences become conscious material only for those North Americans who possess a great deal of sensitivity as well as culture. There are, naturally, very few of these in Puerto Rico. It is in them, nevertheless, that one can best observe all the complexities of the North American psychology. There is an undercurrent of anguish in their dealings with Puerto Ricans. The urgency to belong causes them to make a sincere and honest effort to understand the Puerto Rican and sympathize with his idiosyncrasies and his cultural patterns. But they never accomplish this completely, perhaps because their uneasiness over their "betrayal" of North American values disturbs them too much. Black sheep among the North American residents, they cannot help but see themselves as "ugly ducklings" in the Puerto Rican social group. Some, unable to stand the external tensions, arrive at the illusory compromise of pretending to be, simultaneously, North Americans among the North American residents and Puerto Ricans among the Puerto Ricans. Such psychological acrobatics in the long run cause their moral, spiritual, and intellectual deterioration. (Their sociologists and psychologists then cite the enervating tropical climate as the cause of this deterioration.)

On confronting the North American, the Puerto Rican for his part sets in motion his colonial guilt complex. In order to tolerate his humiliating condition he has to find an excuse for it and admit that he is *inferior* to the North American. This motivates his obsequiousness (the traditional "courtesy," "hospitality," and "generosity"), expressed in ways which closely approach servility. This unconscious admission of inferiority cannot help but hurt his ego, often provoking extreme compensatory reactions such as violent antagonism or total surrender. The most interesting from the psychological point of view is, without doubt, the latter, since by surrendering he is able to dispense with his defense mechanisms and open himself up, without resistance, to all that is North American. He hopes in this way to acquire or to incorporate the "superiority" of that feared and envied being, but, of course, he never can. In many Puerto Ricans who have some sensitivity as well as education and culture, these extreme manifestations never appear in all their brutal clarity. They develop a strange ambivalence in their social dealings with the North American, similar, in its undercurrent of anguish, to that of the sensitive North American when he tries to fraternize with the Puerto Rican.

Only in authentically bilingual individuals who believe they have resolved their ambivalence toward the politico-cultural problem into which they were born—and in Puerto Rico there are scarcely a handful of these tropical icebergs—can the painful defense mechanism be reduced to a minimum. When they communicate with a North American, there appear to be no barriers. The few Puerto Ricans who, because they were raised or educated in the United States, speak English fluently but Spanish less so, are not true bilingual speakers. With them the mechanism functions inversely: they are made uneasy by Spanish. This is aggravated by the fact that, forced to use the native tongue of their compatriots in their communication with other Puerto Ricans, they develop an additional guilt complex precisely because they cannot handle it perfectly. So they avoid it, using it as little as possible. Then they advocate English as the "official" language in the circles in which they move or they retire to narrow little social islands—no-man's-lands—where other cultural pariahs like themselves have already imposed the use of the foreign tongue.

It is becoming clear that English in Puerto Rico is not simply another foreign language, like French or Italian, but the painful site of many conflicting experiences—political, cultural, spiritual, and psychological—which exacerbate the Puerto Rican's colonial anguish.

The imposition and social acceptance of English in Puerto Rico can be viewed, then, without risk of error, as one more manifestation of Puerto Rican docility.

ESMERALDA SANTIAGO

The American Invasion of Macún

FROM *WHEN I WAS PUERTO RICAN*

Lo que no mata, engorda.
What doesn't kill you, makes you fat.

> *Pollito,* chicken
> *Gallina,* hen
> *Lápiz,* pencil
> *y Pluma,* pen.
> *Ventana,* window
> *Puerta,* door
> *Maestra,* teacher
> *y Piso,* floor.

Miss Jiménez stood in front of the class as we sang and, with her ruler, pointed at the chicks scratching the dirt outside the classroom, at the hen leading them, at the pencil on Juanita's desk, at the pen on her own desk, at the window that looked out into the playground, at the door leading to the yard, at herself, and at the shiny tile floor. We sang along, pointing as she did with our sharpened pencils, rubber end out.

"*¡Muy bien!*" She pulled down the map rolled into a tube at the front of the room. In English she told us, "Now gwee estody about de Jun-ited Estates gee-o-graphee."

It was the daily English class. Miss Jiménez, the second- and third-grade teacher, was new to the school in Macún. She looked like a grown-up doll, with high rounded cheekbones, a freckled *café con leche* complexion, black lashes, black curly hair pulled into a bun at the nape of her neck, and the prettiest legs in the whole *barrio*. Doña Ana said Miss Jiménez had the most beautiful legs she'd ever seen, and the next day, while Miss Jiménez wrote the multiplication table on the blackboard, I stared at them.

She wore skirts to just below the knees, but from there down, her legs were shaped like chicken drumsticks, rounded and full at the top, narrow at the bottom. She had long straight hair on her legs, which everyone said made them even prettier, and small feet encased in plain brown shoes with a low square heel. That night I wished on a star that someday my scrawny legs would fill out into that lovely shape and that the hair on them would be as long and straight and black.

Miss Jiménez came to Macún at the same time as the community center. She told us that starting the following week, we were all to go to the *centro comunal* before school to get breakfast, provided by the Estado Libre Asociado, or Free Associated State, which was the official name for Puerto Rico in the Estados Unidos, or in English, the Jun-ited Estates of America. Our parents, Miss Jiménez told us, should come to a meeting that Saturday, where experts from San Juan and the Jun-ited Estates would teach our mothers all about proper nutrition and hygiene, so that we would grow up as tall and strong as Dick, Jane, and Sally, the *Americanitos* in our primers.

"And Mami," I said as I sipped my afternoon *café con leche*, "Miss Jiménez said the experts will give us free food and toothbrushes and things . . . and we can get breakfast every day except Sunday . . ."

"Calm down," she told me. "We'll go, don't worry."

On Saturday morning the yard in front of the *centro comunal* was filled with parents and their children. You could tell the experts from San Juan from the ones that came from the Jun-ited Estates because the *Americanos* wore ties with their white shirts and tugged at their collars and wiped their foreheads with crumpled handkerchiefs. They hadn't planned for children, and the men from San Juan convinced a few older girls to watch the little ones outside so that the meeting could proceed with the least amount of disruption. Small children refused to leave their mothers' sides and screeched the minute one of the white-shirted men came near them. Some women sat on the folding chairs at the rear of the room nursing, a cloth draped over their baby's face so that the experts would not be upset at the sight of a bare breast. There were no fathers. Most of them worked seven days a week, and anyway, children and food were woman's work.

"Negi, take the kids outside and keep them busy until this is over."

"But Mami . . ."

"Do as I say."

She pressed her way to a chair in the middle of the room and sat facing the experts. I hoisted Edna on my shoulder and grabbed Alicia's hand. Delsa pushed Norma out in front of her. They ran into the yard and within minutes had blended into a group of children their age. Héctor found a boy to chase him around a tree, and Alicia crawled to a sand puddle where she and other toddlers smeared one another with the fine red dirt. I sat at the door, Edna on my lap, and tried to keep one eye on my sisters and brother and another on what went on inside.

The experts had colorful charts on portable easels. They introduced each other to the group, thanked the Estado Libre Asociado for the privilege of being there, and then took turns speaking. The first expert opened a large suitcase. Inside there was a huge set of teeth with pink gums.

"*Ay Dios Santo, qué cosa tan fea,*" said a woman as she crossed herself. The mothers laughed and mumbled among themselves that yes, it was ugly. The expert stretched his lips into a smile and pulled a large toothbrush from under the table. He used ornate Spanish words that we assumed were scientific talk for teeth, gums, and tongue. With his giant brush, he polished each tooth on the model, pointing out the proper path of the bristles on the teeth.

"If I have to spend that much time on my teeth," a woman whispered loud enough for everyone to hear, "I won't get anything done around the house." The room buzzed with giggles, and the expert again spread his lips, took a breath, and continued his demonstration.

"At the conclusion of the meeting," he said, "you will each receive a toothbrush and a tube of paste for every member of your family."

"*¿Hasta pa' los mellaos?*" a woman in the back of the room asked, and everyone laughed.

"If they have no teeth, it's too late for them, isn't it," the expert said through his own clenched teeth. The mothers shrieked with laughter, and the expert sat down so that an *Americano* with red hair and thick glasses could tell us about food.

He wiped his forehead and upper lip as he pulled up the cloth covering one of the easels to reveal a colorful chart of the major food groups.

"*La buena* nutrition is *muy importante para los niños.*" In heavily accented, hard to understand Castilian Spanish he described the necessity of eating portions of each of the foods on his chart every day. There were carrots and broccoli, iceberg lettuce, apples, pears, and peaches. The bread was sliced into a perfect square, unlike the long loaves Papi brought home from a bakery in San Juan, or the round *pan de manteca* Mami bought at Vitín's store. There was no rice on the chart, no beans, no salted codfish. There were big white eggs, not at all like the small round ones our hens gave us. There was a tall glass of milk, but no coffee. There were wedges of yellow cheese, but no balls of cheese like the white *queso del país* wrapped in banana leaves sold in bakeries all over Puerto Rico. There were bananas but no plantains, potatoes but no *batatas*, cereal flakes but no oatmeal, bacon but no sausages.

"But, *señor*," said Doña Lola from the back of the room, "none of the fruits or vegetables on your chart grow in Puerto Rico."

"Then you must substitute our recommendations with your native foods."

"Is an apple the same as a mango?" asked Cirila, whose yard was shaded by mango trees.

"*Sí,*" said the expert, "a mango can be substituted for an apple."

"What about breadfruit?"

"I'm not sure . . ." The *Americano* looked at an expert from San Juan who stood up, pulled the front of his *guayabera* down over his ample stomach, and spoke in a voice as deep and resonant as a radio announcer's.

"Breadfruit," he said, "would be equivalent to potatoes."

"Even the ones with seeds?" asked Doña Lola, who roasted them on the coals of her *fogón.*

"Well, I believe so," he said, "but it is best not to make substitutions for the recommended foods. That would throw the whole thing off."

He sat down and stared at the ceiling, his hands crossed under his belly as if he had to hold it up. The mothers asked each other where they could get carrots and broccoli, iceberg lettuce, apples, peaches, or pears.

"At the conclusion of the meeting," the *Americano* said, "you will all receive a sack full of groceries with samples from the major food groups." He flipped the chart closed and moved his chair near the window, amid the hum of women asking one another what he'd just said.

The next expert uncovered another easel, on which there was a picture of a big black bug. A child screamed, and a woman got the hiccups.

"This," the expert said scratching the top of his head, "is the magnified image of a head louse."

Following him, another *Americano* who spoke good Spanish discussed intestinal parasites. He told all the mothers to boil their water several times and to wash their hands frequently.

"Children love to put their hands in their mouths," he said, making it sound like fun, "but each time they do, they run the risk of infection." He flipped the chart to show an enlargement of a dirty hand, the tips of the fingernails encrusted with dirt.

"Ugh! That's disgusting!" whispered Mami to the woman next to her. I curled my fingers inside my palms.

"When children play outside," the expert continued, "their hands pick up dirt, and with it, hundreds of microscopic parasites that enter their bodies through their mouths to live and thrive in their intestinal tract."

He flipped the chart again. A long flat snake curled from the corner of the top of the chart to the opposite corner at the bottom. Mami shivered and rubbed her arms to keep the goose bumps down.

"This," the *Americano* said, "is a tapeworm, and it is not uncommon in this part of the world."

Mami had joked many times that the reason I was so skinny was that I had a *solitaria*, a tapeworm, in my belly. But I don't think she ever knew what a tapeworm looked like, nor did I. I imagined something like the earthworms that crawled out of the ground when it rained, but never anything so ugly as the snake on the chart, its flat body like a deck of cards strung together.

"Tapeworms," the expert continued, "can reach lengths of nine feet." I rubbed my belly, trying to imagine how long nine feet was and whether I had that much room in me. Just thinking about it made my insides itchy.

When they finished their speeches, the experts had all the mothers line up and come to the side of the room, where each was given samples according to the number of people in their household. Mami got two sacks of groceries, so Delsa had to carry Edna all the way home while I dragged one of the bags full of cans, jars, and bright cartons.

At home Mami gave each of us a toothbrush and told us we were to clean our teeth every morning and every evening. She set a tube of paste and a cup by the door, next to Papi's shaving things. Then she emptied the bags.

"I don't understand why they didn't just give us a sack of rice and a bag of beans. It would keep this family fed for a month."

She took out a five-pound tin of peanut butter, two boxes of cornflakes, cans of fruit cocktail, peaches in heavy syrup, beets, and tuna fish, jars of grape jelly and pickles, and put everything on a high shelf.

"We'll save this," she said, "so that we can eat like *Americanos cuando el hambre apriete.*" She kept them there for a long time but took them down one by one so that, as she promised, we ate like Americans when hunger cramped our bellies.

One morning I woke with something wiggling inside my panties. When I looked, there was a long worm inside. I screamed, and Mami came running. I pointed to my bottom, and she pulled down my panties and saw. She sat me in a basin of warm water with salt, because she thought that might draw more worms out. I squatted, my bottom half in, half out, expecting that a *solitaria* would crawl out of my body and swim around and when it realized it had come out, try to bite me down there and crawl back in. I kept looking into the basin, but nothing happened, and after a long time, Mami let me get up. That night she gave us only a thin broth for supper.

"Tonight you all get a *purgante*," she said.

"But why," Delsa whined. "I'm not the one with worms."

"If one of you has worms, you all have worms," Mami said, and we knew better than to argue with her logic. "Now go wash up, and come get your medicine."

The *purgante* was her own concoction, a mixture of cod-liver oil and mugwort, milk of magnesia, and green papaya juice, sweetened to disguise the fishy, bitter, chalky taste. It worked on our bellies overnight, and in the morning, Delsa, Norma, Héctor, and I woke up with cramps and took turns at the latrine, joining the end of the line almost as soon as we'd finished. Mami fed us broths, and in the evening, a bland, watery boiled rice that at least stuck to our bellies and calmed the roiling inside.

"Today," Miss Jiménez said, "you will be vaccinated by the school nurse."

There had never been a school nurse at Macún Elementary School, but lately a woman dressed in white, with a tall, stiff cap atop her short-cropped hair, had set up an infirmary in a corner of the lunchroom. Forms had been sent home, and Mami had told me and Delsa that we would be receiving polio vaccines.

"What's polio?" I asked, imagining another parasite in my belly.

"It's a very bad disease that makes you crippled," she said.

"Is it like meningitis?" Delsa asked. A brother of one of her friends had that disease; his arms and hands were twisted into his body, his legs splayed out at the knees, so that he walked as if he were about to kneel.

"No," Mami said, "it's worse. If you get polio, you die, or you spend the rest of your life in a wheelchair or inside an iron lung."

"An iron lung!?!?" It was impossible. There could not be such a thing.

"It's not like a real lung, silly," Mami laughed. "It's a machine that breathes for you."

"*¡Ay Dios Mío!*" Polio was worse than *solitaria*.

"But how can it do that?" Delsa's eyes opened and shut as if she were testing to see whether she was asleep or awake.

"I don't know how it works," Mami said. "Ask your father."

Delsa and I puzzled over how you could have an iron lung, and that night, when Papi came home from work, we made him draw one for us and show us how a machine could do what people couldn't. He drew a long tube and at one end made a stick figure face.

"It looks like a can," Delsa said, and Papi laughed.

"Yes," he said, "it does. Just like a can."

Miss Jiménez sent us out to see the nurse two at a time, in alphabetical order. By the time she got to the *S*'s, I was shaky, because every one of the children who had gone before me had come back crying, pressing a wad of cotton against their arm. Ignacio Sepúlveda walked next to me, and even though he was as scared as I was, he pretended he wasn't.

"What crybabies!" he said. "I've had shots before and they don't hurt that much."

"When?"

"Last year. They gave us shots for tuberculosis." We were nearing the lunchroom, and Ignacio slowed down, tugged on my arm and whispered, "It's all because of politics."

"What are you talking about? Politics isn't a disease like polio. It's something men talk about at the bus stop." I'd heard Papi tell Mami when he was late that he'd missed the bus because he'd been discussing politics.

Ignacio kept his voice to a whisper, as if he were telling me something no one else knew. "My Papá says the government's doing all this stuff for us because it's an election year."

"What does that have to do with it?"

"They give kids shots and free breakfast, stuff like that, so that our dads will vote for them."

"So?"

"Don't you know anything?"

"I know a lot of things."

"You don't know anything about politics."

"Do so."

"Do not."

"Do so."

"Who's the governor of Puerto Rico, then?"

"Oh, you could have asked something really hard! . . . Everyone knows it's Don Luis Muñoz Marín."

"Yeah, well who's *el presidente* of the Jun-ited Estates?"

"Ay-sen-hou-err."

"I bet you don't know his first name."

I knew then I had him. I scanned Papi's newspaper daily, and I had seen pictures of *el presidente* on the golf course, and of his wife's funny hairdo.

"His first name is Eekeh," I said, puffed with knowledge. "And his wife's name is Mami."

"Well, he's an imperialist, just like all the other *gringos!*" Ignacio said, and I was speechless because Mami and Papi never let us say things like that about grown-ups, even if they were true.

When we came into the lunchroom, Ignacio presented his arm to the nurse as if instead of a shot he were getting a medal. He winced as the nurse stuck the needle into him and blinked a few times to push back tears. But he didn't cry, and I didn't either, though I wanted to. There was no way I'd have Ignacio Sepúlveda calling me a crybaby.

"Papi, what's an imperialist?"

He stopped the hammer in mid-strike and looked at me.

"Where did you hear that word?"

"Ignacio Sepúlveda said Eekeh Aysenhouerr is an imperialist. He said all *gringos* are."

Papi looked around as if someone were hiding behind a bush and listening in. "I don't want you repeating those words to anybody . . ."

"I know that Papi . . . I just want to know what it means. Are *gringos* the same as *Americanos?*"

"You should never call an *Americano* a *gringo*. It's a very bad insult."

"But why?"

"It just is." It wasn't like Papi not to give a real answer to my questions. "Besides, *el presidente's* name is pronounced Ayk, not Eekeh." He went back to his hammering.

I handed him a nail from the can at his feet. "How come it's a bad insult?"

He stopped banging the wall and looked at me. I stared back, and he put his hammer down, took off his hat, brushed his hand across his forehead, wiped it on his pants, sat on the stoop, and leaned his elbows back, stretching his legs out in front of him. This was the response I expected. Now I would hear all about *gringos* and imperialists.

"Puerto Rico was a colony of Spain after Columbus landed here," he began, like a schoolteacher.

"I know that."

"Don't interrupt."

"Sorry."

"In 1898, *los Estados Unidos* invaded Puerto Rico, and we became their colony. A lot of Puerto Ricans don't think that's right. They call *Americanos* imperialists, which means they want to change our country and our culture to be like theirs."

"Is that why they teach us English in school, so we can speak like them?"

"Yes."

"Well, I'm not going to learn English so I don't become American."

He chuckled. "Being American is not just a language, *Negrita*, it's a lot of other things."

"Like what?"

He scratched his head. "Like the food you eat . . . the music you listen to . . . the things you believe in."

"Do they believe in God?"

"Some of them do."

"Do they believe in phantasms and witches?"

"Yes, some Americans believe in that."

"Mami doesn't believe any of that stuff."

"I know. I don't either."

"Why not?"

"I just . . . I believe in things I can see."

"Why do people call *Americanos gringos*?"

"We call them *gringos*, they call us spiks."

"What does that mean?"

"Well," he sat up, leaned his elbows on his knees and looked at the ground, as if he were embarrassed. "There are many Puerto Ricans in New York, and when someone asks them a question they say, 'I don spik inglish' instead of 'I don't speak English.' They make fun of our accent."

"*Americanos* talk funny when they speak Spanish."

"Yes, they do. The ones who don't take the trouble to learn it well." He pushed his hat back, and the sun burned into his already brown face, making him squint. "That's part of being an imperialist. They expect us to do things their way, even in our country."

"That's not fair."

"No, it isn't." He stood up and picked up his hammer. "Well, I'd better get back to work, *Negrita*. Do you want to help?"

"Okay." I followed him, holding the can of nails up so he wouldn't have to bend over to pick them up. "Papi?"

"Yes."

"If we eat all that American food they give us at the *centro comunal*, will we become *Americanos*?"

He banged a nail hard into the wall then turned to me, and, with a broad smile on his face said, "Only if you like it better than our Puerto Rican food."

The yard in front of the *centro comunal* teemed with children. Mrs. García, the school lunch matron, opened the door and stepped out, a bell in her hand. We quieted before she rang it. She beamed.

"Good." There was whispering and shoving as we crowded the door to be the first in for breakfast. Mrs. García lifted the bell in warning. We settled down again.

"Now," she said in her gruff voice, "line up by age, youngest first."

The smaller children, who had been pushed to the back of the crowd by bigger ones, scurried to the front. I took my place halfway between the younger and the older ones, who scowled at us and jammed the line forward with rough shoves.

"Stop pushing!" Mrs. García yelled. "There's enough for everyone."

She opened the double doors and we rushed ahead in a wave, goaded from behind by boys who crushed against us with their chests and knees.

The *centro comunal* had been decorated with posters. Dick and Jane, Sally and Spot, Mother and Father, the Mailman, the Milkman, and the Policeman smiled their way through tableau after tableau, their clean, healthy, primary-colored world flat and shadowless.

"Wow!" Juanita Marín whispered, her lips shaped into a perfect O.

People who looked like Mother and Father held up tubes of Colgate toothpaste or bars of Palmolive soap. A giant chart of the four basic food groups was tacked up between the back windows. In a corner, the Puerto Rican seal, flanked by our flag and the Stars and Stripes, looked like a lamb on a platter. Above it, Ike and Don Luis Muñoz Marín faced each other smiling.

"What's that smell?" I said to Juanita as we shuffled closer to the counter lined with steaming pots.

"It's the food, silly," she giggled.

It was a sweet-salty smell, bland but strong, warm but not comforting, lacking herbs and spices.

"It's disgusting!"

"I think it smells good." She pouted and took a tray, a pale green paper napkin, and a spoon.

The server picked a blue enamel tin plate from a stack behind her and scooped out a bright yellow blob from the pot in front of her. She dumped a ladleful on Juanita's plate and slid it onto the tray.

"You'd like some eggs too, wouldn't you?" she asked me with a smile.

"Those are eggs?"

"Of course they're eggs!" she laughed. "What else could they be?" She heaped a mound of it in the middle of my plate, where it quivered, its watery edges green where they met the blue.

"They don't look like eggs."

Ignacio Sepúlveda poked his tray into my ribs. "You're holding up the line!"

"They're *huevos Americanos*," said the next server, whose job it was to spear two brown sausages with a fork and slip them onto the plate. "They're powdered, so all we do is add water and fry them." She arranged my sausages to flank the eggs. "And here are some *salchichas Americanas*, so you can put some meat on those bones." She laughed, and I gave her a dirty look. That only made her laugh harder.

The next server slapped margarine on two bread squares, which he laid like a pyramid over the eggs. Next, a girl not much older than the kids behind us poured canned juice into a bottom-heavy glass, which she put on our trays so carelessly it splashed out and made watery orange puddles that ran to the corners of our trays.

We sat on long benches attached to plastic tables, Juanita and I across from one another.

"This is great!" she chirruped in her reedy voice, lips wet with anticipation. Her black eyes took in the colors of our American breakfast: maroon tray, blue plate, yellow eggs, brown sausages, milky white bread with a thin beige crust, the hueless shimmer of margarine, orange juice, pastel-green paper napkin, silvery spoon. "Wow!" she oohed again.

I rearranged the food so that none of it touched and dipped my spoon into the gelatinous hill, which was firmer than I expected. It was warm and gave off that peculiar odor I'd smelled coming in. It tasted like the cardboard covers of our primers, salty, dry, fibrous, but not as satisfyingly chewy. If these were once eggs, it had been a long time since they'd been inside a hen. I nicked the tip of the sausage with the spoon and tongued it around before crushing it between my teeth. Its grease-bathed pepperiness had a strong bitter aftertaste like anise, but not sweet. The bread formed moist balls inside my mouth, no matter how much I chewed it. The juice might have had oranges in it once, but only a faint citrus smell remained.

I was glad the food wasn't tasty and played it around the blue plate, creating yellow mountains through which shimmering rivers of grease flowed, their edges green, the rolled-up balls of white bread perfect stones along strips of brown earth studded with tiny black flecks, ants perhaps, or, better yet, microscopic people.

> *Are ju slippin? Are ju slippin?*
> *Bruder John, Bruder John.*
> *Mornin bel sar rin ging.*
> *Mornin bel sar rin ging.*
> *Deen deen don. Deen deen don.*

Miss Jiménez liked to teach us English through song, and we learned all our songs phonetically, having no idea of what the words meant. She tried to teach us "America the Beautiful" but had to give up when we stumbled on "for spacious skies" (4 espé chosk ¡Ay!) and "amber waves of grain" (am burr gueys oh gren).

At the same time she taught us the Puerto Rican national anthem, which said Borinquén was the daughter of the ocean and the sun. I liked thinking of our island as a woman whose body was a garden of flowers, whose feet were caressed by waves, a land whose sky was never cloudy. I especially liked the part when Christopher Columbus lands on her shores and sighs: "¡Ay! This is the beautiful land I've been searching for!"

But my favorite patriotic song was *"En mi viejo San Juan,"* in which a poet says good-bye to Old San Juan and calls Puerto Rico a "sea goddess, queen of the coconut groves."

"Papi . . ." He was on his knees, smoothing the cement floor of the new kitchen he was attaching to the house.

"Sí . . ." He put his trowel down and squeezed his waist as he stretched his back. I squatted against the wall near him.

"Where was Noel Estrada going when he was saying good-bye to Old San Juan?"

Papi reached over and turned the radio down. "I think he was sailing from San Juan Harbor to New York."

"It's such a sad song, don't you think?"

"At the end he says he'll come back someday."

"Did he?"

"The last verse says he's old and hasn't been able to return."

"That makes it even sadder."

"Why?"

"Because he says he's coming back to be happy. Doesn't that sound like he wasn't happy in New York?"

"Yes, I guess it does."

"Maybe he didn't want to go."

"Maybe." He picked up his trowel, slid a thin layer of cement on it, and leveled it on the floor, smoothing and stretching it in arcs that formed half circles, like gray rainbows.

"Look how pretty this is!"

Mami held a yellow blouse with a ruffled collar against her bosom, patted the neckline into shape, and stretched it across her shoulders to check the fit. It was a wonderful color against her skin, making the freckles on her nose look like gold specks.

"I'll put it away for now. It's a little small." She was pregnant again, and her belly pressed against the fabric of her dress and strained the seams that zigzagged down the sides, where bits of flesh showed pale and soft between the stitches. She folded the blouse and pulled a dress out of the box. Delsa and I both grabbed for it, but Mami yanked it out of reach and crossed her arms, crushing it against her.

"Stop that! Let me see what size it is." She held it up. It was perfect for me. It had red dots on white puffy sleeves, a white bodice, a white skirt with a stripe of red dots at the hem, and two dotted heart-shaped pockets.

"Negi, I think this one is for you."

I grabbed it and ran to the other end of the room, where Norma was already trying on pink shorts with a matching tee-shirt. I stuck my tongue out at Delsa, who sent daggers with her eyes, but only until Mami pulled out a sky-blue dress with ruffles and lace on the collar. Perfect for Delsa.

Tata, Mami's brother, had sent us a box from New York full of clothes that Mami's cousins no longer wore. Clothes that were almost new, with no stains or tears or mended seams. Héctor, the boy in our family, was the only one to get new pants and shirts, because none of Mami's New York relatives had boys his age. But for us girls there were shiny patent-leather shoes with the heels hardly worn, saddle shoes that had already been broken in, a red sweater with a bow at the neck and only one button missing, pleated skirts with matching blouses, high heels for Mami, a few nightgowns, and a pair of pajamas that I claimed, because I loved the cowboys and Indians chasing each other across my body, down my arms and legs.

"Our cousins must be rich to give up these things!" Norma said as she tried on a girl's cotton slip with embroidered flowers across the chest.

"Things like these are not that expensive in New York," Mami said. "Anyone can afford them."

She sat on the edge of the bed and unfolded a letter that had been taped to the inside of the box. A crisp ten dollar bill fell out. Héctor and Alicia dove for it and wrestled one another to be the first to get it. While they fought, Delsa calmly picked it up and handed it to Mami.

"What does the letter say, Mami?" I asked.

"It says she hopes we like the presents." She looked up at me, her eyes shiny. "Maybe you could write Tata a letter and tell her we love them."

"Sure!" I liked writing letters. Especially if they were going far away. I had often written things for Mami, like addresses on envelopes she sent to Tata in New York, or notes for my teachers, which I wrote and she signed.

That night I wrote Tata a letter. It took me a long time, because we were just learning cursive in school, and I had to look up the shapes of some letters on the back of the book Miss Jiménez had given us for penmanship practice. I found it difficult to form the capital *E* of my first name, with its top and bottom curlicues and uneven-size bulges that faced in what seemed like the wrong direction no matter how many times I wrote it. So I signed it Negi, which I considered to be my real name. When I finished the letter, Mami read it out loud.

" 'Dear Tata, We liked the presents you sent us. The dress with the polka dots fits me and Delsa looks pretty in the blue dress. Mami is saving the yellow blouse for after the baby. We love you and thank you for the things you sent. Love, Negi.' . . . You made a mistake. . . ."

"What?"

"You didn't start with a salutation."

"Yes I did. See? Dear Tata."

"I know, but you also have to write, 'I hope when you receive this letter you are feeling well. We are all well here, thank God.' You can abbreviate 'A Dios Gracias' by writing 'A.D.G.' if you want to."

"Why does it have to start that way?"

"All letters start that way."

"But why?"

"I don't know!" she said, exasperated. "That's how I learned it. And every letter I get starts that way. If you don't have a salutation at the beginning, it's not a real letter. . . . Besides, it's rude not to wish the reader good health, and God has to be thanked first thing. . . . You'd better write it again."

"I don't want to write it again."

"You have to." She set it down on the table. "Finish it and I can take it to the post office tomorrow." She walked away.

"I'm not doing this stupid letter over," I mumbled.

"What was that?" She'd whirled in her tracks and was at me before I could blink my eyes, her left hand gripping my arm.

"Nothing! I didn't say anything."

Mami stood over me, crushing my arm, right hand at her side, the fingers trembling. I wanted to grab her fingers, to bite into them, to make them hurt, those fingers that sometimes soothed but so many times splayed against my skin in smacks, or, fisted, knuckled my head in *cocotazos* that echoed inside my brain. She slammed me against the chair. The rungs dug into my bony back.

"Finish it." I could almost touch the heat she gave off, the faint sweaty smell of her anger. Hot, quiet tears dribbled down my cheeks in a steady flow, like the faucet at the public fountain. The drone inside my head was louder, my ears felt warm, red, too big for my head. Mami stood there watching, as I picked up the pencil, carefully tore a sheet from my notebook, and, in labored script, wrote, "Dear Tata, I hope when you receive this letter . . ."

> *My bonee lie sober de o chan,*
> *My bonee lie sober de sí,*
> *My bonee lie sober de o chan,*
> *O breen back my bonee 2 mí, 2 mí . . .*

"What's that smell?" The breakfasts at the *centro comunal* had fallen into a pattern of *huevos Americanos* alternating with hot oatmeal, which at least tasted like oatmeal, except it was not as smooth, sweet, and cinnamony as the oatmeal Mami made.

"They must be giving us something new today," said Juanita Marín.

The steaming pots were gone. Instead, there was a giant urn in the middle of the table and a five-pound tin of peanut butter. One of the servers scooped a dollop of peanut butter into the bottom-heavy glasses, and another filled them with warm milk from the urn.

"Here's a spoon so you can stir it," she said as she put the glasses on our trays.

I carried my tray to the usual table Juanita and I shared. Even she, who loved the breakfasts, had a suspicious expression on her face. We faced each other, looked down at the glass full of milk with the brown blob on the bottom, looked at each other again, then at the milk.

"Are you going to taste it?" I asked her.

"Sure," she said, unconvinced. "Are you?"

"Sure." I stirred the milk, and beige pellets floated up from the bottom, like sand encased in a shimmery oil that skimmed the top and bubbled around the whirlpool I made with my spoon. Juanita stirred hers too. I took a sip from the spoon but couldn't really taste much except the milk. Juanita spooned a dribble into her mouth. She smiled.

"Yum!" But it wasn't her usual happy "Yum!" It was more of an "I'm going to pretend to like this in case it's good" kind of "Yum!"

I wrapped my hands around the glass, lifted it to my lips, and drank. A consoling warmth compensated for the milky smell, and the gritty, salty-sweet taste. The peanut butter, which was supposed to dissolve in the milk, broke off into clumps, like soft pebbles.

I gagged, and the glass fell out of my hand, spilled over my uniform, and crashed to the tile floor, where it broke into large chunks that gleamed in the pebbly milk. I threw up what little I'd swallowed, and children around me jumped and receded into a tittery circle of faces with milky mustaches. Mrs. García pushed through the crowd and pulled me away from the mess, while one of the servers dragged a dirty mop across it.

"*Now* look what you've done!" she said, as if this were something I did every day of the week to annoy her.

"I couldn't help it!" I cried. "That milk tastes sour!"

"How can it taste sour?" she yelled as she wiped me down with a rag. "It's powdered milk. We made it fresh this morning. It can't get sour."

I remembered a word Mami used for food that made her gag. "It's . . . *repugnante*!"

"I suppose you'd find it less repugnant to go hungry every morning!"

"I've never gone hungry!" I screamed. "My Mami and Papi can feed us without your disgusting *gringo* imperialist food!"

The children gasped. Even Ignacio Sepúlveda. Mrs. García's mouth dropped open and stayed that way. From the back, a loud whisper broke the silence: "Close it, or you'll trap flies!" My face burned, but I couldn't stifle a giggle. Mrs. García closed her mouth and forgot about me for a moment.

"Who said that?" Everyone looked innocent, eyes cast down, lips fighting laughter. She grabbed me by the arm and dragged me to the door. "Get out! And tell your mother I need to speak to her."

Before she could push me, I pulled my arm from her grip and ran, not sure where I should go because the last thing I wanted to do was go home and tell Mami I'd been disrespectful to an adult. I dragged my feet down the dirt road, leaving my body behind, burying it in dust, while I floated in the treetops and watched myself from above, an insignificant creature that looked like a praying mantis in a green and yellow uniform. By the time I got home, I had decided to lie to Mami. If I told her the truth, she was sure to hit me, and I couldn't bear that humiliation on top of the other. When I came into the yard, my sisters and brother surrounded me, their curiosity comforting, as they pulled on my dirty clothes with remarks that I smelled bad.

"What happened to you?" Mami asked, all eyes. And all of a sudden I felt very sick. "I threw up in the lunchroom," I said, before falling into a faint that lasted so long that by the time I woke up from it, she had taken off my soiled uniform and washed me down with *alcobolado*.

For days I lay sick in bed, throwing up, racked by chills and sweats that left the bedcovers soaked and sent Delsa to sleep with Norma and Héctor, swearing that I was peeing on her. If Mrs. García ever talked to her, Mami never said anything. After what seemed like weeks, I went back to school, by which time the elections had been won, the breakfasts ceased, and my classmates had found someone else to tease.

PART 5

URBAN REALITY

"We accepted everybody ... Nobody accepted us."
—FROM *CARLITO'S WAY* BY EDWIN TORRES

PEDRO PIETRI

Monday Morning

Monday morning
the end of the world returns
Everybody has a hangover
Everybody has lost their temper
All thru the night nobody slept
and now is time to wake up again
and take more instructions
from the instigators of destruction

The race for the toilet begins
The table is empty
There is plenty of nothing to eat
Black coffee without toast
A few words with the holy ghost
And is time to forget
the definition of time
as you lose your mind
trying to get to work on time
to say good morning
to your well-dressed
clean-cut white-collar executioner
who has never worked a day
in his remote-control existence

Everybody has bad breath this morning
switchblade tempers anti-social eyeballs

cemetery erections wash-and-wear headaches
as downtown trains faint on top of them
Farts of protest
are heard by the wind
as the working
day and night begins
for the tenants
of condem buildings
in el barrio
the south bronx
lower manhattan
fort greene
astoria queens
and wherever else
we are concentrated
castrated and liquidated
in the name of democracy
that raped our nation
with deadly weapons
and dumped us into
the garment district
and other places
Unemployed faces
drop dead working
for spice ham
and cheese salaries
and the next
legal paid holiday

Everybody hates their jobs
Everybody hates their take-home pay
Everybody hates new york state taxes
Everybody is praying for better days
Everybody is waiting for the messiah
the same one who left after he got elected
Everybody must work until they have saved
enough money for a good down payment
on a semi-decent credit card funeral

Spic take the broom
and sweep the place
till you make it look
cleaner than heaven
Spic take the mop
and baptize the floor
with soap and water
Spic the garbage can
looks like your salary
make it look like
my salary immediately
Spic I feel hungry
run faster than the speed
of light and get me
a tailored made sandwich
Spic skip your lunch today
for coming late yesterday
Spic I is feeling bored
amuse me with your
broken english humor
Spic the floor is sinning
again do your thing
with the salvation broom
Spic the windows are blind
restore their vision
Spic you have five minutes
to make ten deliveries
Spic stick your tongue out
I want to mail a letter
Spic say goodnight
to your employer he is
exhausted from looking
at you work so hard

Day is done
The night that never comes is over
Sober or not is time to wake up again
The alarm clock is alive and well

and ringing at six o'clock in the morning
Wake up chico! snap out of that dream
If you get to work one minute late
you will be deducted for fifteen

FREDDIE PRINZE

"Looking Good"

COMEDY PERFORMANCE AT MR. KELLY'S IN CHICAGO, ILLINOIS (CBS RECORDS, 1974)

I'm not all Puerto Rican.

I'm half Hungarian: HungaRican.

That was a weird combination to grow up with because I could never figure out how my parents met. A Gypsy and a Puerto Rican.

I asked my mother and she told me that they were on a bus trying to pick each other's pocket.

My mother is great! She has always been a romanticist. She is always talking about her wedding:

"Oh Freddie, my wedding was so beautiful. The flowers. The orchestra playing. Your father looked so handsome—you should have been there."

I was there.

There are not many Puerto Ricans where I live now. I live in Los Angeles. There's about 200,000 Puerto Ricans—in one room.

But it's better than the neighborhood I grew up in. I grew up in New York City in an area called Washington Heights, which was like a ghetto suburb.

Slums with trees. Even the birds were junkies.

Dope addict sparrows that didn't know how to fly. Just fall out of trees and bother people:

"Tweet! tweet! sucka, gimme a quarter."

A lot of people think that Puerto Ricans are responsible for cockroaches. I want to clear that up right now! We didn't bring them here. When we got here they were living in the apartments we live in now.

But they're strong. I'm afraid of them. They adapt to any environment. They learned how to talk in my building.

They would threaten me before I went out:

"Freddie! Where are you going? To the grocery store, huh? Don't come back with no roach poison or we lock you out!"

The guy I talk about most and when I first started I talked about him a lot, was Mr. Rivera, who was the landlord of the apartment building I grew up in.

He was the kind of landlord that never wanted to fix anything in your apartment, but he wanted the key anyway.

In case of an emergency, like he was broke.

You couldn't complain to him.

My father would tell him:

"Hey! Rivera! There's no ceiling in our apartment!"

"That's okay, the guy upstairs don't walk around much! He don't complain he don't have a floor! You just like to make trouble, Mr. Prinze!"

"Never mind that—when are you going to fix it?"

"It's not my job, man!"

Other things that gives people the wrong impression of Puerto Ricans are movies. Like, *West Side Story* set us back a hundred years—and we were only in the country twenty!

Because if you saw the movie it made people think that all we did was stand in streets whistling and dancing.

They thought we were gay ballet dancers!

And the movie became such a hit that the New York Chamber of Commerce had to keep up the image about Puerto Ricans in New York. So they hired Gene Kelly and Fred Astaire to choreograph every Puerto Rican wino in Harlem.

This was for the bus tours from the Midwest that would come in, see Harlem and tour the city.

And the winos are on the corner going:

"Hey man, if that bus don't show up by four-thirty I ain't dancing for nobody!"

But the bus would always show up. And they would go into the act.
And people on the bus would go:

"Look at that, Marge! It's just like on TV, honey. Those people can dance, boy!"

The most unbelievable scene in the picture was two A.M., the young lovers Tony and Maria are out on the fire escape—vowing their love for each other.

And Tony goes:

"Maria, I love you."

"Shh! My papa will hear you."

"But I'm whispering."

"Shhh!"

The next thing you know, they sing:

"TONIGHT! TONIGHT!"

Her father must have been deaf or have pillows in his ears!

If that had been a black neighborhood at two A.M. in the morning singing, they would have gotten shot!

"What you doing on the fire escape singing, sucker?! People trying to sleep here! Gimme my gun, Mama! You gonna sing all the way to the funeral parlor, baby!"

Another thing that gave people the wrong impression of Puerto Ricans is most people think that all we do is stand in the streets going:

"MIRA! MAMI! LINDA! OYE! MIRA! Oh, what's the matter you can't talk with me? Who needs you, ugly. I got two wives, man. Eighteen kids I don't know about!"

When streaking was popular we loved it because the girls were already naked before we made noise:

"MAMI! DAMN! Hey Bobby! Bobby! Come look at this, man!"

"Hey, that's my sister, man! What the hell are you looking at, sucka? You gonna marry her now!"

There is a code among the muggers and criminals in New York. No mugger in New York will hit you if you have money at the time of the holdup.

So my mother would give me a dollar a day—criminal money.

She'd say:

"Freddie, if the criminal bothers you, don't fight, give him the money. You can always make more money but you can never get your life back."

So this one guy Henry would mug me every day. Yeah, I knew him. If he was sick, I would take the money to his house.

One day it was snowing really hard and I said, Well, Henry is not coming out in this weather. And I am not going to his house—so I spent the dollar.

Sure enough, after school Henry was right out there waiting for me.

"Where is the dollar, Fred?"

"I spent it, Henry."

"I'm gonna tell your mother!"

Soon as I got home my mother says:

"Henry called me. You spent his money?"

POW!

No fun where I grew up. In my neighborhood, my best friend was this dude, Nat. Black dude that played trumpet. I was in a band and I played drums. We were hanging out. Nat was about six-eight—but five inches was his hair, three inches was platform.

He initiated me into an all-black gang called the Royal Lords. It was the only gang in the neighborhood. They never fought anybody. They just had a gang to have a gang.

The first day they initiated me they said:

"Fred, come here. This ain't the usual procedure for the Royal Lords, but we're gonna take a Puerto Rican in. We've been getting alot of static—about we're not an equal opportunity gang. So, we are going to let you in, my man. But, you got to get your initiation. The initiation is ask Ralphy—see that fellow eating the building?—ask Ralphy how his father dances."

I didn't know any better, so I asked Ralphy:

"Ralphy, how does your father dance?"

"MY FATHER AIN'T GOT NO LEGS, MAN! I'LL KILL YOU— WHAT'S WRONG WITH YOU, SUCKA!"

I got arrested once. I was driving without license, insurance, or registration. Wasn't my car. I didn't care. I had my man Nat with me. We were driving in the South, and I'm going at the speed limit. I'm not breaking any laws. All of a sudden I hear a siren.

Oh, God. I pull over.

A cop comes out.

"You know what you did?"

"No, officer—"

188 · "Looking Good"

"Hell you don't. Where you from?"

"New York."

"Bit out of your way, ain't you? Where are you going?"

"School."

"You know your left rear taillight is out of order?"

"No."

"Tell your friend to get his head out of the glove compartment, will you. I'm going to let you go. Okay, school boy. Give you a break today, but if I see you tomorrow you are in big trouble—beat it!"

The cop let me go. The cop gave me a break.

Nat says—"HOLD ON, YOU GOT RIGHTS! COME BACK HERE, PIG! YOU LOOKING TO MAKE A BRIBE? DON'T MESS WITH MY FRIEND WHEN HE'S BEEN DRINKING!"

People talk in the wrong situations.

Junkies. They go to court. They know how to lie.

"Your honor, man, I'm straight now, baby! This cop is just trying to get a promotion from me, man. I didn't steal no car. Do I look like I can drive? I don't need your lousy car. I'm a track star. Look at me, I am in great shape, I run a hundred yards in nine seconds with a color TV in each arm."

Gotta believe him. Because of junkie burglars we didn't believe in Santa Claus.

Christmas Eve my father would tell me:

"Someone comes down the chimney, you blow his damn head off! Ho! Ho! Shit, you shoot him!"

I'll tell you how bad the burglars were. I once bought a stereo that was originally mine.

He comes up to me and says: "It's from your house, buy it again, you know it works!"

That's the thing with crime. People are buying dogs, guns, taking kung fu lessons.

Most people buy German shepherds because they are great with the door bell.

BUZZ!

"WOOF! WOOF! WOOF!"

Neighbors move.

I bought a Puerto Rican shepherd. Very macho.

BUZZ!

"WHO IS IT!"

I tried to paper train him. I put newspaper in the bathroom and he would go sit on the bowl and read them.

The reason I knew he was a Puerto Rican shepherd, if I took him out in the street and he would see a French poodle, he'd go:

"BOW! WOW! HONEY! OYE! LOOKING GOOD!"

EDWIN TORRES
Carlito's Way

Sooner or later, a thug will tell his tale. We all want to go on record. So let's hear it for all the hoods. The Jews out of Brownsville. The Blacks on Lenox Avenue. The Italians from Mulberry Street. Like that. Meanwhile, the Puerto Ricans been gettin' jammed since the forties and ain't nobody said nothin'. We been laid, relayed, and waylaid and nobody wants to hear about it. Well, I'm gonna lay it on you one time, for the record.

Who these people? Puerto Ricans. They come from an island a hundred long by thirty-five miles wide. They come in all sizes, colors, and shapes. They got a little of everybody. Heart like the Jews, soul like the Blacks, balls like the Italians. They hit New York in the 1940s, the wrong time. But like when is it right, when your face don't help, your accent ain't French, and your clothes don't fit? They hung in anyway—most of the tickets were one-way. So they filed into the roach stables in Harlem and the South Bronx. They sat behind the sewing machines and stood behind the steam tables. In other words, they busted their ass, they went for the Dream. Most of them.

A handful couldn't handle the weight at the bottom of the totem pole. They wouldn't squat, couldn't bend. Had to take their shot. Them was the hodedores, *hoodlums. Hard nose. And like the thugs from any group, they went for the coin of the realm, head on.*

I'm talking from the far shore looking back on thirty years. At least I made it to the other side. Most of my crew got washed on the way. And if survivors don't talk about it, who's gonna know we was here, right? So here's how it went down for one P.R., me, Carlito Brigante.

I came on the scene in the 1930s. Me and my moms. Brigante Sr. had long since split back to Puerto Rico. Seem like we was in every furnished room in Spanish Harlem. Kind of hazy some of it now, but I can remember her draggin' me by the hand from place to place—the clinic on 106th Street, the home relief on 105th Street, the Pentecostal church on 107th Street. That was home base, the church. Kids used to call me a "hallelujah"—break my chops. My mom was in there every night bangin' on a tambourine with the rest of them. Sometimes they'd get a special *reverendo* who'd really turn them on. That's when the believers, *feligreses*, would start hoppin' and jumpin'—then they'd be faintin' on the floor and they'd wrap them in white sheets. I remember I didn't go for this part. I was close to my mom, it was just me and her.

I was comin' into my teens in the 1940s when they laid her out at Gonzalez's Funeral Home on 109th Street. Looked like she was into one of her faints, like she'd be all right. Wasn't like that. I ain't sayin' my way would have been any different if she'd been around. That's all you hear in the Joint—aw, man, I didn't have a chance. Bullshit. I was already a mean lil' fucker while my mom was alive, but I always respected women because of her.

Anyway, the court put me on to this jive uncle who come out of nowhere up in the Bronx. I got promoted from the basement to the sub-basement. No good. I cut out. Back down to Harlem. Sleepin' on the roof. Stayin' with friends. Then the juvenile people put me in the Heckscher home near 104th Street. But I was always takin' off on them. I was still in my teens. World War II was over but they was warrin' in the streets. Kiddie gangs was goin' strong. The Puerto Ricans was boxed in. Irish on the south, Italians to the east, Blacks to the north and west. Wasn't none of that brotherhood jive in them days. Git that Po'Rican! We was catchin' hell.

The crazy part is me comin' up rumblin' against these groups as a kid—it should end up that the only two cats that was ever in my corner was Earl Bassey, a black dude, and Rocco Fabrizi, a wal-yo. Unbelievable. But I'm jumpin' ahead.

Lemme tell you about them rumbles. The wops said no spics could go east of Park Avenue. But there was only one swimming pool and that was the Jefferson on 112th Street off the East River. Like, man, you had to wade through Park, Lexington, Third, Second, First, Pleasant. Wall-to-wall guineas. The older guys be standing around in front of the stoops and stores, evil-eyeing us, everybody in his undershirt; the kids would be up on the roof with the garbage cans and in the basements with the bats and bicycle chains. Mostly busted heads, black eyes in those days. First into the street was always me, loved a swingout. That's when I first saw Rocco Fabrizi. He was running with a wop gang, the Redwings. One day we went down to the pool with about twenty or thirty P.R. guys—a hell of a rumble—and right up front is this guy, Rocco, swinging a stickball bat. Stuck in my mind, tough kid. We took a beating—their turf, too many guys. A while later we get the word that this Rocco is sneaking up on a roof with a Latin chick named Carmen—fine head—near Madison Avenue and 107th Street. The balls. He caught some beatin', but he stood up; the Lopez brothers wanted to throw him off the roof but I said enough. He remembered.

The spooks said no Ricans could go west of Fifth Avenue. So if they caught you in Central Park, shame on you. The Copiens, the Socialistics, the Bachelors, the Comanches—all bad motherfuckers—these were the gangs that started using hardware. Then the rumbles got mean—like if the Copiens caught you, you knew they were going to stick you. Then the zip guns came out, metal tubes with door latches as firing pins set off by rubber bands—if the pin hit the .22 on the primer and the piece was held close to your head, you were in trouble. Lucky for a lot of diddy boppers it wasn't often. I once got caught by the Copiens in Central Park by the lake near 106th Street. Me and this black kid duked it out after he said, "Let me hold a quarter." I said, "Let yo' mammy hold it." We got it on, I was kicking him on the ground when his boys arrived on bikes—my blood was up; I said, "I'll take any one of you motherfuckers." "No, motherfucker, we gonna kill yo' ass," and they started pulling the rubber bands on the zip guns. So like I quit the scene, they chased me all the way to 110th Street. That was the last chase on me like that. I always carried a piece from then on. I wasn't about to take no shit. You step up, I'm gonna knock you down.

Summers were hotter in them days. No air-conditioning—the asphalt could burn your sneakers. Took the bus up to Highbridge Pool in Washington Heights. The Irish jumped us in the locker room—we fought with the metal baskets. Know what the pool guard said? "You don't belong up here." No sooner we was on the bus back, we had to bail out the windows on to Amsterdam Avenue, a mob of micks was comin' through the door after us.

That same summer I got hit in the head with a roller skate by some spade in Central Park by the boats near 110th Street. Another time I got my neck all scraped up from a bicycle chain some eye-talian wrapped around me. We caught it from everybody. Don't get me wrong, we gave good as we got—but you remember your own lumps better. We was tryin' to melt into the pot but they wouldn't even let us in the swimming pool. *Hijos de puta.*

Irregardless, I was never a race man. Us P.R.'s are like that—maybe 'cause we come in so many shades. We always had a stray wop or Jew-boy and plenty of spades with our gangs. Anyway, I figure them beatings get you ready for later on—when you gotta get the money.

But the clubs wasn't always fightin'. There was a lot of stickball playing—we had the Devils, the CBCs, the Home Reliefers (dig it), the Turbens (that's the way they spelled it), the Viceroys, the Zeniths, the Falcons, the Tropical Gents, the Royal Knights, the Boca Chica—these all claimed to be S.A.C.—social and ataletic club—ha.

Pimping was popular. Tony Navarro, the Cruz brothers, Bobby Roldan, all had whores. We looked up to these guys—big cars, always a ringside table at the Palladium; always clean, none of that zoot-suit shit—wingtip shoes, conservative-cut clothes. Imagine lookin' up to a pimp! Later on we wouldn't let one of them scumbag motherfuckers stand near us at the bar.

About that time *motherfucker* came into style—it came down from black Harlem in a game called "the dozens." Two cats would meet on the street and start playin' the dozens; one guy would say, "Ashes to ashes, dust to dust, your mother has a pussy like a Greyhound bus," and the other guy come back with, "The dozens ain't my game but the way I fuck your mother is a goddamn shame!" Rough on the mothers. From then on everything was motherfucker.

Mostly we stood around corners on Madison Avenue. Just like Middletown, U.S.A.—ha. The schools, Patrick Henry, Cooper—forget about it. No YMCA, no Boys' Club, no gym, raunchy houses, scummy streets. If you inclined to plea-cop, them streets contributed to the delinquency of a whole lot of minors. But who wants to hear that shit? Only plea I ever copped cost me three years in the slams. A man got to stand up. Take his shot.

Like when the junk started arrivin' about this time. And where did the wops first arrive it? Right on ol' 107th Street between Lexington and Third. A punk-ass kid I was, but I looked it over. I'm gonna ride the horse, or the horse gonna ride me? That was the question on a lot of them corners, 'cause the junk was still a new scene in the forties. All the losers went for the spike and the dynamite high behind it. Only a skag high ain't but good the first few times out, then you hooked, all they gotta do is reel you in, by the crotch now, and squeeze till you cough up another five dollars for a bag. I seen the horse play with them junkies like a cat with a rubber mouse.

Age fourteen, I saw that. I said, uh-uh. Them's the humped—I'm goin' with the humpers. The dealers had the pussy, the clothes, and the cars. That's what I wanted, in that order. The dope fiends had the sores, the scabs, the O.D.'s. Maybe that's what they wanted. Must be crazy—couldn't see it then, can't see it now.

I was thinkin' myself, among other things, half a pug in them days. I didn't really know the science of the game, but I was heavy-handed, with a lot of snap in my shoulder, so when I tagged a stud, he was hurtin'. So now I'm gonna go in the Gloves, this must have been 'round '48 or '49. With a little trainin' everybody said Carlito was a natural. I was gonna fight for the Police Athletic League. Ha. And who was the man there? Moran of the Twenty-third Precinct, my sworn enemy. "What, this fuckin' troublemaker on my squad?" So I ended up fightin' unattached. My trainin' was drinkin' wine and smokin' pot. One time I ran around the 106th Street lake in the park—finished up puffin' on a joint. Some program for a contender. Irregardless, I kicked some ass down in Sunnyside and Ridgewood, including a bad spook from the Salem-Crescent A.C. But then they busted my jaw in a street fight on 105th Street and I had to drop out of the tournament. What a laugh on Moran if I had gone all the way to Chicago. Him with his squad breakin' their ass runnin' around the reservoir every day.

Anyway, I'm too good-lookin' to be a pug. I'm gonna be a pimp. I'm runnin' 'round with these fly broads from 111th Street and Fifth Avenue. That's where all the whores were trickin' in them days. Whores galores. But I could take a knock-around broad but so long. I didn't go for that scene too touch. Pimp got to hate women. That sure wasn't me.

There was some nice chicks around but their mothers wouldn't let them out of the house. Specially with *delincuentes* like me waitin' on the stoop. Them was not "free sex" days. Leave it to me to come up at the wrong time. The good girls held on to their cherry. And it was a big deal. If a broad dropped her drawers, right away she lost her rating—even to the scrounge who copped them; "I ain't gonna marry no broad what lost her cherry!"

I used to get laid in Central Park, but you had to have a long switchblade ready 'cause always some degenerate motherfucker would be sneakin' up on you and your girl from behind the bushes. I didn't mind a guy lee-gating (peeping), I used to do it myself, but these pre-verts would want to gang-bang your broad. I chased more than one around that park at night. One guy tried to hit me with a wooden Keep Off the Grass sign, which he pulled out the ground while he was running from my sticker. He missed, I didn't. Many a piece I missed out on, gettin' interrupted by this element.

I was a big pussy-hound. Ain't changed much either.

Was a big movie fan too. Knock-around kids was always in the movie house. No TV in them days. The Fox Star on 107th Street and Lexington Avenue was our show. There was some bad guinea racketeers in there. You had to go with a gang, 'cause if the wops caught you alone on the balcony, you was a flyin' Po'Rican. I remember once they had a singin' contest on the stage on a Saturday. They was givin' ten dollars to the winner. I was there with a whole mob of guys smokin' pot in the balcony. I ran up on stage and sang "Bei Mir Bist Du Schön," which I sang as "My Dear Mr. Shane." I couldn't sing worth a damn, but you rated on applause and my people made the most racket. I won. Then I did "Playmate" and the dirty version of "La Cucaracha," which was my best number—they couldn't get me off the stage.

I was into being a musician too. This was 'cause I noticed they was gettin' all the fine women. Some ugly clown be shakin' maracas or a cowbell in front of a band and all the chippies be saying, oh, he's showbiz! Jive-ass bitches. Showbiz is the guy giving enemas to the elephants in the circus. Anyway, I got me a big conga drum out of the pawnshop and thought I was Chano Pozo, the great Cuban conga player used to work the skins for Dizzy Gillespie. Chano was the greatest. Bad too, big stud, used to be strongarm for the politicals in Havana. Came to Harlem, was bad there too. Somebody forgot how bad and blew him away. But he had some tough hands while he was around. My hands couldn't keep no beat, I was not about to be no great *conguero*. So be it. I'll get me that trim some other way.

Used to play at block parties—everybody in Harlem be there, dancin', drinkin', smokin', 'n fightin'. Had one on 107th Street, Copiens or Dragons came around—forget who—anyway, they started shooting pistols. My friend, Tato—"Carlito, they got me"—fell on his back under the lamp post. *Coño*, Tato, he's dead! No way, cap hit him on his belt buckle—didn't have a scratch. Just like in the movies. After that, I used to throw myself on the ground—"Tato, they got me!" I was a big ballbreaker as a kid.

But don't get me wrong, I used to do a lotta good things too. Although later on they never showed up in any of my probation reports. Like God forbid somebody abuse a buddy of mine. I'd travel for blocks to duke with a cat that would try to gorilla a friend—I tangle-assed with Sabu from 104th Street and Flash from 110th Street, bad motherfuckers in the first degree, and it wasn't even my beef. "This ain't witchoo, Carlito"—"Never mind, take to the street." That's the kind of guy I was. But sometimes could backfire on you. Like m'man Polito—went up to 113th Street to straighten a kid out for somebody. Polito told me he was a stringbean black kid. Skinny arms and legs. Polito was a regular lil' buzz saw. He said shee-it, I'll tear 'im up. Polito say that spook kid like to bust him every way but loose. Later on he found out the kid was Sandy Saddler.

One time I had to rumble a deaf-mute guy. On me like white-on-rice. Couldn't get off on this guy. Whipped me. I had respect for the handicapped after that.

A lot of Hollywood names in Harlem at the time. We had Tarzans and Sabus and Cheyennes. I remember a guy used to call himself Naiyoka—like from Pago Pago. We had Cochise and we had Apache. Sometimes a name could cause a problem. Like Cheyenne from the

Bronx would come down with ten or twelve guys to see Cheyenne from Harlem—"Who said your name was Cheyenne?"—"Not me, my name is Jacinto Quinones." I seen that one. Then you had a pimp name of Red Conk on account of he conked his hair red (hair was straight in them days one way or the other—Dixie Peach or Sulfur 8). We had a white guy named Negro, and we had a black guy named Indio. We had a lot of Louies—Louie the Jew (crazy Jew got killed in a stickup, spoke better Spanish than me), Louie Lump-Lump (had a funny-shaped head), Louie Push-Push (used to run fast). We had Tobacco, Chuleta, Machete, Frankie *La Cagona* (Frankie the Shitter).

How'd I exist on the street? Sometimes legit—like delivery boy on an ice truck, or a grocery, or a dry cleaner's. But mostly hustlin', thievin', break and entry—shootin' pool was my main stick. I used to catch merchant marines for a hundred, hundred-fifty dollars playin' nineball—this when I was fourteen or fifteen years old—always had good wrists. Then there was boostin' in department stores—and there was dice, cards, writin' numbers (single action) for Jakie Cooperman, one of the few Jew bookies left around. We had a little scare with Jakie once. Jakie used to book out of a candy store on 108th Street and Fifth Avenue—he was a degenerate gambler himself. Me and some other kids were hangin' around one night. This big black car pulled up with four rays of sunshine—older wops from the East 107th Street mob out of the Fox Star. Two stayed in the car, two came into the candy store. Skinny guy, Nino, he had half a button, cool head, he'd talk to you. The other guy, Buck, was a terror—looked like a buffalo, only bigger—and he used to carry a softball bat—was the bouncer at the Fox Star. God forbid he should catch you sneakin' in the side door. Buck stands by the door, Nino walks up to the counter and pulls an empty bag out of his coat (the two of them was wearin' black coats and black hats with the brim turned up—wops got this Al Capone shit down to a science). Anyway, the bag was a cement bag. Nino gives the bag to Moe, owner of the store—"This is for Jakie." Moe shit a milk shake right there. Then Nino turned to me and the rest of the kids—"Anybody here seen Jakie around?" No, not us, never happen. They split. We was shook up. Seems Jakie was into the shylocks for fifty thou. The wops said he ran away to the coast on them, but Jakie himself would have given you five hundred to one he was planted on Long Island. Wops was already leery about goin' up to Black Harlem. Not Buck (really Buccia)—he'd jump out of a car on 116th Street and Lenox Avenue bat in hand—"C'mere"—spook would run—one shot—lay 'im out. Buck didn't give a fuck. He went up in the mob later on. Stayed mean.

There was other guys like Buck around. *Abusadores*, we called them—abusers or ballbreakers. Uptown Harlem had one named Jenks, or Jinx. Bad nigger. Big—didn't fit through no door, 'cept sideways. Take everybody off. Take your money, your welfare check, your watch, your dope—take a wheelchair, glass eye. Mean. When he was outa jail, people stayed home. Jinx had a pretty long run, then he tried to run a game on a friend of mine. Shakedown. So much per week 'cause I'm bad. My buddy was hardnose, so he had to deal with Jinx. Shot him in the legs—kept coming. Shot him in the chest—kept coming. Finally stopped Jinx with a bullet through his head. All this time Jinx was chasing him around the bar. My friend had to do time for this. Judge said, "Victim was unarmed"—that motherfucker was armed when he was unarmed. Some judges will say, "Why didn't you go to the police?" The fuckin' police only want to know you as one of two "de's"—de deceased or de defendant. In between—"Don't bother me, I got a lotta paper work." If the judge took time to check out a "victim" like Jinx, he'd give the defendant the Distinguished Bronze Cross, first degree. And if His Honor had to live in the same tenement with a Jinx or a Buck, he'd put the contract out hisself. Buck and Jinx—some neighbors we had.

Another source of livelihood for me was a first-class Murphy game I used to run up on 111th Street with the tricks looking for whores. Me and m'partner Colorado used pencil and paper (that would impress the Johns)—"Okay, write it down, eh, Chico? These two gentlemen, ten dollars apiece—that's twenty dollars. No rough stuff or fancy fuckin', boys; Lolita is only sixteen and just startin' out. I'll hold the money." Colorado would go upstairs, then he'd call down, "Lolita wants to see the money and the list first, Pancho." Wait right here, boys, she's very shy—I'll call you from upstairs. You could come back an hour later and they'd still be waiting with their hard-on. Lo-leeta, Lo-letta, they'd be yodelin' in the canyon. Sometimes me and Colorado would fall down on the roof from laughing.

Them roofs was busy for us. Flyin' pigeons, flyin' kites, flyin' dope. Somebody was always jumpin' off the roof too. Usually some Rican who couldn't cut it on the street. But the street got him anyway—unless he jumped in the backyard.

Anyway, I was a busy lil' snot in them days.

Sometimes Moran the cop would get a bug up his ass and grab me or Colorado on the street and put us back in the Home. Maybe a kick in the ass and a few smacks in the face from a telephone book in the Twenty-third Precinct before he took us over. He wanted me to go over to another precinct to break chops—I said I was a citizen of this precinct and he couldn't deport me. To this day I don't pick up a phone that I don't say, "Moran of the Twenty-third Precinct." I used to do it then, figuring the phones in the poolroom or the bar was tapped and Moran's name would get on some shoo-fly tape. He was a tough sombitch. One night, one of them traveling carnivals came to the lot on 108th Street and Madison Avenue. This guy Lucky ran out of luck in a fight with some marine tiger who cut him to pieces with a butcher knife. I remember him on his back on the ground trying to kick up at the guy. He never made it to the emergency table at the Flower Hospital. Moran was there with some photographers from *Life* magazine and he got a write-up with pictures and all. Lucky was a sharp dresser, used to be in the furnished rooms on 107th Street between Park and Madison. He didn't come out too good in the pictures though. Moran, believing his own publicity, became a worse ballbuster than ever.

Another ballbuster cop was Schula or Schuler, known as "Cara de Palo" (Woodface). He was a fat guy with glasses, but he could move, 'specially the time they threw the garbage can off the roof at him.

Baddest of the bad was Big Jeff from the "Mutt and Jeff" detective team from the Twenty-third. One was a little wop, Lil' Jeff, the other a big mick, Big Jeff; you couldn't call either one Mutt or they'd break yo' ass. When they'd pull up to the poolroom on 106th Street and Madison, everybody start walkin'. Nearly everybody. Legend says that one time they wanted everybody lined up against the wall in the poolroom—"All you Puerto Ricans up against the wall"—this smart guy wouldn't get up—"Me no Puerto Rican, me Cuban"—*wap!* "Same shit." None of that "move-along-boys" jive in them days.

Little Jeff give you sass, Big Jeff look around like he ain't even listening, but if you gave backlip—wap!—Big Jeff laid you out. I ain't seen nobody, in the ring or out, hit harder than him. Elbow close to body, leverage—lights out. Better you fell off a roof than he should land on you. Big Jeff finally got put out of commission by a little P.R. name of Augie Robles. Robles was a contract killer, one of the few we had around there. I mean this dude would travel to other states on hits. Around Harlem, he'd feed off the policy bankers. Like, "You know me, Augie Robles; you got a thousand for me by Saturday, okay?" Everybody was scared shit of him. Big Jeff and Augie finally got around to it on 112th Street. There must have been ten thousand people watching that shootout. Just like in *Scarface*. Big Jeff, as usual, was the first bull through the door. Imagine, Augie Robles, cornered, with four, count 'em, four pistols, waiting on you. Shee-it. The bulls killed Augie that night, but not before Big Jeff got his knee blown up with a dum-dum. They tried to do this gunfight in a jive movie, *Madigan*. Big Jeff make Madigan look like a faggot. He was bad. But he wasn't no flake artist. He let me walk away from one that wasn't my doing even though he could have laid it on me. Bulls ain't never been my bag—but here's to you, anyway, Big Jeff. You done the right thing.

The Ricans had some other hairy guys. Was a guy, Cabezon, sat down in a barber chair at Lino's on 107th Street off Madison—"Lino, cut my hair short today. Tonight I'm going to settle with a guy. No telling where I'm gonna go afterward." That's cold. He goed it too. Electric chair.

Then was a guy, Johnny Lata, had his face cut by a rival pimp, Tony Navarro. Lata kept a straight razor in a pan filled with onions and water so that when he got his revenge, the scar on Tony's face would never heal. Lata did cut a forget-me-not on Tony's face, but the onion bit never checked out because Tony's liver gave out from too much coke not longer after. Tony had in his stable of four the best-lookin' whore in Harlem, a German war bride. When that *fenomeno* used to walk down the street I used to lay right down on the pavement— "Vee gates, fraulein"—but I was too broke to hit on her. When I think of all them fine women I didn't get nothin' of! Years later, after Tony died, I went to a party at Birdland and there she was with a spook band leader, one of the biggest in the country. Being broke never was no fun. I'll be dead or in jail, but I ain't ever gonna be broke. Believe that.

That's all I was ever interested in, makin' a dollar without hurtin' nobody. By my lights, I wasn't nasty or no troublemaker like them other motherfuckers around there; them guys was just burnin' up inside—the streets was battery acid to them. But the streets never whipped me that bad. I always saw the signs leading out—they was always painted green. Right this way, Mr. Brigante.

That guy Lino, the barber, used to worry about me. He was from the same mountain town in P.R. as my moms. They gonna kill you on the street, Carlito, they gonna lay you out in Gonzalez's Funeral before you're twenty-one. He wanted me to go to school like this guy on the block Wilfredo—imagine a grown man still going to school. Never learn nothin' out of no book. Keep your eyes and ears open, maybe read the *Daily News* to know who's gettin' locked up. If the smarts are there, you be all right—if they ain't, you can read books from shit to Shinnecock, ain't gonna help. Lino was a okay guy, used to bring me Baby Ruths when I was in the Home. He beat me to Gonzalez's. Here's to you, Lino—you done the best you could.

In the matters of race, the Puerto Ricans was ahead of their time in the forties. We accepted everybody. Nobody accepted us. Since black was not in style in them days, us P.R.'s declared ourselves white. We had a few variations but that didn't bother us none. The Cubans say, *El que no la tiene del Congo, la tiene del Carabalí.* Myself, I don't go for colored guys—but what about colored gals? This country can't do without them fine women—no kinda way. This country can make all them cars, toasters, ice boxes—goin' to the moon—meanwhile, it's still hung up on the race watzis. Bunch o' bullshit. If the rest of the country had listened to us it wouldn't be in the mess it is now. You take me for instance. I been light enough to sit in the front of a Jim Crow bus but dark enough to be worried about it. I been taken for spook, wop, and one faggot (used to come to the door jay-naked when I was delivering clothes for a cleaner) said I was Armenian. You're better off having a little bit of everything. That way you are what you have to be whenever you got to be. But who gives a shit, the main thing is to be good-lookin' so the broads will go for you.

Ricardo Montalban I ain't. But many a kitty has gone for me even when I didn't have big bread behind me. Believe that. It is true I spend all my time pursuin' good trim and, thank God, have a good rap. It is also true I have had knocked-out-lookin' broads. *Tremendos pollos.* White, black, tan, green, 'n in b'tween (never had no Chinese broad). In other words, I have done all right with the fair sex. I got no squawks in that apartment.

Fact is, I got no beef about my first twenty years. Had me a hell of a time. Warts and all, the streets was my playground. Couldn't ground me down—not the bulls, not the thugs, not the landlord, not the welfare, not nobody. I ran all over them. Fact is when I was in the get-o I didn't even know I was there. I didn't even know how dee-prived I was or that I was one of the downtrotted—it was news to me when the socio workers told me about it. I was happy as a pig in shit.

I would say by and large and mainly Carlos Brigante, mainly known as Carlito, had a good time as a kid. The next twenty years is more tricky. In other words, in the 1950s I was mostly a criminal. I have to admit that. And I did a lot of time for it too. But then Earl Bassey wised me up and Rocco Fabrizi gave me a break into the heavy wood. So like the sixties was big-time for me and I was less into bein' a thug and more like a class guy. But I'm runnin' ahead again.

Okay, the end of the forties saw me into the slams at Elmira Reception Center, Elmira, New York. Thereafter known as "the El." First whiff of country air. Alma mater for many a mope majorin' in thievery, roguery, lechery, and mopery. Thirty-six-month bit I did. I had been on probation for sticking a guy who'd busted my jaw with brass knuckles made out of ashcan handles. Probation don't mean I didn't have a few things going—burglaries, cars, like that. So like I'm shooting dice on 105th Street off Madison Avenue on a Saturday afternoon when this bad-ass named Chago grabs all the money on the ground and says, "These dice are loaded. You guys are robbing me; I'm taking the money," and he pulls out the difference, size .38, so I say, "Motherfucker, you ain't going nowhere with my bread."

"I'll kill you, Carlito."

"Kill me, *hijo de puta*, kill me—"

Everything is real quiet now except for Chago's breathing—he ain't got no heart. I grab the piece, bust him in the face with it; he falls down some basement steps, and I grab a garbage can full of ashes and throw it on him. That night I'm shooting nineball in

Ramon's parlor on 106th Street and Madison when Mutt and Jeff from the two-three squad come in.

"Chago's over at the Flower Hospital. He's asking for you, Carlito."

"Chago who? What right you—"

Smack. Right off my ear.

"Okay, let's go see him."

No lineup, no reading of rights—they even gave me an admission. Times were rough. Judge put me away—felonious assault, violation of probation. For Chago, they shoulda give me a medal.

In the Joint, thirty-six months. Up there I meet a lot of the boys, including Rocco Fabrizi, who was up for stealing cars. He was tight with Earl Bassey. Earl was up there for dealing in pot. I'd been hearing about him on the street in Harlem, he was the war counselor of some click uptown on Lenox Avenue. Earl was around our age but he was slick beyond his years. He could see something coming around the corner, like he'd say, "So-and-so is a faggot," and there would be this big stud with tattoos and muscles blowing everybody in the Joint. He knew things. I can't explain it; he never went to school but he could read people in minutes. His skin was black, but his eyes were like yellow, and when he put them on you everything was cool, like calm. Nothing went down without discussing it with Earl. Even the hacks would check out a beef with Earl.

Me and him got real tight when I started boxing again. Even in the street when I was smoking pot and drinking wine, my hands were quick and my wind wouldn't quit. Like I'd get inside a cat and hook to the body—I'd catch a few or be pushed off, but I'd get back inside—I'm swinging without stop—most guys couldn't stay with me. Earl had fought pro in the ring. He was my trainer, taught me how to hook to the head, how to finish a cat when you hurt him. I took a few guys out and my rep was made. Like Earl used to say, "Don't mess with Hoppy." Being Earl was smarter than me, I'd listen to him. He'd come on with, "Look here, Holmes, you got to dig yo'self—you gonna be on the street soon, forget about that okey-doke shit— gorilla-ing people, robbing pads—the shit is on, Briss, I got the word from Rocco—the junk is already here. And we is in—you think some guinea is going up to 125th and Lenox to deal with the niggers or to 111th and Fifth to deal with the spics? They gonna need distributors with brains and with heart—stand-up motherfuckers. I don't know about you, but I'm declaring myself in. These wops don't fuck around, bro—you got to play with their rules. Your word is your life—they make a meet, be there! This Mickey Mouse jive with the pussy and the coke and the booze don't mean nothin'. Got to be cool, stay clean. Make the move a few times a year—that's it. After a while, I'll have my own crew—then I'm gonna make my own world. I ain't gonna be a nigger all my life, pushing wooden Cadillacs on 37th Street—not Mrs. Bassey's boy. I'm going all the way—they got to kill me, Jack, kill me!"

"What about me, Earl, what about me?"

"You gonna be my man with the Ricans, Chappie—they ain't nothing but niggers turned inside out."

Rocco was from another garage—but a boss-type. Tall, lean, with light hair, he didn't look like no eye-talian to me. And he didn't give you the wise-guy jive. He was mobbed up with the Pleasant Avenue outfit. But his uncle was a made-guy, a lieutenant with the Mulberry Street crew—a heavy hitter—so like you knew that Rocco was marked. He couldn't miss, he was a down cat, and he was connected. Rocco didn't talk with no *dese* and *dose*; he spoke nice and soft—like dignity—but he wasn't no punk. Word was he had already iced some greaseball in the Bronx whose bail had dropped too low. The only thing wrong with Rocco was his love life; he had this thing for a P.R. chick, which in those days was unheard of, so like his uncle kept him in the boondocks—but I know he'd work it out. Like I say, he was a natural boss-type.

The three of us used to pal out. They'd rap and I'd listen.

"Earl, I'm out of the doghouse, so I'll be moving downtown—you know where to reach me. I'm not promising you guys anything, but if I get a shot, then I'm dealing you in. We may connect once a year, or even five years—in the meantime I don't even know if you guys are alive. We meet, we deal, good-bye. Now I'm not talking Harlem shit, I'm talking kilos, up to ten thou a kilo. On my okay you're going to get stuff on consignment at the beginning. You cross me, I'm dead, because I'm responsible for you—but you know you go right behind me. I'm moving up; you guys can move with me or stay in the shithouse hustling quarters."

"I'm your man, Rocco."

"Deal me in, Rocco."

It's hard to explain, but when you're doing time with a man you can read him faster than when you're on the street. He can't hide behind his rep or his clothes—shit like that don't work inside. Inside, all you got is mostly yourself. Like Earl used to say, yo' hole and yo' soul is buck neck-id in the Joint. So that's how come three cats from different alleys got close and stayed close for twenty years. The time was ripe, was overdue—but that don't mean nothin' if the right people ain't on the scene. Me and Earl was the right people, and we was ready. We needed a break. Rocco—Rocco had the inside rail from before, what with his uncle, Dominick Cocozza, who was a boss. But he saw their thing had to open up—open up or it was gonna bust open.

So he brought us in out of the rain. He didn't do it overnight, 'specially for me; I was still a cowboy for years yet. But I knew he knew I was stand-up, and later than sooner he would cut me loose into the big bucks. Earl first, then me. Rocco was the icebreaker and he done the right thing. And it took balls, because there was fool wops that couldn't see it—no put grits, rice, and beans in the pasta. Prejudiced old fucks like Rocco's boss, Pete Amadeo (*maldita sea su madre*), who thought they could sit inside the one tent with a whole bunch of Indians like me and Earl runnin' around outside bare-ass in the cold. Not to forget the hole the feds was diggin' under the floor.

Sick—some of them guys is sick too. You take Amadeo—a/k/a Petey A. One night at the Copa—this is when Tom Jones was at his peak. All the wise guys 'n dolls was jammed in—place was hysteria. Broads throwin' their keys, their drawers even, at Jones. Pete says to this button-guy with him,

"He's a fuckin' nigger. All this noise over a fuckin' nigger."

"No, Pete, you got it wrong—he's English."

"I say he's a fuckin' nigger, awright?"

"Eh, yeah, you're right, Pete—lookit the way he dances."

We split from the El in the order we came in. First Rocco, then Earl, then me. I hit Harlem like Sonny hit Floyd.

MIGUEL PIÑERO

Short Eyes

BROWN   On the gate.

(Gate opens and CLARK DAVIS *enters, goes to stage center.* BROWN *closes gate and exits)*

CUPCAKES   Hey, Longshoe . . . one of your kin . . . look-a-like sin just walked in. . . .

EL RAHEEM   Another devil.

LONGSHOE   Hey . . . hey, whatdayasay . . . My name's Longshoe Charlie Murphy. Call me Longshoe. What's your name?

CLARK   Davis . . . Clark . . . Ah . . . Clark Davis . . . Clark is my first name.

PACO   Clark Kent.

CUPCAKES   Mild-mannered, too.

OMAR   No, no, Superman.

(Other ad-libs: "Faster than a speeding bullet," etc.)

PACO   Oye . . . Shoe . . . Está bueno . . . Pa' rajalo . . .

LONGSHOE   Back . . . back . . . boy . . . no está bueno . . . anyway, no mucho . . . como Cupcake.

PACO   Vaya.

LONGSHOE   Pay them no mind . . . crazy spics . . . where you locking?

CLARK   Upper D 15.

LONGSHOE   Siberia, huh? . . . Tough.

CLARK   First time in the joint.

LONGSHOE   Yeah? Well, I better hip you to what's happening fast.

ICE   Look out for your homey, Shoe.

OMAR   Second.

LONGSHOE   Look here, this is our section . . . white . . . dig? That's the

Rican table, you can sit there if they give you permission . . . Same goes with the black section.

ICE Say it loud.

OMAR I'm black and proud.

ICE Vaya!

LONGSHOE Most of the fellas are in court. I'm the Don Gee here. You know what that mean, right? Good . . . Niggers and the spics don't give us honkies much trouble. We're cool half-ass. This is a good floor. Dynamite hack on all shifts. Stay away from the black gods. . . .

(NETT appears outside gate)

NETT On the gate.

LONGSHOE You know them when you see them.

(NETT opens gate and enters)

NETT On the chow.

ICE What we got, Mr. Nett?

NETT Baloney à la carte.

ICE Shit, welfare steaks again.

(All exit except CLARK and LONGSHOE. Gate stays open. The men reenter with sandwiches and return to their respective places. NETT closes gate and exits)

LONGSHOE Black go on the front of the line, we stay in the back . . . It's okay to rap with the blacks, but don't get too close with any of them. Ricans, too. We're the minority here, so be cool. If you hate yams, keep it to yourself. Don't show it. But also don't let them run over you. Ricans are funny people. Took me a long time to figure them out, and you know something, I found out that I still have a lot to learn about them. I rap spic talk. They get a big-brother attitude about the whites in jail. But they also back the niggers to the T.

ICE *(Throws LONGSHOE a sandwich)* Hey, Shoe.

LONGSHOE If a spic pulls a razor blade on you and you don't have a mop wringer in your hands . . . run . . . If you have static with a nigger and they ain't no white people around . . . get a spic to watch your back, you may have a chance . . . That ain't no guarantee . . . If you have static with a spic, don't get no nigger to watch your back 'cause you ain't gonna have none.

OMAR You can say that again.

ICE Two times.

LONGSHOE You're a good-looking kid . . . You ain't stuff and you don't want to be stuff. Stay away from the bandidos. Paco is one of them . . . Take no gifts from no one.

(NETT appears outside entrance gate)

NETT Clark Davis . . . Davis.

CLARK Yes, that's me.

NETT On the gate.

(NETT opens gate, enters with CLARK's belongings, leaves gate open)

Come here . . . come here . . . white trash . . . filth . . . Let me tell you something and you better listen good 'cause I'm only going to say it one time . . . and one time only. This is a nice floor . . . a quiet floor . . . There has never been too much trouble on this floor . . . With you, I smell trouble . . . I don't question the warden's or the captain's motive for putting you on this floor . . . But for once I'm gonna ask why they put a sick fucking degenerate like you on my floor . . . If you just talk out the side of your mouth one time . . . if you look at me sideways one time . . . if you mispronounce my name once, if you pick up more food than you can eat . . . if you call me for something I think is unnecessary . . . if you oversleep, undersleep . . . if . . . if . . . if . . . you give me just one little reason . . . I'm gonna break your face up so bad your own mother won't know you. . . .

LONGSHOE Mr. Nett is being kinda hard—

NETT Shut up . . . I got a eight-year-old daughter who was molested by one of those bastards . . . stinking sons of bitches and I just as well pretend that he was you, Davis, do you understand that . . . ?

PACO Short eyes.

LONGSHOE Short eyes? Short eyes . . . Clark, are you one of those short-eyes freaks . . . are you a short-eyes freak?

NETT Sit down, Murphy . . . I'm talking to this . . . this scumbag . . . yeah, he's a child rapist . . . a baby rapist, how old was she? How old? . . . Eight . . . seven . . . Disgusting bastard . . . Stay out of my sight . . . 'cause if you get in my face just one time . . . don't forget what I told you . . . I'll take a nightstick and ram it clean up your asshole . . . I hope to God that they take you off this floor, or send you to Sing Sing . . . The men up there know what to do with degenerates like you.

CLARK I . . . I . . .

NETT All right, let's go . . . Lock in . . . lock in . . . for the count . . . Clark, the captain outside on the bridge wants to see you. I hope he takes you off this floor. . . .

LONGSHOE Hey, Davis . . .

(Walks up to him and spits in his face. Men exit)

NETT Juan, stay out and clean the dayroom. Omar, take the tier.

(CAPTAIN ALLARD appears on the catwalk above. CLARK joins ALLARD and they carry on inaudible conversation. Crossing from stage right to stage left on the catwalk are CUPCAKES, ICE, and LONGSHOE, followed by MR. BROWN. As LONGSHOE passes he bumps CLARK. MR. BROWN stops beside CLARK, and CAPTAIN ALLARD chases after LONGSHOE to catwalk above left)

ALLARD Hey, just a minute, you. That's just the kind of stuff that's going to cease.

(BROWN and CLARK exit catwalk above right and appear at entrance gate stage right)

BROWN On the gate.

(BROWN opens gate, CLARK enters dayroom, BROWN closes gate. CLARK says something inaudible to BROWN)

You're lucky if you get a call before Christmas.

(BROWN exits. CLARK leans on gate)

LONGSHOE Get off that fuckin' gate.

(While the above was going on, JUAN has taken his cleaning equipment from the shower upstage left and placed can of Ajax and rag on the toilet area upstage center, and broom, mop, bucket, dust-

pan, dust broom, dust box in downstage left corner. JUAN *sits at table,* CLARK *at window.* JUAN *pours coffee, offers* CLARK *a sandwich.* CLARK *crosses to table and sits)*

JUAN Hey, man, did you really do it?

*(*OMAR *starts chant offstage)*

CLARK I don't know.

JUAN What do you mean, you don't know? What you think I am, a fool, or something out of a comic book.

CLARK No . . . I don't mean to sound like that, I . . . I . . .

JUAN Look, man, either you did it or you didn't.

*(*JUAN *stands)*

That all there is to it. . . .

CLARK I don't know if I did it or not.

JUAN You better break that down to me

(Sits)

'cause you lost me.

CLARK What I mean is that I may have done it or I may not have . . . I just don't remember . . . I remember seeing that little girl that morning . . . I sat in Bellevue thirty-three days and I don't remember doing anything like that to that little girl.

JUAN You done something like that before, haven't you?

CLARK I . . . ye . . . yes . . . I have . . . How did you know?

JUAN Your guilt flies off your tongue, man.

(Stands)

Sound like one of those guys in an encounter session

(Starts to sweep)

looking to dump their shit off on someone . . . You need help . . . The bad part about it is that you know it. . . .

CLARK Help? I need help? Yes . . . yes, I do need help . . . But I'm afraid to find it . . . Why? . . . Fear . . . just fear . . . Perhaps fear of knowing that I may be put away forever . . . I have a wife and kid I love very much . . . and I want to be with them. I don't ever want

to be away from them . . . ever. But now this thing has happened
. . . I don't know what to do . . . I don't know . . . If I fight it in
court, they'll end up getting hurt . . . If I don't, it'll be the same
thing . . . Jesus help me . . . God forgive me.

JUAN 'Cause man won't.

(JUAN at downstage left corner sweeping up dust)

CLARK No, man won't . . . Society will never forgive me . . . or accept me back once this is openly known.

(JUAN begins to stack chairs stage right. CLARK hands JUAN a chair)

I think about it sometimes and . . . funny, I don't really feel disgusted
. . . just ashamed . . . You wanna . . .

JUAN Listen to you? It's up to you . . . You got a half hour before the
floor locks out unless you wanna go public like AA.

(JUAN picks up stool)

CLARK No . . . no . . . no . . . I can't . . . I didn't even talk with the
psychiatrist in the bughouse.

JUAN Run it. . . .

(JUAN puts down stool)

CLARK You know, somehow it seems like there's no beginning.
Seems like I've always been in there all my life. I have like little picture incidents running across my mind . . . I remember being . . .
fifteen or sixteen years old

(JUAN crosses upstage center to clean toilet)

or something around that age, waking up to the sound of voices coming from the living room . . . cartoons on the TV . . . They were
watching cartoons on the TV, two little girls. One was my sister,
and her friend . . . And you know how it is when you get up in the
morning, the inevitable hard-on is getting up with you. I draped
the sheet around my shoulders . . . Everyone else was sleeping . . .
The girl watching TV with my sister . . . yes . . . Hispanic . . . pale-
looking skin . . . She was eight . . . nine . . . ten . . . what the difference, she was a child . . . She was very pretty—high cheekbones,
flashing black eyes . . . She was wearing blue short pants . . . tight-

fitting . . . a white blouse, or shirt . . . My sister . . . she left to do number two . . .

(*JUAN returns to stage right*)

She told her friend wait for me, I'm going to do number two, and they laughed about it. I sneaked in standing a little behind her . . . She felt me standing there and turned to me . . . She smiled such a pretty little smile . . . I told her I was a vampire and she laughed . . . I spread the sheets apart and she suddenly stopped laughing . . . She just stood there staring at me . . . Shocked? Surprised? Intrigued? Don't know . . . don't know . . . She just stood and stared . . .

(*JUAN crosses to downstage left*)

I came closer like a vampire . . . She started backing away . . . ran toward the door . . . stopped, looked at me again. Never at my face . . . my body . . . I couldn't really tell whether or not the look on her face was one of fear . . . but I'll never forget that look.

(*BROWN crosses on catwalk from left to right with a banana. Stands at right*)

I was really scared that she'd tell her parents. Weeks passed without confrontation . . . and I was feeling less and less afraid . . . But that's not my thing, showing myself naked to little girls in schoolyards.

(*JUAN crosses to downstage right corner and begins to mop from downstage right to downstage left*)

One time . . . no, it was the first time . . . the very first time. I was alone watching TV . . . Was I in school or out . . . And there was this little Puerto Rican girl from next door . . . Her father was the new janitor . . . I had seen her before . . . many times . . . sliding down the banister . . . Always her panties looked dirty . . . She was . . . oh, why do I always try to make their age higher than it really was . . . even to myself. She was young, much too young . . . Why did she come there? For who? Hundred questions. Not one small answer . . . not even a lie flickers across my brain.

OFFSTAGE VOICE All right, listen up. The following inmates report for sanitation duty: Smalls, Gary; Medena, James; Pfeifer, Willis; Martinez, Raul. Report to CO grounds for sanitation duty.

CLARK How did I get to the bathroom with her? Don't know. I was standing there with her, I was combing her hair. I was combing her hair. Her curly reddish hair . . .

(JUAN crosses upstage right, starts to mop upstage right to upstage left)

I was naked . . . naked . . . except for these flower-printed cotton underwears . . . No slippers, barefooted . . . Suddenly I get this feeling over me . . . like a flash fever . . . and I'm hard . . . I placed my hands on her small shoulders . . . and pressed her hand and placed it on my penis . . . Did she know what to do? Or did I coerce her? I pulled down my drawers . . . But then I felt too naked, so I put them back on . . . My eyes were closed . . . but I felt as if there was this giant eye off in space staring at me . . .

(JUAN stops upstage left and listens to CLARK, who is unaware JUAN is in back of him)

I opened them and saw her staring at me in the cabinet mirror. I pulled her back away from the view of the mirror . . . My hands up her dress, feeling her underdeveloped body . . . I . . . I . . . I began pulling her underwear down on the bowl . . . She resisted . . . slightly, just a moment . . . I sat on the bowl . . . She turned and threw her arms around my neck and kissed me on the lips . . . She gave a small nervous giggle . . . I couldn't look at her . . . I closed my eyes . . . turned her body . . . to face away from me . . . I lubricated myself . . . and . . . I hear a scream, my own . . .
. . . The next day I went home and met the little Puerto Rican girl again . . . Almost three times a week . . . The rest of the time I would be in the playground or in the children's section of the movies . . . But you know something? Er, er . . .

(CLARK moves toward JUAN, who is in downstage left corner)

JUAN Juan.
CLARK Yes, Juan . . . Juan the listener . . . the compassionate . . . you know something, Juan . . .
. . . I couldn't help myself . . . I couldn't help myself . . . Something drove me to it . . . I thought of killing myself . . . but I just couldn't go through with it . . . I don't really wanna die . . . I wanted to stop, really I did . . . I just didn't know how. I thought maybe I was

crazy . . . but I read all types of psychology books . . . I heard or read somewhere that crazy people can't distinguish right from wrong . . . Yet I can . . . I know what's right and I know what I'm doing is wrong, yet I can't stop myself . . .

JUAN Why didn't you go to the police or a psychiatrist . . .

(JUAN crosses to shower room upstage left)

CLARK I wanted to many a time . . . But know that the police would find some pretext to kill me . . . And a psychiatrist . . . well, if he thought he couldn't help me he'd turn me over to them or commit me to some nut ward . . . Juan, try to understand me.

(JUAN comes out of shower room and starts putting away his cleaning equipment)

JUAN Motherfucker, try to understand you . . . if I wasn't trying to, I would have killed you . . . stone dead, punk . . .

(JUAN, at downstage left corner, picks up broom and bucket)

The minute you said that thing about the Rican girls . . . If I was you I'd ask transfer to protection . . . 'cause

(JUAN returns to shower room)

if you remain on this floor you're asking to die . . . You'll be committing involuntary suicide . . .

(JUAN again crosses to downstage left corner, picks up remaining equipment, crosses to toilet, picks up Ajax and rag, and crosses to shower room)

Shit, why the fuck did you have to tell me all of it . . . You don't know me from Adam . . .

(JUAN comes out of shower room and crosses to CLARK, stage center)

Why the hell did you have to make me your father confessor? Why? Why didn't you stop, why?

CLARK 'Cause you asked. 'Cause you . . . What I told you I didn't even tell the doctors at the observation ward . . . Everything is coming down on me so fast . . . I needed to tell it all . . . to someone . . . Juan, you were willing to listen.

(Whistle blows)

JUAN What you want to see me about, Clark?

CLARK Look, what I told you earlier . . . er . . . that between me and you . . . like, I don't know why I even said that, just . . . just that . . . man, like everything was just coming down on me . . . My wife . . . she was at the hospital . . . She . . . she didn't even look at me . . . once, not once . . . Please . . . don't let it out . . . please . . . I'll really go for help this time . . . I promise.

JUAN What happened at the PI stand?

CLARK Nothing . . . nothing . . . happened . . .

JUAN Did she identify you? Did she?

CLARK I don't know. I didn't see anybody. They put me next to a bunch of the other men about my size, weight . . . You—the whole lineup routine. I didn't see anybody or anything but the people there and this voice that kept asking me to turn around to say, "Hello, little girl." That's all.

JUAN Nothing else?

CLARK No.

JUAN You mean they didn't make you sign some papers?

CLARK No.

JUAN Was there a lawyer for you there? Somebody from the courts?

CLARK Juan, I really don't know . . . I didn't see anybody . . . and they didn't let me speak to anyone at all . . . They hustled me in and hustled me right out. . . .

JUAN That means you have a chance to beat this case . . . Did they tell you what they are holding you for?

CLARK No . . . no one told me anything.

JUAN If they are rushing it—the PI—that could mean they only are waiting on the limitation to run out.

CLARK What does that all mean?

JUAN What it means is that you will get a chance to scar up some more little girls' minds.

CLARK Don't say that, Juan. Please don't think like that. Believe me, if I thought I couldn't seek help after this ordeal, I would have never—I mean, I couldn't do that again.

JUAN How many times you've said that in the street and wind up molesting some kid in the park?

CLARK Believe me, Juan . . . please believe me. I wouldn't anymore.

JUAN Why should I?

CLARK 'Cause I told you the truth before. I told you what I haven't told God.

JUAN That's because God isn't in the House of Detention.

CLARK Please, Juan, why are you being this way? What have I done to you?

JUAN What have you done to me? What you've done to me? It's what you've done, period. It's the stand that you are forcing me to take.

CLARK You hate me.

JUAN I don't hate you. I hate what you've done. What you are capable of doing. What you might do again.

CLARK You sound like a judge.

JUAN In this time and place I am your judge.

CLARK No . . . no. You are not . . . And I'm sick and tired of people judging me.

JUAN Man, I don't give a fuck what you're sick and tired about. What you told about yourself was done because of the pressure. People say and do weird things under pressure.

CLARK I'm not used to this.

JUAN I don't care what you're used to. I got to make some kind of thing about you.

CLARK No, you don't have to do anything. Just let me live.

JUAN Let you live?

CLARK I can't make this . . . this kind of life. I'll die.

JUAN Motherfucker, don't cry on me.

CLARK Cry . . . why shouldn't I cry . . . why shouldn't I feel sorry for myself . . . I have a right to . . . I have some rights . . . and when these guys get back from the sick call . . . I'm gonna tell them what the captain said to me, that if anybody bothers me to tell him . . .

JUAN Then you will die.

CLARK I don't care one way or the other. Juan, when I came here I already had been abused by the police . . . threatened by a mob the newspaper created . . . Then the judge, for my benefit and the benefit of society, had me committed to observation. Placed in an isolated section of some nut ward . . . viewed by interns and visitors like some abstract object, treated like a goddamn animal monster by a bunch of inhuman, incompetent, third-rate, unqualified, unfit psychopaths calling themselves doctors.

JUAN I know the scene.

CLARK No, you don't know . . . electros—sedatives—hypnosis—therapy . . . humiliated by some crank nurses who strapped me to my bed and played with my penis to see if it would get hard for "big girls like us."

JUAN Did it?

CLARK Yeah . . . yes, it did.

JUAN My father used to say he would fuck 'em from eight to eighty, blind, cripple, and/or crazy.

CLARK Juan, you are the only human being I've met.

JUAN Don't try to leap me up . . . 'cause I don't know how much of a human being I would be if I let you make the sidewalk. But there's no way I could stop you short of taking you off the count.

(NETT appears at gate)

CLARK Mr. Nett. Mr. Nett . . .

(CLARK runs to window ledge upstage center. OMAR jumps on ledge with him. NETT appears at gate, opens it, walks in, sees what's happening, and turns to go, but remains)

Okay. Okay. Don't hurt me any more. Go 'head, do what you want. Go 'head, you filthy bastards. Go 'head, Mr. Nett, don't think you can walk away from this. I'll tell the captain. I'll bring you all before the courts. You bastards. You too, you fat faggot.

JUAN Shut up . . . shut up.

PACO You gonna do what?

(PACO pulls out homemade knife)

LONGSHOE He's gonna squeal. He's gonna rat us out.

(OMAR jumps off window ledge)

JUAN Ice, let him go.

EL RAHEEM You're in this, too, Ice. We'll all get more time.

CLARK I'll make sure you get life, you son-of-a-bitch.

MR. NETT I'll lose my job.

(Opens gate to look down corridor)

CLARK I'll make sure you go to jail. My father has money . . . plenty
money.

JUAN Shut up, Clark . . . shut up.

(PACO runs toward CLARK to kill him. EL RAHEEM restrains him)

PACO I ain't doing no more time than I have to.

OMAR Paco, that murder.

CUPCAKES What are we going to do?

LONGSHOE Kill the motherfucking rat.

MR. NETT Kill him—it's self-defense.

EL RAHEEM Suicide . . . suicide . . . He did it to himself.

JUAN It's murder. Ice, it's murder. You'll be part of it, too.

PACO Hold him, Ice.

CUPCAKES I don't want to do more time.

LONGSHOE Kill him . . . kill him . . . kill the sick motherfucker.

(LONGSHOE pulls CLARK off window ledge)

PACO Here, El . . . He's a devil . . . kill him . . . You said the devil is
gonna die anyway.

(PACO gives the knife to EL RAHEEM)

OMAR Kill him, El . . . kill him.

EL RAHEEM Hold him . . . hold him. . . .

*(CLARK runs to downstage right corner. OMAR and LONGSHOE grab
him and hold him)*

PACO Stab him.

MR. NETT No, cut his throat.

EL RAHEEM Cut his throat.

PACO Do it, El . . . Do it, El.

(EL brings the knife down to CLARK's neck)

LONGSHOE Go on, nigger, kill him.

EL RAHEEM I can't . . . I can't . . . I don't have the heart . . . I can't . . .
do it.

LONGSHOE What you mean? You can do it . . . You talk of killing
Whitey every day.

EL RAHEEM   I can't do it. I just can't kill a man like that. Not that way. Get up and fight, honky. Let him up and I could do it.

LONGSHOE   Kill him . . . standing up . . . laying down . . . sitting . . . Either way, he's dead.

EL RAHEEM   It's not the same thing . . . I just can't do it.

LONGSHOE   Kill him . . . kill him.

PACO   He's a devil, El Raheem.

CUPCAKES   Oh, my God.

(CUPCAKES pushes EL RAHEEM to shower and restrains him)

JUAN   Don't, El, don't do it. That's not the way a black god kills. That's a devil's way.

CLARK   Please . . . don't kill me . . . please, I didn't mean what I said. I didn't mean it. I won't tell anybody . . . please do what you want but don't kill me. I got a wife and kids. Please don't . . . please.

EL RAHEEM

(Breaking loose from CUPCAKES, tries once more to kill CLARK)

Allah Akbar, Allah Akbar, I can't do it—I just can't do it.

LONGSHOE   Give that knife, punk.

(Swings knife, cutting CLARK's throat)

Scream, bastard . . . rat . . . Scream . . . monster . . . die . . . die. . . .

(Everyone is silent. NETT closes gate and exits)

REINALDO POVOD

Poppa Dio!

CHARACTERS

ANGELO: *Mid-thirties. Hispanic. Is tall, restless and commanding. Angelo is a man consumed with that drive to have it all. Happiness, money, women.*

MAFIA: *Is her stage name—from when she was performing in Boston's "Combat Zone" as a stripper. She is the mother of Angelo, and she is fifty years old. But she looks as old as her son, somewhere between her late thirties and early forties. Young, eager, well-built. Clearly a woman from the backwoods of Puerto Rico. Still eager, desirous, even anxious—keenly in search of life and for love. Trembling on the brink of despair. Also not afraid to take the final leap.*

SCENE: Angelo and Mafia's kitchen in the South Bronx. Basically, it is a kitchen similar to the one in "Nijinsky Choked His Chicken." The only difference is that Angelo and Mafia's kitchen is littered with garbage, beer bottles, and clothes. The major difference is that this particular family possesses a telephone! The lights in this kitchen are dimmed—to 15 watts. A typical and undistinguished unhappy home.

TIME: Autumn.

SCENE 1

AT RISE: Midnight. All LIGHTS are down but the corner STREET-LAMP, shining through the window lighting the stage dimly. The faint sounds of a WOMAN CRYING are heard and increase in volume. It is more in anguish than hysteria. The audience will only see her bare legs. MAFIA is in her nightgown, laying on the floor where she had fallen from being struck.

ANGELO. *(In a fury. HE enters the stage, looking around the kitchen.)* I hate you! God, I hate you! I hate you so fuckin' much! *(Crosses over to the refrigerator, looks to the side of it and takes out a baseball bat. ANGELO silently stands, holding the baseball bat, glaring down on Mafia. MAFIA wakes instantly, perceives his action, and crawls over to Angelo.)*
MAFIA. *(Sobs.)* No, no, no, no. *(ANGELO raises the baseball bat over his head. MAFIA sobs uncontrollably.)* No, no, no, no!

(MAFIA turns away, too weak to stand and run. SHE crawls, rushing toward the exit. ANGELO pursues her. Silently. Calmly. When SHE has exited, ANGELO will stop at the edge of the exit, raise his

hand, and proceed to beat Mafia with it. Taking sharp, precise, shots at her. The audience is only seeing ANGELO lift and come down with the bat. They will also be hearing the thud and her GROANS. ANGELO will swing the bat until he is exhausted, building his swing until the bat falls from his grasp.)

ANGELO.   *(Turns and faces the audience, eyes full of tears.)* Poppa Dio! . . . *(Drops to his knees.)* Poppa Dio . . . *(Sobs.)* I beat her to death. *(Covers his face with his hands, sobbing uncontrollably.* "Poppa Dio," *he repeats over and over.)* I beat her to death . . . My mother . . . Poppa Dio! I killed her, Poppa Dio! . . . I killed my mother. *(Sobs, and covers his face again.)* Poppa Dio! Poppa Dio! . . . *(LIGHTS slowly dim out.)*

SCENE 2

TIME: A few hours earlier.

AT RISE: The RADIO on top of the refrigerator is going. ANGELO stands at the window looking down at the street below. HE is dressed soberly in a dark suit, shirt and tie. Is smoking a cigarette. Presently, MAFIA is by the stove stirring a pot of rice with a large cooking spoon. SHE is in her nightgown, and is barefooted. MAFIA looks over at her son in fascination. ANGELO loudly snorts—three times.

MAFIA.   Spit that out.
ANGELO.   *(Without looking over at her.)* Too late. I swallowed it.
MAFIA.   . . . It turns my stomach.
ANGELO.   It coats mine. *(SHE gives up on him and starts to stir the pot of rice again. ANGELO listens to the music, with his eyes far away—MAFIA is dumbfounded. SHE purposely slams her cooking spoon against her pot of rice.)* What was that? The phone?
MAFIA.   No!

(The TELEPHONE rings.)

ANGELO.   That's for me. *(MAFIA turns off the RADIO. It is obvious that SHE wants to listen.)* Why you turn off the radio? (HE an-

swers the telephone.) Hello? Yeah, this is Angelo. What's wrong? *(MAFIA looks at her son, not stirring the rice. A long silence.)* Why you doin' this? What did I do wrong?!

MAFIA. Who's that—Virgin?

ANGELO. *(Pauses heavily. Depressed. Deeply hurt.)* That's not a reason.

MAFIA. It's Virgin—I know it's Virgin.

ANGELO. I wanna see you.

MAFIA. Hang up—hang up on her.

ANGELO. Please, Virgin.

MAFIA. *(Angry)* Gimme the phone. *(Reaches out for it.)*

ANGELO. *(Turns on her.)* What are you doing?!!!!

MAFIA. Gimme the phone.

ANGELO. I'm on the phone.

MAFIA. It's my phone.

ANGELO. I wanna see you, Virgin.

MAFIA. *(Angry)* E'tupido.

ANGELO. *(Gives her a hard stare.)* You at yer mother's?

MAFIA. That phone is mine—I pay for it.

ANGELO. She called me!

MAFIA. So what?

ANGELO. Here. Here, here. *(HE goes into his pocket—counts off a few dollars—and throws them on the floor at his mother's feet.)*

MAFIA. *(Furious—kicks the money.)* E'tupido. Animal!

ANGELO. Come over, Virgin.

MAFIA. I don't want that slut here. *(ANGELO punches the wall.)*

MAFIA. Good. That's good. Bang your face! Go 'head. Better.

ANGELO. Don't leave me, Virgin.

MAFIA. *(Laughs)* Ha! I told you.

ANGELO. Don't go to Puerto Rico. Lemme talk to you.

MAFIA. Oh—I thank God.

ANGELO. I love you, Virgin.

MAFIA. *(Furious)* Que 'stupido!

ANGELO. Virgin? . . . Virgin? Hello, Virgin?

MAFIA. Hang up—she's gone.

ANGELO. *(About to break down.)* Virgin?

MAFIA. *(SHE roughly snatches the phone from him.)* Hang up.

ANGELO. *(HE snatches back the phone.)* Virgin? *(HE is quietly sob-*

bing. The words pour out with urgency and desperation.) Virgin? I'm not feeling good ... *(MAFIA gestures with bitter disgust.)* I know you're still there—I love you, Virgin—Come over, Virgin? Come over. *(HE sobs.)*

MAFIA. *(Snatches the phone and hangs it up.)* You got no shame. It turns my stomach. *(SHE walks over to her stove—stirs her pot of rice. ANGELO walks over to the window and loudly sobs.)* Go to bed. Lay down. *(SHE loudly strikes her spoon against the pot of rice.)*

ANGELO. Stop that! Stoppit! *(HE sobs. Opens the window.)*

MAFIA. Why are you opening the window? Don't open the window— it's cold outside. *(ANGELO sobs, pacing.)* Close the window.

ANGELO. *(Lunges for the window with a loud sigh. MAFIA screams!)* I wanna die!

MAFIA. *(Leaps forward and wraps her arms tightly around his waist. ANGELO sobs on the windowsill. SHE is angered.)* Come inside. C'mon. You want people to see you?

ANGELO. I don't care. *(Loudly sighs. MAFIA leaves him at the window. Walks over to her stove. Stirs her pot of rice. Long silence. SHE loudly strikes the pot with her cooking spoon.)* Stoppit! Stop that.

MAFIA. Close the window. *(Long pause. Strikes the pot again loudly.)*

ANGELO. Okay. Okay. *(HE closes the window.)*

MAFIA. Siddown—eat something.

ANGELO. *(Sits. To himself.)* I want her.

MAFIA. What did you say?

ANGELO. Nothing. *(HE stands and walks over to the phone.)*

MAFIA. You're not gonna call her. *(Slams her pot loudly.)* You better not call her.

ANGELO. I want to.

MAFIA. *(While serving him, filling his plate with rice and beans.)* Not on my phone.

ANGELO. *(Angry)* Why not?!

MAFIA. *(Disgusted)* 'Cause this ... this ... bitch—don't love you!

ANGELO. Her name is Virgin.

MAFIA. Bitch.

ANGELO. Virgin.

MAFIA. Bitch. She don't love you.

ANGELO. That ain't true.

MAFIA. Bitch! *(Slams her pot.)* It's true.

ANGELO. *(Walks over to her, snatches the cooking spoon away from her, and repeatedly bangs the pot of rice with it.)* Ha? Ha?! *(HE stops.)* Okay?

MAFIA. Animal. *(Slams the plate of rice and beans on the table. AN-GELO snorts loudly.)* Spit that out. *(ANGELO sits down to eat.)* She only loved you when you had money.

ANGELO. *(Lifts the fork.)* I'm eating. Awright?

MAFIA. *(Everytime ANGELO attempts to eat, MAFIA will interrupt him—by speaking. At which time HE simply lowers his fork and stares out into space.)* When you were shot in Brooklyn—

ANGELO. Not again—don't bring that up again.

MAFIA. When you were shot at the bar in Brooklyn.

ANGELO. I'm eating.

MAFIA. They told me she was there with you.

ANGELO. *(Drops the fork on his plate loudly.)* Who told you that, huh? Who the frig' told you that?! Who?

MAFIA. Somebody.

ANGELO. Who—somebody?! *(ANGELO lifts his fork.)*

MAFIA. They told me—she ran—out into the street—with all the other people who were at the bar.

ANGELO. *(Angry)* That's a lie. Who told you all this?

MAFIA. They told me the bartender dragged you outta the bar—

ANGELO. That's about the only thing you said that's true.

MAFIA. And he locked the bar and left you on the street to die.

ANGELO. Yeah. So?

MAFIA. *(Angry)* Where was this bitch?

ANGELO. *(Angry)* I don't know, awright?! Lemme eat! *(ANGELO attempts to put the fork in his mouth.)*

MAFIA. You're an old man. *(ANGELO loudly drops the fork on his plate.)* What she gonna do with an old man?

ANGELO. Lemme eat!

MAFIA. She's a twenty-year-old girl. You went—like a fool—you went out—and spent all this . . . this . . . money you made—I don't know how—I don't wanna know. I just know you—like a fool—spent it all on her.

ANGELO. I made it bartending.

MAFIA. Bartending? Bartending, my beautiful fat ass. You was a barfly maybe, but not a bartender. She took your money.

ANGELO. Nobody takes my money. I'm not a puta.

MAFIA. Ha!!

ANGELO. I'm a puta?!

MAFIA. You bought her a car.

ANGELO. I bought her a car—yeah.

MAFIA. 'Cause she wanted it.

ANGELO. 'Cause I wanted too.

MAFIA. 'Cause she wanted it.

ANGELO. Lemme eat—please.

MAFIA. What did you buy me?

ANGELO. These rice and beans. I'd like to eat 'em.

MAFIA. Ralphie.

ANGELO. *(Nasty. Mimics MAFIA.)* May he rest in peace.

MAFIA. May he rest in peace. Yeah, that's right. May he rest in peace.

ANGELO. *(Angry)* Okay.

MAFIA. He was your best friend.

ANGELO. He was my only friend.

MAFIA. I remember. May he rest in peace. I remember the day he told me—you could—

ANGELO. I know—I could—

MAFIA. Yeah. You could have—

ANGELO and MAFIA. *(Together)* Bought a house!

MAFIA. Bought me a house, that's right.

ANGELO. *(Upset)* With what?

MAFIA. With what?!

ANGELO. All I want to do is eat and go, awright? I didn't come here to argue.

MAFIA. What happened to all the money you had?

ANGELO. What money I had?

MAFIA. Ralphie told me you had thousands.

ANGELO. Oh, yeah, I had millions—not thousands—millions!

MAFIA. That's right.

ANGELO. Get outta here. I didn't have that much.

MAFIA. Enough for a down payment on a house.

ANGELO. Okay, I did. Awright—lemme eat something.

MAFIA. Enough to send Esa Pendeja—that four-legged garbage pickin' cat—to Spain.

ANGELO. You know—you're beautiful.

MAFIA. I'm fuckin' mad.

ANGELO. Not with my food—okay?

MAFIA. What did she do to get all this money outta you? Did she rub a piece of steak between her legs and feed it to you?

ANGELO. Rub what?

MAFIA. If a woman wants to tame a man—have him by his pride— his nuts—

ANGELO. I know where his pride is.

MAFIA. All she has to do before she cooks 'im his steak is rub it on her pussy.

ANGELO. And that'll tame 'm? *(HE laughs.)*

MAFIA. How many steaks did she feed you?

ANGELO. *(ANGELO is still laughing.)* Nah—I just ate her—no steaks. Why you always wait till I sit down to argue with me?

MAFIA. It's the only time—you won't walk out on me. Leave me with my words in my mouth.

ANGELO. Can I eat? I'd like to put something in my mouth.

MAFIA. Here, lemme cook you a steak.

ANGELO. That's awright. *(A long silence as HE finally gets an opportunity to eat. MAFIA looks at him. HE stops.)* Don't look at me, okay? I don't like to be looked at when I'm eating.

MAFIA. *A hora se yo?* I'm not looking at you.

ANGELO. No, that's right, I was looking at you.

MAFIA. Yeah, you were lookin' at me!

ANGELO. I'm sorry—my mistake.

MAFIA. So delicate. *(A long silence.)*

ANGELO. No!

MAFIA. I know.

ANGELO. Huh?

MAFIA. I know you ain't delicate. I carried you inside here. *(Smacks her stomach loudly.)* Nine months—you scratching and kicking every day of those months—like a brute.

ANGELO. I am a brute.

MAFIA. I didn't say you were a brute.

ANGELO. I am.

MAFIA.   You ain't delicate.

ANGELO.   I ain't delicate, awright. You're the boss and I'm the hoss.

MAFIA.   I gave you life.

ANGELO.   Yeah. You're the boss and I'm the hoss. Now, you mind if I put on the feedbag?

MAFIA.   I mind seeing you going around borrowing money to pay for her car.

ANGELO.   What's that got to do with you?

MAFIA.   Everything.

ANGELO.   Am I taking food outta yer mouth?!

MAFIA.   It has everything to do with me.

ANGELO.   Do you see me taking food outta yer mouth??

MAFIA.   *(Furious)* What the hell have you given me?

ANGELO.   Am I taking food outta yer mouth?

MAFIA.   A house?!

ANGELO.   You can't eat a house.

MAFIA.   *(Slams her hand down on the kitchen table loudly.)* I want to live in one.

ANGELO.   Go 'head—who's stoppin' you?

MAFIA.   *(Suddenly, with hate and agony, screaming.)* YOU! *(SHE throws his plate of food onto the floor.)*

ANGELO.   *(Not disturbed)* That was nice. Why don't you throw the whole pot of rice on the floor? *(MAFIA does.)* It's only money. I can always buy a bag of potato chips.

MAFIA.   Eat on the floor, you animal—only an animal treats his mother the way you do.

ANGELO.   I treat you bad?

MAFIA.   YES!

ANGELO.   Whatta I do? Do I throw yer food on the floor like you always do to me?

MAFIA.   *(In anguish)* You've left me here . . . in this place.

ANGELO.   What do you want me to do? Go out and hold up people?

MAFIA.   Yes.

ANGELO.   You do?!

MAFIA.   Yes.

ANGELO.   Awright. *(HE stands up to leave.)* How many people you want me to rob?

MAFIA.   . . . As many as I had to go to bed with! *(There is total si-*

lence. ANGELO looks at his mother without recognition.) You stand there—actin' like you didn't know? Innocent!

ANGELO. *(Not wanting to believe her.)* You mean .... you were a 'ho?

MAFIA. *(Accusing him.)* Guilty!

ANGELO. . . . You mean . . . I'm guilty? Guilty of what?!

MAFIA. Of being innocent.

ANGELO. *(In sudden anger, frightened agony. Turning madly.)* . . . Don't do it . . . please don't do it . . . Man, not with me. *(Furious)* I'm not gonna let you do it.

MAFIA. *(Slowly, maliciously. Slowly for effect.)* Like violin notes on blue marble, I landed on the beds of cops, doctors, and lawyers, and creeps. But I ain't tellin' you nothin' you didn't know.

ANGELO. I was a kid.

MAFIA. Innocent.

ANGELO. Innocent—yeah.

MAFIA. But you had eyes—

ANGELO. Innocence.

MAFIA. You were blind?

ANGELO. Innocent.

MAFIA. Blind to what was going on.

ANGELO. I saw.

MAFIA. And you didn't care.

ANGELO. You were my mother. How could I really believe my eyes?

MAFIA. I watched you—I watched you—watch me. Think.

ANGELO. No.

MAFIA. Think back.

ANGELO. No. I was a kid.

MAFIA. Innocent.

ANGELO. Yeah.

MAFIA. Guilty.

ANGELO. Why am I guilty?

MAFIA. 'Cause you didn't stay innocent.

ANGELO. *(Adamantly)* You're not gonna drive me crazy.

MAFIA. Not for long. You didn't stay innocent—for long. *(Advances)* You continued to watch me. You wanted food—so you watched me. You wanted a bed to sleep in. So you watched me. You wanted clothes—so you watched me. You wanted money—so you took it from me. *(SHE takes on a sensuous mood. Takes his face in her hands and passionately kisses her son on the lips.)* My pimp. *(Long pause)* Remember how I used to always kiss you on the lips?

ANGELO.   Remember how I never liked it.

MAFIA.   . . . I haven't kissed you—

ANGELO.   In a long time.

MAFIA.   Years.

ANGELO.   Don't ever kiss me like that again. I swear, don't. *(Long pause)*

MAFIA.   I can do anything I want—I carried you nine months in pain. I gotta right to enjoy the fruit of my labor.

ANGELO.   That's what you call enjoying?

MAFIA.   What did you call it when you came down to the club and watched me dance . . . Naked . . . in front of all those men?

ANGELO.   Nothing.

MAFIA.   I saw your eyes—felt 'em all over me. Beckoning—felt 'em beckoning me to hurry and take it all off.

ANGELO.   No—that's wrong.

MAFIA.   No—you wasn't innocent. Over twenty-one, an' a man.

ANGELO.   You were a pro. You raised me to always think you were a professional. You never took your job home.

MAFIA.   That's right.

ANGELO.   I came down to the club—jus' to come down.

MAFIA.   I was a professional.

ANGELO.   Yeah.

MAFIA.   Mafia—they called me down in the "Combat Zone" when I worked in Boston. Mafia. Presenting Mafia! I was big. I was powerful. Mafia! You watched me.

ANGELO.   Yeah—I watched you.

MAFIA.   I love you.

ANGELO.   I hate you . . .

MAFIA.   *(Looking at him.)* Mafia!

ANGELO.   . . . for making it all so damn casual. Natural. I thought it was natural for me to go and see you. Since I was a kid—

MAFIA.   Innocent.

ANGELO.   No.

MAFIA.   You watched me.

ANGELO. I watched you . . . From one strip joint to another. From Boston to Baltimore.

MAFIA. You watched me.

ANGELO. I watched you.

MAFIA. I hate you.

ANGELO. I love you. I watched you.

MAFIA. *(Shouts)* Mafia!

ANGELO. I hate myself.

MAFIA. I love you.

ANGELO. I hate myself.

MAFIA. I love you.

ANGELO. I hate myself.

MAFIA. Watch me. *(SHE throws her arms up above her head and slowly comes down feeling her breasts, hip, and thighs.)*

ANGELO. I remember . . . *(MAFIA continues to repeat the action of caressing herself.)* One time, I dropped by—when you were working at the Pink Pussy Cat. We were living in Boston. That night you wasn't dancing. You were—just working for the car—commission.

MAFIA. I was hustling for drinks.

ANGELO. *(Gives her a hard stare for a long moment.)* I was around twenty-two—

MAFIA. *(SHE stops caressing and begins to slowly dance.)* I wanted you to take care of me.

ANGELO. I know.

MAFIA. You work and I take care of the house.

ANGELO. I know, Ma.

MAFIA. I cook for you.

ANGELO. I sat down next to you—you were sitting next to this old guy.

MAFIA. I remember—I kissed you.

ANGELO. Yeah.

MAFIA. On the lips.

ANGELO. *(Upset)* Yeah. You told the guy I was yer boyfriend.

MAFIA. How could I tell 'im you was my son? What kinda son would let his mother work in a place like that? *(Stops dancing)* Without feeling ashamed for his mother, or himself!

ANGELO. I hate you . . . for raising me to feel no shame.

MAFIA. I love you.

ANGELO. The worst was when you told me one time to buy yer boss a drink. I was 18 years old—and you were working down on the block in Baltimore. I didn't have a job. I was outta school and didn't have any money to buy 'im a drink.

MAFIA. I know. I asked the man sitting next to me to gimme five dollars.

ANGELO. And you kissed him.

MAFIA. I love you.

ANGELO. I turned my head—made believe I didn't see you.

MAFIA. I watched you.

ANGELO. You gave me the five and I bought yer boss a drink with it. I hate you. I felt no shame. *(Their feelings hang in the room. MAFIA stares out into space. ANGELO stares out the window.)*

MAFIA. I don't like you.

ANGELO. I know.

MAFIA. *(Very quietly)* You know.

ANGELO. I did nothing.

MAFIA. I've done everything for you.

ANGELO. You did.

MAFIA. I still do everything for you.

ANGELO. . . . You do.

MAFIA. I don't like you.

ANGELO. I know.

MAFIA. No more.

ANGELO. O.K. I won't come around.

MAFIA. You need a bed to sleep—

ANGELO. I know.

MAFIA. The door is always—

ANGELO. I know.

MAFIA. It's always open.

ANGELO. O.K.

MAFIA. Awright?

ANGELO. It's O.K.

MAFIA. I can't rely on you.

ANGELO. No.

MAFIA. I can't see you—

ANGELO. No.

MAFIA. Not doing anything for me.

ANGELO. No. *(A heavy silence. ANGELO crosses, moving toward the exit. Quiet. MAFIA, without looking up at him, crosses over to the window.)*

MAFIA. . . . I pass this window every evening.

ANGELO. Lemme give 'ya a few bucks.

MAFIA. I gotta few bucks on the floor.

ANGELO. That . . . I was mad. *(Bends down to pick up the three dollars he threw on the floor when he was on the phone.)*

MAFIA. Leave it.

ANGELO. *(Annoyed)* What?

MAFIA. I pass this window every evening.

ANGELO. What—What are you saying?

MAFIA. During my "Happy Hour."

ANGELO. Happy Hour?

MAFIA. I have a Happy Hour. An hour where I stand here in front of this window—in my negligee—with a beer in my hand and I cough.

ANGELO. Cough? For what—what are you talkin' about?

MAFIA. Cough. Like this . . . *(Coughs into the window.)* See . . . it fogs up.

ANGELO. Yeah. So, big deal.

MAFIA. And I write, real fast, b'fore the fog fades away: "Be Happy."

ANGELO. *(Shakes his head from side to side, knowing what is coming next. SHE is going into one of her many self-pitying moments.)* Here's forty bucks.

MAFIA. *(Not looking at him.)* No.

ANGELO. What?!

MAFIA. I wait each dusk for 'em.

ANGELO. . . . Who you wait for?

MAFIA. For the men to come home from work.

ANGELO. I don't wanna hear it.

MAFIA. There's one.

ANGELO. You want this? *(Meaning the forty dollars.)*

MAFIA. *(Waves)* No. I want all of it.

ANGELO. All of it?!

MAFIA. All of it.

ANGELO. What about me?

MAFIA. Linger.

ANGELO. What?!

MAFIA. *(Shouts at the window.)* Linger, honey, linger, in the twilight. Stand on the stoop, at the bottom step, ignore the cold, honey, linger.

ANGELO. Ma?

MAFIA. Mafia—the name is Mafia. Look up here, honey, that's right . . .

ANGELO. What are you doing?

MAFIA. Now that you've gotten yer look—take a walk . . .

ANGELO. What do you get outta teasing these assholes?

MAFIA. What I put in it. Satisfaction.

ANGELO. You get called a "cock-tease."

MAFIA. Coming from an asshole, it's not much of an insult. The asshole always gets screwed. You should know—this broad—whatever her name is—gave you a screwing.

ANGELO. Nobody screws me.

MAFIA Oh, no?

ANGELO. Nobody.

MAFIA. I want all yer money.

ANGELO. I give you all my money—I ain't gonna have any money—

MAFIA. That's right.

ANGELO. I ain't gonna have nothin' for myself.

MAFIA. Nothing but a single smile. The smile of a good deed. What is it they say? "Smile, and the whole world smiles with you." Do you believe that?

ANGELO. I'm gonna give you an extra ten. How's that? You got $50.

MAFIA. Smile.

ANGELO. I don't feel like smiling.

MAFIA. Refusing yer mother a smile.

ANGELO. I don't like smiling.

MAFIA. You want me to smile?

ANGELO. Do I want you to smile?

MAFIA. I wanna smile.

ANGELO. For what?

MAFIA. Smile and the whole world smiles with you.

ANGELO. Yeah, I know, you awready said that.

MAFIA. I wanna crack yer face with a smile.

ANGELO. Why?

MAFIA. I hate you.

ANGELO. I love you.

MAFIA. Gimme all yer money.

ANGELO. I hate you.

MAFIA. I love you.

ANGELO. I'll give you another ten—so you got sixty, awright?

MAFIA. I don't wanna argue about money . . . it's my "Happy Hour." *(Takes a beer out of the refrigerator—stands by the window.)* Open this. *(Hands him the beer. Does not look at him.)* Open it gently. The POP sound—twitches my hips, and I might all of a sudden forget where I am and start to strip.

ANGELO. *(Glares at her.)* What's wrong with you—are you flippin?

MAFIA. *(Still not looking at her son.)* Leave yer money on the table.

ANGELO. Or—are you being mean?

MAFIA. My beer. *(Extends her hand out to him—does not look at Angelo. ANGELO hands her the beer.)*

ANGELO. I'm leaving sixty dollars.

MAFIA. No! All of it—or nothing. *(ANGELO is frustrated—exhales heavily.)* Ammonia. It's the smell of ammonia. The super must of just mopped. The super always when he mops the building—starts from the top floor—from this staircase here—that leads to the roof. And he works his way down. Ammonia, ugh. Supers. The super super. Me and him sat . . . the landing was cold and damp then. My skirt was raised and hugged the shape of my hips—like an alligator sandwich bag. You see, baby, I was a virgin. And this guy knew it . . . His eyes . . . anxious—raised my skirt up to my waist. And I wondered. Wondered how will he spread my legs apart? Will he take 'em like he takes a wishbone—and pull 'em apart? Or is he gonna get on one knee and wear my panties away by scraping with his teeth—words of love. "I love you." *(Sharply, boldly, saucily.)* Money, honey. Gimme some money! I really didn't think . . . Something done so fast—in the blink of an eye—on yer mark, get set, go! . . . Something done so quick . . . didn't even work up a sweat—got offa me—didn't turn around to look back . . . Coulda gotten me pregnant!

ANGELO. Are you talkin' about me?

MAFIA. I couldn't see—

ANGELO. Look at me.

MAFIA. . . . nothing ahead of me—except my pointed belly. *(MAFIA finally looks at Angelo.)*

ANGELO. Just what I needed to hear.

MAFIA. Don't tell me you didn't know.

ANGELO. I knew.

MAFIA. So what's wrong with hearing it from the horse's mouth?

ANGELO. I don't like the way you're saying it . . . Like yer trying to hurt me.

MAFIA. Yeah, it does seem that way. Not outta love—but outta love for money.

ANGELO. Thank you for tellin' me how I was born.

MAFIA. I screamed. Gamblin' with the throw of the dice. Seven—the winner—a baby boy. Craps the loser. A girl. *(Growls, shaking her fist as if she held in her hands a pair of dice.)* Seven—give mama—a pair of baby shoes . . . SEVEN!! The winner . . . I won. Believe it or not—I won. Down in the gutter. I had you.

ANGELO. . . . You want all my money?

MAFIA. *(Pause)* I want it—and more.

ANGELO. *(Long pause)* I've known you.

MAFIA. *(Very noble)* You know me.

ANGELO. Yeah, so it's no surprise.

MAFIA. You know how I am.

ANGELO. I know.

MAFIA. This is the way I've always been.

ANGELO. I know.

MAFIA. An' you've known me to be worse.

ANGELO. With people—yeah.

MAFIA. What do you mean—with people?

ANGELO. With other people, not with me.

MAFIA. . . . Well . . . it's rough.

ANGELO. On who?

MAFIA. *(Shocked)* On who?

ANGELO. You—or me?

MAFIA. On me . . . of course.

ANGELO. Not me?

MAFIA. *Mira*—you? The cash they threw on the stage was not for me—but for you! You took every penny. You tellin' me it was rough living—like a king? I served you hand and foot!

ANGELO. Awright—forget it.

MAFIA. Yeah, how easily we forget.

ANGELO. I'm sorry.

MAFIA. Don't let me say—I'm sorry.

ANGELO. What do you mean?

MAFIA. I'd be sorry for a lot of things. *(Long pause. Steadying him. Her tone changes. Strutting like a sport.)* D'you think I'm worth the price of a ticket? Worth everything you have in yer pocket? . . . C'mon . . . Not as yer mother—but as a woman—I'm still . . . splendid in black garters. Soaked in sweat—black garters that snap—stinging—faces with twisted grins, and crooked smiles. *(Shouts)* MAFIA! Look, but don't touch—boys . . . *(Quietly)* You can touch.

ANGELO. . . . Why should I touch you?

MAFIA. 'Cause you want to. Why did you come down to the clubs and watch me—perform? 'Cause you wanted to. Like everybody there—you like what you saw. *(Long pause. ANGELO is shaken by her remarks. HE is speechless. MAFIA advances. Sensuous.)* Here. Touch.

ANGELO. Who do you think I am? You don't know me.

MAFIA. I know you—you came outta me.

ANGELO. You don't know me.

MAFIA. You was to be my knight in shining armor.

ANGELO. You don't know me.

MAFIA. You was my knight—

ANGELO. Stoppit.

MAFIA. —in shining armor.

ANGELO. You don't know me.

MAFIA. *(Defeated)* I no longer want to know you. *(SHE pauses. Then, in a sudden change of mood.)* God! Dammit! What do you want from me? . . . You seen me—like no son has seen his mother . . . We're not mother and son . . .

ANGELO. What are we? *(Studying her.)*

MAFIA. *(A glimmering of truth spreads across her face like a smile—and sparkles in her eyes. Awkward silence. SHE dramatically takes hold of both his hands and caresses her face with them.)* What are we?

ANGELO. I'm gonna slap this shit outta you.

MAFIA. Go 'head. Do whatever it is you have to do. *(SHE has his*

hands around her neck.) But leave me all yer money on the table.
That's how much it's gonna cost you. All of it. Every cent you
have. *(SHE places his hands on her chest.)* I don't want to see
you again. I don't want to see you up here. I don't like being left
behind—here. It's terrible awful the way you don't lift a finger for
me. *(No response from ANGELO. MAFIA edges toward him. Long
silence. Places his hand on her breasts. Awkward silence.)*

ANGELO.   *(In deep thought)* . . . You know? Just the way you're
standin' there—

MAFIA.   I'm not just standin' here.

ANGELO.   I know. *(Long pause)* I know . . . *(Long pause)* You remind me of someone.

MAFIA.   The woman—you loved . . . Loved to see on stage. *(Shouts)*
Mafia!

ANGELO.   No.

MAFIA.   Mafia!

ANGELO.   No.

MAFIA.   Mafia!

ANGELO.   Virgin. *(MAFIA shoves him back violently.)* What the hell
is wrong with you?! Are you jealous?

MAFIA.   Depends on your intentions.

ANGELO.   I wanna marry her.

MAFIA.   For what?

ANGELO.   I love her.

MAFIA.   For what?

ANGELO.   For what?!

MAFIA.   I'll give it to you.

ANGELO.   *(Angry. Long pause.)* You're gonna gimme it . . .

MAFIA.   Whatever it is·you want from her . . .

ANGELO.   I want her.

MAFIA.   You don't want her. You want what you always wanted.
(Slowly, for effect.) When you first squashed yer cigarette butt on
the floor—and stood alongside the other men sitting at the bar—

ANGELO.   I knew—

MAFIA.   You knew—when you looked up between my legs—you
wanted me. I'm a woman—don't you think I can tell by jus' lookin'
at ya?

ANGELO.   You're my mother.

MAFIA. I love you.

ANGELO. *(Long pause)* Don't make me say some things I'm gonna regret. Please—don't make me talk.

MAFIA. I wish you would.

ANGELO. I don't wanna.

MAFIA. Do it. I want you to—

ANGELO. No.

MAFIA. Yeah—it makes it easier to hate you.

ANGELO. . . . I don't like—

MAFIA. I don't care.

ANGELO. I don't like—

MAFIA. I don't care. I don't care.

ANGELO. *(Pause)* I don't like—disliking myself.

MAFIA. I don't care.

ANGELO. *(Displeased. Daring.)* . . . I think of you all the time . . .

MAFIA. Good.

ANGELO. All the time.

MAFIA. Very good!

ANGELO. Naw, it's . . . I got you on my mind for all the wrong reasons.

MAFIA. Go 'head, say 'em . . . I wanna hear 'em . . .

ANGELO. . . . It's not about you . . . It's about me. *(No response from MAFIA.)* . . . I been puttin' myself down so much—I got heel marks on the back of my neck.

MAFIA. Good.

ANGELO. *(Long pause)* Yer right.

MAFIA. Yeah.

ANGELO. 'Cause yer fuckin' right about everything.

MAFIA. *(Smirking)* Uh-huh . . . Mother is always right.

ANGELO. But how come . . . you know . . . it don't affect you? Knowing . . . Knowing it—knowing I wanted to—

MAFIA. You want to . . . not wanted to, but still want to. You still want to!

ANGELO. *(Long pause)* I use to always have dreams about you.

MAFIA. You still do.

ANGELO. I had a . . . a picture of you—a colored photograph of you dressed in yer . . . what do you call it? ·

MAFIA. In my pasties and G-string.

ANGELO. Yeah.

MAFIA. And you did what with it? What did you do alone with my picture?

ANGELO. *(Shakes his head from side to side. Solemnly. Bewildered. Frightened at what may happen—or be said next—but determined to forge ahead under his own steam.)* I'm gonna tell you this is . . . this is low-life shit. This goes against everything. *(Sudden change in mood.)* Yeah . . . I want to. But I won't! I won't. I'm a lot of things. I'm a whole lotta things . . . I committed some nasty-looking sins—

MAFIA. But you're not a "motherfucker."

ANGELO. Here. *(Goes into his pocket.)* You want all my money? . . . Here. *(Puts all his cash on top of the kitchen table.)*

MAFIA. Is that all of it?

ANGELO. Yeah.

MAFIA. Are you sure? *(Pause)* I want it all—

ANGELO. I gave you all of it.

MAFIA. That's not what I'm saying. I want it all—I don't wanna leave a penny for you to split in two—no. For what? So you can give the half that should by all rights be going to me—to some broad?! I want my half. But since you don't see it that way—I'm taking it—taking it all. This mother and son relationship is terminated.

ANGELO. We were never mother and son.

MAFIA. I'm exhausted.

ANGELO. We were never mother and son.

MAFIA. I'm tired of expecting—something.

ANGELO. We were never mother and son.

MAFIA. Anything. Even you on top of me—I'm willing to go that far—anything is better than nothing. It beats a blank. I'm sick. I'm sick. Sick and tired . . .

ANGELO. We were never mother and son.

MAFIA. I wish I could die. *(Turns on Angelo.)* SHUT-UP!

ANGELO. I never cared for you. I love you 'cause you're my mother. But I never cared for you.

MAFIA. We are all—all of us are born in a strange fashion—so what is yer hang-up?

ANGELO. I don't care about you.

MAFIA. That's why there is a God . . . for that reason. So we can all look up to him. *(SHE shouts.)* Help me—God—my son don't care about me!

ANGELO. . . . I'm glad. Man, I'm fuckin' glad you're taking all my money. It proves, it proves—it proves what it was all about— "money." I was kinda like an investment! I was gonna, gonna . . .

MAFIA. Reciprocate. The word is—

ANGELO. The word is nothing. I was—right?

MAFIA. I don't know what you was. You was a five dollar misunder- standing . . . You came cheap. How much you got there on the table? Looks like a couple of hundred dollars . . . Not bad for a five dollar investment.

ANGELO. I hate you.

MAFIA. *(Teasing, smiling.)* I love you . . . Look at all this money. *(Counts the money. Jubilantly. Relishing the moment.)* Lookit all these twenties. Wow! *(SHE stops counting the money. Stares down at it. Ponders for a moment. An uneasy silence prevails. Sneering—SHE deliberately takes each bill and one after the other throws it at Angelo's face.)* How's it feel? How does this feel?! Huh?

ANGELO. . . . No different.

MAFIA. How's it feel to have it thrown in your face?! *(SHE continues to throw the money in his face. Increases the force with which she flings the money at him.)*

ANGELO. I feel the same. It feels the same way it always felt.

MAFIA. You love it!!

ANGELO. It hurts . . .

MAFIA. It doesn't hurt enough.

ANGELO. No.

MAFIA. *(SHE smacks him.)* How's that?!

ANGELO. *(A heavy silence. A thought strikes him. Looks at Mafia intently.)* You . . . You went in to work on days you didn't have to.

MAFIA. I had to.

ANGELO. No.

MAFIA. Yes.

ANGELO. You had it off with pay.

MAFIA. So?

ANGELO. You didn't have to go in.

MAFIA. *(Evades)* You're steppin' on one of my twenties.

ANGELO. Why you go in?

MAFIA. It's my job.

ANGELO. 'Cause you liked yer job.

MAFIA. You're still steppin' on one of my twenties.

ANGELO. You liked yer job.

MAFIA. Move your foot!

ANGELO. You was the star. *(MAFIA stoops and begins to pick up the money.)* Mafia! . . . My mother . . . It played tricks with my mind. It was nice—you bigger than life. It was something else, for a kid, it was a hell of a sight. I didn't know any better. I thought it was Hollywood. Showbiz. As a man . . . it was too late . . . I didn't care . . . I didn't care . . . I got the feelin'—if you were to hit the Lotto you'd still be down at the club. You were in control—Mafia!

MAFIA. I had 'em by all their balls. What do you think? Sure, I was in control.

ANGELO. Mafia—huh?!

MAFIA. Lift yer foot.

ANGELO. Then it's true—huh—what I said?

MAFIA. It's true—so what?

ANGELO. *(Exhales heavily)* I always thought.

MAFIA. Move yer foot—I want to pick up my twenty.

ANGELO. I always thought I'd—been seeing things. Imagining things. Maybe . . . the guy I saw you kiss was an old-time friend of yours. Or—the guy who was feelin' you up—maybe he was a long-lost relative or something. And not a guy who jus' walked in—an asshole who dropped in for a beer and a peek.

MAFIA. Lying to yerself—softens the blow—when you keep telling 'em to yourself enough times. Move yer foot.

ANGELO. Yeah, whatever you say.

MAFIA. Move!

ANGELO. . . . The night you didn't move. The night you had noodles for legs—and you had to leave all yer tips on the stage—'cause yer legs got so trembly. Everybody had to take their drinks off the bar—or else you woulda shooked 'em off. That's how bad—

MAFIA. *(With great force.)* Fucked up.

ANGELO. You was. Yeah . . .

MAFIA. Lift yer foot—c'mon!

ANGELO.   It was then I knew nobody would ever hire you to dance again.

MAFIA.   I'm still beautiful.

ANGELO.   Yeah ... Yeah ... After all them years of shuffling you around in my head—with yer bad feet and aching legs, having my back patted like if I was yer man. "She's some woman!" Grinning when I was losing my mind ... After all that I was gonna ask—for more by putting my head on the chopping block. Getting a job as a super in one of these tenement buildings here in the Bronx. So I could get free rent and put some kinda roof over yer head.

MAFIA.   I want a house!

ANGELO.   ... Yeah ... But a house ain't in me. It ain't in you. Don't you know what I'm saying? We belong right here—where we are ... You danced yer last dance. You had yer times of fallin' outta sight. And you had enough troubles to fill a dozen eight-foot graves. You gotta face it—it's gotten away from us. We the last of the big-time losers.

MAFIA.   You're a loser.

ANGELO.   Instead of investing yer money in me—you shoulda put it away somewhere for yer house.

MAFIA.   I blew a lot of money on you.

ANGELO.   You did. And I'm doing my best to pay back a little of it.

MAFIA.   I want it all back—every cent of it.

ANGELO.   I can't do that.

MAFIA.   You owe me.

ANGELO.   I think I've given you enough.

MAFIA.   No.

ANGELO.   I'm gonna take this twenty.

MAFIA.   No, you're not. That twenty is mine.

ANGELO.   I'm gonna use it for cab fare.

MAFIA.   Not my twenty.

ANGELO.   I'm gonna try to get as far away from here as I can.

MAFIA.   I don't care where you go—as long as you keep sending me money.

ANGELO.   I'm not gonna send you no more money. I'm gonna live, man. You got food stamps to live. You're collecting welfare. You got Medicare. I got to hustle for every buck I put in my pocket.

MAFIA. Good.

ANGELO. I hate you.

MAFIA. I hate you, too. *(Long silence. SHE moves back toward the stove, where SHE will take from behind it a large carving knife. Menaces him with it.)* You're not gonna take my twenty dollars.

ANGELO. Lend me it.

MAFIA. No, you walk.

ANGELO. Lend me it—O.K.?

MAFIA. No. *(Long silence. HE stoops down to pick up the twenty dollars. SHE rushes at him and stabs Angelo with the knife. The knife falls to the floor. ANGELO groans. MAFIA laughs hysterically. ANGELO slowly stands in pain—approaches her.)*

ANGELO I was gonna send you money. *(MAFIA laughs.)* I was gonna send it. I wasn't gonna do something like that to you. You're my mother. *(MAFIA continues to laugh. ANGELO smacks her hard. The force of it knocks her over near the exit, where SHE falls. The audience only sees her bare legs. SHE is now in the exact position she was in the beginning of this piece. MAFIA continues to laugh loudly and to sob faintly. After concentrated attention, ANGELO approaches her.)* Here's yer twenty dollars. *(Drops the twenty dollar bill at her feet. MAFIA, still laughing and sobbing, proceeds to rip the twenty dollar bill. SHE will also tear to shreds the rest of the money. Her sobbing will increase louder and louder. Crosses over to the refrigerator—looks to side of it and removes a baseball bat.)* I hate you. God I hate you. I hate you so fuckin' much. *(Turns, advances, lifting the baseball bat high above his head. The ACTION FREEZES. The LIGHTS all will dim out, except for a SPOTLIGHT on ANGELO. HE will drop the baseball bat and will fall to his knees crying. To the audience.)* Poppa Dio! . . .

SLOW BLACKOUT

PEDRO JUAN SOTO

Bayaminiña

From the distance, if one went by its colors, it was a snappy little cart parked on the corner of 116th street. It had blue, red, and yellow stripes, and the box on top—full of cod fritters, blood sausage, and banana fritters—had glass on all four sides. From close, however, you could see that its snappiness was no more than a front that disguised the wear and tear and the rot which were consuming it from the wheels up to the push bar. On a piece of tin nailed to the front you could read in red, shaky letters: BAYAMINIÑA.

But no one paid attention to the cart. The crowd was watching the argument between the vendor and the policeman. The black women heading toward Lenox Avenue stopped in their rapid, ass-swinging tracks to see how it would all end. The customers in the nearby bar neglected their drinks and the TV set to follow the altercation through the glass window. And curiosity even turned heads in passing cars and buses.

"I pay no more," the vendor was saying, tense. "I pay las' year other fine . . ."

The policeman only shook his head as he finished scribbling in his notebook.

"This has nothing to do with last year, buddy."

"I got no money. I no pay more."

"And the fine you'll have to pay next year will be a bigger one, if you don't get rid of that thing there."

"You're killing me," said the vendor. "Why you do this?"

"The Department of Health . . .".

"Okay, you gimme a job an I . . ."

". . . is after you guys."

"I have to eat," said the vendor. "Don't gimme no fine, gimme a job."

"I have nothing to do with that," said the policeman. He put the summons in one of the vendor's pockets and added: "You keep that . . . And remember to go to court."

The vendor took out the summons, furious, and tried to read it. But he could understand no more than the numbers.

"All right, break it up," the policeman said to the crowd. And to the vendor: "And you get going before I lose my patience."

The vendor turned to the school kids, slight and cinnamon-colored like him.

"These bastards," he said to them in Spanish. "Sia la madre d'ehtos policías!"

"C'mon," said the policeman. "Get the hell out of here."

Suddenly the vendor bent over, picked up the rock which served as the cart's brake, and stood up again with it in his fist. His face was already crumpling with a coming sob.

"Gimme a job, saramabich!"

"You'd better get your ass out of this neighborhood before I throw you in jail!" said the policeman, not raising his eyes from the threatening fist while moving his hand to his gun holster.

The vendor hesitated, grimaced angrily, turned, and threw himself on the cart. Crash! went the panes and crack! the wood. And he shrieked: "Gimme a job, saramabich, gimme a job!"

And the tin—clank! clank!—where you could still read BAYAMINIÑA, turned dirty with blood, spattered with tears, and, freed from its nails, once again became a tin can.

FELIPE LUCIANO

Roots

FROM *PALANTE! YOUNG LORDS PARTY*

The first ten years of my life were spent in the projects. Long, long, vertical buildings, shit-encrusted walls—there were no rats and roaches, but it was its own prison. It's always reminded me of a mental institution—people closed in, not allowed to expand at all. I grew up there like most of the other Puerto Rican Black brothers and sisters in *El Barrio*.

When I went to public school, I was a bright student, very bright, but I was always a behavior problem—that's what the teachers told me. I rebelled against everything. There was something that I was always looking for as a child. I always knew that I had to do something, as romantic and as weird as this may sound. What that thing was, I didn't really know. I had images and dreams of becoming a doctor, becoming a social worker. Of course before any of those very legitimate dreams, I wanted to be a cowboy on a horse, riding through the plains in my big sombrero. I read *Cowboy Sam* and *Curious George* and Dr. Seuss—very, very entranced. My world was expanded because I was able to read a lot at a very early age.

We were very, very poor. My mother was separated from my father when she was three months pregnant with my sister. They had been married for about three years, and had had one baby right after the other. We went through the welfare scene—the welfare syndrome as I call it—always waiting for that check, anticipating that check, heart beating, mouth dry, arguing with each other. My brother, sister and myself used to fight each other for scraps of food on the table. When that welfare check was supposed to come, we used to run downstairs, open that mailbox. You played a game with yourself—you turned the key very slowly and peeked in the box very slowly, and if that welfare check wasn't there, there were two reactions you used to have. Like when we wanted to be cruel, when we wanted to get back at my mother for a beating she'd given us, we used to go and tell her the check had come and then we'd tell her it hadn't. Otherwise we'd come up with morose-looking faces and say "The check didn't come." I remember those days, I remember almost begging for food.

You resign yourself to poverty—my mother did this. Your face is rubbed in shit so much that you begin to accept that shit as a reality. You've never seen anything else. Like the only thing we knew was that block. You never went out of that block. I didn't know there was a Museum of Modern Art. I didn't know that there were people who were living much, much better. I didn't know about racism. I mean we were just on that block—and that block was our home, it was all we knew.

The images of that poverty . . . My stomach rumbling. My mother beating me when I knew it was because of my father—you know, they just had an argument where he almost hit her. The welfare investigator cursing out my mother because what she wants is spring clothing for her children and he's telling her how she just can't have it—when I read in the magazines that people—you know, other people—had spring clothes. Why couldn't we have clothes for Easter? And he's telling her, like, in a sense, "Fuck you." And I remember images of my saying, "When I grow up I'm gonna kill every welfare investigator I see, every one of them—you know, strangle them."

There's nothing extraordinary, you know, in my childhood— maybe just that I learned very early how to become accepted, how to rise above and beyond, as they say. Even at that point we knew that to the extent that we became white—we would advance in school. To the extent that we spoke properly—we would get Satisfactory or Excellent on our report cards. To the extent that we conformed—we were accepted. And since I read well, and I spoke well, I rose in terms of classes. And I remember the teachers always saying, when I hit a teacher or would throw a chair through a window, or would lead a group of cats through a riot in the cafeteria—a near-riot in the fourth or fifth grade—the teachers grabbed me by the side, grabbed me by my ear, you know. Wrenching my ear and saying, "You know you have so much potential. Why do you act like that? I mean look at your marks—you have so much potential. . . ." That thing went through all my school life—those words were uttered time and time again: "You have so much potential." Of course, what they considered potential was certainly not what I later became.

And my mother was very frustrated also. She couldn't get a job, she wanted to get off welfare. I never looked upon my mother as a woman; she was always my mother. I never looked upon her as a Black Puerto Rican woman who was oppressed—she was just Mommy. She's fat, she is a *bear*, you know, and I remember snuggling between her neck and . . . peace, you know it's peace, 'cause nobody can hurt you when you're with Mommy, 'cause Mommy's the big protector. Not Daddy, but Mommy—Daddy wasn't ever there. And she too wanted to get out, but she didn't know how. You know, she always wanted me to do something, since I was the first-born. I was getting into a lot of trouble. But she had these images of me becoming something.

Finally we moved to California to get away from New York and because my mother wanted to go back to my grandmother. California was such an enlightening experience because I saw all these people—Japanese, Chinese, white people—they lived together without the kind of separation that you see in New York. And it was sunny all the time, like there was no snow, you know—just eighty-five-degree weather all the motherfuckin' time. I got *black*; I got black as the sun, man, and I got fat and healthy. I entered the fourth grade and got good grades in school. We had fields—this was in Wilmington, California, before they industrialized—we had fields that we used to run through. After school that's all we'd be doing. I got into track because I always wanted to do that, but I didn't have the chance to do it in New York. I had a lot of happiness, a lot of fun there because the environment was completely different. There were trees, there were horses, which I had never seen. They had a corral, a stable just a block away from the house. Just to see a horse, just to touch him, was like another kind of world for me.

But it wasn't to last long. We stayed there only four months. My father was supposed to send us money in a legal separation. But he didn't send it. He got very bitter when my mother took us away, it seems. And though he hadn't done a motherfucking thing for us—

remember that when I say that, I'm just remembering the bitterness of my younger years, because I really don't hate him—at that point, he felt my mother had slighted him by taking the kids away. Without the money from him we couldn't survive because my grandmother couldn't take the burden. So we had to go back. And we had to ask the welfare in Wilmington for the money. I remember the very degrading experience of my mother having to go there and be insulted three, four times during that week.

We only had enough money to pay our train fare; we had no money for food. So my grandmother, in a little handkerchief, tied up all of the coins she had. Of course, it didn't last us beyond Union Station in L.A. But we left, and I'll never forget, man, we were starving, you know, literally starving on that train coming back. Big, plush train and no food. We would look at people—you learn how to look at a person to let him know that you're hungry—and they'd give us a little tidbit, but it wasn't much. And I was very concerned for my mother, because throughout the whole trip she held her head in her hands. And it was traumatic, it was horrible, having to see my mother go through shit like that. I felt so responsible for her that I felt like a little man, since I was the oldest. And I was always to my mother lover, confidant, trustee, everything rolled into one.

On that train, hungry as we were, the only thing that saved us were some Black brothers working in the kitchen, and they saw us and we would walk in, we sat down and had some water in front of us. My mother with those little pennies bought some pastries and some coffee and tea because she couldn't afford any more. And the cats knew we were starving, I don't know how they knew, but they just started bringing things to us—burnt blueberry pie, I'll never forget it was burnt, but it was all they could afford, and they gave it to us. And that's how we survived—by them giving us little things. I don't know where they are, man, but all power to them wherever they are. I mean they saved us, I don't know how we would have gotten through that trip without them, 'cause I would've started robbin' or something.

Anyway, we got to New York and we ended up living right back on 112th Street, but in a different project. And for three years we lived there. I went to another school, and again, the same shit. I was, as my mother says, fucking up. I was still into my thing.

At that stage I was living a double life. On the one hand I was going with my mother to church. I grew up in the Puerto Rican Pentecostal Church, which is a scene unto itself—I mean it's a different world. The Holy Spirit, speaking tongues, body contortions, jumping on the floor, vomiting out demons, people entering trances—*vabilias*, as we call them in Spanish—which are just séances almost, that are held overnight . . . all those things I was very involved in. Man, I was a *fervent* churchgoer. Even with all the streetfighting I was getting into. That's not unusual. We find in our community—the Puerto Rican community—that things are compatible. For instance, people have Catholic saints and at the same time they'll have a Voodoo doll, you know, or a piece of bread above the door so that the evil spirits can eat that and leave in peace.

So I made the church and the fighting compatible, you know. I would always just shut up about the fighting. I would never tell her. After church or before church she would talk about people beating up each other and be condemning them for it. I might be coming in from a fight myself, but I'd be coming in goodie-goodie and go to church with her, right. And so I just led that kind of a double life.

In school, the same kind of thing happened. I happened to *love* to read. In fact I just raped books. I used to go to the library, get ten at a time, and just shut myself in my room, because that was my way of escape. Like getting into another world—with horses and trees and flowers, and fighting and adventures—going up on a mountain, and doing all those things that, you know, white folks do.

There were only a very few people that you could talk to about it. I mean, we still hadn't gotten to the point where we were that close to each other. But I had one or two friends—Big Ben, Richard as we called him, and June Bug, right, and we used to sit down and say, "Man, you know, Mount Everest is the highest mountain. I wish we could climb that one, man." We used to talk about riding horses, we used to talk about, oh, so many things.

But at the same time, I was of the street. I had to prove to my friends that I was just as bad as they were. I was always into fighting and scullies—Crack-top as we called it—using spinning tops to crack another guy's top. . . . That's really a ghetto game. Whoever couldn't spin his top had to put his in the middle, and all of us would take turns trying to crack his top—and yet each one cost fifteen cents, and for us that was a lot of money, right. Hot Peas and Butter, that's another game we played. Whoever is It takes a belt and screams "Hot Peas and Butter," and goes around and whips the *hell* out of whoever he catches. Very violent games on *each other* . . . We laugh about it now, but it was very rough, as you begin to think about it, how we murdered each other every day. I was vicious when it came to fighting, simply because I didn't want to be considered a schoolboy, you know.

When I was in eighth grade, I had a teacher—I'll never forget her—Mrs. Shapiro—she introduced us to Shakespeare. Here we were in eight-two, which is, of course, a step below eight-one, and they had told her she'd never be able to have us accept Shakespeare—but we loved it, you know. I was Puck in *A Midsummer Night's Dream*. We read *Twelfth Night*. We did *Romeo and Juliet*, which I thought was corn shit, and all kinds of things—but we began to enjoy Shakespeare.

And again I had to lead that double life. I enjoyed the fighting, you know. I enjoyed it—it was a release for all of us from whatever we were running from. We had our gang, we had our identity, we had our own community. We didn't realize it then—that the oppressor had taken away our community. What America has done is cause groups to fight each other to keep them from seeing the *real* cause of oppression. We didn't understand that then, man, we just understood that as far as we were concerned, you know, we wanted to be together. And we were very close to one another, and we used to goose each other—of course, had you called us homosexuals then, we would have just had a *fit*, but it was. . . . I mean, it's a natural stage for young cats to go through. And that was another factor involved in it. . . .

Oppression binds you together, sometimes in a negative manner, because you have nothing else to look forward to, you have nothing else to look at. You bind yourselves in locales, and one locale will fight against another. All of the energy that we had against the oppressor was perpetrated on our own people. . . . If I just begin to add up the number of brothers and sisters who had lye thrown in their faces—'cause we used to mix red lye in Pepsi-Cola and throw it in a cat's face—the number of brothers who are now crippled, the number of brothers who are *dead* because of those gang fights, it would number into the thousands.

There are very, very few survivors. Big Ben is a dope fiend, Charlie is a dope fiend. . . . June Bug is a very frustrated man—he was brilliant, brilliant as a child, brilliant mind, so was Big Ben, by the way. June Bug ended up as a hospital orderly, and that's what he's doing now. Peachhead is on drugs. Leon, his brother, was shot in the streets and died. The others have died in Vietnam, or are out on drugs now. One, Angelo, is in Harvard—no, he went to MIT—but he's now working for anti-poverty and lost to the world.

And for me I saw no future. College was to me like a dream, I could never get there. I think that's one of the things—that fear—that led me into, you know, like, vicious, man, vicious fighting. Not knowing what to do with your life, even though you've been taught the American Dream. America has sown her own seeds of destruction, because she's made oppressed people eat that dream up hook, line and sinker, and when they found it shattered, they decided that the only way to begin to build that dream for themselves—interpret it for all oppressed people—is to shatter it, shatter the reality that is ugly, and begin to build a new one. America should never have taught us how to read, she should never have given us eyes to see.

PART 6

LOVE, FAITH, AND TRANSCENDENCE

"Who will be able to detain me with useless dreams/when my soul begins to fulfill its task, . . ."

—FROM *POEM FOR MY DEATH* BY JULIA DE BURGOS

JULIA DE BURGOS

I Became My Own Path

I wanted to be like men wanted me to be—
an attempted life
in a game of hide and seek to find the real me.
But I was living for the moment
and my feet firmly planted on promising land
refused to backtrack.
Instead, they continued plodding ever forward
eluding the ashes to reach the embrace
of uncharted paths.

With each advancing step along the way,
desperate flailings from old decrepit men
thrashed my back.

With the tender frond hacked off forever
and each shocking lash, my gaze
withdrew from familiar horizons
ever more and more distant.
My face began to express what came from inside
a demeanor defined by a sense of inner freedom,
a feeling that welled up
from the balance sustained by my life
and true rapture for untraveled paths.

With my route so defined in the present,
I felt like I had sprouted out of a mix

of all matter dissolved in earth's soil
from soils without history
depleted soils
and soils vastly infinite
piecemealed by all peoples from every epoch.

And I meant everything to myself as life was in me.

I had wanted to be like men wanted me to be—
an attempted life
in a game of hide and seek to find the real me.
But I was living for the moment
and as heralds announced my presence
in the royal parade of wooden patriarchs.
The desire to follow in their footsteps, I turned aside
and the homage that kept waiting and waiting for me.

———

MIGENE GONZÁLEZ-WIPPLER

Yoruba

FROM *THE SANTERIA EXPERIENCE*

Arecibo, tucked in a fold of Puerto Rico's northeastern coast, is one of the oldest towns in the western hemisphere. Originally an Indian village ruled by a Taíno chieftain called Aracibo, it was founded by the Conquistadores in 1616.

In the late nineteen forties, when I was three years old, my mother hired María, a black woman of mammoth proportions, to be my nanny. María's skin was like shiny mahogany with almost iridescent tones, and her smile was radiant. I never saw María angry or sad, and if she was ever prey to these dismal human moods, she was quite adept at hiding them from me. I thought her very beautiful, and soon

I would take my meals only if María ate with me and would not fall asleep unless María sat by my side.

María took me everywhere she went. To the marketplace where she did our daily shopping and to the shantytown where her numerous family lived. To daily mass, for she was a devout Catholic, and to the neighborhood store where she placed her occasional bets with the numbers. My mother took a dim view of these escapades, but I was so healthy and so happy in María's care that my mother eventually relented and let her take full charge of me.

Each morning María would put me in a frothy sundress with a matching sunbonnet, white sandals, and socks which she bleached daily to ensure their whiteness. Underneath the bonnet, my long black hair would be meticulously braided and tied with silk ribbons matching the color of my dress. María was partial to the scent of Parma violets, and all my clothes exuded a faint violet fragrance.

Once my morning toilet was finished, María would march me proudly into our dining room, where my parents and grandparents would make proper sounds of praise and admiration at my dazzling pulchritude. Then, under María's watchful eyes, I would sit to breakfast without wrinkling my skirts or soiling my ruffles. After a substantial breakfast, María sailed majestically out of the house with me in tow, her long, immaculate skirts crackling with starch. On her shoulder was a huge parasol to protect us from the fiery Caribbean sun, while from her wrist dangled a fan to bring us relief from the stifling heat. Since air conditioning had barely made its appearance on the island, the fan was more than an ornament. But female vanity had long turned a necessary instrument into a thing of beauty, and fans had become the objects of both pride and delight, some of them made of fine sandalwood and hand-painted with exquisite landscapes by renowned artists. Others were of peacock or ostrich feathers, or of Chantilly lace embroidered with seed pearls. María had purchased her fan from a merchant marine sailor who had brought it from Spain. Its unusually wide span was of ebony, carved with intricate flowery designs and highlighted with delicate touches of color that made the flower patterns dance with light.

It was María who first taught me that with a flick of the wrist and the opening and closing of a fan, a woman can tell an admirer that she is angry or jealous, that she welcomes his advances or finds him a crashing bore. María taught me all this and more during the twelve years I remained in her care.

I was thrilled at the idea of going to school, which opened the day after I turned five, and talked about it incessantly with María. My mother had promised me an especially nice party to celebrate my birthday, and my grandfather had a famous designer in San Juan make a special dress of pink organdy, hand-embroidered with tiny flowers and musical notes. The shoes and socks were also pink, as were the silk ribbons for my hair. But early in the morning, María dressed me in an old white dress and took me to mass. She did not take me in to my family and have breakfast with them. I kept questioning the departure from our daily routine, but María said to be silent and do as I was told.

After mass was over, María brought me to an altar over which stood a statue of the Virgin Mary. While I knelt down before the image, María pulled from her capacious handbag a large wooden rosary, and proceeded to pass the beads. She stood behind me, praying in muted tones, with her hand on my shoulder as if she were introducing me to the Virgin.

Even if you don't pray the litanies, a compilation of fifty-three Hail Marys and seven Pater-nosters is a lengthy business if you are a child of five. My stomach was empty. My knees ached and throbbed and threatened to buckle, and I had to keep balancing my weight first on the one knee, then on the other. I must have presented a most unhappy picture to Our Blessed Lady. But not once did I think to complain to María. One did not question her orders, one simply did what one was told.

It was already midmorning when we left the church. My knees were functioning again after María rubbed them briskly with her handkerchief, but my stomach was grumbling louder than ever.

"María, are we going to the market place or back home?"

"I know you're tired and hungry," she said evasively, opening her parasol and pulling me under it. "But you must never let your body tell you what to do. It must obey you, not the other way around."

I trotted obediently by her side. "But how does my body tell me what to do?"

"By making you feel things," she answered. "It makes you feel hungry, so you eat. Tired, so you sit down. Sleepy, so you go to bed.

Sometimes it makes you feel angry, so you scream and yell and stomp your feet."

My face colored, remembering my occasional temper tantrums.

"But, María, then my body isn't good."

"Oh yes it is, *florecita* [little flower]. Because of your body, you can see the sky and the sun and the sea. You can smell the perfume of the flowers and sing and play, and love your mother and father."

"And you," I added, drawing closer to her.

"And me," she laughed her great throaty laugh. "But you see, florecita, your body is like a little child. It must be taught good habits and to obey. It must learn we can't always eat when we're hungry or sit down when we're tired or sleep when we're sleepy. And the best way to teach your body these things is by sometimes not doing the things it wants you to do. Not always," she emphasized. "Only sometimes."

"Like now?" I asked.

"Like now."

We reached the bus stop. With delight, I thought we were going home, where I could eat some breakfast and play before my party in the afternoon.

"But I will only eat a little," I promised myself, remembering María's words, "and I will play with only one doll."

But I was not to eat a little breakfast or play with any dolls that morning.

The bus chugged along the country road to our home. Palm trees and banana plants heavy with fruit grew profusely on both sides of the road, as did the brilliant blossoms of the hibiscus, the poinciana, and the bougainvillea. To our left, gently sloping hills alternated with narrow valleys carpeted in a dazzling variety of greens. To our right, the Atlantic melted with the sky in a majestic display of aquamarine and gold. A few peasant huts, known as *bohíos*, were scattered on the hillside, while on the ocean side rose elegant, luxurious *quintas* of white stucco ornamented with costly mosaics and Spanish ironwork.

We were still about ten minutes from home when María pulled the cord to get off. Before I knew what was happening I found myself standing by the road, watching the bus disappear in the distance. María opened her parasol and gathered her parcels together.

Directly in front of us was a rough path, largely overgrown with vegetation. María and I trudged along this path until we emerged directly onto a part of the beach hidden from the main road by a series of large boulders imbedded in the sand. Among the dunes grew a profusion of tropical sea grapes, their hard, bitter fruit shining like amethysts among their harsh round leaves. Some palm trees bent their trunks so close to the sand one could easily grab the clusters of coconut growing among the fan-shaped leaves.

We stopped under the shadow of a palm while María removed my shoes and socks, her own heavy brogans, and the thick cotton stockings she always wore. Thus barefoot we trampled through the warm sand.

I did not bother to ask María the reason for our detour, used as I was to being taken along on all her outings. I had the vague feeling this surprise visit to the beach I had always admired from a distance, but never had walked on before, was María's birthday present to me. Intoxicated by the sharp, tangy smell of the sea, I wanted to stay on the shore for the rest of my life.

When we finally arrived at the water's edge, Maria set her parcels down, closed her parasol, and then calmly proceeded to tear the clothes from my body.

I felt no shame. María washed and dressed me every day and put me to sleep every night. I had stood naked in front of her many times before. I had not yet learned to be ashamed of my own body. But her action had a certain ominous authority that made me feel destitute and vulnerable beyond description. Deprived of more than my own clothes, I felt stripped of identity, of a sense of being. It was as if I had died somehow, standing there on the golden sand, with the sun like a halo around me and the taste of salt water on my lips. I stood there in shock and utter humiliation, tears rolling steadily down my cheeks. I did not understand María's actions, but I knew there was always a reason for everything she did. (Many years later I would find an echo of María's teachings, in the philosophies of some of the world's greatest religions, especially Zen Buddhism. When María tore my clothes and left me naked facing the sea, without any sense of ego or identity, she was echoing Zen's concept of the prefect Initiate, who must be "devoid of selfhood, devoid of personality, devoid of identity, and devoid of separate identity.")

Out of her handbag's unfathomable depths, María extracted a bottle of sugarcane syrup and the red handkerchief, tied in a knot, where she kept all her loose change. Only then did she turn to look at me, all at once the picture of consternation.

"Ah, my little flower, don't cry. You afraid of María? You think María can hurt you?" She rocked me gently against her bosom as she spoke her soothing words. "Why, my florecita, María would cut out her heart for you. María could never hurt you."

Slowly my tears stopped flowing. I lifted my wet face from her shoulder. I felt I could question her now.

"Why, María?" I asked, with still trembling lips. "Why did you do that?"

"Because I want you to be protected from all harm. Now that you're going to school, you'll be alone, florecita, without María to watch over you. You need protection, and only God and the Blessed Lady can give it to you and give you her blessings. And now I bring you to the Lady and her true power, the sea."

As she spoke, María opened the bottle of sugar cane syrup. Tasting it with her forefinger, she anointed my temples, lips, wrists, and ankles with the thick liquid. I automatically licked the heavy, cloying syrup on my lips.

"It's too sweet," I grimaced. "I don't like it."

"It has to be sweet for the Lady, as sweet as possible. Nothing can be too sweet for her."

María undid the knot of her red handkerchief. Counting seven pennies, she pressed them in my hand.

"Here, florecita," she said, closing my fingers around the coins. "This is the payment, *el derecho*, of the Lady. I give you seven pennies because seven is her number. You remember that. Seven is the number of the Lady, of Yemayá."

"Of who?" I asked, staring at the pennies. "What Lady are you talking about, María? The Blessed Lady is in the church and in heaven."

"Yes, florecita, but her true power is in the sea and the seawater. She stands in heaven, but where the bottom of her mantle touches the earth, it turns into the ocean. The waves and the sea foam are her ruffles and her lace. And here, in the sea, her name is Yemayá."

She enunciated the strange name carefully so that I could grasp its melodious rhythm, "Say it, florecita. Ye-ma-yá."

I repeated it after her. "It is the prettiest name I ever heard, María!"
"The prettiest name in the whole world," María laughed delight-
edly. "It is the name of the Lady in African, in Yoruba. My mammy
taught it to me. And now, my little flower, your black mammy
teaches it to you." She took my hand gently and guided me to the water. "Come, let me show you how to salute Yemayá."

Lifting her voluminous skirts so that the waves would not wet
them, she turned her body to the left and forced me to do the same.
We both stood ankle-deep in the water, our bodies at right angles to
the sea.

"See, florecita, you never enter into the ocean facing front. To do
so is a challenge to Yemayá, it's like saying, 'I'm here, come get me.'
So then maybe she does. Always, always enter on your side, better
the right side. Then you say, 'Hekua, Yemayá, hekua.' Say it, little
flower."

I looked dubiously at the water, then at María. Like most Puerto Rican children I had been raised as a very strict Catholic, and I had the
vague feeling that our parish priest would not approve of what María
was saying. But my trust in her had been firmly reestablished and I
did not want to offend her. "Hekua, Yemayá, hekua," I repeated.

As soon as I repeated these words, I felt relieved and relaxed, as if
an unseen link had been established between the sea and myself. My
soul was overwhelmed by a great love for the sea, that has never
stopped growing within me. I have never bathed in the sea again
without remembering that incredible feeling of love illuminating my
entire being.

"See, florecita," María said joyously. "Yemayá blesses you, she accepts you. She will always protect you now."

I looked up at her with wondering eyes. "Is that what hekua
means?"

"Yes, hekua means blessings. And see how Yemayá blesses you?"

María pointed to the water frothing softly around my feet. Small
whirlpools of foam enveloped my ankles, then my knees. Then suddenly an unexpetedly huge wave rose from the sea like a great green
arm. As the wall of water collapsed over my head, I heard María cry
out, "The coins! The coins! . . . Let go the coins!"

I felt myself being drawn out to sea inside a glimmering cocoon,
with the rushing sound of a thousand crystal bells. I opened my arms

to embrace the sea, and the seven pennies fell from my fingers. Almost immediately, the water receded and the waves resumed their usual gentle motion. I stood as before, ankle-deep in foamy water, blinking at the morning sunshine.

I recall little of what happened inside the water. The lingering memory is one of silky green depths, of sun rays shining through the water; of softness, warmth and safety. It was almost as if I had returned to the womb of the world, and felt reluctant to be born anew. This episode at the beach was my first initiation in the Yoruba religion known as Santería.

María used to tell me that the presence of Yemayá is always much stronger in very deep waters. Off the north coast of Puerto Rico, in an area known as Bronson's Deep, the ocean floor plunges down to 27,000 feet. Measured from this depth, the mountains of Puerto Rico would be among the highest in the world, with an approximate height of 31,500 feet. Anything that falls within these waters is lost forever—says the legend—unless Yemayá is offered a prize in exchange for her bounty. Truly, her demands are modest. Seven shiny copper pennies, a bit of sugar cane syrup, and sometimes a few candles are enough to please her. Perhaps it is not the value of the gift that Yemayá really wants, but the faith with which it is given.

In these same waters, on August 16, 1977, off the coast of San Juan, an incident took place which was fully reported in the San Juan *Star*. For several weeks I had been in one of the hotels lining El Condado Avenue, working against a deadline on one of my books. One afternoon, a friend went snorkeling in the deep waters off the San Juan coast. When he returned several hours later, he had a tragic story to tell.

A family from nearby Santo Domingo had come to visit Puerto Rico for the first time. Their thirteen-year-old son disregarded the warnings of the dangerous undercurrents surrounding the coast of San Juan, and the great depths of the waters, and he swam out far from shore. Probably too weak to fight against the currents, the boy suddenly sank under the water and did not surface again. Local lifeguards and members of the Police Rescue Squad tried to locate his body, but all their efforts proved fruitless.

The story spread throughout El Condado, and all the hotels sent out search parties to find the body. The boy's mother was determined not to leave her son's body in the sea, as she wanted to bring it back to Santo Domingo for proper burial. But late in the afternoon of the following day, the authorities called off the search. All the desperate entreaties of the boy's mother fell on deaf ears. The police were sure the powerful undercurrents in these waters had driven the body toward the ocean floor or wedged it in one of the reef's many underwater crevices. But the mother asked to go along with a search party—the very last one, she pleaded. If the body was not found during this last search, she would not insist any further.

After some consideration, the authorities agreed. As the story unfolded in the San Juan *Star*, she brought along with her four white candles. When the boat had gone sufficiently out to sea, she asked the officers to stop the engines. Here, she felt, they would find her son's body. More to humor her than for any other reason, the Rescue Squad officers stopped the boat's engines.

The mother then approached the boat's gunwale and began an impassioned plea to the sea. Kneeling on deck, her hands linked together in prayer, tears streaming down her face, she called out to the sea to return her son's body to her. Reminding the sea that the boy was dead, she proposed that it exchange his body for the candles she had brought along. Since four candles are burned around a coffin, these also represented her dead son.

As she spoke, she pulled the candles from her handbag and threw them overboard. A few minutes later, the Rescue Squad officers aboard the boat watched, aghast, as the boy's body surfaced on the same spot where the candles had sunk into the water.

Had María been aboard that boat, she would not have been at all surprised. Without any doubts she would have stated that Yemayá, the Great Supernal Mother, had taken pity on another mother and had accepted the exchange willingly, and with her blessings. As to the apparent cruelty of the sea in taking the boy's life, María would have probably answered that the sea had been kind, saving him from a life of suffering and giving him eternal life instead.

María held the view that life was an illusion. So, for that matter, was death.

"It's just another way of life, florecita," she would say. "A far better way of life."

I would wrinkle my forehead. "But María, then why do we live this life? Wouldn't it be better to die and live in a better life in the other world instead?"

"No, florecita, we're here for a reason. We're here to learn, to become better so that we can enjoy that other, better life. If we're bad here, we don't go to the better life after this one. Instead, we have to come back, again and again, until we learn to be good."

This simple explanation is exactly the same as the theory of reincarnation expressed by Buddha to his disciple Subhuti in the Diamond Sutra:

"Furthermore, Subhuti, if it be that good men and good women ... are downtrodden, their evil destiny is the inevitable retributive result of sins committed in their mortal lives. By virtue of their present misfortunes, the reacting effects of their past will be thereby worked out, and they will be in a position to attain the Consummation of Incomparable Enlightenment."

The Consummation of Incomparable Enlightenment was the same concept expressed by María as a "better life in the other world."

After she took me out of the water, María dried me, braided my hair and tied it with pink silk ribbons, and then dressed me with the pink organdy dress my grandfather had given me for my birthday. She seemed in very high spirits and hummed a popular tune. When I told her I was happy to have come to the sea and hoped that she would bring me back again, she laughed and hugged me.

"We'll see, florecita, we'll see," she said, putting the finishing touches on a satin bow. "But I'm happy that Yemayá has accepted you. Now you can go to school without María and no harm can come to you."

To my lips came a question that was burning in my mind. "María, why did you tear my clothes?"

She looked at me briefly. Her smile widened, and she returned her attention to my hair.

"Why? Because you had to be presented to Yemayá without clothes, like a newborn baby. I tore the clothes to tell Yemayá you gave up your old life and wanted to start living again with her as your mother."

"And now my mother is not my mother anymore?" I asked in alarm, my eyes filling with tears.

María hugged me again, brushing away my tears with expert fingers. "Of course she is, florecita. But she's your mother on earth, while Yemayá is your mother in heaven and in the sea."

"But who is Yemayá, the sea?" I asked, still confused.

"Yemayá is the Yoruba name of the Virgin Mary, florecita," explained María patiently. "She's the mother of all, of whites and blacks, of yellows and greens; of everybody. But in Africa she's always black because the people there are black, and she wants them to know she's black too."

"But María, the Virgin is not black, she's white. I've seen her in the church." ·

"No, florecita, the Virgin is like your ribbons. She has many colors. Sometimes she's white, sometimes yellow, sometimes she's red, sometimes black. It depends on the color of the people who adore her. She does this to tell the world she loves everybody the same, no matter what their color is. To the Yorubas she's always black because they're black.

"Who are the Yorubas, María?"

María paused in the middle of a braid, her eyes lost in reverie.

"The Yorubas were a great black people." She continued her braiding. "My mammy was Yoruba," she said, with evident pride. "She come to Puerto Rico in 1872, year before abolition."*

When she spoke of her mother, which was often, María reverted to broken Spanish, with African words interspersed. "She comes with two hundred fifty Yorubas from Ife, that's the name of Yoruba land in black country," she added. "Come from Africa, they did, in them slave boats. In chains they brought them, the mean slave merchants—*los negreros*. Many of the black people die on boat, of hunger and sickness, but mostly of broken heart. Yorubas is proud people. Don't like white man."

"I'm white, María," I reminded her sadly.

"No you aren't, florecita," María cried, holding me tight against her. "You aren't white, and you aren't black. You're like the sun and the stars—all light, no color."

*Slavery was abolished in Puerto Rico on March 22, 1873.

She finished tying the last ribbon and stood up with great efforts from her stooped position. Her usually immaculate clothes were drenched with seawater and covered with sand, but she paid no attention to them.

"Old María is not as strong as she used to be," she grunted, flexing her back. "Not like my mammy. My mammy real strong," she said with relish. "She only ten when she come to island. But white man leave my mammy alone. She knew how to talk to the *orishas*."

"What is orisha, María?" I asked.

"Orisha?" she mused. "Yemayá is orisha. Elegguá is orisha. Changó is orisha. Orisha is a saint, a force of the good God. But come," she added, taking me by the hand. "It's no good to ask too many questions all at once. Later, I tell you more."

"But María," I insisted. "Are there many . . . orishas?"

"As many as the grains of sand on the beach. But I only know a dozen or two. There are too many. Someday you'll know them too. But now is time to get back home, florecita, or your mammy will be really worried. And then your cake will be eaten, your presents gone, and the ice cream melted."

The thought of the promised birthday party came rushing back to my five-year-old mind, erasing all thoughts about the shadowy orishas, the Yorubas, and even the black Virgin known as Yemayá.

The pink shoes and socks remained in María's handbag until we emerged from the sand into the path that led back to the road. Free from their confinement, I ran ahead of María toward the bus stop, oblivious of my fine embroidered dress, pigtails dancing in the sun, my small feet encrusted with wet sand. She followed behind me slowly, dragging her heavy brogans, her parcels, and her parasol, tired but always smiling.

NICHOLASA MOHR

Aunt Rosana's Rocker

Casto paced nervously, but softly, the full length of the small kitchen, then quietly, he tiptoed across the kitchen threshhold into the living room. After going a few feet, he stopped to listen. The sounds were getting louder. Casto returned to the kitchen, switched on the light, and sat down trying to ignore what he heard. But the familiar sounds were coming directly from their bedroom, where Zoraida was. They grew louder as they traveled past the tiny foyer, the living room and into the kitchen, which was the room furthest away from her.

Leaning forward, Casto stretched his hands out palms down on the kitchen table. Slowly he made two fists, squeezing tightly, and watched as his knuckles popped out tensely under his skin. He could almost feel her presence there, next to him, panting and breathing heavily. The panting developed into moans of sensual pleasure, disrupting the silence of the apartment.

"If only I could beat someone!" Casto whispered hoarsely, banging his fists against the table and upsetting the sugar bowl. The cover slipped off the bowl, landed on its side and rolled toward the edge of the table. Casto waited for it to drop to the floor, anticipating a loud crash, but the cover stopped right at the very edge and fell quietly and flatly on the table, barely making a sound.

He looked up at the electric clock on the wall over the refrigerator; it was two-thirty in the morning.

Again, Casto tried not to listen and concentrated instead on the night noises outside in the street. Traffic on the avenue had almost completely disappeared. Occasionally, a car sped by; someone's footsteps echoed against the pavement, and off at a distance, he heard a popular tune being whistled. Casto instinctively hummed along until the sound slipped away, and he then realized he was shivering. The old radiators had stopped clanking and hissing earlier; they were now ice-cold. He remembered that the landlord never sent up heat after ten at night. He wished he had thought to bring a sweater or blanket with him; he was afraid of catching a cold. But he would not go back inside; instead, he opened his special section of the cupboard and searched among his countless bottles of vitamins and nutrient supplements until he found the jar of natural vitamin C tablets. He popped several tablets into his mouth and sat down, resigned to the fact that he would rather stay here, where he felt safe, even at the risk of getting a chill. This was as far away as he could get from her, without leaving the apartment.

The sounds had now become louder and more intense. Casto raised his hands and covered his ears. He shut his eyes, trying not to imagine what she was doing now. But with each sound, he could clearly see her in her ecstasy. Casto recalled how he had jumped out of bed in a fright the first time it had happened. Positive that she had gone into convulsions, he had stood almost paralyzed at a safe distance looking down at her. He didn't know what to do. And, as he helplessly watched her, his stomach had suddenly turned ice-cold with fear. Zoraida seemed to be another person. She was stretched out on the bed pulling at the covers; turning, twisting her body and rocking her buttocks sensually. Her knees had been bent upward with her legs far apart and she had thrust her pelvis forward forcefully and rhythmically. Zoraida's head was pushed back and her mouth open, as she licked her lips, moaning and gasping with excitement. Casto remembered Zoraida's eyes when she had opened them for brief moments. They had been fixed on someone or something, as if beckoning; but there was no one and certainly nothing he could see in the darkness of the room. She had rolled back the pupils and only the whites of her eyes were visible. She had blinked rapidly, shutting her eyes and twitching her nose and mouth. Then, a smile had passed her lips and a stream of saliva had run down her chin, neck, and chest.

Now, as he heard low moans filled with pleasure, interrupted by short painful yelps that pierced right through him, Casto could also imagine her every gesture.

Putting down his hands, Casto opened his eyes. All he could do was wait patiently, as he always did, wait for her to finish. Maybe tonight won't be a long one; Casto swallowed anxiously.

He remembered about the meeting he had arranged earlier in the evening without Zoraida's knowledge, and felt better. After work, he had gone to see his mother; then they had both gone to see Zoraida's parents. It had been difficult for him to speak about it, but he had managed somehow to tell them everything. At first they had reacted with disbelief, but after he had explained carefully and in detail what was happening, they had understood his embarrassment and his reluctance to discuss this with anyone. He told them that when it all had begun, he was positive Zoraida was reacting to a high fever and was simply dreaming, perhaps even hallucinating. But, it kept happening, and it soon developed into something that occurred frequently, almost every night.

He finally realized something or someone had taken a hold of her. He was sure she was not alone in that room and in that bed!

It was all bizarre and, unless one actually saw her, he explained, it was truly beyond belief. Why, her actions were lewd and vulgar, and if they were sexual, as it seemed, then this was not the kind of sex a decent husband and wife engage in. What was even harder for him to bear was her enjoyment. Yes, this was difficult, watching her total enjoyment of this whole disgusting business! And, to make matters more complicated, the next day, Zoraida seemed to remember nothing. In fact, during the day, she was normal again. Perhaps a bit more tired than usual, but then, who wouldn't be after such an exhausting ordeal? And, lately she had become even less talkative with him, almost silent. But, make no mistake, Casto assured them, Zoraida remained a wonderful housekeeper and devoted mother. Supper was served on time, chores were done without fuss, the apartment was immaculate, and the kids were attended to without any problems. This happened only at night, or rather early in the morning, at about two or two-thirty. He had not slept properly since this whole affair started. After all, he had to drive out to New Jersey to earn his living, and his strength and sleep were being sapped away. He had even considered sleeping on the living room couch, but he would not be driven out of his own bed. He was still a man, after all, a macho, master of his home, someone to be reckoned with, not be pushed out!

Trying to control his anger, Casto had confessed that it had been a period of almost two months since he had normal and natural relations with his wife. He reminded them that he, as a man, had his needs, and this would surely make him ill, if it continued. Of course, he would not touch her . . . not as she was right now. After all, he reasoned, who knows what he could catch from her? As long as she was under the control of something—whatever it might be— he would keep his distance. No, Casto told them, he wanted no part of their daughter as a woman, not as long as she remained in this condition.

When her parents had asked him what Zoraida had to say about all of this, Casto had laughed, answering that she knew even less about it than he did. In fact, at one point she did not believe him and had sworn on the children's souls, claiming her innocence. But Casto had persisted and now Zoraida had finally believed him. She felt that she might be the victim of something, perhaps a phenomenon. Who knows? When Zoraida's parents and his mother suggested a consultation with Doña Digna, the spiritualist, he had quickly agreed.

Casto jumped slightly in his chair as he heard loud passionate moans and deep groans emanate from the bedroom and fill the kitchen.

"Stop it . . . stop, you bitch!" Casto clenched his teeth, spitting out the words. But he took care not to raise his voice. "Stop it! What a happy victim you are! Puta! Whore! Some phenomenon . . . I don't believe you and your story." But, even as he said these words, Casto knew he was not quite sure what to believe.

The first loud thump startled Casto and he braced himself and waited, anticipating what was to come. He heard the legs on their large double bed pounding the floor as the thumping became louder and faster.

Casto shuddered and folded his arms, digging his fingers into the flesh of his forearms. After a few moments, he finally heard her release, one long cry followed by several grunts, and then silence. He relaxed and sighed deeply with relief; it was all over.

"Animal . . . she's just like an animal, no better than an alley cat in heat." Casto was wet with cold perspiration. He was most frightened of this last part. "Little hypocrite!"

Casto remembered how she always urged him to hurry, be quiet, and get it over with, on account of the children. A lot she cares about him tonight! Never in all their years of marriage had she ever uttered such sounds—he shook his head—or shown any passion or much interest in doing it.

Casto looked up at the clock; it was two minutes to three. He thought about the noise, almost afraid to move, fearful that his downstairs neighbor Roberto might knock on the door any moment. He recalled how Roberto had called him aside one morning and spoken to him, "Two and three in the morning, my friend; can't you and your wife control your passions at such an ungodly hour? My God . . . such goings on! Man, and to tell you the truth, you people up there get me all worked up and horny. Then, when I touch my old lady, she won't cooperate at that time, eh?" He had poked Casto playfully and winked. "Hey, what am I gonna do? Have a heart, friend." Casto shook his head, how humiliating and so damned condescending. They were behaving like the most common, vulgar people. Soon the whole fucking building would know! Roberto Thomas and his big mouth! Yes, and what will that sucker say to me next time? Casto trembled with anger. He wanted to rush in and shake Zoraida, wake her, beat her; he wanted to demand an explanation or else! But, he knew it wouldn't do any good. Twice he had tried. The first time, he had spoken to her the following day. The second time, he had tried to wake her up and she had only become wilder with him, almost violent, scaring him out of the bedroom. Afterwards, things had only become worse. During the day she withdrew, practically not speaking one word to him. The next few nights she had become wilder and the ordeal lasted even longer. No, he could not confront her.

Casto realized all was quiet again. He shut off the light, then stood and slowly, with trepidation, walked through the living room and entered the small foyer leading to their bedroom. He stopped before the children's bedroom, and carefully turned the knob, partially opening the door. All three were fast asleep. He was grateful they never woke up. What could he say to them? That their mother was sick? But sick with what?

As he stood at the entrance of their bedroom, Casto squinted, scrutinizing every corner of the room before entering. The street lights seeping through the venetian blinds dimly illuminated the overcrowded bedroom. All was peaceful and quiet; nothing was disturbed or changed in any visible way. Satisfied, he walked in and looked down at Zoraida. She was fast asleep, breathing deeply and evenly; a look of serene contentment covered her face. Her long dark hair was spread over the pillow and spilled out onto the covers. Casto was struck by her radiant appearance each time it was all over. She had an air of glamour, so strange in a woman as plain as Zoraida. He realized, as he continued to stare at her, that he was frightened of Zoraida. He wanted to laugh at himself, but when Zoraida turned her head slightly, Casto found himself backing out of the room.

Casto stood at the entrance and whispered, "Zoraida, *nena* . . . are . . . are you awake?" She did not stir. Casto waited perfectly still and kept his eyes on her. After a few moments, Casto composed himself. He was sure she would remain sleeping; she had never woken up after it was all over. Slowly, he entered the room and inched his way past the bulky bureau, the triple dresser and the rocking chair near the window, finally reaching his side of the bed.

Casto rapidly made the sign of the cross before he lay down beside Zoraida. He was not very religious, he could take it or leave it; but, now, he reasoned that by crossing himself he was on God's side.

Casto glanced at the alarm clock; there were only two and a half hours of sleep left before starting the long trip out to the docks of Bayonne, New Jersey. God, he was damned tired; he hardly ever got enough sleep anymore. This shit had to stop! Never mind, wait until the meeting. He remembered that they were all going to see Doña Digna, the spiritualist. That ought to change things. He smiled and felt some comfort knowing that this burden would soon be lifted. Seconds later he shut his eyes and fell fast asleep.

Everyone finished supper. Except for the children's chatter and Junior's protests about finishing his food, it had been a silent meal.

Casto got up and opened his special section of the cupboard. The children watched the familiar ritual without much interest as their father set out several jars of vitamins, two bottles of iron and liver tonic, and a small plastic box containing therapeutic tablets. Casto carefully counted out and popped an assortment of twenty-four vitamin tablets into his mouth and then took several spoonfuls of tonic. He carefully examined the contents of the plastic box and decided not to take any of those tablets.

"Okay, Clarita, today you take vitamin C . . . and two multivitamin supplements. You, too, Eddie and Junior, you might as well . . ."

The children accepted the vitamins he gave them without resistance or fuss. They knew by now that no one could be excused from the table until Casto had finished taking and dispensing vitamins and tonic.

"Okay, kids, that's it. You can all have dessert later when your grandparents get here."

Quickly the children left.

Although Casto often suggested that Zoraida should eat properly, he had never asked her to take any of his vitamins or tonic, and she had never expressed either a desire or interest to do so.

He looked at Zoraida as she worked clearing the table and putting things away. Zoraida felt her heart pounding fiercely and she found it difficult to breathe. She wanted him to stop staring at her like that. Lately she found his staring unbearable. Zoraida's shyness had always determined her behavior in life. Ever since she could remember, any attempt that others made at intimate conversations or long discussions created feelings of constraint, developing into such anxiety that when she spoke, her voice had a tendency to fade. This was a constant problem for her; people often asked, "What was that?" or "Did you say something?" These feelings extended even into her family life. When her children asked impertinent questions, she would blush, unable to answer. Zoraida was ashamed of her own nakedness with Casto and would only undress when he was not present. When her children chanced to see her undressed at an unguarded moment, she would be distraught for several days.

It had been Casto's self assurance and his ability to be aggressive and determined with others that had attracted her to him.

Casto looked at Zoraida as she worked. "I'll put my things back and get the coffee started for when they get here," he said. She nodded and continued swiftly and silently with her chores.

Zoraida was twenty-eight, and although she had borne four children (three living, one stillborn) and had suffered several miscarriages, she was of slight build and thin, with narrow hips. She had a broad face and her smile revealed a wide space between her two front teeth. As a result, she appeared frail and childlike, much younger than her years. Whenever she was tired, dark circles formed under her eyes, contrasting against the paleness of her skin. This evening, she seemed to look even paler than ever to Casto; almost ghostlike.

Casto was, by nature, hypochondriacal and preoccupied with avoiding all sorts of diseases. He was tall and robust, with a broad frame; in fact, he was the picture of good health. He became furious when others laughed at him for taking so many vitamins and health foods. Most people ignored his pronouncements of ill health and even commented behind his back. "Casto'll live to be one hundred if he lives a day . . . why, he's as fit as an ox! It's Zoraida who should take all them vitamins and then complain some. She looks like a toothpick, *una flaca*! That woman has nothing to show. I wonder what Casto ever saw in her, eh?"

Yet, it was her frail and sickly appearance that had attracted him the first time he saw her. He was visiting his married sister, Purencia, when Zoraida had walked in with her friend, Anna. Anna was a beautiful, voluptuous young woman with an olive tone to her skin that glowed; and when she smiled, her white teeth and full lips made her appear radiant. Zoraida, thin and pale by contrast, looked ill. In Casto's presence, she had smiled sheepishly, blushing from time to time. Anna had flirted openly, and commented on Purencia's brother, "You didn't tell me you had such a gorgeous macho in your family. Trying to keep him a secret, girl?" But it had been Zoraida that he was immediately drawn to. Casto had been so taken with her that he had confided in a friend that very day, "She really got to me, you know? Not loud or vulgar like that other girl, who was acting like a man, making remarks about me and all. No, she was a real lady. And, she's like, well, like a little sick sparrow flirting with death and having the upper hand. Quietly stubborn, you know? Not at all submissive like it might seem to just anybody looking at Zoraida. It's more as if nobody's gonna make the sparrow healthy, but it ain't gonna die either . . . like it's got the best of both worlds, see?"

Yet, in all their nine years of marriage, Zoraida had never become seriously ill. Her pregnancies and miscarriages were the only time that she had been unable to attend to her family. After the last pregnancy, in an attempt to prevent children, Casto had decided on the rhythm system, where abstention is practiced during certain days of the month. It was, he reasoned, not only sanctioned by the Catholic

Church, but there were no drugs or foreign objects put into one's body, and he did not have to be afraid of catching something nor getting sick.

Even after this recent miscarriage, Zoraida appeared to recover quickly, and with her usual amazing resiliency, managed the household chores and the children all by herself. She even found time to assuage Casto's fears of sickness and prepare special foods for him.

Casto could feel his frustration building inside as he watched her. What the hell was the matter with this wife of his? Quickly he reached into his cupboard and took out some Maalox; God, the last thing he wanted was an ulcer on account of all of this.

"I think I'll coat my stomach." Casto chewed several Maalox tablets vigorously, then swallowed. "This way, I can have coffee later and it won't affect me badly." He waited for a response, but she remained silent. Casto sighed, she don't even talk to me no more . . . well, that's why I invited everybody here tonight, so they could see for themselves! He waited, staring at her, and then asked, "You got the cakes ready? I mean, you got them out of the boxes and everything?"

Zoraida nodded, not looking in his direction.

"Hey! *Coño*, I'm talking to you! Answer!"

"Yes," Zoraida whispered.

"And the cups and plates, you got them for the coffee and cake?"

"Yes," Zoraida repeated.

"I don't know, you know? It's been almost three months since Doña Digna did her job and cured you. I didn't figure you were gonna get so . . . so depressed." Zoraida continued to work silently. "Wait. Stop a minute. Why don't you answer me, eh? Will you look at me, for God's sake!"

Zoraida stopped and faced Casto with her eyes lowered.

"Look, I'm trying to talk to you, understand? Can't you talk to me?" Zoraida kept perfectly still. "Say something, will you?"

"What do you want me to say?" Zoraida spoke softly, without looking at him.

"Can't you look at me when you talk?"

Swiftly and furtively, Zoraida glanced at Casto, then lowered her eyes once more.

"*Coño*, man, what do you think I do all day out there to make a living? Play? Working my butt off in those docks in all kinds of weather

. . . yeah. And for what? To come home to a woman that won't even look at me?" Casto's voice was loud and angry. He stopped, controlled himself, then continued, lowering his voice. "I get up every morning before six. Every freaking morning! I risk pneumonia, rheumatism, arthritis, all kinds of sickness. Working that forklift, eight, ten hours a day, until my kidneys feel like they're gonna split out of my sides. And then, to make it worse, I gotta take orders from that stupid foreman who hates Puerto Ricans. Calling me a spic. In fact, they all hate Puerto Ricans out there. They call me a spic, and they get away with it because I'm the only P.R. there, you know? Lousy micks and dagos! Listen, you know what they . . . ah, what's the use, I can't talk to you. Sure, why should you care? All you do is stay in a nice apartment, all warm and cozy. Damn it! I can't even have my woman like a normal man. First you had a phantom lover, right? Then, ever since Doña Digna took him away, you have that lousy chair you sit in and do your disappearing act. That's all you're good for lately. I can't even come near you. The minute I approach you like a human being for normal sex, you go and sit in that . . . that chair! I seen you fade out. Don't think I'm blind. You sit in that freaking thing, rocking away. You look . . . you . . . I don't even think you're breathing when you sit there! You should see yourself. What you look like is enough to scare anybody. Staring into space like some goddamned zombie! You know what I should do with it? Throw it out, or better yet, bust that piece of crap into a thousand splinters! Yeah, that's what I ought to do. Only thing is, you'll find something else, right? Another lover, is that what you want, so you can become an animal? Because with me, let me tell you, you ain't no animal. With me you're nothing. *Mira*, you know something, I'm not taking no more of this. Never mind, when they get here they can see your whole bullshit act for themselves. Especially after I tell them . . ."

Zoraida barely heard him. The steady sound of the television program and the children's voices coming from their bedroom filled her with a pleasant feeling. How nice, she thought, all the children playing and happy. All fed and clean; yes it's nice and peaceful.

The front doorbell rang.

"There they are." Casto had finished preparing the coffee. "I'll answer the door, you go on and get things ready."

Zoraida heard voices and trembled as she remembered Casto's threats and the fury he directed at her. Now he was going to tell them all sorts of things about her . . . untruths.

"Zoraida, where are you?" She heard her mother's voice, and then the voices of her father, mother-in-law, and sister-in-law.

"Mommy, Mommy," Clarita ran into the kitchen, "Nana and Granpa, and Abuelita and Titi Purencia are here. Can we have the cake now?"

"In a little while, Clarita." Zoraida followed her daughter out into the living room and greeted everybody.

"Mommy, Mommy!" Junior shouted, "Tell Eddie to stop it, he's hitting me!"

"I was not, it was Clarita! Eddie walked over to his little brother and pushed him. Junior began to cry and Clarita ran over and smacked Eddie.

"See?" Casto shouted, "Stop it! Clarita, you get back inside." He jumped up, grabbing his daughter by an elbow and lifting her off the ground. "Demonia, why are you hitting him? Zoraida, can't you control these kids?" He shook Clarita forcefully and she began to whine.

"Casto," Zoraida's thin shriek whistled through the room. "Don't be rough with her, please!"

"See that, Doña Clara, your daughter can't even control her own kids no more." He turned to the children, "Now, all of you, get back inside your room and watch television; and be quiet or you go right to bed and nobody gets any cake. You hear? That means all three, Clarita, Eddie, and you too Junior."

"Can we have the cake now?" Eddie asked.

"I'll call you when it's time. Now go on, go on, all of you." Quickly, the children left.

"Calm yourself, son." Doña Elvira, Casto's mother, walked over to him. "You know how children are, they don't know about patience or waiting; you were no angel yourself, you and your sister."

"Let's go inside and have coffee, everybody." Casto led them into the kitchen. There were six chairs set around the kitchen table. Doña Clara and her husband, Don Isidro, Doña Elvira and her daughter, Purencia, squeezed in and sat down.

"Cut some cake for the kids and I'll bring it in to them," Casto spoke to Zoraida, who quickly began to cut up the chocolate cake and place the pieces on a plate. Everyone watched in silence. "Milk," snapped Casto. Zoraida set out three glasses of milk. Casto put everything on a tray and left.

"So, *mi hijita*, how are you?" Doña Clara asked her daughter.

"I'm okay." Zoraida sat down.

"You look pale to me, very pale. Don't she, Papa?" Doña Clara turned for a moment to Don Isidro, then continued without waiting for an answer. "You're probably not eating right. Zoraida, you have to take better care of yourself."

"All right." Casto returned and sat down with the others. "They're happy now."

"Son," Doña Elvira spoke to Casto. "You look tired, aren't you getting enough rest?"

"I'm all right, Ma. Here, everybody, have some cake and coffee."

Everyone began to help themselves.

"It's that job of his. He works so hard." Doña Elvira reached over and placed an extra large piece of chocolate cake on Casto's plate before continuing, "He should have stayed in school and become an accountant, like I wanted. Casto was so good at math, but . . . instead, he . . ."

"Pass the sugar, please," Doña Clara interrupted, "and a little bit of that rum cake, yes. Thank you."

They all ate in silence.

Doña Elvira looked at Zoraida and sighed, trying to hide her annoyance. What a sickly looking woman, *bendito*. She looks like a mouse. To think my handsome, healthy son, who could have had any girl he wanted, picked this one. Doña Elvira could hardly swallow her cake. Duped by her phony innocence is what it was! And how could he be happy and satisfied with such a woman? Look at her, she's pathetic. Now, oh yes, now, he's finding out who she really is: not the sweet innocent one, after all! Ha! First a phantom lover and now . . . who knows what! Well, we'll see how far she can go on with this, because now he's getting wise. With a sense of smug satisfaction, Doña Elvira half-smiled as she looked at her daughter-in-law, then ate her cake and drank her coffee.

Purencia saw her mother's look of contempt directed at Zoraida. She's jealous of Zoraida, Purencia smiled. Nobody was ever good enough for Casto. For her precious baby boy, well, and there you have it! Casto finally wanted Zoraida. Purencia smiled, serves Ma right. She looked at her sister-in-law who sat with her head bowed. God, she looks sicker than ever, but she never complains. She won't say nothing, even now, when he's putting her through this whole number. Poor goody-two-shoes Zoraida, she's not gonna get on Casto's case for nothing; like, why is he jiving her? I wonder what it is she's doing now? After that whole scene with Doña Digna, I thought she cured her of whatever that was. Purencia shrugged, who knows how it is with these quiet ones? They're the kind that hide the action. Maybe she's doing something nobody knows about . . . well, let's just see.

Doña Clara looked at her son-in-law, Casto, with anger and a scowl on her face. *Bestia* . . . brute of a man! He doesn't deserve anyone as delicate as Zoraida. She has to wait on that huge monster hand and foot. With all his stupid medicines and vitamins when he's as fit as a horse! Ungrateful man. He got an innocent girl, pure as the day she was born, that's what. Protected and brought up right by us. Never went out by herself. We always watched out who her friends were. She was guarded by us practically up until the moment she took her vows. Any man would have been proud to have her. *Canalla! Sinvergüenza!* She's clean, hardworking and obedient. Never complains. All he wants to do is humiliate her. We already went to Doña Digna, and Casto said Zoraida was cured. What now, for pity's sake? Doña Clara forced herself to turn away from Casto because the anger fomenting within her was beginning to upset her nerves.

Don Isidro sat uneasily. He wished his wife would not drag him into these things. Domestic disputes should be a private matter, he maintained emphatically, between man and wife. But, his wife's nerves were not always what they should be, and so he had to be here. He looked at his daughter and was struck by her girlish appearance. Don Isidro sighed, the mother of three children and she hasn't filled out . . . she still has the body of a twelve-year-old. Well, after all, she was born premature, weighing only two pounds at birth. Don Isidro smiled, remembering what the doctors had called her. "The miracle baby," they had said, "Mr. Cuesta, your daughter is a miracle. She should not be alive." That's when he and Clara had decided to give her the middle name of Milagros. He wanted a son, but after Zo-

raida's birth, his wife could bear no children, and so he had to be satisfied with what he had. Of course, he had two grandsons, but they
wouldn't carry on his last name, so, in a way it was not the same.
Well, she's lucky to be married at all. Don Isidro nodded slightly, and
Casto is a good, honest, hardworking man, totally devoted. Don't
drink or gamble; he don't even look at other women. But, he too was
lucky to get our Zoraida. After all, we brung her up proper and right.
Catholic schools. Decent friends. Don Isidro looked around him at
the silent table and felt a stiffness in his chest. He took a deep breath;
what had she done? This whole business confused him. He thought
Doña Digna had made the situation right once more.

"So, Casto, how are you? How's work?" Don Isidro asked.

"Pretty good. The weather gets to me, though. I have to guard
against colds, and sitting in that forklift gives me a sore back. But, I'm
lucky to have work, the way things are going."

"You're right, they're laying off people everywhere. You read
about it in the news everyday."

"Zoraida, eat something," Doña Clara spoke to her daughter.

"I'm not hungry, Mami," Zoraida's voice was just above a whisper.

"Casto, you should see to it that she eats!" Doña Clara looked at her
son-in-law, trying to control her annoyance. "Whatever this problem
is, I'm sure part of it is that your wife never eats."

"Why should he see that she eats or not?" Doña Elvira interjected,
"He has to go to work everyday to support his family . . . he hasn't
got time to . . ."

"Wait a minute, Ma," Casto interrupted, "the problem here ain't
food. That's not gonna solve what's going on."

"It seems to solve all your problems, eh?" Doña Clara looked at
Casto with anger.

"Just hold on now . . . wait," Don Isidro raised his hand. "Now, we
are all arguing here with each other and we don't even know what
the problem is. Why don't we find out what's going on?" Don Isidro
turned to Casto and waited.

Everyone fell silent. Don Isidro continued, "I thought that Doña
Digna's treatment worked. After all, you told us that yourself."

"It's not that no more," Casto looked around him, "it's something
else now."

"What?" Doña Elvira asked.

Casto looked at Zoraida, who sat with her hands folded on her lap and her eyes downcast.

"Weren't things going good for you two?" Don Isidro asked. "I mean, things were back to normal relations between you, yes?"

"Yes and no," Casto said. "Yes for a while and then . . ."

"Then what?" Doña Elvira asked. "What?"

Casto looked at Zoraida. "You want to say something, Zoraida?" She shook her head without looking at anyone.

"All right, then like usual, I gotta speak. You know that rocking chair Zoraida has? The one she brought with her when we got married?"

"You mean the one she's had ever since she was little? Why, we had that since Puerto Rico, it belonged to my *titi* Rosana." Doña Clara looked perplexed. "What about the rocker?"

"Well, she just sits in it, when . . . when she shouldn't." Casto could feel the blood rushing to his face.

"What do you mean she sits in it?" Doña Clara asked. "What is she supposed to do? Stand in it?"

"I said *when she shouldn't.*"

"Shouldn't what?" Doña Clara turned to Don Isidro, "Papa, what is this man talking about?"

"Look," Casto continued, "this here chair is in the bedroom. That's where she keeps it. All right? Now when, when I . . . when we . . ." Casto hesitated, "you know what I mean. Then, instead of acting like a wife, she leaves the bed and sits in the chair. She sits and she rocks back and forth."

"Does she stay there all night?" Doña Elvira asked.

"Pretty much."

Everyone looked at Zoraida, who remained motionless without lifting her eyes. A few moments passed before Don Isidro broke the silence.

"This is a delicate subject, I don't know if it's a good thing to have this kind of discussion here, like this."

"What do you want me to do, Isidro? First she has those fits in bed, driving me nuts. Then we call in Doña Digna, who decides she knows what's wrong, and puts me through a whole freakin' rigama- role of prayers and buying all kinds of crap. After all of that *pendejá*, which costs me money that I frankly don't have, then she tells me my wife is cured. Now it starts again, except in another way. Look, I'm only human, you know? And she," Casto pointed to Zoraida, "is denying me what is my right as a man and as her husband. And I don't know why she's doing this. But I do know this time you're gonna be here to know what's going on. I ain't going through this alone. No way. And get myself sick? No!"

"Just a moment, now," Doña Clara said, "you say Zoraida sits in the rocker when you . . . approach her. Does she ever sit there at other times? Or only at that time?"

"Once in a while, at other times, but always . . . always, you know, at that time!"

"Ay . . . *Dios mío!*" Doña Elvira stood up. "I don't know how my son puts up with this, if you ask me." She put her hands to her head. "Casto has the patience of a saint, any other man would do . . . do worse!"

"What do you mean, the patience of a saint?" Doña Clara glared at Doña Elvira. "And do worse what? Your son might be the whole cause of this, for all I know . . ."

"Now, wait." Don Isidro stood up. "Again, we are fighting and blaming this one or that one. This will get us nowhere. Doña Elvira, please sit down." Doña Elvira sat, and then Don Isidro sat down also. "Between a man and wife, it's best not to interfere."

"Okay then, Papa, what are we here for?" Doña Clara asked.

"To help, if we can," Purencia spoke. Everyone listened; she had not spoken a word before this. "I think that's what my brother wants. Right, Casto?" Casto nodded, and then shrugged. "Let Zoraida say something," Purencia continued. "She never gets a chance to say one word."

"Nobody's stopping her." Casto looked at Zoraida. "Didn't I ask her to say something? In fact, maybe she can tell us what's going on. Like, I would like to know too, you know."

"Zoraida," Doña Clara spoke firmly to her daughter, "*mira*, you better tell us what all of this is about."

Zoraida looked up, meeting her mother's angry stare. "I don't know what Casto means about the chair."

"Do you sit in the rocker or do you not sit there, like he says?" her mother asked.

"Sometimes."

"Sometimes? What times? Is it like the way he says it is? Because, if this is so, we want to know why. Doña Digna told me, you and all of us, that there was an evil spirit in you that was turning your thoughts away from your husband, so that you could not be a wife to him. After she finished her treatment, she said the evil spirit or force was gone, and that you would go back to a normal husband-and-wife relationship. We have to accept that. She is a woman of honor that has been doing this work for many years, and that she is telling us the truth, yes?" Doña Clara took a deep breath. "But, if you feel anything is wrong, then it could be that Doña Digna did not succeed." She turned to Casto. "That's possible too, you know. These things sometimes get very complicated. I remember when the Alvarez household was having the worst kind of luck. Don Pablo had lost his job, his wife was sick, and one of their boys had an accident; all kinds of problems, remember? You remember, Papa? Well, Doña Digna had to go back, and it took her a long time to discover the exact cause and then to make things straight again." She turned to Zoraida. "*Bueno, mi hija*, you have to tell us what you feel, and if you are doing this to your husband, why." Doña Clara waited for her daughter's response. "Go ahead. Answer, *por Dios!*"

"I . . ." Zoraida cleared her throat in an effort to speak louder. "I just sit in the rocker sometimes. Because I feel relaxed there."

"Yeah!" Casto said. "Every time I go near her at night, or at two or three in the morning, she relaxes." He raised his hand and slammed the table, "Goddamned chair!"

"*Calmate, mi hijito*, calm yourself." Doña Elvira put her hand over her eyes. "I don't know how long my son can put up with all of this. Now she's got an obsession with a chair. *Virgen, purisima!* Somebody has to tell me what is going on here!"

"Listen to me," Don Isidro spoke in a firm voice, "if it's the chair that bothers you, then we'll take it back home with us. Right, Mama?" He turned to Doña Clara, who nodded emphatically. "There should be no objection to that, eh?"

Everyone looked at Casto, who shrugged, and then at Zoraida, who opened her mouth and shook her head, but was unable to speak.

"Very good." Don Isidro clasped his hands and smiled. "There, that ought to take care of the problems pretty much."

"Except, she might find something else." Casto said. "Who knows with her."

"Well, but we don't know that for sure, do we?" Don Isidro replied, "and in the meantime, we gotta start somewhere."

"I feel we can always call Doña Digna in again if we have to." Doña Clara poured herself a cup of coffee. "After all, she was the one that told us Zoraida was cured."

"I agree," Doña Elvira said, "and even though she don't ask for money, I know my Casto was very generous with her."

"That's right, they don't charge, but after all, one has to give these people something, or else how can they live?" agreed Doña Clara.

"Isn't the weather funny this spring?" Doña Elvira spoke amiably. "One minute it's cold and the next it's like summer. One never knows how to dress these . . ."

They continued speaking about the weather and about television programs. Purencia spoke about her favorite movie.

"That one about the professional hit-man, who has a contract out to kill the President of England . . . no, France, I think. Anyway, remember when he goes into that woman's house and kills her? I was so scared, I loved that movie."

Everyone agreed, the best kinds of movies were mysteries and thrillers.

Zoraida half listened to them. They were going to take away the rocker. She had always had it, ever since she could remember. When she was a little girl, her parents told her it was a part of their history. Part of Puerto Rico and her great Aunt Rosana, who was very beautiful and had countless suitors. The chair was made of oak with intricate carving and delicate caning. As a little girl, Zoraida used to rub her hands against the caning and woodwork admiringly, while she rocked, dreamed, and pretended to her heart's content. Lately it had become the one place where she felt she could be herself, where she could really be free.

"*Bueno*, we have to go. It's late."

"That's right, me too."

"Wait," Casto told them, "I'll drive you people home."

"You don't have to . . ." Don Isidro protested. "We know you are tired."

"No, I'm not. Besides, I gotta drive Ma and Purencia home anyway."

"That's right," Purencia said, "my old man doesn't like me going out at night. It's only because of Mami that he let me. So, Casto has to take me home."

"I gotta get you the chair, wait," Casto said. "And, you don't wanna carry that all the way home. It's not very big, but still, it's a lot to lug around."

"All right then, very good."

Everyone got up and Zoraida began to clear away the dishes.

"Let me help you," Doña Clara said as she stood up.

"Me too," Doña Elvira said, without rising.

"No, no thanks. That's all right. I can do it myself," Zoraida said. "Besides, I have to put the kids to bed and give them their milk and all."

"I don't know how she does it. Three little ones and this place is always immaculate." Doña Clara turned to Doña Elvira. "It's really too much for her, and she has no help at all."

Doña Elvira stood. "She keeps a very clean house," she said, and walked out with Purencia following after Casto and Don Isidro.

Doña Clara looked at her daughter, who worked silently and efficiently. "*Mira, mi hija*, I better talk to you." She stood close to Zoraida and began to speak in a friendly manner, keeping her voice low. "You have to humor men; you must know that by now. After all, you are no longer a little girl. All women go through this difficulty, eh? You are not the only one. Why, do you know how many times your father wants . . . well, you know, wants it? But I, that is, if I don't want to do it, well I find a way not to. But diplomatically, you know? All right, he's older now and he bothers me less; still, what I mean is, you have to learn that men are like babies and they feel rejected unless you handle the situation just right. Now, we'll take the rocker back home with us because it will make him feel better. But you must do your part too. Tell him you have a headache, or a backache, or you can even pretend to be asleep. However, once in a while you have to please him, you know. After all, he does support you and the children and he needs it to relax. What's the harm in it? It's a small sacrifice. Listen, I'll give you some good advice; make believe you are enjoying it and then get it over with real quick, eh? So, once in a while you have to, whether you like it or not; that's just the way it is for us. Okay? Do you understand?" Zoraida turned away and, without responding, continued with her work. "Did you hear what I just told you?" Doña Clara grabbed Zoraida's shoulder firmly, squeezing her fingers against the flesh. "You didn't even hear what I said to you!"

Zoraida pulled away and turned quickly, facing her mother. She looked directly at Doña Clara, "I heard you . . ." Zoraida stopped and a smile passed her lips. "I heard every word you said, Mami."

"Oh, all right then . . ." Doña Clara said, somewhat startled by her daughter's smile. "I only wanted to . . ."

"Mama! Come on, it's time to go," Don Isidro's voice interrupted her.

Doña Clara and Zoraida went into the living room. Casto carried the rocking chair and waited by the door. The children had come out of their room and were happily jumping about.

"Look, Mommy, Granpa gave me a quarter," Clarita said.

"Me too," said Eddie. "He even gave Junior one."

"All right, get to bed!" Casto shouted. "Zoraida, put them down, will you?"

Everybody said goodbye and, in a moment, Casto and the others left.

"Mommy, where is Daddy taking your chair?" Clarita asked.

"To Nana's."

"Why?"

"Because they want it now."

"Don't you want it no more?"

"I already had it for a long time, now they need to have it for a while."

Zoraida gave the children their milk, bathed them and put them to bed. Then, she finished rapidly in the kitchen and went to bed herself. She looked over at the empty space near the window. It was gone. She wouldn't be able to sit there anymore and meet all her suitors and be beautiful. The last time . . . the last time she was dancing to a very slow number, a ballad. But she couldn't remember the words. And she was with, with . . . which one? She just couldn't remember him anymore. If she had the rocker, she could remember; it would all come back to her as soon as she sat down. In fact, she was always able to pick up exactly where she had left off the time before. She shut her eyes, deciding not to think about the rocker, about Casto, Doña Digna, or her mother. Instead, Zoraida remembered her children, who were safe and asleep in their own beds. In a short while, she heard the front door open and recognized Casto's footsteps. She shut her eyes, turned over, facing away from his side of the bed. Casto found the apartment silent and dark, except for the night-light.

In the bedroom, Casto looked at Zoraida, who seemed fast asleep, then at the empty space near the window where the rocker usually stood. Their bedroom seemed larger and his burden lighter. Casto sighed, feeling better. He reached over and lightly touched Zoraida; this was a safe time of the month, maybe she would wake up. He waited and, after a moment, decided to go to sleep. After all, he could always try again tomorrow.

ANA LYDIA VEGA

Aerobics for Love

Ce n'est pas la personne de l'autre qui m'est nécessaire, c'est l'espace: la possibilité d'une dialectique de désir, d'une imprévision de la jouissance: que les jeux ne soient pas faits, qu'il y ait un jeu.

—ROLAND BARTHES

It is not the other's being that I need, it is the space: the possibility of a dialectics of desire, of a randomness of jouissance; that the die be not cast, that all remains to be played for.

I

Your head starts nodding during the news at eleven, but you make the effort and keep those eyes open until after the late show so you'll be totally and irremediably zonked.

You toss and turn in the bed, with your rollers digging into your scalp and the alarm clock ticking like a time bomb in your ear. You close down the shop, count sheep, breathe as deep as you can. You squeeze, relax, squeeze, relax. You repeat the mantra to exorcise tension and keep those stressful thoughts at bay. You relive the boss's nasty remark, the latest fight with the ex over the kid's child-support check, the note from the landlord saying you can't water your plants after dark. You suddenly remember the five gray hairs that subvert the blackness of your hair, the creeping cellulitis, the tiny pain in the breast every time you assert yourself a little more forcefully than usual. And it's good-bye to sweet dreams, hello to those bewitching dark circles under your eyes. You spend another insomniac night. Until exhaustion finally takes over and you faint dead away just as the alarm sounds—not a single Z.

You peel the sheet off you the best you can. You look for those slippers but you can't find them. You walk that chilly floor and try not to think about catching cold. And you turn up your toes because the grit on the floor makes the bottom of your feet prickle. You avoid thinking about the mop.

You wash out the coffeepot, throw out yesterday's grounds, turn on the stove and close the refrigerator that the kid left open as he went off for the weekend with good ol' Dad. You take out the melted margarine. You put the dried out three-day-old bread in the toaster, put the coffeepot on the only burner that works. And you sprint to the bathroom to rinse out your mouth, wipe the cold cream out of the wrinkles with a cotton pad moistened with witch hazel. You throw the obscene nightgown that dates from when you were happily married into the clothes hamper. You fly into the kitchen naked when you smell burnt toast. You don't have time to toast another slice, but it's an ill wind that blows nobody good—a hundred calories less isn't bad. And you go back to the bathroom and brush your teeth and grab your feet and pull them up into the sink so you can save yourself another shower before you put on the new high heels you just bought yourself the other day.

You hook the bra, slip on the panties. The blouse with the drop-dead neckline gets caught on your rollers when you try to pull it on over your head. You yank off the offending roller and discover that your hair isn't dry yet. So you get desperate and try to find the hair dryer that's never where you left it last time and, oh thank god, you find it and plug it in and turn it on. And your hairdo is punk before its time. So now you're dripping with sweat and the bad mood is creeping up on you. That precarious line you tremblingly, breathlessly draw along the crow's-foot at the outside edge of your right eye wavers and takes a detour. And from your soul you dredge up the energy to say Shit.

The mauve skirt is wrinkled. But it's a straight skirt, so you climb in, wriggling your backside and exercising your triceps, and hoping your curves will put a nice press in it. You grab your purse and are about to be out of there when you remember one last important detail. You stand on the landing and you open your purse, you take out your compact, you pucker up, you aim, and your smile is suddenly wreathed in mauve glory.

This is the moment when you regret having given up the car so you could keep the furniture. Because now you have to take the bus. And Saturday is not a weekday. And the driver takes his own sweet time. And people badmouthing at the bus stop. And you know it's late, you've barely got time, if that bus doesn't come in the next few seconds, your life'll be set back seven days.

The pumpkin-disguised-as-a-bus comes. You grab the life-saving bar. Your perfume fuddles the air. The looks go u-u-u-p, the looks go do-o-o-wn.

But the bell doesn't work. A disgusted passenger has ripped it out. You're obsessed that you'll pass your stop. And the bus goes on, and on . . . You squeeze your way through the people, dancing clumsily toward the door. And naturally you get off at the wrong stop.

You click your way up the street. Walking fast in a straight skirt is excellent exercise. You gain on the bus. And then little by little you slow down. The lines on the sidewalk make you dizzy. You try to synchronize your steps and your breathing.

Deliberately slow, deliberately fabulous, you come to the corner where you're to stake everything. Your feet want to beat it. Your hands turn to ice. Your heart is about to jump out your throat. But you walk, a marvel of mind control, eyes fixed on some distant spot, as indifferent as a duchess, past the door.

And you see without looking—it's the smell, or the sweetness of the air, or that nice warm feeling, or all of it at once, or nothing at all—that He is standing there at the counter, and that today, like every Saturday of the world, you're about to be swept off your feet and into the orbit of those eyes.

II

He gives a blow-by-blow description of the scene—there he stood, like an African king out of *Tarzan*, one foot upon the toilet seat, the other holding the door closed, a wall of wild graffiti at his back, a slave kneeling at his feet, while outside a gang of bearers bearing bursting bladders awaited their chance to drop their loads—and he had had the orgasm of the century, only surpassed in intensity by the more lasting thrill of retelling it.

She proceeds, immediately thereafter, to recall the secret hand-job with which one Monday afternoon, in the first row of a movie-house in Santurce, she had rewarded the patience of her cousin, who sat goggle-eyed in contemplation of the Triple XXX epic *Coitus Uninterrupted*.

To which He counters with a faithful and detailed recounting of the threesome he had with his boss's wife and daughter in the family room (oh yes) of his boss's house one night while that asshole was drunkenly cheering Roberto Durán on to a championship K.O., a story She immediately one-ups with another domestic tale—this one taking place in her kitchen one morning when, offering to teach her best girlfriend's husband some special homemaking skills, she had showed him a new way of cookin' with Crisco.

Which evokes from Him the nostalgic recollection of his younger days as a male hustler on the beach in the Condado, the strains of an old-time orchestra playing in the background, the smell of suntan lotion and barbecues in the air, as he knelt in the shadow of one of the most luxurious hotels on the beach and planted his hot dog in a gringo tourist's buns.

Which in turn brings to Her the now-fading memory of the experimental lessons in lesbianism she had so kindly given—a special introductory offer, one time only—to her ex-sister-in-law the day after her divorce.

Which leads Him to remember his German shepherd and Her her palomino pony and Him his soft papayas and Her her green bananas and Him his telepathic orgasms and Her her metaphysical orgies.

And then there is silence, in spontaneous tribute to all that still remains to tell.

He looks at Her. And smiles. And He says, in a voice that tries but fails to be objective and detached:

"Oh baby, thank goodness you and I never tied the knot . . ."

III

Everybody else has either split up or is headed that way. Except, of course, for us. Ten years and counting—a record for domestic stability. Not that I'm against breaking up, when you have to. When things don't work out, it's better to cut your losses, save what can be saved, and get on with your life.

But it's that . . . I'm almost embarrassed to say this . . . we're, like, *happy*. No, really, I'm not kidding. Perfectly compatible, I'd say—which is really pretty amazing. The same likes and dislikes, the same way of looking at things, the same sense of humor, the same tastes. No kids? We haven't wanted kids. We're busy just trying to get by.

There are people that can't quite cope with how long we've lasted. "Still together?" they'll say, like they expect us to say "Nope, not anymore." People have bets going, there are surveys, estimates— *I'll give 'em one more week. How many is it now?*

Us? Get real, we just laugh. Although it's no joke. A person could begin to feel . . . I don't know, *weird*. Is something wrong with us, are we brain-dead, or just bored? Are we stupid, is that it? Or are we too profound? Do you have to be stupid to be happy? But even our complexes don't affect our contentment.

To avoid stress, which everyone's got all they need of anyway, we never go to parties. We don't have any big tragedies to talk about, any traumas we care to discuss. And when we run into some divorced friend of ours, we just wave and keep on going.

We just cross ourselves discreetly and keep on going. And we don't look back. Hell or high water, come what may—two may be company, but three, so far as we're concerned, three's the only way.

JACK AGÜEROS

Malig; Malig & Sal; Sal.

FROM *DOMINOES AND OTHER STORIES FROM THE PUERTO RICAN*

I

MALIG

Malig stepped out of the bath wondering why they didn't put showers in the bathrooms of public housing projects. A bath always takes far longer than a shower, even when you hurry. When Sal offered to hook up a shower for them, the housing manager had said it was prohibited. Her dumb mother had asked instead of just doing it. Now they sent a guy around to look at the apartment regularly. Before that, you never saw one of them bastards. Sal was right, you should never tell a landlord nothing.

Standing in front of the mirror still wet, she began to place a few large rollers in her hair and a few small ones. Her mouth full of pins and a cigarette, her hair brush held under her arm, she was leaning close to the mirror, trying hard to keep all the elements under control, straining to see what she was doing. She had promised herself a pair of contact lenses. One of the salesmen at RexCo had told her that she could get a pair and full exam for $230 and that included insurance against loss. She was terribly nearsighted and had to wear thick glasses, but even if they had been thin, she was ready for a drastic change in her life, and that had to include her appearance.

The rollers were in place nice and tight. And she sprayed them with a new "Wet Fixer" she picked up at the drugstore the day before. She was going to cut her hair still shorter, and dye it a different color, and start some exercises to make her breasts a size, and maybe two, bigger. And Sal was right—she had to do something about her round shoulders—other exercises and more concentration on how she stood.

She left the bathroom and went to the kitchen, opened her refrigerator, and took out a bottle of Tom Collins mix and a bottle of Maraschino cherries. On the table she had laid out a bowl full of ice cubes, some lemons, an orange, a sharp knife, and a candle. She was going to give Sal a party tonight. She plunked two cubes into a glass, poured in the mix, added a cherry and some syrup. Then she walked to her room and pulled the gin bottle from where it was hidden, poured a drink into the mix, stirred it, took a slug, and then took out the pint of Bacardi Rum and the bottle of wine from the same hiding place. She never knew what Sal would be drinking, but she had gotten everything he liked including twelve cans of Schaefer beer. He could drink when he felt like it. She brought the bottles back to the kitchen and with her drink in her hand she took a tour of the apartment looking for anything out of place, discovering something slightly erotic in the idea of being very naked, very free.

When she saw the clock in the decorated mirror hanging over the sofa in the living room, she gulped another quantity of her drink and headed back for the bathroom, where she started to put her makeup on. Almost immediately she could see that someone had been in her makeup bag, and her little brush for applying eye liner was gone. Straight for her kid sister's room, she decided, since her mother always was decent enough to put things back. She hated anybody using her makeup because she paid so much for it and here she was stuck with a mother, a grandmother, two kid sisters, and her own daughter to raid her things. She wondered why they didn't put doors on the closets in the public housing projects, or on the openings into the rooms. These damn curtains over everything made her feel stuffed up. More reasons she should leave.

She found her brush and a couple of tubes of old lipsticks which she thought she had lost, and began putting her makeup on again. How would she tell Sal?

Look Sal, I'm twenty-two and have a daughter almost three, and I am getting old and I ain't getting any prettier and I need to get away from my family, from you and from my lousy job, and I need somebody to take care of me, to give me a house and a car and the life of a housewife, and good weather and a nice place to live without crowded trains and people inspecting your apartment. I'm tired of life with not enough and debts and too many people in one apartment and no privacy about anything, not even a private tube of toothpaste that somebody else won't use and misuse.

But she couldn't put it like that to Sal because he would say, "move in with me." And then he would say something funny like "I won't brush my teeth ever again." And she couldn't tell him she thought his apartment was a terrible dump and she couldn't understand why he wouldn't take his parent's apartment in the Bronx. That was the whole trouble with him. He wanted just the opposite of the things she wanted. He wouldn't take a real job and she knew he could get one. He didn't want the nice apartment in the Bronx—wanted a shitty one on the Lower East Side because it was "closer." Closer to what she didn't know. But she had known him ten years, gone out with him for two, and instead of getting better he was getting worse. Always talking about leaving school, about how he didn't like the people there. But he wouldn't leave, and he steadily was changing, he seemed more unsure of himself, more unsure of what he wanted to do. "Don't you want to make money?" she would ask him, and he would say "I don't know. I don't think so." And what was this bullshit about poetry and writing? And he was getting more complicated and he enjoyed everything less. He didn't want to go to parties, he wouldn't dress up. When he was a teenager he had a reputation for being smart. He had folks who worked and they bought everything he wanted as long as he did well in school. He always had good clothes. And after the service he started to change. Same time he started school. It was a pity, that college was messing up the smartest man she knew. Only he wasn't a man, he might be sometime, but he wasn't one now. The man she had been seeing off and on for a year now from RexCo, he was a man, and ready to take care of her—but he also lacked something. He didn't move her—sex appeal—maybe it was just that he wasn't Latin. He was ready to put up an apartment for her, pay her rent, and furnish the place too. And he didn't want any entanglements, he was married and he wanted to stay married. She had thought a lot about his offer. He just wanted a place to get

away to, and a girl who would treat him right. He didn't want to
know what she did all the time, she just had to reserve some time for
him. And he wasn't bad looking, nor stiff like some of the other men
at RexCo, and he would take her on a trip now and then. And she
was very tempted. She had ideas about letting him keep her and then
having Sal around all the time. Nobody moved her like Sal, that was a
fact. And she knew that Sal loved her, truly loved her, or else he
wouldn't, couldn't, put up with all the shit she gave him. But she was
afraid of Sal too. She could play with him, but he wasn't a punk. The
guy at the office would accept Sal, but it wouldn't work the other
way around. There was a story that Sal had shot a gang kid once in a
playground at point blank, and that he had a very violent side, that
luckily didn't come out very often. But being kept was only part of an
answer, for Howard wasn't rich enough to keep her all the way. She
would have to work and there was Linda, her baby. How would she
fit in to being kept by Howard and living with Sal part time? It was
too crazy but the offer of the apartment had been tempting and she
had begun to see in it a real solution. She had to simplify the formula.
Find a man who would keep her well, full time. Reduce the men to
one instead of two. She couldn't give up Sal for Howard. It was not
right. Howard was not enough and Sal was true. So she had decided
to leave them both, go to Puerto Rico, and start again. Change her
looks and her way of life. That would hurt Sal, but it was fair. It was
fair for what he had given her that was good.

And that was one of the painful parts. Sal had given her good, very
good things and feelings. He was a man in so many ways that she had
come to be very fascinated with him. He knew how to move her and
that was special. And he had a way of holding her, possessive and
proud. But when they went to parties or in public like at the club, he
let her have her freedom to come and go and dance with whomever
she wanted. And he was jealous, he admitted it, but he said he had to
stay in control of things like that, "Or I'll have to kill every man that
looks at you, every creep who ogles that behind of yours." And he
was generous with his praise and made her feel sexy and attractive
and wanted. He didn't do those little things like try to flirt with other
girls or act disinterested in her while she was around other men or
women. And he had been good to Linda, giving her his time and

showing in the way he was with her, the way he talked to that little girl, that he could be a real father, better than her flesh and blood father.

"Sal," she said out loud to the mirror, "I love you but we can't make it." She washed off her right eye and began again. If only he had stayed the way he was when he came out of the service. He had a beautiful little sports car and he dressed in the latest things. Late at night he would take her through the drive in the park going at incredible speeds and doing things with his shift, downshifting he called it, so she thought the car would explode. And when they got to that part of Central Park that was called Snake Hill, she had to close her eyes sometimes the way he would go down that hill the car swaying from side to side and going round on two wheels. Yes he was wild, he couldn't stop driving hard, couldn't stay home one night, not one night in the week, and if he went to a movie then he'd find another place to go afterwards, and it was out 'til one or two in the morning every night. And two or three times a week he borrowed his father's red and white Oldsmobile and they would wind up in the backseat and he would ball her. Sometimes in his father's garage, sometimes in Central Park. They would leave the car and go off into the bushes. The first time they ever balled was in the park. He had said, "Goddamn it, Malig, if you blow in my ear again, I'm gonna ball you right here." It had been a crazy scene that night since she was wearing skin-tight slacks. And they were afraid together, and afraid of being in the park, and of being seen. And she blew in his ear again. So they took her slacks off only one leg and her panties the same, and they made love in a most uncomfortable position but it had been good good. Once they had been caught making love in the park. Sal had stopped in one of the parking areas, and next thing they knew they were balling right in the front seat. The windows of the car were all steamed up and a cop knocked on one of them. Sal, without getting up, rolled down the window and said, "Yes Sir?" The cop said, "I'm going to be back in fifteen minutes. You better not be here." Sal didn't like that, didn't like the police, and after that he never stopped in the park again. "Too many stories of cops raping girls who are afraid to talk because they have to explain too much. I'm not putting you in that spot again." After that he had started sneaking her in and out of his mother's apartment and finally he had gotten a sort of begrudged permission to have Malig over as a "guest" now and then. It meant that they could sleep late.

Then he sold the sports car. Then he said he was not going to the movies anymore. Then he quit a really good job he had. Then one night he walked into her apartment and pulled the cord out of the T.V. Yanked it right out. While the set was on. What a fight they had that night. That's when her family decided he was crazy. After that her grandmother called him *El Loco. "Como esta El Loco, Malig?"* And then she would roar with laughter as if she could see the scene of Sal pulling the cord out of the T.V. The live wire sparking in his hands. Then he moved out of his mother's house, took a nice apartment in Brooklyn. Big rooms and he left in three months. Moved to the Lower East Side to the awful apartment he had now. A bathtub in the kitchen. Even the projects didn't have bathtubs in the kitchen. And then he disappeared for a whole week. Nobody knew where he was and when he reappeared he said he had been drunk—drunk for five days or seven days or eight days maybe. And when he was asked why he had done that, he said he "didn't know." And he read more and more and said he was doing worse and worse in school, and he started writing. Carrying papers with him and scratching at them all the time, but that gave him no peace either. He had no peace and she didn't know why. And when his mother and father decided to go to Puerto Rico and offered him their very nice apartment in the Bronx and he said no, that was the beginning of the break. That same week she took up Howard's offer of a drink. And she felt that Sal had driven her away.

Exactly.

That's just what she would tell him. She looked at her eyes now. They seemed right. And she started working on her face with a powder brush.

"Sal," she was gonna say, "you drove me away. Not that you stopped loving me or you weren't nice to Linda, or that you found other women, or started flirting, or became careless or cruel. You started driving me away with your behavior—looking sloppy all the time. And the things you said like you weren't going to finish college, or that you didn't wanna work. Those things drove me away. And when you started writing I liked that. I thought it would be good for you because writers don't work like other people work, but they use their brains and they make good money. But you don't write anything. Anything you write you cross out or throw away, or say you have to write it again. A writer has to write. How can I believe you will be a writer if you haven't written anything in more than a year?"

Malig ran to the living room to check the time. She had time for another drink and made herself one. Then she stood in the door of the living room staring at the clock set in the mirror. On the ends of the mirror were two pink flamingoes and around the top edge of the mirror, over the clock, there was a bouquet of many flowers in green and gold. God, it was ugly. Sal was always saying that it was so ugly it was actually beautiful, and that the world was going to begin when the two terrible flamingoes came alive.

When he talked like that it bothered her. Because he could be so serious about it and use all his Sunday words to say that the world had not yet actually begun. That we were all here on earth as a trial. That there would be so many generations and no more. When that time came the clock would decide if man had done well enough to let the world begin. If the discoveries of science and the contributions of art were greater than the evils of war and poverty and exploitation and the misery of people who had to live in rotten conditions, then the world would begin. He hoped now wasn't the time, Sal said, because if now was the time the world would not begin. The clock was God, the flamingoes were angels, and the mirror was the whole universe including heaven because you could see everything in it.

When he talked like that it displeased her because she wasn't sure whether he was serious or not. He sounded serious but she had the feeling that he was making fun of something, himself, her religion, everything. Had college made him crazy? Her mother used to say that too much studying, too much reading, could make people go crazy. It was bad for the *cerebro*. A well-known fact in Puerto Rico. Especially if the person doing the reading and studying does not eat nourishing foods like eggs, avocados, breadfruit and fresh coconuts, water and flesh. That's what Sal's father told her once. And here was Sal eating nothing, drinking too much, not sleeping well, just reading and going to school and doing odd jobs. Maybe he had gone crazy. Maybe all he needed was vitamins. What was it he had said had made him get drunk for a week? He said he had read three books in one week that had depressed him. What were their names? If for no other reason, she should remember them just to be sure not to read them. And who was forcing him to live in rotten conditions? And it was not nice to fool around with God, to say that God was a clock. She had met a girl who had gone out with Sal when he was fifteen, and the girl had said, "Sal's too smart for himself. Smart people are unhappy. Get yourself a nice dumb guy. Sal's been too spoiled by his family, too spoiled by his brains. He don't know what work is, what wanting something is. He never had to do it."

She began to dress, put her eyeglasses on, was satisfied with the thin black lines she had drawn and the faint blue shadow on the upper lids. How well her eyes would look when she would be rid of her glasses. She began to pull the rollers out carefully from her hair and to brush as carefully. She had put on her white dress, the one Sal said drove him wild. No stockings over her beautifully tanned legs. And no panties tonight either. The dress fit beautifully and even the sheerest panties made lines. Tonight she wanted Sal to jump right out of his skin. For she was going to give him a good, very good, good-bye. She wanted him to remember her. Even if she didn't read the books he gave her, and if she hadn't taken the courses or gotten interested in anything that he recommended. They had had sex between them in a beautiful way. She wanted to be remembered by him powerfully, perhaps, because she was afraid that that was how she would remember him. She had difficulty remembering herself in bed with her husband. Tried to remember her dismal marriage, her dismal furnished room with a toilet in the hall. God, everyone in one room, sleep, eat, watch TV, cook. After a while she was grateful that the toilet was outside. It was a break from the monotony of that little cell and it was a chance to be alone although not for long, not with four other families sharing two toilets. She could not remember sex with her husband, although it wasn't that long ago, just that it wasn't pleasant. More like washing dishes, that kind of thing you have to do which ain't really terrible but you don't ever enjoy it. And Howard was boring. And anyway he was so white he looked like a boiled fish and so she was put off. Poor Howard. In a way he took more shit than Sal. Howard spent money on her—restaurants, perfumes, clothing here and there, a very nice watch last Christmas, and what did he get for it? A very moody girl who had gone to bed with him three times in one year, once because she was curious to see the hotel he offered. But she was not going to waste her sympathy on Howard. Howard was a big wheel at RexCo, he was knocking down big bucks and had his wife and house in the country somewhere. His wife could go to the beauty parlor twice a week. She had her own car. What the shit more could she want? And Howard had the story straight from the beginning. Malig had told him he would get nowhere. He persisted in spending his money on her. If he thought what he spent was worth three cold bangs in one year that was his business. After each rotten time with sex, Malig had told Howard she was sorry. She had apologized and told him it would not be any better ever. She had tried to spare his feelings. In fact hadn't she gone to bed with him in the first place because she cared about his feelings? What the hell—it was true he was a *gringo,* but that did not mean she could be cruel to him. No, there was absolutely no point in being sorry for Howard. She had been straight, very straight, with him. But not with Sal. Imagine if Sal ever found out about Howard! Holy shit. There would be hell to pay. It was a frightening thought because Sal was capable of killing her for something like that. He tried to fight his jealousy and she knew it, and she took advantage of the fact, often manipulating him into something simply by asking him if he was jealous. But being unfaithful, and with a *gringo*! And with a *gringo* that she didn't even love or respect. How would she say to him "Look I just felt sorry for the man, so I went to bed with him. There was no feeling, I wasn't even disgusted." How could she expect Sal to understand such a thing. Sal who was so straight, so honest, so childlike when it came to these things.

No.

The best idea was had. She had to say good-bye to Sal. Good-bye to Howard. Howard would be easy. One phone call. Sal would require a night, perhaps two nights, passionate love making and careful, very careful explanations. He would respect anything that was well thought out. She would have to lie and say she already had a job in Puerto Rico. Sal would never accept a scheme which did not include a job. If she presented the plan in terms of personal goals of her own fulfillment, her own freedom, he would accept it. Because he gen- _uinely only wanted the best for her. He had told her once, "If I thought I was bad for you, or that I was keeping you back, I would get out of your life." And it wasn't just a line. Sal had a way of saying and meaning things like that. He said them very simply and very directly, and those were the things he meant. He had also said, "If I thought you were fucking around on me I would take it very badly and I don't know what I would do." And that was true. Sal didn't like to make threats and he also disliked violence. "Only people who can't think use violence. Violence is for stupid people. Smart people never need it, they know better ways of achieving the things they want."

Perhaps she was making a big undue fuss over this parting. She could do it more easily through one or two small lies. She could start by saying that her grandmother's sister was dying and that she had to go to Puerto Rico. Then once she was in Puerto Rico, she could write and say she had been offered a nice job. Then she could write and say she took it. Sal was too wild to sit around waiting for her, too smart not to figure out what was happening after a short time. This way it would seem more natural, his feelings would be spared. She could say she met a nice man. He was proposing marriage. She intended to accept. She would never forget Sal, but she knew he would understand.

No.

She looked at herself in the mirror. A white-dressed devil. She took a short gulp from her drink. Said, "Sal, the world is about to begin for me. I cannot do it by small lies."

And then she took a long gulp from her drink.

ED MORALES

My Old Flame

To celebrate a lost lust is a matter of taste and smell. The smell, a sweet odor around the mouth and nose, the taste, a salty neck. It's also the sight of a candle flickering between two bodies, sitting and facing each other, abdomens thrusting and meeting in the center of the bed. The eros of absence is a deep, yearning one, and when M. stopped sleeping with me, she became the essence of my sexuality.

The architecture of our connection was secret, not for general consumption, which seemed to free us from messy contradictions. We watched John Woo shoot-'em-ups in dark, smelly theaters and then, after the wine, made the most tender love, sprawled, standing, slung across the sofa. Inevitably, we developed a language problem. I couldn't say *it* fast enough. I had suffered previously from several instances where I said *it* early and often, and had made so many sacrifices and fought so hard for *it* that this time I was reluctant to come out and say *it*.

When she finally left, I decided I wasn't going to give up easy. It was time for me to finally consider the mystic arts. I remembered that when my friend Darius was writing his essay "The Blackman's Guide to Seducing White Women," he tried to explain hoodoo to me. "You must know about this stuff. Don't you have an aunt or *abuela* that was into it, putting spells on people?" I sheepishly admitted that I hadn't, that all my relatives were unrelievedly Christian, and that their idea of being Puerto Rican was to denounce spiritualism and Santería as savage paganism.

In Migene González-Wippler's controversial text, *Santería, the Religion: A Legacy of Faith, Rites, and Magic*, she describes a spell to bring back a lover: "A santero hollows a pumpkin and puts inside it five toenails from a rooster, along with an egg, pepper, marjoram, Florida Water, a personal article of the person, and name written on a piece of paper. He spits three times inside the pumpkin and places it in front of Oshun's image, where it remains for 10 days. At the end of this period he throws it into the river." This seemed a little too complicated for me, I wasn't too thrilled about the spitting part, and I worried that I'd draw unwanted attention if seen dumping a funky-looking pumpkin into the East River.

Acting instinctively, I took the 6 train up to 116th Street and stopped by the biggest *botanica* I know, Otto Chicas Rendon, and started asking around for advice. The middle-aged *comadres* were skeptical and bored, so they stuck me with this cheesy purple glass-encased candle that's supposed to be for praying for the secret desires of one's mind, body, and heart. I took it home and made a little altar ("Set up your altar with previously selected, emotion-evoking objects," advised Darius), including the last letter M. wrote me explaining once again why she still wasn't seeing me, and some reed-like twiggy things she'd once brought me from her family's house in the Northwest.

I burned the candle every night for weeks, watching its reflection gleam faintly in the blank TV screen. A full moon passed, then another. ("Always keep the menstrual cycle in mind," said Darius.) These were sexless days, but the candle kept burning, teasing with its fake erection. I began to doubt whether I was capable of making magic. One night I picked the candle up to see if I had scrawled M.'s name clearly enough in the designated space and got stung—the glass was still hot, blistering my fingertips. As I walked over to the sink to stick them into cold running water, I could see my hands slipping under her skirt, thick black nylons protecting the flesh underneath, the home of my craving. But just as quickly, the image flickered and died.

———

MIGUEL ALGARÍN

HIV

1) Revelation: to tell in strength. "The telling," when to tell, leads to a discovery between the teller and the listener. Acquiring knowledge; the teller holds his/her information as a tool for health, movement towards truth.

2) Salvation: to converse as a movement towards recuperating, a holding on not to die.

3) Speech: to acquire "language" for talking about a plague in the self.

4) Sharing secrets: who to tell? Is there someone? The search for what to tell.

5) Mature Masculinity: welcome the responsibility to do the work of building verbs, adjectives and nouns for mortality and its subsequent eternal breaking of concrete.

Revelation
Revel at ion,
rebel at I on a course
to regret erections,
to whip the cream in my scrotum
till it hardens into unsweetened,
unsafe revved elations
of milk turned sour
by the human body,
of propagation of destruction:
the epiphany: I am unsafe,
you who want me,
know that I who want you,
harbor the bitter balm of defeat.

Salvation
If I were to show you
how to continue holding on,
I would not kiss you,
I would not mix the fluids
of my body with you,
for your salvation
can not bear the live weight
of your sharing liquids with me.

Language
To tell,
to talk,
to tongue into sounds
how I would cleanse you with urine,
how my tasting tongue would wash your body,
how my saliva and sperm would bloat you,
to touch you in our lovemaking
and not tell you

would amount to murder,
to talk about how to language this
so that you would still languish
in my unsafe arms and die,
seems beyond me,
I would almost rather lie
but my tongue muscle moves involuntarily
to tell of the danger in me.

Of Health
To use my full and willing
body to reveal and speak
the strength that I impart
without fear,
without killing,
without taking away what I would give,
to use my man's tongue
to share,
to give,
to lend,
to exact nothing,
to receive all things,
to expand my macho
and let the whole world
into the safety of my mature masculinity.

Quarantine
Sometimes I fear touching your plump ear lobes,
I might contaminate you.
Sometimes I refuse odors that would
drive my hands to open your thick thighs,
sometimes closing my ears to your
voice wrenches my stomach
and I vomit to calm wanting,
can it be that I am the bearer of plagues?
Am I poison to desire?
Do I have to deny yearning for firm full flesh

so that I'll not kill what I love?
No juices can flow 'tween you and me,
only dry sands
will suck me in.

JULIA DE BURGOS

Poem for My Death

I WANT

To die by myself, abandoned and alone,
on the most solid rock of a deserted island.
At that moment, a supreme longing for carnations,
and from the landscape, a tragic horizon of stone.

My eyes to brim full with the graves of stars
and my passion, lying prone, be exhausted, dispersed.
My fingers like children watching clouds vanish
and my mind be taken over by an immense savannah.

My pale devotions to return to silence,
even love—a brother melting in my path.
My name unraveling yellow on the branches, and my hands
clenched turning myself over to the blades of grass.

To internalize the last final second,
and to offer myself to the fields chaste as a star,
to fold the leaf of my simple flesh,
and without smiles or witness sink into an inert state.

I had no one protane my death by indulging in sobs,
nor tuck me in forever under a mantle of innocent soil,
so that at the precise instant of release I may freely dispose
of the one and only freedom on the planet.

With what fierce joy my bones will begin
to look for small windows in my brown flesh
and I, giving myself, giving myself, wild and foot-loose
to the open air and all alone, will be breaking my chains!

Who can stop me with useless reveries
when my soul begins to fulfill its task,
making from my dreams a fertile dough
for the fragile worm that will knock at my door?

Each time smaller my smallness rendered,
each instant much greater and simpler the surrender;
perhaps my breast will stir to start a seedling,

———————

LUCKY CIENFUEGOS

Dedicated to María Rodriguez Martínez—
February 24, 1975

Translation by Miguel Algarín

I admire and love you mother

Rose necklace

lilac rose beloved
mother
today in front of you
I show my love
without hesitation
without fear
on the road
the rain and its cold drops
and the wind without the will
to caress
the sky winds
sky, soul heart
I wait for the day of my struggle
today I think of you
my mother
sick but always
with a smile
Mother underneath that smile
I know the pain
but today will be the memory
of tomorrows
pay attention, look at me
above my tomb I do not want cold roses
beloved mother
I love you, I remember
the cold ice creams of my youth,
when I was a child
we'd both enjoy my ice cream
and Saturdays
are like clarity
and like that
feeling that comes
with the struggle for clarity
rose necklace
lilac rose
loyalty forever mother
and if tomorrow's grass
cloaks its birds

with memories of today
I await that day
Mother.

MARIA GRANIELA DE PRUETZEL WITH

JOHN A. BARBOUR

The Freddie Prinze Story

PREFACE

This is not a story about drugs or Hollywood or morality. It is a story about a human being in show business. And it starts not on Sunset Boulevard but in the now-faded elegance of Washington Heights, Upper Manhattan.

It is the story of Freddie Prinze, a young man with a very mature sense of direction, with a determination to obtain success, with a desire to be a living example that—in spite of evil influences and hard times—there is always a chance to get ahead, to build a better world for yourself and those around you.

Freddie Prinze was my son. He was extremely bright and talented—he studied ballet, he danced, and he played piano, organ, guitar, bass guitar, and drums. Almost obsessively ambitious, he left New York's School of the Performing Arts at the age of nineteen, one month before graduation, in pursuit of his dream. And in less than one year he had become the Chico who won the hearts of more than forty million television viewers. That was 1974.

But in January 1977, just ten days after his last personal appearance—at the Preinaugural Ball for President Jimmy Carter—depressed, lonely, brokenhearted, emotionally and physically exhausted, a bullet in the brain ended it all for Freddie.

The Freddie Prinze Story is the story of a whole lifetime of accomplishments compressed into three years. It began, really, with his appearance on *The Tonight Show* with Johnny Carson in December 1973. He became a television personality, a standup comic commanding top fees for personal appearances along the Las Vegas–Lake Tahoe–Miami Beach circuit. He made a record for Columbia and starred in the NBC movie *The Million Dollar Rip-Off*. He hosted the Johnny Carson show many times and was loved and respected by many of the biggest names in show business.

And then, only twenty-two and already brutalized by a life he did not fully comprehend, he died—thirty-three hours after a shooting accident in the apartment of a hotel on Wilshire Boulevard—at the UCLA Medical Center, only a short distance from the Hollywood studio where his television career began.

Some will ask, "Where is Freddie's father in this story?" To be frank, it is not *our* story, it is *my* story—the story of a mother and her son.

Freddie and his father, Karl, had something in common. They both were the only child of a second marriage, and Karl, like Freddie later on, was unusually close to his mother. Even now in 1978, Karl's mother, who lives in New York and is ninety years old, calls him frequently to see "if there is anything I can do for you."

But for the record, some things have to be said. There was a tragedy in Karl's first marriage that left its mark on him. Maybe deep down psychologically this experience explains why Karl took so little responsibility for Freddie—maybe because he was afraid to.

You see, one day Karl was painting the porch of their home in the Bronx. At the same time he was supposed to be looking after their five-year-old daughter, Alice, who was playing outside. Concentrating on his job, he forgot about the little girl until he became aware that she was no longer underfoot. He called her, but she did not answer. Looking for her, he found her lying on the bottom of the unfenced swimming pool in their front yard. He jumped in and a neighbor responding to his screaming gave her artificial respiration—but it was too late.

Karl blamed himself for his daughter's death. He took to drinking and for the first few days he practically lived on cognac, enshrouded in a protective haze. He continued to drink heavily in his flight from his feelings and from reality, but I must say his drinking never interfered with his work as a tool-and-die maker and he continued to be a good provider. Yet without a doubt, Karl's heavy drinking had an impact on Freddie's life when he was growing up, and seriously undermined their relationship.

When Freddie was born, Karl's fear of taking responsibility for his child became almost an obsession. Oh yes, he and Freddie did things together like on Saturday outings and on trips to the Greenport, Long Island, resort where we spent our summer vacations. It was there where he taught Freddie how to drive, and there they went horseback riding together. On the way back from Greenport one year, they bought King, the German shepherd Freddie wanted.

Karl worked nights and was usually heading out the door when Freddie was coming home from school, so it was just a "Hi, Freddie!" kind of thing as Karl went on his way. Since I worked during the day, Freddie and I had more time to be with each other. He'd watch for me coming home from my job and we would sit down to talk in the kitchen night after night.

So I practically raised Freddie by myself. Life was not easy for me, but I needed to be strong because Freddie needed me then and today Karl needs me, especially since his recent battle with throat cancer.

So this is my story, the story of a mother and her son—*The Freddie Prinze Story.*

Maria Graniela de Pruetzel
Van Nuys, California . . .

. . . In Freddie's Bible, I found a note he wrote about that time dated August 1976. The writing is barely legible, very scratchy and spidery, as if he was stoned or greatly agitated while writing it. The notations were in the form of numbered paragraphs:

1. Dear Lord, stop disappointing me. I am sugar myself. [I don't know what he meant by that.]

2. Make it Your way. Who can beat the Lord, the Son of God. "Dear Lord, help me be strong where I am weak, if it be Your will!"

3. Help me get straight.

4. Help me with my problem. If You can hear me please, and if it be Your will, give me grace. Let me be a good man.

I cried when I read those words.

On another piece of paper in the same spidery writing were the words, "Pop [Freddie's nickname for himself] is a great husband. I love Kathy. Don't let me lose her. In Jesus' name I pray. If it be Your will let me win the Jonas case. Amen."

There were other words which I could not make out and then:

What I leave to all the children after I am dead: You are all that is real and pure and, no matter what you go through, strive to keep that. Regardless of your race or religion, have faith.

1. Go for no temporary happiness.
2. Have faith and persevere.
3. And love yourself and all your brothers! Believe!

These notes were scrawled on pages torn from a Chicago Playboy Towers telephone scratch pad.

Freddie's many problems were weighing on him more and more, like a big stone growing heavier and heavier. Between September 1 and September 23 he called me constantly—sometimes two and three times a day. Again and again, he said in Spanish, "*No soy feliz*—I am unhappy." . . .

. . . When Dusty arrived at Freddie's apartment in the Comstock, Freddie got up from the couch and opened the door. He was wearing his karate pants and was moving sluggishly. Dusty saw the gun—whether in Freddie's hand or on the coffee table in front of the long sofa, he is not sure. But he saw it.

Freddie sat down again on the sofa, his telephone nearby. And on the table in front of him lay an open telephone book, some stationery, and a pen. As Dusty sat down on the love seat he saw Freddie write something on the paper.

"Is this legible?" Freddie asked.

Dusty read the message.

"I can't go on," Freddie said. "I must end it." He repeated the words over and over again.

Dusty picked up the phone and called Dr. Kroger. He told him what Freddie had written and how he was acting.

Dr. Kroger replied, "I just left him. He's been behaving that way all this week. He's just crying out for attention and help. But I'm not concerned about his doing harm to himself."

After Dusty hung up the phone, Freddie made several more calls to Kathy and to Carol. He also called me.

Throughout most of the thirty minutes that Dusty was with him, the gun was in Freddie's hand. At one point, he made a quick movement with the gun.

"Give me that," Dusty said.

Freddie pulled back as if to say, "Don't come near me."

"I kept my distance," Dusty remembers. "But I knew that the two things he really cared about in life were his mother and his baby. So I reminded him about the insurance and that it had a suicide clause which had four months to run."

The next few moments are hazy in Dusty's recollection. As Freddie sat on the sofa Dusty was aware of what he could only describe later as one fluid movement. The gun was at Freddie's head and there was a muffled sound which Dusty scarcely recognized as a shot until he saw Freddie slump sideways.

In shocked disbelief, he called the police . . .

. . . Even to this day, I cannot help but feel the terrible turmoil that tortured our son for so long. Even during those long hours of his last day, everything he said and did was a plea for help. He sought the help of others.

Yet Freddie was left alone. Why? No one ever called us, his parents, to see what we might be able to do to help him. Why?

The people around Freddie knew his problems. They knew of his bouts with depression. They knew about his court struggles, his marriage problems, his battle with drugs. They knew he was physically and mentally wasted, on the edge of a complete breakdown, yet no one seemed to notice.

Freddie's compulsive use of Quaaludes was also a cry for help. Even today I hear that cry as I read his medical history and see date after date when Quaaludes and other drugs were prescribed for him by his physician, Dr. Ablon:

December 3, 1974. 100 Quaaludes, 300 milligrams.

April 4, 1975. 100 Quaaludes, 300 milligrams.

October 27, 1975. 50 Valiums.

November 7, 1975. Two Ritalins, 20 milligrams.

February 25, 1976. Six Quaaludes, 300 milligrams.
February 26, 1976. 50 Quaaludes, 300 milligrams.
November 16, 1976. 24 Quaaludes, 300 milligrams.

I have no doubt that Freddie also spent money for dope on the streets. And I am saddened at how easily young people get whatever they want on the streets.

Freddie had come to Hollywood with a dream he believed about to come true. But in Hollywood he stopped being a person and became—as he put it one day—"only a piece of merchandise." Even his sayings became merchandise. He was offered a fortune to endorse lunchboxes bearing his trademark quip: "It's not my job." Freddie the product had replaced Freddie the person.

He saw his efforts, everything he had worked for, taken away from him. In his litigation with David Jonas, his ex-manager ended up with $205,000. Besides that amount, Freddie had to pay legal fees amounting to approximately $100,000.

The decision blew Freddie's mind. No one that young is that strong. It seemed to my son that he had lost everything. The dream turned into a nightmare so terrible it frightened our son to death.

Was all this what killed Freddie? Was it that the dollar was more important than the human being with feelings and emotions? Was the image more important than the real person? Is society responsible for the Freddie Prinzes that die from drugs and pressures? If this is the case, then we live in a society suffering from spiritual malnutrition.

In studying my Bible, I know that there was agony in God's heart far greater than any agony of mine when His own Son died. And in that death, He became my Savior and my Friend. He is the one who has given me strength to go beyond Freddie's death in the desire to bring some hope to others.

So I walk around today and I try to do the best I can for others. The tragedy of Freddie's death is a wound that will never heal, but today I feel closer to God than ever before. And I know that I will meet my son again.

Many mothers and wives have written to me and said, "I lost my daughter" or "I lost my son" or "I lost my husband" and have asked me, "What can I do? Tell me your secret. How can I be strong?"

To them I say, my dear friends, positive faith may be the missing link in your life. Faith is not just a five-letter word. It has dynamic power. It is a force that can be an unrelenting influence in your life.

Whatever your problem is, reach out to Jesus. He is the answer. He will give you strength. I hope all of you can find the inner peace that I have found through His love and mercy.

And my advice to young people is this: Be aware who your friends are if loneliness and depression have caught up with you. Drugs or a divorce court are not the answer.

Believe in a Supreme Being and in the power of prayer. And in the importance of faith. Don't go for temporary happiness. What happened to Freddie doesn't have to happen to you.

Freddie loved life. He was grateful to be alive. He loved the streets and the street people. He once said, "The truth is everywhere you find it, and you find a lot of it in the streets."

Freddie was not as poor as he claimed to be. He talked about being from the ghetto, but he never really lived in a ghetto. He seemed to have a guilt complex about being more privileged than other kids he knew. And because he was sensitive, he felt the hurt that some of his less fortunate friends experienced.

His ethnic humor was a channel to bring a message about minority groups. "I make people laugh, but I want people to go home and think," he said on more than one occasion.

Freddie was a sucker for a sad tale, and many people who professed to be his friends took advantage of his generosity. He gave a lot of money away to so-called friends, and he lent money to people who never bothered to pay him back.

Freddie seemed to feel that he had a mission in life to solve the world's problems, but he was disappointed.

In Freddie's handwriting I have the following: "A friend is faithful, trusting and helpful, someone that realizes your imperfections and stands by you. A friend makes your problems his problems. He will be with you when you need him most. He is never too busy to listen to you. That is what a friend means to me."

Freddie's description of a friend is the description of The Friend who has helped me live through the hurt of my son's living and dying. That Friend is my silent partner, now and always.

I feel blessed, fortunate, and proud that I am Freddie Prinze's mother. He lives in my heart. He is—and always will be—my prince.

GERALDO RIVERA

A Special Kind of Courage: Bernard Carabello

The scene at the institution had been horrible and revolting. In three years as a newsman in New York City, I had seen poverty, hunger, and people dead from fire, drug overdoses, and gunshot wounds. They were things that seemed the absolute pits of human misery and despair. But this had been worse. Willowbrook. It was such an ironically lyrical name, much more befitting a pastoral painting than a foul and overcrowded human warehouse. It was the world's largest and one of the nation's worst institutions for the mentally retarded.

Filled to overflowing with almost six thousand children, the air in the place had been heavy with the stink of feces and neglect. The two dozen buildings were all divided into four wards, each haphazardly littered with naked or barely dressed boys and girls. The wards are large rooms, maybe thirty feet square. Into that space were jammed between sixty and eighty children. Most were severely or profoundly retarded. They had either never learned to speak or had lost the ability, but their nightmarish moaning echoed from the hard cinder-block walls.

Concentration was necessary to perceive them even as human children. They were so filthy, and frighteningly out of control.

The kids who weren't groping toward our camera lights were just sitting on one of the four wooden benches strategically placed in the corners of the otherwise furnitureless space. These rocked back and forth, oblivious to everything and everyone around them.

There was virtually no supervision, just one hopelessly overburdened attendant. She was a heavyset black lady, who held a squirming child under each chubby arm, while patiently trying to talk with a third retarded child who was pulling insistently at her uniform skirt. I tried to listen in on what she was saying, but the undulating moans in the background, like the sounds of a crashing sea, made it impossible to hear.

With that sound, and the nauseating smell, the institution would have been more at home in Dante's *Inferno* than on Staten Island, in the supposedly cosmopolitan and sophisticated city of New York.

When our unauthorized filming was completed, we dashed out the back door of B ward in Building 6 and into our waiting car. I was driving. To avoid trouble from the institution guards, we were off the grounds of the huge facility in less than sixty seconds. We drove with the windows open to purge our clothing of the wretched smell. Nobody spoke. For a long time the only sound was the rush of the wind and the screech of the tires.

"It's hopeless. Isn't it?" I finally asked Dr. Mike Wilkins, who was sitting alongside me in the front seat. He was the staff physician who had asked me to bring my cameras into Willowbrook. "I mean . . . nothing can really be done to help those kids . . . can it?"

"Geraldo, you'd be surprised at what can be done—if people care." When Dr. Wilkins spoke, even about an issue he was so deeply and emotionally involved in, it was always in a quiet, scholarly way. He was the teacher. I was the student, made willing to learn by the frightening spectacle he had just shown me. "Those kids weren't freaks," he continued. "They just have brains that are damaged or retarded. Some more than others." He gestured, pointing to me and then back to himself. "They have the same feelings we do, and if you give them half a chance, they respond the same as normal children do to things. They get happy. They get sad. And they need love and attention."

Dr. Wilkins was a young man, bespectacled and slightly built. But as with Gandhi, the strength of his convictions more than compensated for his physical frailty. He went on carefully, conscious of the fact that I had been deeply shocked and needed to be convinced that things didn't have to be the way they were.

"Willowbrook represents the worst possible care for the mentally retarded. That institution just holds them until they die. There is no attempt at education or rehabilitation. Nothing. Just abuse and neglect." He paused for a second. Taking his glasses off, he rubbed his forehead, as if trying to ease the pain of a bad headache. He shook his head. "You know something? The largest single cause of death at Willowbrook is pneumonia. You know how the children get it? They gag on the slop they're fed, because there's nobody around to teach them how to use utensils. Food particles get into their lungs, and it causes an infection. The infection eventually causes the pneumonia, and that causes death."

As we drove, Mike interrupted himself to give me directions. There was one other place where he wanted us to film before going back to the newsroom. It was only about fifteen minutes away from the institution.

"But the ultimate tragedy at Willowbrook," he explained, picking up where he had left off, "is the children who never should have been there at all."

"What do you mean?" I asked, hoping I had heard him wrong. I hadn't.

"Many of the residents aren't even mildly retarded."

"Don't tell me that," I said, almost pleading. The thought that some of the kids in that dreadful place might be there unnecessarily was appalling.

"I know it's terrible even to think about, but we have to think about it, because it's true." Mike went on regretfully, "There was a bad diagnosis when they were very young, or they have some kind of physical disability. Because there was no other, more appropriate place to put them, they get dumped in Willowbrook. . . . Well, after a couple of years spent on one of those wards, they get to seem retarded." Always the professor, Mike spared me none of the unhappy details. "Environment can retard a person almost as much as physical brain damage."

"That must really kill you—to see kids who aren't even retarded, rotting away on those wards."

"Let me answer it this way." He paused for a second, trying to find words. "I think this thing is going to change. As soon as we bring this story to the American people, they are going to be angry, and they are going to demand that that place and others like it be cleaned up."

The three other members of my film crew were sitting in the backseat of the car. Usually when this type of job-related conversation was going on in the front seat, these hard-nosed photojournalists would be completely tuned out—looking out the windows, or napping, or reading the New York *Daily News*. Their personal involvement in a story usually ended when they left the scene, but this was obviously different.

They had been as deeply affected by what we'd seen as I was, and as Mike spoke, they listened intently.

"But the most frustrating aspect of the whole thing is that change doesn't happen overnight," Mike continued. "It's going to take time. Years, probably. And in that time, people who never should have been in that place are going to grow up, grow old, and die there."

I stammered, "But . . . I mean . . . can't we do something to get some of them out in the meantime?"

"We're getting some of them out."

"How are they doing?"

"Not badly. Considering where they've been. You know, it's not easy to adjust to life outside a hellhole like that one. Especially if it's the only life you've ever known."

"Can I meet some of the kids who've gotten out?"

"That's where I'm taking you now..I want you to meet Bernard."

"Who's Bernard?"

"He's twenty-one years old. And he just got out of Willowbrook."

"How long was he in there?"

"Sixteen years."

"And he's not retarded?"

"No. He's not retarded."

"Goddamnit."

"This is where we get off."

We turned off the highway, and I pulled the crew car into the driveway of an old house. It was about three in the afternoon. It was biting cold out, and the January sky was already getting dark. The house was sort of run-down, but at least it had a big yard, filled with trees and shrubbery, which in the summer, especially, would lend a real country feeling, not uncommon in the relatively suburban borough of Staten Island.

The house belonged to Bill Bronston, another young activist doctor from Willowbrook. We walked up to the porch. Mike was leading me; Bob Alis, the cameraman; Davey Weingold, the sound man; and Ronnie Paul, who did the lighting. Hustling in the cold with our portable TV equipment, we went in the front door and into a warm old living room crowded with people.

They all knew we had planned to go into Willowbrook earlier that afternoon to film the conditions there. Since that was expressly forbidden by the Department of Mental Hygiene, everyone had been anxiously awaiting word of our expedition.

"How did you make out?" Dr. Bronston nervously asked before we had even set the equipment down.

"All right, I guess," cautiously answered Dr. Wilkins.

"Great!" I put it more emphatically. (A word of explanation: In the news business, with some exceptions, there is a direct relationship between the importance of the story and the grimness it portrays; so if a cameraman has successfully filmed something that is horrible, a newsman can classify his story as "great.")

"You mean you got the cameras inside?"

"Yeah. We sure did."

"Fantastic!"

Bernard was sitting on the couch. As a living, breathing example of all that was wrong with Willowbrook, he was the star of the show, lavished from both sides with solicitous attention. It was a pleasant but unsettling change of pace for the young man who had spent most, of his life living a grotesque nightmare.

I walked toward him, Mike and Bill guiding me through the crowded room.

"Bernard. I'd like you to meet Geraldo Rivera." Then, looking to me, Mike completed the introduction. "Geraldo, this is the friend I've been telling you about. Bernard Carabello."

"How ya doin', pal?" I asked him, energetically flashing what passes for a warm, friendly smile in embarrassing public situations. I extended my hand, and he tried to do the same. Bernard wanted to shake hands, but his arm and his thought processes seemed badly connected. Finally, after an embarrassing moment, he grabbed for his semiextended right arm and guided it toward me with his more controlled left. It was shaking as I reached for it, pretending not to notice anything extraordinary.

"So what's new, partner?" I asked. He struggled to answer.

Bernard's affliction is cerebral palsy, not mental retardation. His mind is perfect; it's just badly packaged, and that afternoon his handicap was painfully obvious. His speech is severely distorted during the best of times, and that day his physical handicap was compounded by his nervousness. After sixteen anonymous years in the ward, he was unaccustomed to being the center of attention.

"Nnnahot Mmmuch." He painfully forced speech out as I released his hand. Holding it had been unpleasant. Even though I had already done some stories about the physically handicapped, I still wasn't entirely at ease with them. It would have been difficult to estimate which of us, Bernard or me, for our different reasons, was more uneasy.

Although he had greatly improved his ability to control his movements since leaving the institution, this high-pressured situation caused him to relapse temporarily. Much to the dismay of the people sitting next to him, Bernard's arms flailed about in involuntary perpetual motion as he sat there on the old couch. Only with great effort did he manage to get both hands underneath himself, stopping their movement by sitting on them.

Bill asked the eager kids next to Bernard to get up so we could talk with him. As soon as I sat down next to Bernard, Mike skillfully avoided an awkward lapse in our fledgling conversation by telling me the story of how this twenty-one-year-old young man had come to spend most of his life in an institution worse than the worst prison.

Things were bad for Bernard from minute one of his life. There were complications. He had been badly positioned in his mother's womb, so doctors at New York's Bellevue Hospital had to struggle for hours to deliver him. When he came out, it was elbow-first, and his mother, Pedra, was left exhausted and sick from the experience. For five days she was listed in critical condition.

Bernard was the fifth child born to her and Louis Carabello, the janitor of a six-floor walk-up on Broome Street on the Lower East Side of Manhattan. So desperate was the family's financial situation that things would have been impossible for the Carabellos even if Bernard had been a normal child, born without complications. In return for maintaining the tenement building they lived in, Louis was given a three-room apartment, rent-free, and $120 a month. Two adults and five children crowded into a one-bedroom apartment, trying to get by on less than thirty dollars a week.

Mr. and Mrs. Carabello slept on the fold-out couch in what served as the living, dining, and utility room. Bernard slept next to them, in the same cheap crib that had served his brothers, Louie, Tony, and Howard, and his sister, Beverly.

The children, including Bernard, had been born with depressing regularity—one a year for the past five years. Each one made the situation more untenable. Bernard had escalated the deteriorating situation by having been born abnormal.

The week after she got out of the hospital, Pedra went to work. Still weak from her ordeal, she got a job for eighty dollars a week packing underwear at a run-down old factory near their home. The task of watching the children was shared by Mr. Carabello, when his duties around the building permitted, and by Louis junior, age 5½, the oldest of the kids.

Since Mr. Carabello disliked the domestic work, Louis had to diaper and feed his infant brother, whose handicap was already becoming apparent. Pedra would relieve him of his premature and arduous responsibility when she came home from work about six in the evening. She would be exhausted, but before resting she had to make dinner for everyone, including her husband, who was beginning to drink too much. The menu was almost always the same: rice and beans, and once a week, either dried fish or stringy beef.

After the meal, she would put the kids to bed. The four oldest, ranging from 5½ to 1½, all slept on the same big bed that had originally been shared by Pedra and Louis Senior when they had first gotten married. The kids' room was sparsely decorated with cheap, shiny furniture. The bed itself was fringed in red pom-poms and nestled under a plaster-of-paris statue of Jesus.

With Mrs. Carabello bringing a few extra dollars in each week, things started marginally to improve. Then, as often happens in ghetto families with neither the recreation of television nor the protection of birth control, she got pregnant again. Pedra worked until the last minute, because she had to.

Jenny was born almost exactly one year after Bernard, who demanded increasing attention and care as his handicap became more and more pronounced. The house was impoverished and chaotic. The family was held together only by the patience and grim determination of the inexhaustible Pedra.

With relentless timing, David followed Jenny, and Margarita followed David. When there were eight children, all born within less than ten years, Louis Carabello left home.

In a knavish but, in the slums, common maneuver, he left Mrs. Carabello to make the best of the impossible situation by herself, with some public assistance. Bernard was five years old. He still couldn't walk or talk, and he was not toilet-trained. Pedra had to diaper and change this normal-size five-year-old several times each day.

Concerned about Bernard's lack of development, Mrs. Carabello began taking him every two or three weeks to the public-health clinic at Bellevue Hospital. Doctors there had told her that Bernard's only hope for even seminormality was constant physical therapy.

In the beginning, getting her nonambulatory son to the clinic on East Twenty-fifth Street was a difficult but manageable proposition from her relatively nearby home on Broome Street. But because their old apartment there was far too small for all nine of them, Pedra had to move her brood to Brooklyn.

She had applied for and was granted a large two-bedroom apartment in the Scholes Street city housing projects in the Williamsburg section of Brooklyn. As a neighborhood, Williamsburg is neither better nor worse than the Lower East Side. Like the Carabellos' old neighborhood, this new one was predominantly Puerto Rican, with a substantial minority of Eastern European Jews, the two ethnic groups joined by their common poverty.

The projects were located within sight and sound of the old Broadway elevated subway train, which cut a rumbling swath through the area every fifteen minutes or so.

The new apartment was far larger than the one the Carabellos had left behind, but it was still far too small. Another and ultimately more important disadvantage was its distance from the clinic at Bellevue Hospital. Now, not only did Pedra have to struggle to dress and carry the deadweight of her growing son, but they also had to endure a combined subway and bus voyage of an hour and a quarter each way, every two weeks.

At the time, Pedra spoke no English, and since none of the young doctors at the public-health clinic spoke Spanish, an interpreter was always needed. Sometimes Pedra would just find somebody who happened to be at the hospital on the afternoon she brought in Bernard. Other times, she would bring a neighbor along to translate.

In the rushed, harried atmosphere of the clinic, the overworked interns sympathized with Mrs. Carabello's misfortune. But they still avoided serving her and her child whenever possible. She was a brash woman, given to concerned but noisy outbursts at doctors who were patiently trying to explain Bernard's lack of progress. Even when she was docile, it was an inconvenience dealing with Mrs. Carabello. Since she spoke no English, talking with her took twice as long, conversations having to be translated by a middleman, sometimes a stranger.

Finally, one afternoon when Pedra came in complaining loudly, as she usually did, about the slowness of the Broadway train, she quieted abruptly when she saw the head of the clinic somberly walking toward her. With him was the stern-faced Spanish-speaking officer of the hospital's community-relations department. Neither of these exalted gentlemen had ever waited on her and Bernard before.

With the help of a girlfriend, Pedra had plopped Bernard onto one of the waiting-area benches and was in the process of taking off his outer coat when they came up to her.

She awkwardly stopped what she was doing. At the doctor's request, translated into Spanish by the community-relations man, Pedra anxiously and with uncharacteristic quiet followed them into the head man's glass-partitioned clinic office. Before walking off, Pedra had nodded to a friend and then at her son. The body language was easily understood; the neighbor walked over and finished taking Bernard's coat off and kept a protective hand on him.

Inside the glass walls, all the hyperactivity was still visible outside; only the crying and the clanking noises of the busy clinic seemed abated. The community-relations official was a shorter, darker, more active man than his pale and properly professional colleague. He carried the conversation; the doctor just listened. Looking at whoever was talking, the clinic doctor seemed to be following the intense emotional conversation. Even though he couldn't understand Spanish, he could easily approximate what was happening, because he had instructed the other man what to say.

"Señora, these trips all the way in to Manhattan are difficult. Are they not?"

"Yes. Of course, they're a pain in the neck," answered Mrs. Carabello, quickly recovering from her initial uneasiness at being called into the office. "You think it's easy to drag that kid in from Brooklyn all the time?"

"We know you're having a tough time. That's why we called you in here today."

"Why? You got a better way?"

"Yes, señora, we think we do."

"What? Can you get the city to give me some more money? . . . How do they expect me to feed eight kids with $230 a month?"

"That's not what we have in mind."

"What, then?"

"Bernard should be placed in an institution."

"What institution?" she asked, softly now, as if recovering from a punch in the stomach.

"One close to where you live. A place where he could get the kind of help he needs." Mrs. Carabello's brashness was completely gone. Her eyes were beginning to shine wetly. Recognizing the danger signs of a potentially embarrassing emotional outburst, the official started patting her arm smoothingly. "It will be much better for everybody this way," he continued, buttressing his honey-coated presentation still further. "You can't really take care of him at home. Not with all the other children."

Pedra knew he was only saying what was more true than she wished to admit. Recognizing his advantage, the community-relations man pressed home his most convincing argument. Nodding to the silent man sitting next to them, he said, "The doctor thinks it would be much better for Bernard. He knows that you try very hard to care for your son, but you have your hands more than filled." Then the coup de grace: "Think what's best for your son."

"Where will he go?" Pedra's question was phrased in the defeated syntax of a mother whose natural resistance toward giving up her child had been overcome.

"There's a place on Staten Island. You could take the ferry to see him there."

"What's it called?"

"Willowbrook."

"That's a nice name." It was the only thing she could think of to say.

Bernard was only one of thousands of children who grew up almost completely within the institution. At the time he was admitted, at the age of five, there was only a perfunctory screening of prospective residents. So the fact that Bernard was not actually retarded understandably went unnoticed. He had some handicap, and that was more than enough to qualify him for admission.

At the age of 5½ Bernard was placed in Building 25 at Willowbrook. Half of it was used for teenage girls, and at the time, the other half was occupied by younger boys and girls. Until his tenth birthday, Bernard's routine was established, harsh and unrelenting.

At five o'clock each morning, the last official act of the night-shift attendant was to walk through the crowded dormitory area, switching on the lights as she went, shouting, "Wake up! . . . Wake up!" The sixty children were expected to be out of bed before the vigilant attendant made her return trip through the ward. For some of the kids, like Bernard, getting out of bed was a difficult and time-consuming project, because they couldn't walk. But after incurring the painful prodding and pushing of the tired and impatient attendants, Bernard soon developed a technique to get him out of bed and onto the floor within the requisite time period.

Lying on his back, he would start rocking back and forth, picking up momentum until he had rolled almost onto his side. At the farthest point in his motion, he would reach out and grab for the metal frame of the bed. Sometimes he would miss and have to start the rocking movement all over again. When he had finally taken hold of the frame, Bernard would pull himself over to the side of the bed. Poised there, he would make one final roll, off the bed, down onto the hard tile floor, maintaining his hold on the frame as he fell. Bernard did that so that the bottom half of his body, not his head, would hit first, absorbing the punishment of the impact.

Once out of bed and lying on the floor, Bernard had successfully fulfilled the requirements of reveille, but he still had the problem of navigating the one hundred feet to the bathroom. He still hadn't learned to crawl, and the attendant, even if she wanted to help Bernard, couldn't. For one thing, he was too heavy for her to carry. And besides, with sixty children under her supervision, there was simply no time for personalized attention.

Bernard had to use the only method of movement available to him. Rolling. Like normal children at play in a heavy snowfall, he would squirm until his body was pointed in the right direction, and then start flopping over and over. He would frequently have to stop, either from dizziness or to correct his direction. And the trip was fraught with other dangers. In the sleepy, early-morning hours, he wasn't easy to spot on the floor, and would often be stepped on accidentally or tripped over by the attendants or other residents hurrying to do whatever they had to do.

The bathrooms of Willowbrook are the single most unpleasant aspect of life in that institution. They are filthy, and they stink. Many of the residents aren't fully toilet-trained, but they realize that defecation is more acceptable in certain areas than in others. In the long, old-fashioned nightshirts worn by all the children, Bernard would have to roll around, or over, the feces of his co-residents as he made the long trip to the toilet. There, he would have to grab the rim of the bowl and struggle to pull himself onto the toilet seat. The only help he got was from the iron-stomached attendant who wiped him and the others and then lifted him off and back onto the floor. There to endure the three-hundred-foot odyssey into the dining area for breakfast.

The morning meal consisted of an oatmeal-like substance. Once Bernard had successfully pulled himself into one of the chairs at the long dining table, an attendant would feed him with a shoveling motion: scoop, force open his mouth, drop, then scoop again. Bernard quickly learned that the secret to not gagging and choking on the rapid-fire feeding was to swallow as soon as a mouthful was placed on his tongue, whether he wanted to or not. Delay meant that the next spoonful would be dumped on top of the lump already in his mouth, parlaying it into an unmanageably large mass in his throat. According to Bernard, this forced feeding wasn't the work of sadists.

"Naaahot all the aahtendants are baaad peeeople," he explained. "Ttthhere wwwaahsan't enough help." The newly arrived morning shift, two people for sixty children, had to rush if they were to feed everyone and get them ready for the day. Some of the attendants were more caring and compassionate than others, although kindness under those circumstances is really remarkable, considering that they took home less than a hundred dollars a week to work in a cesspool.

"Theyyy had it rough . . . really rough," said the young man who had every reason to hate them. "I don't know why theyyy woooorked in that place."

After surviving the ordeal of breakfast, Bernard would roll back into the "dayroom." It was the large and virtually empty space adjacent to the dormitory area. When all the children had assembled there, the attendants would dump the clean laundry into a large pile near the center of the room. The hill of clothing would be a haphazard collection of garments: gray shirts, pants, and nightshirts provided by the state, mixed in with more colorful and diverse garments donated by the Benevolent Society or some other charitable organization.

The ambulatory, higher-functioning residents would select their own clothing from the pile, often with tragicomic results. Little boys would often select brightly colored old ladies' dresses, while the little girls would frequently end up wearing a man's work shirt. The costumes just added to the insane, surrealistic-nightmare quality of life in the building.

Bernard could only roll himself into reasonable proximity with the clothing distribution point; he couldn't make the selection by himself. The attendants dressed him, almost always selecting an open hospital gown. He usually didn't get underpants. That way, he could go to the bathroom and manage most of that process without their help—help that would have been needed if the hard-pressed attendants had given him a pair of pants to wear.

Willowbrook, until 1974, was called a state school, even though very little formal education went on there. It's now called a developmental center—a much less ambitious and more realistic label. But there was a half-day of classes, even in Bernard's day, for those children who could make it to the classroom. For him, that meant more rolling, and more struggling once he got there, to get himself into his assigned seat. Because these young and very handicapped kids could neither read nor write and would have needed a tremendous amount of individual attention to obtain those skills, the classes consisted primarily of supervised play with educational toys: fitting the circle into the appropriate place on the board, the square into the square, and so on.

"Yaahhou noo whhat ahheye liked best?" asked Bernard. "The readin'." He answered his own question.

The teacher would read fairy tales to the ten children in his class. Most of the time, Bernard had no idea of what was being said. But the gentle, friendly voice was in dramatic and refreshing contrast to the din of the wards. For him, that was enough to make the long roll from the dayroom to the classes, located on the other side of Building 25, worth the trip.

The most unbearable aspect of his early years in the institution was the summers. First of all, there were no classes to relieve the plodding monotony of the dayroom. Then, there was the heat. New York's summers are naturally hot and sticky, and the constant hosing in the bathrooms, much like the keeper's hosing of the animal cages in the zoo, added dampness to the already oppressive humidity in the wards. There was no air-conditioning, and no screens on the small windows near the top of the walls. Mosquitoes and flies shared all Bernard's meals in Willowbrook.

Some of the ambulatory children were occasionally permitted to play outside the building. But only occasionally, since there weren't sufficient attendants to supervise them and still watch for the inevitable crises among the children left inside the building. So the grounds of the huge institution—green, open spaces dotted with big old trees—always seemed deserted. From the outside it still looks like an abandoned, haunted suburban college campus. In any case, Bernard never got out. To him, outdoors was the small, enclosed concrete patio adjacent to the dayroom.

Bernard's day always ended with a shower. The administration had decreed this mandatory—a daily shower for everybody. It was an effort to cut down the incidence of infectious hepatitis, which at the time was striking 100 percent of Willowbrook's residents, being transmitted by the human feces lying in piles everywhere.

In order to comply with this requirement, Bernard had to roll into a shower stall. The water would already be running. Once inside, to prevent himself from drowning, he would be careful not to lie on his stomach. Eventually, years later, he learned to pull himself up off the bottom and onto his knees. It was a milestone, and it led finally to his first heroic breakthrough. When he was about nine years old, he learned to crawl. Imagine his wonder at finally being able to point himself in a direction, and then move without undergoing the disorientation of rolling over and over again to get there. He had learned how to crawl by watching the babies and the very young children living around him. What had come naturally to them was mastered out of necessity by Bernard in just under four years. Even so, he was a very inefficient crawler. His poor coordination caused exaggerated movements in his arms and legs. When he moved, he looked like an old-fashioned steam engine spinning furiously but slowly up an icy grade.

But his newfound skill was important as more than just a means of locomotion. When the physical therapist on one of her weekly visits to the building noticed him crawling, he was implicitly taken off the list of the totally hopeless cases. It ultimately led to a big change in his life. Within a short time he was transferred out of Building 25 and into Building 2, the big building that also housed the hospital.

Everything was better for him in his new home. There were fewer kids in each ward, and a much more comprehensive educational program. The two and a half hours of classes were supplemented by an hour or two of speech therapy or physical rehabilitation. But for Bernard the happiest thing about the whole move was that his best friend, Joey, was transferred along with him.

Joseph Cucchiara is the same age as Bernard, and, like him, is a victim of cerebral palsy, not mental retardation. Even before these boys learned how to speak, Bernard and Joey seemed somehow to understand each other, to take comfort in the other's presence.

They were constant and mutually entertaining companions. Cowboys and Indians was their favorite game. Bernard was usually the Indian/bad guy. They didn't have any of the usual trappings—no cap guns, cowboy hats, or anything like that. But pointing their cocked fingers at each other and ducking behind the benches or under their beds, they did manage to pass the time.

The boys taught each other also. They struggled together to verbalize, one of them learning a new word, then teaching it to his friend as they crawled along the floor.

Joey was the first one to walk. He took his first faltering steps at the age of eleven. Bernard, with the inspiration and guidance of his friend, learned shortly afterward. He would pull himself erect, holding onto his bed, or the back of a bench, or Joey's arm. Once he was standing, he would lurch forward, sometimes taking two or three or four awkward steps before careening back down to the floor. But he always got up. When the surface is slippery, Bernard still sometimes loses his balance. But he'd rather risk injury than resort to a wheelchair.

When they were about twelve years old, Bernard and Joey were transferred to Building 6. The prevailing feeling among the staff of the hospital building they had been living in, apparently, was that all that reasonably could have been done to rehabilitate the youngsters had been done. Besides, the space was needed for other, younger children who didn't even know how to walk.

Number 6 is the building I had seen on that first trip to Willowbrook. It was filled with older, bigger boys, some of them prone to violent, unreasoned outbursts; Joey and Bernard were terrorized there. Constant harassment and physical abuse became part of their daily regimen. The attendants, with some glowing exceptions, also seemed a more cold-blooded bunch. Perhaps it's understandable. In Building 25, at least, some of the children had been cute, or anyway smaller and easier to handle.

As Bernard's vocabulary grew, so too did his problems with the attendants. He would often complain to the building physician when one of them had been unnecessarily cruel to this or that resident. He and Joey were also becoming more doggedly independent. They would, for instance, sneak out of their beds after the official seven o'clock lights-out. Sitting in a corner of the crowded dormitory or in the dark, empty dayroom, they would often talk for hours.

Their favorite conversation was about what they were going to do when they got out of Willowbrook. After a hundred evenings spent in grand speculation, they decided on a mansion in California. Since they had never consciously been off the grounds of the institution, it was a magnificent triumph of their collective imagination. With just the limited knowledge of the outside world gained from the old television set in the dayroom, they constructed an ideal future for themselves. Bernard was even thoughtful enough to provide them with a made-up maid and a conjured butler to help with the housework.

Late one night, as Joey and Bernard whispered and giggled about their blissful futures, an attendant caught them. While most of his co-workers would have either overlooked or dealt mildly with this minor rules infraction, this man exploded. It was as if the boys had been conspiring to humiliate him.

"What the hell is going on here?" he shouted upon discovering them sitting on one of the benches in the half-lit dayroom. "You again, Bernard? This time I'm going to teach you to stay in bed when you're put in bed!" Whap. He slapped Bernard across the face.

"Yyyyuuu kah . . . kahrayzee," was all Bernard could manage as he uncoordinatedly lifted his hands to protect his face.

The attendant pulled Bernard off the bench by his ankles, slamming him to the ground. Joey reached toward him to help. "You want some too?" asked the attendant menacingly.

"Leeeave himmm alone!" cried Bernard as he squirmed on the floor to free his ankles.

Distracted by Bernard's surprisingly vigorous struggle, the attendant started dragging him toward the dormitory, taunting him as they went. "You ain't going to get out of bed anymore. Are you, big boy?"

When they finally reached the sleeping area, he roughly tossed Bernard into a pile at the foot of his bed. With the skirmish over, the attendant walked out of the dormitory, laughing softly at his small victory.

Sticking to the shadows, Joey, who walked with the same awkward gait as Bernard, did his best to make his way to his friend's bed without being noticed. When he got there, he helped Bernard to straighten out. Since they were both so poorly coordinated, the effort caused them to jerk sideways and up and down like two dancers in an amateur puppet show. Finally, after a struggle, they were sitting alongside each other on Bernard's bed.

"You okay?" asked Joey.

"Yeah," answered Bernard. "You okay?"

"Yeah. I'mmm goin' to bed."

"Gaanite, Joey."

" 'Night, Bernard."

When Bernard was nineteen, he was transferred to Building 7. Similar in most respects to Building 6, it was located about a quarter of a mile away. By this time Bernard had learned how to dress himself fairly well, although he could not tie his shoes and had difficulty buttoning his shirts. But this achievement, however limited, added an extra dimension to his life. Since he could dress himself and was basically ambulatory, Bernard was permitted to walk outside his building.

That meant he could still see Joey, either on the grounds or by visiting him in Building 6, where he still lived.

It went that way for a while, until Joey told Bernard the big news. He was leaving the institution. His family had signed the consent forms, and Joey was moving into an apartment on Staten Island. Bernard greeted the momentous tidings with an understandably mixed reaction. He knew that Joey, like himself, wanted desperately to be out of Willowbrook, but he was afraid he wouldn't see his friend anymore. Joey made everything right when he told Bernard that he would still be coming to the institution every day. The administration had given him a paying job as a janitor.

Joey's freedom was an inspiration and a goal for Bernard. Whenever he saw his old friend, Bernard would eagerly ply him with questions about what his apartment was like, and the buses, and the movies, and everything else. Now that Joey was experiencing what life on the outside was really like, they didn't talk about their California mansion anymore.

Bernard was still going to school. He wasn't as advanced as Joey, and still had problems with his reading. So for two and a half hours each day he went to his classes. Until he reached his twenty-first birthday. When he passed that milestone, Bernard was no longer permitted to go to school. He was too old. The fact that he still was in dire need of more instruction was irrelevant. The rules were the rules, and Bernard was out.

When he had first been placed in the institution, his family had paid Bernard frequent visits. But these had gradually tapered off, until he saw his mother and brothers and sisters only occasionally. When he was informed that he could no longer go to school, Bernard did something he rarely did: he called his mother at home. He asked her to sign him out of Willowbrook. It was a dead-end street for him now, he explained; he couldn't even get an education.

Concerned and confused, Pedra came out to Staten Island to see her son and to talk with the staff social workers. They told her what she expected to hear. Bernard was ill-prepared to survive in the rough, tough world outside the institution's gates. So he stayed in Willowbrook, his first real attempt at getting himself out ending in failure.

Despite his disappointment, Bernard chose to follow Joey's example, at least in part. He also got a job as a janitor. But while his friend qualified for the minimum wage, Bernard, as a resident of the institution, did not. He worked three hours each afternoon, cleaning the slop in the bathrooms of Building 7, and for that he was paid two dollars a month. If you break it down, it comes to less than fifty cents a week.

At the time, Bernard was living in a twilight zone. As a working and relatively high-functioning person, he was in a social stratum above most of the residents, many of whom were severely and profoundly retarded. But he was also far below the exalted level of the attendants. This ambiguity, coupled with his intense disappointment at not being able to get out of the institution, caused Bernard great loneliness. The only person he could talk with was Joey—that is, until he met some of the new breed of committed young social workers who had started working in Willowbrook after the public outrage over conditions there generated by Senator Robert Kennedy's visit in 1965. The kids were different from those usually attracted to positions that not only are low-paying but have the additional fringe detriment of atrocious working conditions.

These social workers worked hard to change Willowbrook from the inside. They knew they couldn't change the crusty administration, but they felt they could meaningfully affect the lives of some of the residents. A group of them spotted Bernard one afternoon hard at work with his mop and his pail in the bathroom of Building 7. One of them started complimenting Bernard on his thoroughness, speaking in the simple, flattering sentences grown-ups use when they talk to babies or house pets.

Bernard's response, after he got going, was, to them, surprisingly intelligent. Shocked, almost as if a friendly dog had started suddenly to speak to them, the social workers began to perceive him as a person of some potential. They offered Bernard a job as a messenger, at a heady new salary. Taking up a collection among themselves, the social workers were able to pay Bernard five dollars a week, which qualified him, by Willowbrook's standards, as a member of the nouveau riche.

More important than the money, Bernard, for the first time in his life, was spending time with people who had grown up outside a mental institution. Elizabeth Lee, Tim Casey, and Ira Fischer were all in their mid-twenties, and all were militantly committed to improving conditions at Willowbrook. They were political activists who had decided to channel their activism into something socially beneficial. Bernard became their resident expert on just how bad the quality of life was inside.

He angered and frustrated the social workers with the hapless story of his own experience, and curiously, these conversations had exactly the same effect on Bernard. It was as if he were also hearing the story for the first time. All his life he had seen and lived amid the crap, but the crap was always the norm. It didn't make him angry, because he had nothing with which to compare it. Watching Liz and Tim and Ira reacting to his descriptions, Bernard came to realize a bitter, central truth. He'd been duped. All the pain and most of the unpleasantness in his life had been unnecessary. Willowbrook was not the best that society could reasonably offer the mentally or physically handicapped. It was the worst.

.To fill the time when he was picking up the pieces of his emotional life, Bernard began getting more involved in the extracurricular activities of the institution, such as they were. The sewing class had scheduled a show of fashions made by some of the residents. The teacher, to stir up interest, had offered a prize of a new pair of shoes to the resident who sold the most tickets. While Bernard was too old to attend the class, there was no age discrimination against ticket sellers, so he energetically began canvassing the grounds. He needed a new pair of shoes, and besides, he didn't have anything better to do.

After work, late one afternoon, Bernard decided to go over to Building 6 in his search for potential customers. The social workers had told him that the staff physician there might be interested in a ticket or two.

Walking into his old home, the B ward, Bernard greeted Thomas, a mildly retarded young man who had been one of his closest wardmates. They talked for a while, their conversation interrupted occasionally as Bernard said "hello" and "how are you?" to passing attendants and residents he recognized from his tenancy in the building. Finally Thomas pointed out the doctor Bernard had been looking for. As he walked past, Bernard called after him, and with Thomas' help got quickly off the bench to talk with the white-coated young doctor.

"Excuse me . . ." he said. "Mmmy name is Bernard."

"Well, Bernard. It's a pleasure meeting you finally," answered the young man, smiling. "Elizabeth Lee has been telling me all about you. My name is Mike Wilkins."

"Helllo, Dr. Wilkins . . ."

"Just call me Mike."

Bernard, put completely at ease by the friendly manner of Dr. Wilkins, so unlike most of the other staff doctors, felt no embarrassment at making a pitch for ticket sales. The doctor, while explaining that he would probably not be able to attend the fashion show, did say he would take a few tickets anyway. Mike asked Bernard to bring them over the next day, which was payday.

Bernard was there first thing in the morning. Mike laughed at his promptness. "What did you think—that I was going to skip town?" Bernard laughed with him, explaining tongue-in-cheek, that he knew the doctor was very busy and he didn't want him to forget. Mike decided that he wanted six of the tickets, which were selling for $3.50. The purchase was a big boost in Bernard's sales campaign, and helped him, eventually, to win the pair of shoes, with total sales of fifty tickets. But more important, Bernard had made a friend. With their business dealings over, Mike told Bernard that they should get together. Bernard, thinking the doctor was just being polite, said sure, thanked him warmly, and walked back to Building 7.

The next day, Bernard had to make a phone call. It was his sister Jenny's birthday, and he had promised he would call her. She probably had no idea how great a sacrifice that promise was for Bernard. In order to make a phone call, he had to walk in his careening shuffle the half-mile that separated Building 21 from his home in Building 7. The phone outside 21 was the closest to his ward. After he had made his call, Bernard was resting outside the phone booth in anticipation of the long trek back home. Just as he was about to take his reluctant first step, he heard a familiar voice. "Hey, Bernard!" He turned. It was Dr. Wilkins.

Mike asked Bernard what he was doing, then asked if he would like to join him and another friend for lunch at Palermo's, an Italian restaurant out on Victory Boulevard.

"Nooo thank youuu, Mike," answered Bernard calmly, the tone of his voice giving no clue to what he was feeling inside. "I'mmm not dressed propurrly."

"That's okay. What about tomorrow?"

"All right." Bernard's heart was racing as he and Mike ironed out the details of time and where they'd meet. Bernard had never been off the grounds of Willowbrook before, aside from several short rides with his family when he was very young. Mike was offering a real-life view of a world Bernard had seen only secondhand.

The removal of a resident from the grounds, even if it was by a doctor, and even if it was only for a short time, was a discouraging project requiring compliance with a mile of red tape. First Mike would have had to fill out a volunteer form, because he was spending his own time on a resident. Then he would have had to ask the supervisor of Bernard's building for permission to remove him from the grounds, stating their prospective destination and expected time of return. Bernard, it should be recalled, was twenty-one at the time, and perfectly capable of making his own decisions about whom he was going to lunch with. This procedure was just another of the countless minor outrages at the institution.

To avoid the bureaucracy, Bernard met Mike outside, about twenty feet down from Building 7, and climbed into his car. Liz, the social worker, was already there, sitting alongside Mike in the front seat. In a happy mood, they drove to the Italian restaurant and sat down at a table for three. Although Palermo's can best be described as modest, it was full of wonders for Bernard. There were colorful prints of Italy on the walls, glittery goldlike little chandeliers that brightly lit the red-vinyl decor, and a menu filled with scenic shots of the Mediterranean.

After Bernard had been scanning the menu for a few minutes, Mike asked him what he wanted to order. Since Bernard was still having trouble with his reading, but was a bit embarrassed saying so, he said, "Roast beef." It was the first thing that came into his mind, and while it wasn't exactly the house specialty, it was, luckily, on the menu.

After the meal, which Bernard describes as "fantastic," he began telling Dr. Wilkins the story of why he was in Willowbrook and what it was like for him. Mike listened, not with anger so much as with anguish.

When one of the assistant directors of Willowbrook later reprimanded Dr. Wilkins for taking Bernard off the grounds without permission, the almost always composed young man experienced a rare outburst. "I had Bernard's permission. And, sir . . . so far as I'm concerned, that's the only permission I needed."

A month after that, in late December 1971, with Bernard as the catalyst and Dr. Wilkins and Elizabeth Lee as the leaders, many of the professional employees staged a low-keyed protest over living conditions at Willowbrook. The protest took the form, finally, of a list of grievances submitted to the administration, specifying the most glaring deficiencies. The official response was to terminate the employment of Mike and Liz, while temporarily suspending some of the other, and presumably less guilty, "troublemakers."

If the administration had calculated that the firings would end this infant upheaval, they had guessed very wrong. The protesting employees were joined on the newly established picket lines by hundreds of parents with children in those wards being cared for by Dr. Wilkins. He was a good doctor, they said, who only wanted to make things better for the children. It was the beginning of the first large-scale protest in the institution's history. When the administration refused to back down, more and more parents and employees joined in what was essentially a spontaneous expression of revulsion at conditions that for years had seemed inevitable. "We can do better . . . we must do better" became their unspoken slogan.

I was called to do the story, just a week after Mike had been fired; to be exact, it was January 5, 1972. I had met Dr. Wilkins a year or so before while covering a different story at the Public Health Service Hospital, where Mike had been working at the time as an intern. I was probably the only newsman he could think of when things started happening at Willowbrook, so he telephoned me with the information.

"Geraldo. You have to see this place."

"Tell me a little about it." I was frequently called with tips about supposedly "hot" stories, but after a couple of years in the news business I was more cautious and slower to excite than I had been in the beginning.

"It's awful here."

"How is it awful, Mike?" I was polite but slightly impatient.

"Well . . ." There was so much to say, I know now, that Mike's frustration was at having to select which of the many horrible realities to talk about. "The children . . ." he chose. "You should see the way they treat the children."

"Oh?"

"There are sixty or seventy retarded kids to a ward. And most of them are naked and smeared with their own mess."

"Can I get my cameras inside the place?" Children being abused had always been a "favorite" story of mine—the word "favorite" being used in the inverted news sense I spoke of earlier.

"I think so," Mike answered, and we set to planning how we could secretly get inside to film the conditions he had started to describe.

The next day, by the time Dr. Wilkins and Bernard had finished telling me some of the details of the time he'd spent in the institution, it was already four o'clock and dark outside. I looked at my watch, realized how late it was, and jumped up.

"I've got to split, or I'll miss the deadline."

The early edition of the local news goes on at six in the evening. We hurried, so we made it into Manhattan in forty-five minutes, with another forty-five minutes once we got in for developing the film; there was less than a half hour to write the script and edit the film and get to the studio.

In the beginning of the report, I was fairly calm in my delivery. But as I talked about the conditions I had seen that day, calm exploded into fury. When I got to the part about Bernard, my voice cracked with pain and slurred with sorrow.

It was the start of one of the most massive local-news exposés in recent history. Within a few days every local newspaper, television news program, and national news magazine was reporting the obscene story of Willowbrook. When the story was first breaking and the public was learning the full magnitude of the horrors within the institution, I interviewed Bernard no less than four times. Although his speech was strained and difficult to follow, nobody, not even my news director, complained. Bernard was the undisputed expert, and he had earned the patience of the viewing audience by spending sixteen unnecessary years in what Senator Robert Kennedy had earlier labeled a "snakepit."

At first, the reaction of the State Department of Mental Hygiene was scandalously to resist the demands that Willowbrook be cleaned up. They claimed initially that the press reports were overstated and that conditions were not nearly as bad as we were telling people they were. But finally, in late February 1972, with extra millions appropriated by the state legislature on an emergency basis, the department dropped all pretense of denying the reality of the institution, and the painfully slow process of change began.

A month later, in March, Bernard's family signed him out of Willowbrook for the last time. He got an apartment on Staten Island, near his friend Joey, whom he still sees all the time. On the outside, Bernard didn't become Pollyanna. It was an extremely difficult time for him; nothing came easy, and there were times when he wondered whether he hadn't been better off inside the institution. Willowbrook had been grim, but at least it was predictable, not like the mile-a-minute, dazzlingly uncertain outside world.

Finally, with help from his friends, things started to work for Bernard. He took additional speech therapy, improved his reading, and eventually got a job with One to One, a charity we had established to fund humane alternatives to institutional life for the mentally retarded. Now he's sort of the goodwill ambassador/public-relations man, giving speeches at high schools and colleges in the New York metropolitan area, drumming up support for the movement to improve the plight of the retarded.

On April 22, 1975, after more than three years of relentless pressure from the media and the federal courts, the Department of Mental Hygiene capitulated. The commissioner resigned, and the newly elected governor, Hugh Carey, announced that he was signing a consent judgment settling a federal lawsuit that had been filed on behalf of the residents of Willowbrook, shortly after Mike and Liz had been fired.

The federal court commanded that "straitjackets never be used again in Willowbrook, nor shall any resident be tied spread-eagled to a bed, or subjected to either corporal punishment, or degradation, or seclusion." It went on to prohibit "physically intrusive, chemical or biomedical research or experimentation," and to demand that "health and safety hazards be corrected, radiators and steam pipes covered to protect residents, windows repaired and screened, lead paint removed, buildings air-conditioned, and cockroaches and vermin be eradicated."

The major sections of the agreement stipulated that the population of Willowbrook, which had been more than six thousand, be reduced to no more than two hundred and fifty residents. It further stipulated that training programs be immediately instituted to prepare more than three thousand residents for their return to society. And finally, the agreement called for the funding of more than two hundred small, community-based residences for the retarded, each housing no more than ten people.

Bruce Ennis, the counsel for the New York Civil Liberties Union, who had argued the case on the residents' behalf, said that the agreement "recognizes that retarded persons are capable of physical, emotional, and social growth." It was a historic agreement that stated, essentially, that there would be no more Willowbrooks in New York State.

The next day, I helped Bernard send off a telegram to Governor Carey, thanking him for his great humanity. We were all pleased, Bernard most of all.

VICTOR HERNÁNDEZ CRUZ

Loíza Aldea

Loíza
Who is there   in you took
a walk   Sandy walks
y Jose y Jane   in Loíza
the rain
The Coconut that had wings
of rum
In that bar-café   Sunday
night
Palm trees are the first
to wake in the mornings
and walk around the streets
Loíza—who was you

"who that in deep natural
woods . . . who that walking
naked in the forest rain . . .
who that . . . if it's as sweet
as the dulce de coco then
come here we would like to
eat"
She came when she came in
dreams
When she came
Above her Flamboyant red feathers
She hears laughter and song
She hears all the salsa that
is played on her ground
They hit six drums with one hand
She knows all the Aldea
Lit up with la Fiesta de
Santiago Lit up like natural
glow from the mangos hanging
from the trees
Horses dressed with gowns
Coconut faces parading
Mediania Baja
Tumba/unquinto from the night
If legs played drums
The body moves like the drum
drum/in motion tumba The song
jumps on the head—the head jumps
like the leg/sounds like the drum
drum talk to body tumba
Body talk for drum
fingers make it laugh Body
come so close Loíza is the
wind you like to blow
Above the town your legs
unfold Everywhere you
look carnaval a sea of laughter
dancing coming

The plaza is full
In brown sandals we walk
the walks   we stand to eat the
food   shirts are opened
Breeze Loíza you are soft and
warm
The waves
The red dresses
The pink and yellow
La plaza la plaza lit
The merry go round the smell
of shuffling bodies
Loíza
Loíza Aldea
On fire
Over there where fruits dance
into your mouth
& love comes gently
We sit till the morning
The wind blows festive sleep
Loíza you are always there
Silent with your African swing
Salsasa.

EPILOGUE

REDEMPTION

"And I will rise, holding a flag once a shroud."
—FROM *THE FINAL ACT* BY JOSÉ DE DIEGO

JOSÉ DE DIEGO

The Final Act

Translation by Roberto Santiago

Shroud me, moments after my death,
with the shield of my nation.
Shroud me, head to foot,
with the three colors of my flag.

Above my tomb,
as patient as the sea,
will sit a lonely Hope,
testing the patience of eternity.

But there will arrive a great day when
my tomb will be unsealed.
And Hope's joyous cry will ring.

My bony remains will lift that shield.
And I will rise, holding a flag once a shroud.

Hoisted high, before the world, before Infinity.

ABOUT THE CONTRIBUTORS

Jack Agüeros was born in New York City in 1934. Recipient of numerous awards, he has published poetry, plays, and children's stories, and has written for "Sesame Street" and WNBC-TV Channel 4. For almost ten years he was director of the Museo del Barrio in East Harlem, the only Puerto Rican museum in the United States. Agüeros is the author of the short-story collection *Dominoes* (Curbstone Press) and the forthcoming *Sonnets from the Puerto Rican*, to be published by Hanging Loose Press in 1996.

Miguel Algarín is a distinguished scholar, poet, and editor and the founder of the Nuyorican Poets Cafe. His anthology, *ALOUD—Voices from the Nuyorican Poets Cafe* (Henry Holt), won the 1994 American Book Award. His poetry includes *Mongo Affair* (Nuyorican Press) and *Body Bee Calling from the 21st Century* (Arte Publico Press). He is a professor at Rutgers University.

Zoë Anglesey edited *Stone on Stone / Piedra Sobre Piedra: Women of Diverse Heritages, !Word Up! Hope for Youth Poetry* and *Ixok Amar Go: Central American Women's Poetry for Peace*. Her translations are in *These Are Not Sweet Girls: Poetry by Latin American Women Poets; Costa Rica: A Literary Travel Companion*; and *Mouth to Mouth: Poems by Twelve Contemporary Mexican Women*.

Julia de Burgos remains Puerto Rico's greatest literary icon. Her most famous poem, "Grand River of Loiza," has influenced generations of

Puerto Rican artists and writers and firmly established her as the finest Puerto Rican poet of the 20th century. De Burgos was born in Puerto Rico in 1914 and moved to New York City where she wrote and struggled in poverty. She died in 1953.

Pedro Albizu Campos was the greatest hero in the history of Puerto Rico. A gifted orator, he headed the Puerto Rican Nationalist Party in the 1930s, struggling to raise consciousness among the Puerto Rican people to fight for independence.

Lucky CienFuegos was a Nuyorican poet whose work has appeared in numerous anthologies. He lived in New York City up until his death.

Judith Ortiz Cofer is the author of the 1995 short-story collection *An Island Like You: Stories of the Barrio* (Orchard Books). An award-winning essayist, Cofer is an associate professor of English and creative writing at the University of Georgia. She has written for *Glamour* and the *Kenyon Review*.

Jesus Colon was best known for his 1961 landmark book, *A Puerto Rican in New York* (Masses and Mainstream), which chronicled, for the first time, the experience of Puerto Ricans migrating to the United States. Colon was born in Cayey, Puerto Rico, and moved to the United States in 1918. He died in 1974.

Victor Hernández Cruz is an award-winning poet whose books include *Red Beans* (Coffee House Press), *Rhythm, Content and Flavor: Selected Poems* (Arte Publico Press), and *Snaps* (Random House). He received a Guggenheim Fellowship in 1991. Cruz has read and lectured throughout the world. He lives in Puerto Rico

José de Diego was a visionary poet who, in the 19th century saw that Puerto Rico's goal must always be independence. Through the discipline of being an attorney and the artistry of being a poet, de Diego forged two intellectual skills to impact his nation. His poetry urges the Puerto Rican people never to give up—to rise and continue the struggle to victory.

Martin Espada is a poet/attorney/scholar who follows in the tradition of José de Diego. His poetry books include *Rebellion Is the Circle of a Lover's Hand* (Curbstone Press), which won the PEN/Revson Foundation Award for Poetry. A professor at the University of Massachusetts at Amherst, Espada has been published in numerous anthologies and literary magazines.

Poet **Sandra Maria Esteves** was born and raised in the South Bronx and studied art and writing at the Pratt Institute in Brooklyn. Her books include *Bluestown Mockingbird Mamba* (Arte Publico) and *Yerba Buena: Dibujos y Poemas* (Greenfield Review Press). In 1985 Esteves was awarded a poetry fellowship from the New York Foundation for the Arts.

Ronald Fernandez is a professor at Central Connecticut State University and, as a Spaniard, is this anthology's honorary *Boricua*. He is the author of *Los Macheteros* (Prentice Hall Press) and specializes in social psychology and sociology.

José Luis Gonzalez is a scholar/social critic whose 1980 book *Puerto Rico: The Four-Storeyed Country* remains his most controversial work. Gonzalez is considered one of the island's leading intellectuals. He is of Puerto Rican and Dominican heritage.

Migene González-Wippler is a national expert of the Santeria religion. She is the author of *Santeria: African Magic in Latin America* (Original Publications) and lectures around the nation.

Pablo Guzman is a broadcast journalist who was one of the founding members of the Young Lords Party. He has written for the *New York Daily News* and the *Village Voice*.

Felipe Luciano is a broadcast journalist who has won two Emmy Awards for reporting. In the late 1960s he was one of the founders of the Young Lords Party and The Last Poets. Luciano has written for the *Village Voice* and the *New York Times*.

René Marqués is a renowned intellectual and playwright whose landmark essay, "The Docil Puerto Rican," remains controversial over thirty years after its publication. He is the author of the play *La Carreta*.

Luis Muñoz Marín in 1948 was Puerto Rico's first elected governor, a post he held until he retired in 1964. Muñoz Marín is credited for shifting the sentiment from independence to a continued alliance with the United States. He declared Puerto Rico's ties with the United States not as colonial based but as "commonwealth state" or "free associated state," terms he is credited for having coined.

Nicholasa Mohr is a prolific writer best known for her fiction. Among her books are *Going Home* (Dial Press) and *Nilda* (Harper & Row). Her awards include the 1990 Edgar Allan Poe Award from the Bronx Historical Society, the 1981 American Book Award, and the 1973 *New York Times* Outstanding Book of the Year. She has taught and lectured throughout the country.

Aurora Levins Morales is a Puerto Rican Jewish poet best known for her book *Getting Home Alive* (Firebrand Books), which she co-authored with her mother. Her work has appeared in numerous anthologies. She is completing work on *Threads*, a collection of short stories.

Ed Morales is a Nuyorican poet and editor at the *Village Voice* whose poetry has appeared in numerous anthologies. He has written for *Rolling Stone*, *Details*, and *Entertainment Weekly*.

Martita Morales is a Nuyorican poet who is best known for her poem "The Sounds of Sixth Street," which spoke directly about the political and cultural struggle Puerto Rican women endure in the face of racial self-hatred. It is a poem of working-class feminism—that intellectualism must always serve as a predicate for change.

Rosario Morales is the author of *Getting Home Alive* (Firebrand Books), which she coauthored with her daughter. She has an M.A. in anthropology from the University of Chicago.

Willie Perdomo is a Nuyorican poet who frequently gives readings around the world. His book *Where a Nickel Costs a Dime* will be released by W. W. Norton in 1996. Perdomo has written for *New York Newsday*.

Pedro Pietri is a renowned poet whose books include the landmark *Puerto Rican Obituary* (Monthly Review Press), *Lost in the Museum of National History* (Ediciones Huracan), and *The Masses Are Asses* (Waterfront Press). He lives in New York City.

Miguel Piñero was known as the best Puerto Rican playwright born in the United States. Among his award-winning plays are *Short Eyes* (based on his prison experiences), later made into a film, and *The Sun Always Shines for the Cool*. His poetry collection includes *La Bodega Sold Dreams* (Arte Publico Press). Piñero died in 1988.

Reinaldo Povod was known as the best Puerto Rican playwright of the 1980s. His debut play, *Cuba and His Teddy Bear*, played on Broadway and starred Robert DeNiro and Burt Young. His trilogy of one-act plays, *La Puta Vida—This Bitch of a Life*, was produced at New York's Public Theater. Povod, of Puerto Rican and Irish heritage, died in 1994.

Freddie Prinze was known as the best Puerto Rican comedian there ever was. In the 1970s he starred in NBC's "Chico and the Man," performed stand-up comedy around the country, and recorded the now-rare album *Looking Good* for CBS Records. Prinze, of Puerto Rican and Hungarian heritage, died in 1977.

Maria Graniela de Pruetzel is the mother of late comedian Freddie Prinze and author of the biography *The Freddie Prinze Story*. She lives in Puerto Rico.

Geraldo Rivera is the host of the syndicated talk show "Geraldo" and has won numerous prestigious awards for his breakthrough journalism in the 1970s. He changed the way the mentally retarded are treated in this country with his landmark reporting on abuses of the mentally retarded in Willowbrook, New Jersey. Rivera, of Puerto Rican and Jewish heritage, was the original attorney for the Young Lords Party.

Abraham Rodriguez, Jr., is a writer born and raised in the South Bronx. He is the author of *Spidertown* (Hyperion) and the short-story collection *The Boy Without a Flag* (Milkweed Editions). He has written for *Story* magazine.

Clara E. Rodriguez is a professor at Fordham University in New York City. She is the author of *Hispanics in the Labor Force: Issues and Policies* (Plenum Press) and *Puerto Ricans: Born in the USA* (Westview Press). She writes for numerous academic journals.

Esmeralda Santiago is a writer whose first book, an autobiography entitled *When I Was Puerto Rican*, caused a sensation in 1994. Santiago was born in Macun, Puerto Rico, and moved to the United States. She is a graduate of Harvard University and earned her M.F.A. from Sarah Lawrence College. She currently lives with her husband in Boston, where she runs Cantomedia, a film production company.

Pedro Juan Soto is the author of the landmark short-story collection, *Spics*. He lives in Puerto Rico.

Piri Thomas is best known for his landmark autobiography, *Down These Mean Streets* (Knopf), banned in more schools than J. D. Salinger's *Catcher in the Rye*. He is the author of *Stories from El Barrio* (Knopf), and *Savior, Savior Hold My Hand* (Doubleday). Raised in Spanish Harlem, he lives in Berkeley, California.

Edwin Torres is a judge in New York City who doubles as a mystery writer. His two crime novels have been made into hit films—*Carlito's Way*, starring Al Pacino, and *Q&A*, starring Nick Nolte.

José Torres is a living national hero of Puerto Rico. He was the first Puerto Rican light heavyweight champion of the world for three years. After retiring from the ring, Torres embarked on a career as a successful journalist. In 1971, he wrote the bestseller *Sting Like a Bee: The Story of Muhammad Ali*. In 1988 he authored the controversial bestseller *Fire & Fear: The Inside Story of Mike Tyson*, which was made into an HBO film in 1995. Torres has won 380 awards—including the 1992 Hispanic Heritage Award and the Life Achievement Award of the National Puerto Rican Coalition. He has written for *Playboy*, *GQ*, and *Parade*.

Joseph B. Vasquez was an independent filmmaker whose works include *Hangin' (Out) with the Homeboys*, which was a hit at the Sundance Film Festival in 1990, and *The Bronx War* and *Manhattan Merengue*. He died in 1995.

Ana Lydia Vega is a novelist who writes about intimate male/female relationships. She is the winner of the 1989 Guggenheim Fellowship for Literary Creation, the 1984 Juan Rulfo Short Story Prize, and the 1982 Casa de Las Americas Prize in Havana, Cuba. She is a professor at the University of Puerto Rico.

AUTHOR INDEX

PERMISSION ACKNOWLEDGMENTS

Grateful acknowledgment is made to the following for permission to reprint previously published material:

Addison-Wesley Publishing Company, Inc.: Excerpt from pp. 63–83 of WHEN I WAS PUERTO RICAN by Esmeralda Santiago. © 1993 by Esmeralda Santiago. Reprinted by permission of Addison-Wesley Publishing Company.

Miguel Algarín: "Mongo Affair" and "HIV" from NUYORICAN POETRY: AN ANTHOLOGY OF PUERTO RICAN WORDS AND FEELINGS. Reprinted by permission of the author.

Arte Publico Press: "Aunt Rosana's Rocker" by Nicholasa Mohr. Reprinted by permission from the publisher of RITUALS OF SURVIVAL: A WOMAN'S PORTFOLIO (Houston: Arte Publico Press-University of Houston, 1985).

Lucky CienFuegos: "Dedicated to María Rodriguez Martínez: February 24, 1975" by Lucky CienFuegos from NUYORICAN POETRY. Reprinted by permission of the author.

Victor Hernández Cruz: "Loíza Aldea" from TROPICALIZATION. © by Victor Hernández Cruz. Reprinted by permission of the author.

Curbstone Press: "Malig; Malig & Sal; Sal" from DOMINOES by Jack Agüeros. "Niggerlips" from REBELLION IS THE CIRCLE OF A LOVER'S HAND by Martin Espada.

Maria Graniela de Pruetzel: Excerpts from THE FREDDIE PRINZE STORY by Maria Pruetzel and John A. Barbour. Reprinted by permission of Maria Graniela de Pruetzel.

ABOUT THE ARTISTS

FRANK DIAZ ESCALET is a painter-storyteller whose work, including the BORICUAS cover art, "Que Bueno," powerfully depicts the lives, hopes, and dreams of Latino people. Born in Ponce, Puerto Rico, he served in the U.S. Air Force before launching an art career in New York City. Mr. Escalet has received numerous art awards in the United States, Canada, and Eastern Europe, including an Award of Excellence from *Manhattan Arts* magazine. His work has been exhibited at the National Gallery and The Smithsonian in Washington, D.C. Mr. Escalet now lives with his wife and family in Kennebunk, Maine.

CLEMENTE FLORES was born and raised in East Harlem. A self-taught artist he began to draw and paint in 1985 when his son bought everyone in the family drawing pads except for him. Mr. Flores actively campaigns to encourage people in the Latino community to engage in art activities. His original line drawings for BORICUAS reflect his belief that Latino artists have a social responsibility to break through the barriers that would relegate art to an exclusive class of people. Clemente Flores's artwork has been exhibited extensively in New York City.

ABOUT THE EDITOR

Dale Omori

ROBERTO SANTIAGO is a journalist who lectures around the nation on Latino issues. He received the 1991 Inter American Press Association Award for Commentary and won first prize in the 1990 *Hispanic Magazine* Short Story Contest. A former reporter for the *Cleveland Plain Dealer,* Santiago has written for *Omni, Rolling Stone,* and *Essence.* He lives in Brooklyn, New York.

Printed in the United States
by Baker & Taylor Publisher Services